MACROECONOMICS
A Contemporary Introduction

FIFTH EDITION

William A. McEachern

Professor of Economics

University of Connecticut

South-Western College Publishing
Thomson Learning℠

Australia • Canada • Denmark • Japan • Mexico • New Zealand • Philippines
Puerto Rico • Singapore • South Africa • Spain • United Kingdom • United States

Acquisitions Editor:	Keri L. Witman
Developmental Editor:	Dennis Hanseman
Marketing Manager:	Lisa L. Lysne
Sr. Production Editor:	Sharon L. Smith
Manufacturing Coordinator:	Georgina Calderon
Internal Design:	A Small Design Studio/Ann Small
Cover Design:	Tin Box Studio
Cover Illustrator:	John Mattos
Photo Researcher:	Feldman & Associates, Inc.
Production House:	Pre-Press Company, Inc.
Printer:	Von Hoffmann Press, Inc.

Printed in the United States of America
4 02 01 00

For more information contact South-Western College Publishing, 5101 Madison Road, Cincinnati, Ohio, 45227. Or you can visit our Internet site at http://www.swcollege.com

For permission to use material from this text or product contact us by
• **telephone: 1-800-730-2214**
• **fax: 1-800-730-2215**
• **web: http://www.thomsonrights.com**

Library of Congress Cataloging-in-Publication Data
McEachern, William A.
    Macroeconomics: a contemporary introduction/William A. McEachern.—5th ed.
      p. cm.
    Includes bibliographical references and index.
    1. Macroeconomics.   I. Title.
    HB172.M375 1999   99-11638
    339—dc21

ISBN: 0-538-88847-4

This book is printed on acid-free paper.

About the Author

William A. McEachern, Professor of Economics at the University of Connecticut, has taught principles of economics since 1973 and has offered teaching workshops since 1980. His research has appeared in a variety of journals, including *Economic Inquiry, National Tax Journal, Journal of Industrial Economics,* and *Public Choice.* He is Founding Editor of *The Teaching Economist,* a newsletter that focuses on teaching economics at the college level, and is Editor in Chief of *The Connecticut Economy: A University of Connecticut Quarterly Review.* Professor McEachern has advised federal, state, and local governments on policy matters and directed a bipartisan commission examining Connecticut's finances. Publications in which he has been quoted include the *New York Times, London Times, Wall Street Journal, Christian Science Monitor, USA Today,* and *Reader's Digest.* The University of Connecticut Alumni Association conferred on him its Faculty Award for Distinguished Public Service, and the Connecticut Academy of Arts and Sciences elected him to membership. He was born in Portsmouth, N.H., earned an undergraduate degree with honors from Holy Cross College and an M.A. and Ph.D. from the University of Virginia.

To Pat

Brief Contents

Contents

PART 1

INTRODUCTION TO ECONOMICS

PART 2

FUNDAMENTALS OF MACROECONOMICS

CHAPTER 11
Aggregate Supply 228

PART 3

FISCAL AND MONETARY POLICY

CHAPTER 12
Fiscal Policy 250

CHAPTER 13
Money and the Financial System 272

CHAPTER 14
Banking and the Money Supply 294

PART 4

THE INTERNATIONAL SETTING

Preface

Economics has a short history but a long past. As a distinct discipline, economics has been studied for only a few hundred years, yet civilizations have confronted the economic problem of scarce resources but unlimited wants for millennia. Economics, the discipline, may be centuries old, but it is new every day as fresh evidence supports or reshapes economic theory. In *Macroeconomics: A Contemporary Introduction*, I draw upon more than a quarter century of teaching experience to convey the vitality, timeliness, and evolving nature of economics.

LEADING BY EXAMPLE

Remember the last time you were in unknown parts and had to ask for directions? Along with the directions came the standard comment "You can't miss it!" So how come you missed it? Because the "landmark" that was obvious to the neighborhood resident who gave the directions might as well have been invisible to you, a stranger. Writing a principles text is much like giving directions. The author must be familiar with the material, but familiarity can also dull one's perceptions, making it difficult to see things through the fresh eyes of new students. Some authors try to compensate by telling all they know, in the process overwhelming students with so much detail that the central point gets lost. Other authors take a minimalist approach by offering little of what students may already know intuitively, and instead talking abstractly about good x and good y, units of labor and units of capital, or the proverbial widget. This turns economics into a foreign language.

Good directions rely on landmarks familiar to us all—a stoplight, a fork in the road, a white picket fence. Likewise, a good textbook builds bridges from the familiar to the new. How? In essence, I try to "lead by example"—I provide examples that draw on the students' common experience. I try to create graphic pictures that need little explanation, thereby eliciting from the reader that light of recognition, that "Aha!" Examples should be self-explanatory; they should convey the point quickly and directly. Having to explain an example is like having to explain a joke—the point gets lost. Throughout, I provide just enough intuitive information and institutional detail to get the point across without overwhelming the student. My emphasis is on economic ideas, not economic jargon.

Students arrive the first day of class with eighteen or more years of experience with economic choices, economic institutions, and economic events. Each student grew up in a household—the central economic institution. As consumers, students are familiar with fast-food restaurants, movie theaters, car dealerships, and dozens of stores at the mall. Most students have been resource suppliers—more than half held jobs while in high school. Students also have experience with government—they know about taxes, drivers' licenses, speed limits, and public education. And, from imported cars to the World Wide Web, students are becoming more familiar with the rest of the world.

Thus, students have abundant experience with the stuff of economics. They may not recognize the economic content of that experience, but they possess it nonetheless. Yet many principles authors neglect this rich lode of experience and, instead, try to create for the student a new world of economics. Such an approach fails to make the connection between economics and what Alfred Marshall called "the ordinary business of life."

Since instructors can cover only a fraction of the textbook material in class, principles texts should, to the extent possible, be self-explanatory, thereby providing instructors with greater flexibility to emphasize topics of special interest. My approach is to start where students are, not where we would like them to be. For example, to explain the division of labor, rather than refer to Adam Smith's pin factory, I call attention to the division of labor at McDonald's. And to explain the most reliable relationship in macroeconomics, that between income and consumption, I point out how easy it is to guess the average income in a neighborhood just by observing the quality of housing and the types of cars in the driveways. This edition is loaded with similar down-to-earth examples.

CLARITY BY DESIGN

In many principles textbooks, chapters are interrupted by boxed material, parenthetical explanations, qualifying footnotes, and other distractions that disrupt the flow of the material. Students remain uncertain about when or if such segregated elements should be read. In contrast, this book has a natural flow. Each chapter opens with a few questions aimed at stimulating interest, then tells a compelling story, using logical sections and subsections. Qualifying footnotes are used sparingly, and parenthetical explanations are used hardly at all. Moreover, case studies are not boxed off but appear in the natural sequence of the chapter. Students can thus read each chapter smoothly from the opening questions to the conclusion and summary. I also employ a "just-in-time" approach to introduce material just as it is needed to develop an argument. Overall, the Fifth Edition is a bit leaner, economic jargon has been reduced, and many tables have been converted to charts and graphs.

In most textbooks, the page design—the layout of the page and the use of color—is an afterthought, conceived without regard to how students learn. No element in the design of this book is wasted, and all elements work together for the maximum pedagogical value.

Page Design. By design, all elements of each chapter have been carefully integrated. Every effort has been made to present students with an open, readable page design. The size of the typeface, the length of the text line, and the amount of "white space" were all chosen to make learning easier. Graphs are uncluttered and are accompanied by captions explaining the key features. These features are all optimal for students encountering college textbooks for the first time.

Use of Color. Color is used systematically within graphs, charts, and tables to ensure that students quickly and easily see what's going on. Throughout the book, aggregate demand curves are blue and aggregate supply curves are red. In comparative statics examples, the curves determining the final equilibrium point are lighter than the initial curves. Color shading distinguishes key features of many graphs, such as output levels that fall short of the economy's potential and output levels that exceed it. In short, color is more than mere face entertainment—it is employed consistently and with forethought to help students learn.

THE FIFTH EDITION

I build on the success of earlier editions to make the material even more student-friendly through concrete examples, more questions along the way, and additional summaries as each chapter unfolds. And by making the material both more personal and more natural, I try to draw students into a collaborative discussion. I have also built on the success of the Fourth Edition's Internet support to make the use of technology even more innovative and helpful. This edition features an even tighter integration of text and technology.

Introductory Chapters Basic material macroeconomics and microeconomics is covered in the first four chapters. Limiting the introductory material to four chapters saves precious class time.

Macroeconomics Core Rather than focus on the differences among competing schools of thought, I use the aggregate demand and aggregate supply model to underscore the fundamental distinction between the active approach, which views the economy as unstable and in need of government intervention when it gets off track, and the passive approach, which views the economy as essentially stable and self-correcting. In developing aggregate supply, I have taken more care in laying out the logic of the model to help students see what's going on. I also provide more review along the way.

Wherever possible, I rely on student experience and intuition to explain the theory behind macroeconomic abstractions such as aggregate demand and aggregate supply. For example, to explain how employment can temporarily exceed its natural rate, I note how students, as the term draws to a close, can temporarily shift into high gear, studying for final exams and finishing term papers.

I have made the graphs more readable and more intuitively obvious by using numbers, such as $8.0 trillion, rather than letters, such as Y. And to convey a feel for the size of the U.S. economy, I usually talk in terms of trillions of dollars rather than billions of dollars. New material in this edition includes discussions of banking consolidation around the globe, banking troubles in Japan, the Fed's targeting of the federal funds rate, balancing the federal budget, and trouble ahead for the Social Security system.

International Chapters This edition reflects the growing impact of the world economy on U.S. economic welfare. International issues are introduced early and discussed often. For example, the rest of the world is introduced in Chapter 1 and comparative advantage and the production possibilities frontier are each discussed from a global perspective in Chapter 2. International coverage is woven into the text. For example, students gain a better perspective about such topics as economic growth, productivity, unemployment, inflation, and central bank independence if the U.S. experience is compared with that of other countries around the world.

New international material includes discussions of the euro, economic troubles in Asia, "crony capitalism", declining fertility rates around the world, and the painful progress of transitional economies. Although international references are scattered throughout the book, including a number of case studies, the final three chapters focus exclusively on international trade, international finance, and developing and transitional economies, respectively.

Case Studies Some books use case studies as boxed-off asides to cover material that otherwise doesn't quite fit. I use case studies as real-world applications that reinforce ideas in the chapter and demonstrate the relevance of economic theory. My case studies are different enough to offer variety in the presentation yet are integrated enough into the flow of the chapter to let students know they should be read. This edition distinguishes among four categories of case studies: (1) "The World of Business" offers students a feel for the range of choices confronted by business decision makers today; (2) "The Information Economy" underscores the critical role of information in the new economy, from the computer revolution to the value of intellectual property; (3) "Other Times, Other Places" involves applications either from economic history or from other economies around the world; and (4) "Public Policy" cases highlight the tradeoffs in the public sector. All case studies are supported by references and relevant Web addresses and are tied to further analysis on the Web with questions, navigation tips, and other information that can be accessed through the McEachern Interactive Study Center at http://mceachern. swcollege.com.

Net Bookmarks Each chapter includes a Net Bookmark. These margin notes identify interesting Web sites that illustrate real-world examples of chapter topics, giving students the opportunity to explore some of those sites and build their economic research skills. And they are extended on the Web with additional information on resources as well as step-by-step navigation hints. They can be accessed through the McEachern Interactive Study Center at http://mceachern.swcollege.com.

The *Wall Street Journal* Edition The Fifth Edition makes it easy to bring the real world into the classroom. This *Wall Street Journal* Edition provides numerous opportunities to relate economic concepts to late-breaking news stories. A special Preface guides students in their use of the *Wall Street Journal*. And there is a question at the end of each chapter that asks students to read and analyze information from the *Wall Street Journal*.

Experiential Exercises New to this edition are end-of-chapter questions that encourage students to develop their research and critical thinking skills. These Experiential Exercises ask students to apply what they have learned to real-world, hands-on economic analysis. Most of these exercises involve the Internet, the *Wall Street Journal*, or other media resources.

The Internet

As mentioned already, we devoted careful attention to capitalizing on the vast array of economic resources and alternative learning technologies the Internet can deliver. I gave much thought to two basic questions: What can this technology do that a textbook cannot do? And how can Web-based enhancements be employed to bring the greatest value to teaching and learning?

It's clear that students learn more when they are involved and engaged. The Internet provides a way to heighten student involvement while keeping the introductory economics course as current as today's news. With these ideas in mind, we have undertaken a major upgrading of our Web site to more tightly integrate the book and the Internet. We have done this in a way that exploits the comparative advantage of each medium, and in a structure that optimizes both teaching and learning experiences.

The McEachern Interactive Study Center (http://mceachern. swcollege.com) Through McEachern Interactive, students benefit from the best textual presentation as well as the most innovative on-line experience. This edition offers a structured approach to the Internet, providing a comprehensive chapter-by-chapter on-line study guide that includes graphical support, interactive quizzes, a glossary, updated and extended applications from the text, and numerous other features. Some highlights include:

> **Over 100 Examples and Exercises** The Internet-enhanced text features such as Net Bookmarks, Case Studies, and end-of-chapter Experiential Exercises are tied to the Study Center where students will find clear links to relevant Web sites. These applications are interesting and easy-to-use. All of the in-text features that are extended on the Web are indicated by a special McEachern Interactive icon (Shown at left).

> **On-Line Graphing Tutorials** Key graphs from the text—also indicated by the McEachern Interactive icon—are brought to life as students explore interactive graphing tutorials that feature helpful audio explanations.

> **Interactive Quizzes** These multiple-choice on-line quizzes provide a perfect review resource and solid exam preparation. They feature detailed feedback for right and wrong answers as well as the option of e-mailing quiz results to the instructor.

It is important to note that none of these features requires detailed knowledge of the Internet. Nor are they required for a successful classroom experience if an instructor wants to assign only the materials contained within the text. The on-line enhancements simply offer optional paths for further study and exploration—new ways for students to employ their individual learning styles and new ways for instructors to experiment with technology and a wider range of assignment materials.

THE SUPPORT PACKAGE

The teaching and learning support package that accompanies *Economics: A Contemporary Introduction* provides instructors and students with focused, accurate, and innovative supplements to the textbook.

Student Supplements

Study Guide. The *Study Guide* was written by John Lunn of Hope College. Each chapter of the *Study Guide* corresponds to a chapter in the text and offers: (1) an introduction; (2) a chapter outline, with definitions of all terms; (3) a discussion of the chapter's main points; (4) a *lagniappe*, or bonus, which supplements material in the chapter and includes a "Question to Think About"; (5) a list of key terms; (6) a variety of true-false, multiple-choice, and discussion questions; and (7) answers to all these questions. Visit the McEachern Interactive Study Center at http://mceachern.swcollege.com for more details.

Graphing Primer One of the most difficult challenges for many introductory economics students is working with graphs. The *Graphing Primer* is a print supplement that helps students create, interpret, and understand graphs.

McEachern Interactive CD-ROM This CD-ROM provides a powerful collection of electronic study tools:

> **PowerPoint Lecture Review Slides** Students can visually review key concepts and exhibits from each chapter, and print the slides to use as note-taking guides during class lectures.

> **South-Western Economics Tutorial Software** James T. Doak has developed tutorial software compatible with Microsoft Windows. It is organized around key topics, and correlated to relevant text chapters. Each topic provides a series of interactive graphing exercises that help students test their understanding of key concepts. Students can also track and record their progress.

> **McEachern Interactive Graphing Tutorials** The graphing tutorials found at the McEachern Study Center are also included on this CD-ROM.

Economics Guide **Tutorial Software** Robert Brooker, of Gannon University, has developed this economics tutorial software, compatible with Microsoft Windows. Through the use of a sophisticated testing engine, it presents students with an unlimited supply of quizzes over the topics covered in each chapter. Students are able to track and record their progress throughout the course. *Economics Guide* software is perfect for review or for test preparation

Macroeconomics Alive! **CD-ROM - Interactive Study Guide** The *Macroeconomics Alive!* CD-ROM, created by Willie Belton, Richard Cebula, and John McLeod, Jr. of the Georgia Institute of Technology, is compatible with Microsoft Windows and with the Apple Macintosh. This multimedia CD-ROM combines interactive lessons, graphing tools, and simulations to bring macroeconomic concepts to life. To learn more about these CDs, visit the *Economics Alive!* Web site at http://econalive.swcollege.com.

The McEachern Web Site The McEachern Web Site at http://mceachern. swcollege.com offers a variety of learning tools. In addition to the helpful tools available at the McEachern Interactive Study Center, students can also find summaries of current news stories, review current and historical economic data, keep up-to-date through current examples and policy applications, access information about saleable supplements, correspond with me, and take advantage of many other benefits.

Instructor Supplements

Instructor's Manual The *Instructor's Manual*, revised by Dorothy Siden of Salem State College, is keyed to the text. For each text chapter, it includes (1) a detailed lecture outline and brief overview; (2) a summary of main points; (3) pedagogical tips that expand on points raised in the chapter; and (4) suggested answers to all end-of-chapter questions and problems. New to this edition is a set of classroom economic experiments developed by Michael Haupert of the University of Wisconsin, La Crosse and Noelwah Netusil of Reed College. Each experiment comes with an abstract, an overview, a clear set of instructions for running the experiment, and forms for recording the results.

Teaching Assistance Manual I have revised my *Teaching Assistance Manual* to provide additional support beyond the Instructor's Manual. It is especially useful to new instructors, graduate assistants, and teachers interested in generating more class discussion. This manual offers: (1) overviews and outlines of each chapter; (2) chapter objectives and quiz material; (3) material for class discussion; (4) topics warranting special attention; (5) supplementary examples; and (6) "What if?" discussion questions. Appendices provide guidance on (a) presenting material; (b) generating and sustaining class discussion; (c) preparing, administering, and grading quizzes; and (d) coping with the special problems confronting foreign graduate assistants.

Test Bank Thoroughly revised for currency and accuracy, the *Macroeconomics Test Bank* contains over 3,100 questions in multiple-choice and true-false formats. All multiple choice questions have five possible responses, and each is rated by degree of difficulty. For this edition, Nathan Eric Hampton of St. Cloud State University has thoroughly reworked the *Test Bank* and has grouped all questions according to chapter subheadings. This makes it easy to find just the questions you want and to make sure your questions are representative of material you teach in class.

Testing Tools—Computerized Testing Software *Testing Tools* is an easy-to-use test creation software package that is available in versions compatible with Microsoft Windows and with the Apple Macintosh. It contains all of the questions in the printed Test Banks. Instructors can add or edit questions, instructions, and answers, and select questions by previewing them on the screen and then choosing them by number, or at random. Instructors can also create and administer quizzes on-line, either over the Internet, through a local area network (LAN), or through a wide area network (WAN).

Microsoft PowerPoint Lecture Slides Tables and graphs from the text, as well as additional instructional materials, are available as PowerPoint slides to enhance lectures and help integrate technology into the classroom.

Transparency Acetates Most of the tables and graphs from this text are reproduced as full-color transparency acetates.

CNN Economics Video The CNN Economics Video provides a variety of brief video clips, taken from Cable News Network (CNN) programs, that illustrate various aspects of economics.

On-line Course Creation and Delivery Systems South-Western College Publishing now makes taking your course to the Web as easy as typing. Visit ITP Electronic Learning (http://www.itped.com) to learn about simple-to-use options for creating an on-line course or a Web site for your traditional course.

The Teaching Economist For nearly a decade, I have edited *The Teaching Economist*, a newsletter aimed at making teaching more interesting and more fun. The newsletter discusses imaginative ways to present topics-for example, how to "sensationalize" economic concepts, useful resources on the Internet, economic applications from science fiction, and more generally, ways to teach just for the fun of it. A regular feature of *The Teaching Economist*, "The Grapevine," offers teaching ideas suggested by colleagues from across the country. The latest issue—and back issues—of *The Teaching Economist* are available on-line at http://economics.swcollege.com.

ACKNOWLEDGEMENTS

Many people contributed to this book's development. I gratefully acknowledge the insightful comments of those who have reviewed chapters for the Fifth Edition. Their suggestions made me think more and made the book better.

Donna Anderson	University of Wisconsin, LaCrosse
Mohsen Bahmani	University of Wisconsin, Milwaukee
Jay Bhattacharya	Okaloosa Walton Community College
Doug Conway	Mesa Community College
Thomas Creahan	Morehead State University
Ron Elkins	Central Washington University
Roger Frantz	San Diego State University
J.P. Gilbert	MiraCosta College
Robert Gordon	San Diego State University
Fred Graham	American University
Nathan Eric Hampton	St. Cloud State University
Mehdi Haririan	Bloomsburg University
Julia Heath	University of Memphis
James Henderson	Baylor University
Bryce Kanago	Miami University
Robert Kleinhenz	California State University, Fullerton
Faik Koray	Louisiana State University
Marie Kratochvil	Nassau Community College
Jim Lee	Ft. Hays State University
Ken Long	New River Community College
Michael Magura	University of Toledo
Richard Martin	Agnes Scott College
KimMarie McGoldrick	University of Richmond
Mark McNeil	Irvine Valley College
Art Meyer	Lincoln Land Community College
Carrie Meyer	George Mason University
Bruce Mills	Troy State University

Shannon Mitchell	Virginia Commonwealth University
Maureen O'Brien	University of Minnesota, Duluth
Jaishankar Raman	Valparaiso University
Mitch Redlo	Monroe Community College
Simran Sahi	University of Minnesota, Twin Cities
George Santopietro	Radford University
Carol Scotese	Virginia Commonwealth University
Alden Shiers	California Polytechnic State University
Frederica Shockley	California State University, Chico
Gerald Simons	Grand Valley State University
Mark Stegeman	Virginia Polytechnic Institute
John Tribble	Russell Sage College
Robert Whaples	Wake Forest University
Mark Wheeler	Western Michigan University
Michael White	St. Cloud State University
Patricia Wyatt	Bossier Parish Community College

To practice what I preach, I relied on the division of labor based on comparative advantage to help put together the most complete teaching package on the market today. John Lunn of Hope College authored the *Study Guide*, which has been quite popular. Dorothy Siden of Salem State College authored the *Instructor's Manual*. And Nathan Eric Hampton of St. Cloud State University undertook a major reworking of the *Test Bank*. I thank them for their imagination and discipline.

The talented staff at South-Western College Publishing provided invaluable editorial, administrative, and sales support. I would especially like to single out the guidance of Dennis Hanseman, Development Editor and Ph.D. in economics, who helped me every step of the way, from the reviews of the previous edition to final proof pages. I also appreciate very much the excellent design work of Joe Devine, the superlative project coordination by Senior Production Editor Sharon Smith, the photography management of Cary Benbow, and the production assistance of Mary Ansaldo of Pre-Press Company, the production house for this edition. Kurt Gerdenich and Vicky True have been particularly helpful in developing the McEachern Interactive Study Center.

In addition I am most grateful to Bob Lynch, President of South-Western, Jack Calhoun, Publishing Team Director, Keri Witman, Acquisitions Editor, and especially Lisa Lysne, the Marketing Manager who knows the book inside and out. As good as the book is, all our efforts would be wasted unless students use it. To that end, I greatly appreciate South-Western's dedicated service and sales force, who have contributed in a substantial way to the success of previous editions.

Finally, I owe an abiding debt to my wife, Pat, who provided abundant encouragement and support along the way.

William A. McEachern

PREVIOUS EDITION REVIEWERS

Polly Reynolds Allen	University of Connecticut
Ted Amato	University of North Carolina, Charlotte
Richard Anderson	Texas A&M University
James Aylesworth	Lakeland Community College
Dale Bails	Christian Brothers College
Andy Barnett	Auburn University
Klaus Becker	Texas Tech University
David Brasfield	Murray State University
Jurgen Brauer	Augusta College
Gardner Brown, Jr.	University of Washington
Judy Butler	Baylor University
Charles Callahan III	SUNY College at Brockport
Giorgio Canarella	California State University, Los Angeles
Larry Clarke	Brookhaven College
Rebecca Cline	Middle Georgia College
Stephen Cobb	Xavier University
James P. Cover	University of Alabama
James Cox	DeKalb College
Jerry Crawford	Arkansas State University
Joseph Daniels	Marquette University
Elynor Davis	Georgia Southern University
Susan Davis	SUNY College at Buffalo
A. Edward Day	University of Central Florida
David Dean	University of Richmond
Janet Deans	Chestnut Hill College
David Denslow	University of Florida
John Edgren	Eastern Michigan University
Donald Elliott, Jr.	Southern Illinois University
G. Rod Erfani	Transylvania University
Gisela Meyer Escoe	University of Cincinnati
Mark Evans	California State University, Bakersfield
Eleanor Fapohunda	SUNY College at Farmingdale
Mohsen Fardmanesh	Temple University
Paul Farnham	Georgia State University
Rudy Fichtenbaum	Wright State University
T. Windsor Fields	James Madison University
Rodney Fort	Washington State University
Gary Galles	Pepperdine University
Edward Gamber	Lafayette College
Adam Gifford	California State University, Northridge
Robert Gillette	University of Kentucky
Art Goldsmith	Washington and Lee University
Philip Graves	University of Colorado, Boulder
Daniel Gropper	Auburn University
Simon Hakim	Temple University
Robert Halvorsen	University of Washington

William Hart	Miami University
Baban Hasnat	SUNY College at Brockport
James Hill	Central Michigan University
Jane Smith Himarios	University of Texas, Arlington
Dennis Hoffman	Arizona State University
Bruce Horning	Fordham University
Calvin Hoy	County College of Morris
Beth Ingram	University of Iowa
Joyce Jacobsen	Wesleyan University
Nancy Jianakoplos	Colorado State University
Nake Kamrany	University of Southern California
John Kane	SUNY College at Oswego
David Kennett	Vassar College
Joseph Kotaska	Monroe Community College
Joseph Lammert	Raymond Walters College
Dennis Leyden	University of North Carolina, Greensboro
C. Richard Long	Georgia State University
Thomas Maloy	Muskegon Community College
Gabriel Manrique	Winona State University
Robert Margo	Vanderbilt University
Wolfgang Mayer	University of Cincinnati
John McDowell	Arizona State University
James McLain	University of New Orleans
Martin Milkman	Murray State University
Milton Mitchell	University of Wisconsin, Oshkosh
Kathryn Nantz	Fairfield University
Reza Ramazani	St. Michael's University
Carol Rankin	Xavier University
Robert Rossana	Wayne State University
Mark Rush	University of Florida
Richard Saba	Auburn University
Rexford Santerre	Bentley College
Ted Scheinman	Mt. Hood Community College
Peter Schwartz	University of North Carolina, Charlotte
Roger Sherman	University of Virginia
William Shughart II	University of Mississippi
Calvin Siebert	University of Iowa
Phillip Smith	DeKalb College
V. Kerry Smith	Duke University
David Spencer	Brigham Young University
Jane Speyrer	University of New Orleans
Houston Stokes	University of Illinois, Chicago
Robert Stonebreaker	Indiana University of Pennsylvania
William Swift	Pace University
Lee J. Van Scyoc	University of Wisconsin, Oshkosh
Percy Vera	Sinclair Community College
Jin Wang	University of Wisconsin, Stevens Point
Gregory Wassall	Northeastern University

THE WALL STREET JOURNAL.

DOWJONES

Educational Edition

What's News—

ss and Finance

World-Wide

STS ARE UPBEAT that
omy will pick up by late
rvey found. They foresee
ending driven by recent
declines.   Separately,
and   construction

BRITAIN'S MAJOR WON
leader of the ruling Conservat
    Twelve days after resign
leader, Major was elected with
Tory members of Parliament
will remain as prime ministe
218 votes, compared with 89
wood, who quit the cabinet to c

How to Read Between the Lines

An Introduction to The Wall Street Journal

THE WALL STREE

MARKET

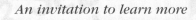

Why Ticket

An invitation to learn more

about the world's business daily.

An opportunity to go behind

the scenes at America's most

important business publication.

FIFTY YEARS IN EDUCATION
50
THE WALL STREET JOURNAL

The Marketplace

The Ears
These alert you to the day's top stories found in that section.

The Rotating Column
Here seasoned Journal writers, who are experts in their fields, inject personal opinion and informed judgements into their news stories.
MONDAY: **Health Journal**
TUESDAY: **Managing Your Career**
WEDNESDAY: **Work & Family, Business & Race**
THURSDAY: **Personal Technology**
FRIDAY: **The Front Lines**

The Top News
News with an individual perspective, you might find front-page articles about autos, travel, advertising, healthcare, pharmaceuticals, technology, law, marketing and the media.

Inside The Marketplace

Marketing & Media
Fifteen reporters and editors, focusing on the big stories first, cover all the news from the media, advertising and entertainment industries.

Net Interest/ Watching the Web
"Net Interest", a monthly column, takes a consumer's perspective to the Internet's promises, failures and personalities. "Watching the Web" is a directory of reviews that focus on must-visit or must-avoid sites.

Enterprise
Here you'll find news on trends, issues and legislation that affects small business, and illuminating news stories on why some small companies succeed while others fail.

Index to Business
Is there a company in which you're particularly interested? The Index, on page B2, lets you know at a glance if we've covered it in today's paper.

Inside The Marketplace (Continued)

Industry/Corporate Focus

Every day, we take a detailed look at a specific corporation – its competitive situation, corporate strategy, problems and successes – or an entire industry. In the latter case, our reporters covering the beat put together an insightful overview of an industry's current situation and future prospects.

Law

Here's legal news from a unique perspective: In our daily "Legal Beat" column and feature articles, we write about the law as a service that most people need, sooner or later. And we do so with uncommon expertise, as four of our seven reporters on the beat are lawyers themselves.

Technology

Our technology coverage may be anchored on a Marketplace page – in columns such as "In the Lab", "Technology & Medicine" and "Technology & Environment" – but it is also found all throughout the publication, from the front page to the last.

Who's News

Make it big in business, and you might find your name and picture in this column, where we chart the comings and goings of the upper reaches of corporate management. If you're thinking of working for a company, or investing in it, you might do well to keep your eye here, to find out who's running it.

Digest of Earnings Report

Public corporations can satisfy their legal obligation to announce quarterly and annual figures by publishing them in the Journal. (Of course, we have to be satisfied of their veracity before we'll print them.) This extensive compilation, which can feature over 200 companies in a single issue, is a must for investors.

Money & Investing: All the Numbers

Expert analysis, straight-forward explanations and comprehensive statistics create an easy-to-navigate guide to the stock market and other markets that affect both America's business and your finances.

Markets Diary

A prominent display of Yesterday's results in the stock, bond and commodities markets as well as the previous week's activity, interest rates, and the performance of the U.S. dollar relative to other major currencies.

The Top News

Here you'll find feature stories that carry the hottest news from the world of finance.

Pan Markets

Here's where you'll find all of yesterday's activity from the stock, bond and dollar markets are brought together in a concise and comprehensive overview of what happened and what it means.

Money & Investing Columns

Abreast of the Market/Small Stock Focus

Look to these columns first, for the authoritative word that explains market activity. While "Abreast" trains its sights on large-capitalization stocks, "Small Stock" does the same for small and medium-cap issues. Together, they constitute the most respected daily analysis of the stock market in print.

Heard on the Street

Every day, "Heard" brings our readers the first word on subjects and stocks that Wall Street denizens are talking about among themselves.

Getting Going

Whether you've got $3,000 to invest or $3 million, "Getting Going" gets you started in the right direction. Because Jonathon Clements has a rare ability to explain the first principles of investing in simple terms. His column every Tuesday will help you learn the most important criteria by which to evaluate what kind of fund is right for you.

Intrinsic Value

Once you've got some trades under your belt, take a look at Roger Lowenstein's "Intrinsic Value", which appears on Fridays. It's a sophisticated analysis of the fundamentals underlying the numbers, written with obvious expertise and marked by a strong ethical underpinning.

Money & Investing Columns (Continued)

Annuities Watch

As more people take responsibility for their own retirement planning, annuities have rapidly grown in popularity. In response, the Journal introduced this column and an accompanying page of variable-annuity statistics.

Fund Track

The mutual fund, an essential financial instrument, is the centerpiece of our news coverage and analysis in "Fund Track." This major daily column's primary purpose is to break news on the industry, but it also takes an advisory tone on matters of personal finance.

Your Money Matters

"Your Money Matters" sticks to the basics of money management and, through the course of a year, covers virtually everything of importance to the individual, from buying a home to financing an education, from evaluating stocks to planning an estate.

World Markets

Sara Webb gained years of expertise covering global equities markets for The Asian Wall Street Journal and the Wall Street Journal/Europe. Now, American readers get the benefit of her insight.

Money & Investing Statistics

The Journal's financial statistics are so comprehensive and extensive, it would take pages to introduce you to them in detail. Suffice it to say this: Whatever you need to know about the markets, either as an investment professional or individual investor, you'll find here. In most cases, you'll also find accompanying news columns that provide daily context and informed perspective on the movements of the particular market. Here's a brief look at some of the broad categories of data you'll find in "Money & Investing" every business day.

Stock Prices & the Stock Market

The Stock Market

The New York Stock Exchange, American Stock Exchange and Nasdaq National Market Issues lead the stock tables, but the Journal also includes regional and foreign stock exchange listings.

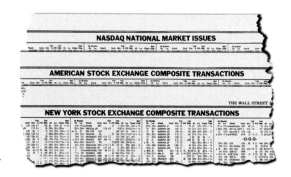

Stock Market Data Bank

Many analysts look at several indexes, not just the DJIA, and a variety of them are published at the top of the Stock Market Data Bank, which appears daily on page C2. Besides the Dow Jones Averages, there are the New York Stock Exchange indexes of all stocks traded on the exchange, and the NYSE indexes of major sectors. Indexes compiled by Standard & Poor's Corp. are market-weighted; the 500-stock index is often used as a benchmark of overall New York Stock Exchange performance. It is made up of 400 industrial, 20 transportation, 40 utility and 40 financial stocks. For each index, the Data Bank shows the latest day's closing level and changes from the previous day, a year earlier and the end of the previous year, both in absolute terms and as a percentage of the previous figure. The high and low for the latest 12 months also are shown. You can also find Nasdaq, American Stock Exchange, the 1,700 -stock Value Line and the 5,000-stock Wilshire indexes.

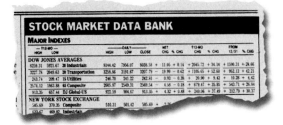

Understanding the Stock Market Tables

52 Week Hi and Lo:
Highest and lowest prices paid for the stock over the past 52 weeks, excluding the latest day's trading

Stock Symbol:
Used when looking up the stock on online systems

Stock Name

Dividend:
Stock's annual cash dividend, if any, based on the rate of the last quarterly payout to shareholders

Vol 100s:
Number of shares traded in each stock in the previous day, expressed in hundreds. Thus 57 means 5,700 shares were traded. Transactions generally take place in units of 100 shares. A "z" footnote before the volume figure means it represents the total shares traded; z57 means 57 shares were traded, not 5,700. Stocks with unusually high volume compared with that stock's average trading volume are underlined.

52 Weeks		Stock	Sym	Div	Yld %	PE	Vol 100s	Hi	Lo	Close	Net Chg
Hi	Lo										
42¾	28⅜	ColesMyer	CM	1.39e	3.6	...	38	39⅛	39¹⁄₁₆	39⅛	...
s78¹¹⁄₁₆	40¹³⁄₁₆	ColgatePalm	CL	1.10	1.7	29	9547	65¹¹⁄₁₆	64⁹⁄₁₆	64¾	− ⅜
12⅜	5½	CollnsAikman	CKC		...	5	340	11⁵⁄₁₆	11	11⁵⁄₁₆	+ ⁵⁄₁₆
s 28⁹⁄₁₆	16¹⁵⁄₁₆	ColBgp	CNB	.60	2.1	17	358	28	27½	27¹⁵⁄₁₆	...

Latest day's price data –
high, low, close and change from the previous day's closing. If one of these is a record for the previous 52 weeks, a small up or down arrow will appear to the far left of that stock's listing that day. The new extreme will be reflected in the 52-week high or low for the next day. A special table lists new highs and lows of NYSE listed stocks established that day. The length of this list can be an indicator of the market's performance. When a lot of issues reach new highs, there probably is a lot of buying pressure in the market. A large number of new lows indicates a bearish tone. Stocks that close up or down more than 5% from the previous day's closing price are printed in boldface.

Yld %:
Yield Percentage is obtained by dividing the cash dividend by the closing price of the stock. This enables dividend yields to be compared with other stocks and with the interest paid on debt instruments.

PE:
The P-E ratio is used as an indicator of relative stock performance. High P-Es indicate a stock price that's a high multiple of a company's earnings – suggesting optimism about the stock. Low P-E stocks often represent lower investor favor, but there isn't any "best" ratio. Reasons for high and low P-Es include the company's growth outlook, the company's industry, accounting policies, riskiness or the stability of the earnings. P-E ratio is the result of dividing the latest closing price by the latest available earnings per share, based on primary per-share earnings for the most recent four quarters.

Footnote:
An explanation of the footnotes appears daily underneath the graphs of the Dow Jones Averages. This box also recaps the meaning of the numbers in each of the stock-listing columns. For example, an "n" indicates a new issue of stock.

Dow Jones Global Indexes

Nearly 3,000 companies from 16 countries and 120 industry groups go into the most extensive foreign listings in any U.S. publication. The groupings divide these stocks into nine sectors that reflect large segments of the world economy; these nine sectors are then further subdivided into more specific industries. Countries are being added to the index as the global economy evolves. Over time, it will include every country whose stocks are available to foreign investors. As investor interest in global markets continues to grow, the Dow Jones World Stock Index has become an increasingly crucial measurement of world-wide stock performance.

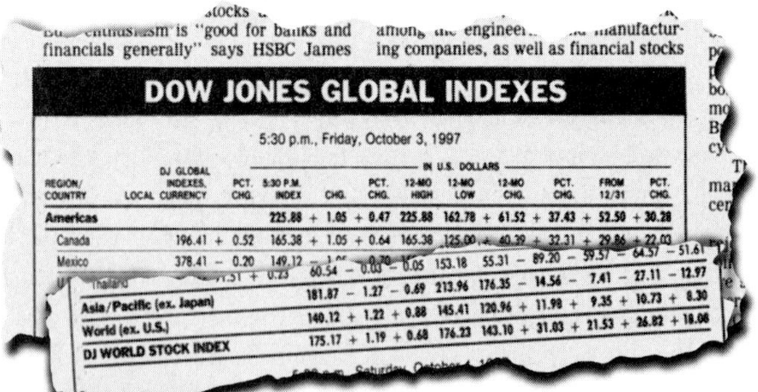

The Index offers superior measures of stock-market performance by providing investors with two comparative views: geographic and industrial. Investors can assess the political, economic and financial forces affecting the global market and measure how an individual issue has performed against its peers globally, regionally or nationally.

Dow Jones Averages

The universal standard barometer that charts the health of the market comes from Dow Jones & Company, the publisher of the Journal. When people ask "How's the market doing?" they usually mean the first of these indicators, the 30 stock Dow Jones Industrial Average. But there are indexes covering 20 transportation company stocks and 15 utility-company stocks, along with a composite index of the 65 stocks in the three indexes. The names of the stocks in each index appear daily next to the respective graph.

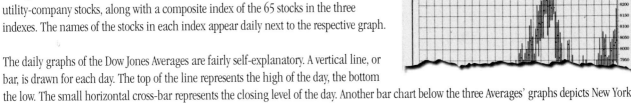

The daily graphs of the Dow Jones Averages are fairly self-explanatory. A vertical line, or bar, is drawn for each day. The top of the line represents the high of the day, the bottom the low. The small horizontal cross-bar represents the closing level of the day. Another bar chart below the three Averages' graphs depicts New York Stock Exchange volume for the days corresponding to the ones in the index charts.

The Dow Jones stock averages are price-weighted. This means a high-priced stock has a greater effect on the index than a low-priced one. There are other market indicators that attach weights to prices to give greater significance to stocks with greater market value. Market value is the price of a stock multiplied by the number of its shares outstanding. This system gives greater significance to larger companies. These are called market-weighted indexes.

You'll find the previous day's Dows detailed on page C3, along with other indexes of interest primarily to financial professionals.

Dow Jones Global Industry Groups

The Dow Jones Global Industry Group Table shows at a glance the relative performance of broad economic sectors both day-to-day and over the long term.

Unlike the Dow Jones Industrial Average, the World Stock Index World Industry Group Performance Table is market-weighted, not price-weighted – companies with large total-market values have the most effect on the movement of the indexes. They are all calculated based on a common value of 100 on June 30, 1982, so that their relative performance can be determined at a glance. Every day, the Journal reports on how each industry group fared compared with its close on the previous day, and the groups with the best and worst performance are displayed at the top of the Industry Group box along with the strongest and weakest stocks in each group.

Investment Funds

In many ways and for many reasons, the 1990s have seen America's first experiment with popular capitalism. In other words, investing is no longer just for the wealthy – it's become part of all our lives. One reason and result of this development is the explosive growth of investment funds, in which large and small investors pool their money and place it in the care of professional money managers. There are now thousands of funds with scores of investment objectives: growth funds, income funds, foreign-stock funds, bond funds...you get the picture. And you get all the data about all of them in the Journal. The best-known and most widely held, open-ended mutual and money-market funds are tracked daily. These funds continuously issue new shares if people wish to buy them back at prices based on the net asset value (NAV), or the value of the fund's portfolio less liabilities, divided by the number of shares outstanding. Unlike open-ended funds, closed-end funds offer a fixed number of shares—influenced by supply and demand but usually at prices that are very close to the net asset value. They trade on exchanges or over the counter; a table of closed-end funds is published on Mondays in the Journal. Each listing includes the closing NAV and exchange or over-the-counter price, the percentage difference and the market return for the latest 52-week period.

Mutual Funds

On Mondays through Thursdays, you'll find the fund's net asset value (NAV, or value per share); change from the previous day; and change for the year to date for every fund with assets of $25 million or more, or 1,000+ shareholders.

Mutual Funds–Friday

On Fridays, the listings expand to include the fund's investment objectives; total return over a month, year, three years and five years; its maximum load, or initial commission; and its annual expenses. In addition, each fund is ranked from A to E to compare its performance to other funds with the same objectives.

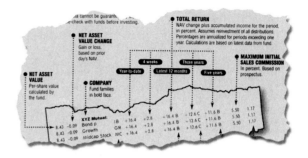

A charge, or sales commission of up to 8.5%, may apply to the mutual fund purchase price. Also, some funds may charge an exit fee when an investor redeems the shares. Other funds are sold on a no-load (NL) basis, i.e., without any sales commission. No-load shares usually are purchased directly from the fund, not through a broker. But these funds, like all others, usually charge an asset-management fee for investment advice or pay a fee to the outside firm that makes investment decisions for the fund. This annual fee is based on the average assets of the fund and typically averages less than 1% but can be higher.

Money Market Mutual Funds

Another type of open-ended fund is the money-market fund, which is limited to short-term instruments, such as CDs in large banks, commercial paper issued by major corporations and Treasury bills.

These money-market instruments often require a minimum investment of $100,000, but money-market funds allow smaller investors to participate in the higher interest rates offered by these instruments for a considerably smaller sum. But unlike bank deposits, money-market funds usually aren't guaranteed by the federal government.

Money-market fund quotes appear weekly on Thursdays. Each listing shows the average maturity for the portfolio in days, the average annual yield as a percentage based on the market for the past seven days, and total assets in millions of dollars.

Foreign Currency

Whether you're working at a company that does business overseas, or traveling to foreign shores, the foreign currency tables are the place to look for exchange rates, foreign currency futures prices and currency cross-rate tables that make it easy to convert one foreign currency into another.

Currency Trading Table

Gives the exchange rates prevailing at 3 p.m. Eastern time, expressed both as dollars per unit of foreign currency and as units of foreign currency per dollar. The former is the U.S. way of looking at things, the latter is the foreign way. Readers may encounter both ways. These rates apply to transactions among banks in amounts of $1 million or more. Rates for smaller transactions will be less favorable. Banks usually offer individuals better rates than commercial establishments do. Some currencies, such as the Belgian franc, have different rates for financial or commercial transactions. For some major currencies, such as the British pound and the German mark, rates also are given for future delivery.

At the bottom of the table is the conversion rate for the SDR, or Special Drawing Right, which is a reserve asset created by the International Monetary Fund for settlements among central banks. It also is used as a unit of account in international bond markets and by commercial banks. Based 42% on the U.S. dollar, 19% on the German mark and 13% each on the British pound, French franc and Japanese yen, the SDR's value fluctuates less than any single component currency. Also in the Journal every day is a currency cross-rates table that makes it more convenient to translate one foreign currency directly into another.

Exchange rates between important currencies used to be fixed, with sudden large changes forced only by the pressures of crises. Eventually the pressures became too great and too persistent, so rates now vary daily among major currencies. The system is known as floating exchange rates.

Since most international trade involves a delay between setting the price of a transaction and getting paid, this means at least one of the parties to such a transaction has a risk of losing money because the exchange rate may vary before payment is made.

This risk can be minimized by purchasing or selling foreign currency for future delivery at a specified exchange rate. For large amounts, this can be accomplished through banks in what is called the forward market; the 30-, 60-, 90- and 180-day rates in the Foreign Exchange table reflect this. Some foreign currencies also can be traded in futures markets, in smaller amounts; these are quoted daily (see "Futures above). There are also foreign currency options and futures options. The futures exchanges are increasingly providing a kind of secondary market in foreign exchange.

Money and Credit Markets *In other words (& very broadly): bonds, interest rates and the money supply.*

This can be a complicated world of secondary markets and over-the-counter trading among securities dealers, so let's just say this: This is the safest realm of investing, where the returns are lower but the security lets you sleep at night. Bonds and other instruments issued or backed by federal, state or local governments are considered virtually risk-free.

All types are covered thoroughly in our tables, with data that includes issue date, maturity, yield and asked/bid prices. We also include complete information on corporate bonds traded on the New York Stock Exchange and four major foreign-government bond markets.

Allied to these data is our information on the supply of and demand for money. The Federal Reserve Report, which we publish every Friday, gives important indicators for both, as do our daily Money Rates box (which lists the current prime lending rate) and the weekly Key Interest Rates table and Consumer Savings Rates List, which shows the rates paid by 100 banks in 10 large cities.

Treasury Issues

The Treasury issues instruments, due after various lengths of time, known as maturities. The shortest regularly issued maturities, three or six months, take the form of Treasury bills. These are issued every Monday in minimum denominations of $10,000 and in increments of $5,000 above the minimum. Investors bid for them at a discount, by offering, say $97.50 for every $100 of bills. At maturity, the investors will receive $100 for every $97.50 they paid. Yields are expressed on an annual basis.

Similar bills due in one year are sold monthly. The Treasury also issues cash-management bills on an irregular basis, generally for short periods, such as a few days. Treasury issues maturing in between one and 10 years are called notes. Those maturing in more than 10 years are called bonds. The process of selling these to the public takes place in the primary market, with the proceeds going to the issuer.

Secondary markets are made by securities dealers in all maturities of Treasury issues. In the secondary market, the prices of bills, notes and bonds fluctuate according to changes in interest rates. But, in one of the more confusing aspects of financial markets, the prices fluctuate inversely to the interest rates. Thus, when interest rates rise, bond prices go down, and when they fall, bond prices go up.

The rationale for this is as follows. Say the Treasury issues some 30-year bonds with an interest rate of 10%, or $10 of every $100. In time, interest rates may rise to 12%. Then, no one in the secondary market will want to pay full price for bonds paying 10% interest when they can buy new ones at 12%. However, they might be willing to pay less than $100 for every $100 of the old bonds. Tables and calculators exist which show the exact price to pay so the yield to maturity on a 10% bond is 12%, taking into account the time left to maturity when the purchase is made.

Similarly, when interest rates fall, bond prices will rise because sellers will hold out for a higher price to compensate for the higher-than-market interest paid on their holdings.

These changing prices are the basis of the Journal's tables for bonds and other debt securities. These issues are traded over the counter by securities dealers.

For bonds and notes, the price quotations are given per hundred dollars of face value.

Bonds issued some time ago may mature sooner than recently issued notes; this list is chronological. Some newer issues, designated "p", are exempt from withholding tax if held by nonresident aliens.

Month and Year of the security "n" designates notes; the rest are bonds.

The original interest rate.

Mid-afternoon bid price at which dealers were willing to buy the issue that day

Asked, or dealer, selling price

Changes in the bid price from the day before

Yield, or effective return on the investment. This is a calculation that takes into account the original interest rate, the current asked price and the amount of time left to maturity.

TREASURY BONDS, NOTES & BILLS

Tuesday, September 9, 1997

Representative and indicative Over-the-Counter quotations based on $1 million or more.

Treasury bond, note and bill quotes are as of mid-afternoon. Colons in bond and note bid-and-asked quotes represent 32nds; 101:01 means 101 1/32. Net changes in 32nds. Treasury bill quotes in hundredths, quoted in terms of a rate discount. Days to maturity calculated from settlement date. All yields are based on a one-day settlement and calculated on the offer quote. Current 13-week and 26-week bills are boldfaced. For bonds callable prior to maturity, yields are computed to the earliest call date for issues quoted above par and to the maturity date for issues quoted below par. n-Treasury note. i-Inflation-indexed. wi-When issued. iw-Inflation-indexed when issued; daily change is expressed in basis points.

Source: Dow Jones/Cantor Fitzgerald.

U.S. Treasury strips as of 3 p.m. Eastern time, also based on transactions of $1 million or more. Colons in bid-and-asked quotes represent 32nds; 99:01 means 99 1/32. Net changes in 32nds. Yields calculated on the asked quotation. ci-stripped coupon interest. bp-Treasury bond, stripped principal. np-Treasury note, stripped principal. For bonds callable prior to maturity, yields are computed to the earliest call date for issues quoted above par and to the maturity date for issues below par.

Source: Bear, Stearns & Co. via Street Software Technology Inc.

GOVT. BONDS & NOTES

Rate	Maturity Mo/Yr	Bid	Asked	Chg.	Ask Yld.
5 1/2	Sep 97n	99:31	100:01		4.81
5 3/4	Sep 97n	99:31	100:01		5.05
8 3/4	Oct 97n	100:09	100:11		4.96
5 5/8	Oct 97n	100:00	100:02		5.07
5 7/8	Oct 97n	100:00	100:02		5.19
7 3/8	Nov 97n	100:09	100:11		5.31

Rate	Maturity Mo./Yr.	Bid	Asked	Chg.	Ask Yld.
5 1/8	Feb 04n	97:27	97:29	+ 1	6.27
7 1/4	May 04n	105:02	105:04	+ 1	6.30
12 3/8	May 04	132:16	132:22	+ 2	6.30
7 1/4	Aug 04n	105:04	105:06	+ 2	6.31
13 3/4	Aug 04	140:31	141:05	+ 2	6.32
7 7/8	Nov 04n	108:23	108:25		
11 5/8	Nov 04	129:30	130:11		

Mat.	Type	Bid	Asked	Chg.	Ask Yld.
Feb 06	ci	58:10	58:15	− 1	6.47
Feb 06	bp	58:19	58:24	− 1	6.41
Feb 06	np	58:21	58:26	− 1	6.40
May 06	ci	57:10	57:15	− 1	6.49
Aug 06	ci	56:13	56:18	− 1	6.49
Nov 06	ci	55:15	55:20	− 1	6.50
Feb 07	ci	54:15	54:20	− 2	6.52
May 07	ci	53:17	53:22	− 2	6.53
Aug 07	ci	52:21	52:26	− 3	6.54
Nov 07	ci	51:25	51:30	− 2	6.54
Feb 08	ci	50:24	50:29	− 2	6.58
May 08	ci	49:29	50:02	− 2	6.58
Aug 08	ci	49:03	49:08	− 2	6.59
Nov 08	ci	48:06	48:11	− 2	6.61
Feb 09	ci	47:11	47:16	− 2	6.62
May 09	ci	46:17	46:22	− 2	6.63
Aug 09	ci	45:24	45:29	− 2	6.63
Nov 09	ci	44:30	45:03	− 2	6.65
Nov 09	bp	44:17	44:22	− 1	6.72
Feb 10	ci	44:05	44:10	− 2	6.66
May 10	ci	43:12	43:17	− 2	6.67
Aug 10	ci	42:20	42:25	− 2	6.68
Nov 10	ci	41:28	42:01	− 2	6.69
Feb 11	ci	41:06	41:11		6.69
May 11	ci	40:14	40:19	− 2	6.70
Aug 11	ci	39:23	39:29	− 2	6.71
Nov 11	ci	39:01	39:06	− 2	6.72
		38:11	38:17	− 2	6.72

In the bond market, a price of 100 is called par and each one-hundredth of par is called a point. Normally, the minimum price fluctuation is 1/32nd of a point. To avoid repeating the figure 32 all the time, and to save space, there is a convention in the bond market that figures after a decimal point in a price represent 32nds. Thus, a quotation of 90.16 means 90 and 16/32nds or $90\frac{1}{2}$.

In the Treasury bill section of this table, however, the decimal takes on its customary meaning: 16.50 means 16μ. Maturities are given as months and dates; 5-28 means May 28. The quotations are for discounts, as explained above. The yield, as for longer-term issues, represents the effective total return and is used for comparison with other investments.

Corporate Bonds,

There are three main types:
- Mortgage bonds: secured by real property, such as buildings
- Debentures: backed by a company's earning power rather than by specific hard assets
- Convertible bonds: can be exchanged for shares of the issue's stock.

Prices of a large number of corporate bonds are given in a table called New York Exchange Bonds. This covers bonds traded on the New York Stock Exchange, where only a small proportion of trading in these bonds takes place. Most bond trading is over the counter among securities dealers.

At the top of this table, there are data on the year's volume to date and a market diary. There is also a set of Dow Jones Averages for bond prices. The main index covers 20 bonds. There are component indexes for the 10 industrials and the 10 utilities. The New York table is followed by a short listing of bonds traded on the American Stock Exchange.

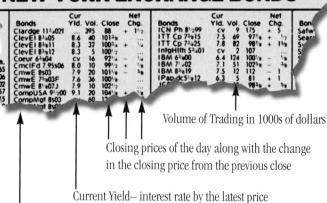

NEW YORK EXCHANGE BONDS

Bonds	Cur Yld.	Vol.	Close	Net Chg.	Bonds	Cur Yld.	Vol.	Close	Net Chg.
Clardge 11 3/4 02†	...	395	88	+ 1 1/2	ICN Ph 8 1/2 99	cv	9	175	+ 5
ClevEl 8 3/4 05	8.6	40	101 3/8	...	ITT Cp 7 3/8 15	7.5	69	97 7/8	+ 1/2
ClevEl 8 3/8 11	8.3	32	100 3/4	+ 1/4	ITT Cp 7 3/4 25	7.8	82	98 7/8	+ 1 3/8
ClevEl 8 3/8 12	8.3	5	100 1/2	...	IntgHlth 5 3/4 01	cv	2	107	...
Coeur 6 3/8 04	cv	16	92 3/4	− 1/4	IBM 6 3/8 00	6.4	124	100 1/8	− 1/8
CmclFd 7.95 06	8.0	10	99 1/2	− 1/4	IBM 7 1/2 02	7.1	51	102 5/8	− 3/8
CmwE 8 03	7.9	20	101 1/8	− 3/8	IBM 8 3/8 19	7.5	12	112	− 1
CmwE 7 3/4 03F	7.6	30	100 5/8	...	IPap dc5 1/4 12	6.3	5	81	− 1
CmwE 8 1/4 07J	7.9	10	102 1/2	...				98 3/4	+ 1/4
CompUSA 9 1/2 00	9.1	20	104 1/4	+					
CompMgt 8 03		60	1						

Volume of Trading in 1000s of dollars

Closing prices of the day along with the change in the closing price from the previous close

Current Yield– interest rate by the latest price

Name of the issuer, the original interest rate and the year of maturity, with an "s" where needed for ease of pronunciation.

Thus, 9s04 means "nines of oh-four," or 9% bonds due in 2004.

Other Government Bonds

Quotations for a selection of Government, Agency and miscellaneous securities are given in a separate table (at right), which is displayed much like Treasury bonds. Indexes measuring the performance of GNMA and FNMA issues are also included daily in the Bond Market Data Bank, as are prices and yields on representative individual mortgage-backed securities. Next to the Mortgage-Backed Securities list in the Data Bank, a small table lists the differential in yield between mortgage-backed securities and Treasury issues of comparable maturity.

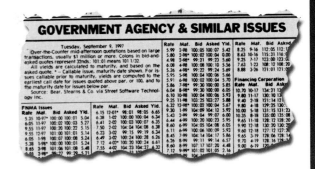

Municipal Bonds

Besides the U.S. government and its agencies, bonds may be issued by a variety of other government bodies that are lumped together under the heading "municipal," even though they include states, highway authorities and other noncity entities, as well as cities and their agencies. Usually, interest on these issues is exempt from income tax by the Federal government and by the state (and sometimes the city) in which the borrower is located. Because of this privilege, the issuer can apply a lower rate of interest, and investors have to consider the after-tax yield, based on their own income-tax situation, when comparing yields on these with those of other bonds. These bonds are also known as tax-exempts. The Journal prints a list of some of the most actively traded tax-exempts each day in the Bond Market Data Bank. The list is supplied by "The Bond Buyer," a New York trade publication.

Bond Market Data Bank

In addition to these market listings of individual bond prices, a further listing of the prices of 20 representative, actively traded corporate bonds is compiled by First Boston Corp. and appears daily in the Bond Market Data Bank. The Data Bank also lists the performance of several other indexes made up of various categories of corporate and convertible bond issues. The Merrill Lynch Corporate Master index, for example, represents a portfolio of about 4,400 nonconvertible bonds with remaining maturities of at least one year, a minimum of $1 million outstanding, and an average credit rating of A-1.

The Data Bank also lists bond prices and yields from four major foreign-government bond markets. All yields are semiannual, and compounded to maturity, to allow investors to make comparisons with domestic bonds. The Total Rates of Return box in the Data Bank provides an overall performance measure of the world's major bond markets.

Federal Reserve Report

One of the main influences on interest rates and the money markets is the supply of and demand for money. The Federal Reserve Report, published every Friday, gives important indicators of both. The level of commercial and industrial loans, for example, is an indicator of the demand for credit. In addition to the weekly report, a monthly chart shows the recent performance of the money supply indicators, compared with the Federal Reserve's targets. If one or more of the indicators is persistently outside the target range, the Fed may adjust its monetary policy and bring about a different level of interest rates.

Interest Rates

The Journal prints several features that track the levels of key interest rates affecting business and consumers. The daily Money Rates box lists the current prime lending rate as well as current yields and rates on a variety of short-term investments and loans. The weekly Key Interest Rates table is put together by the Federal Reserve Board and concentrates on returns for treasury issues. A weekly Consumer Savings Rates List shows the rates paid by 100 banks in 10 large metropolitan areas. Finally, on Wednesdays, the Banxquote Online deposits listings summarize rates paid on bank certificates of deposit.

THE WALL STREET JOURNAL.

WEEKEND JOURNAL.

All the Reasons You Work So Hard

It's Friday. The Wall Street Journal kicks off its shoes, and turns its attention to the world beyond Mondays-to-Fridays, 9-to-5. Every Friday, Journal subscribers smooth the transition from fast-paced to set-your-own speed with Weekend Journal, a regular section that celebrates the proposition that men and women do not thrive on work alone. Look inside, and you'll find great ideas on how to spend your well-earned time and money. If it's in your weekend, it's in Weekend Journal.

Inside Weekend Journal

Futures & Options
Diversions and Excursions. Weekly alerts on upcoming festivals, concerts, performances and gatherings. Previews of exceptional events throughout the U.S.

Travel
Weekend Journal's Travel page alerts you to the trends in airfares, critically examines vacation resorts and accommodations, from off-beat to the lap of luxury.

The Home Front
The Home Front page extols virtues (and vices) in personal real estate, offering one-of-a kind properties, valuable insight on the recoverable costs of improvements – and weekly data that reveals where prices are headed in communities across the country, courtesy of The Dow Jones Real Estate Index.

Sports
Sports page offers unique perspectives and postscripts on teams, individuals, tournaments, finals. You'll find surprising data and indices to change the way you think about, watch and participate in sporting events.

Entertainment
Weekend Journal looks behind the scenes and at the catalysts driving the entertainment business: performers, moguls, impresarios, marketing tie-ins. Reviews, alerts, cautions and catcalls for the performing arts on the road and in major cities.

Tastings
Tough-but-fair critics will get you to the bottom line: Is it worth $45 a bottle? Is it a find at $11? Are the entrees genuinely superb? Are you better served at home? Savory reports every week.

MACROECONOMICS
A Contemporary Introduction

Case Studies

The Art and Science of Economic Analysis

Visit the McEachern
Interactive Study Center
for this chapter at
http://mcisc.swcollege.com

Why are most comic strip characters, such as those in Hagar the Horrible, B.C., Cathy, and Peanuts, missing a finger? And how come Dilbert has no mouth? Why does Japan have twice as many vending machines per capita as does the United States and ten times as many as Europe? In what way are people who pound on vending machines relying on a theory? What's the big idea with economics? These and other questions are answered in this chapter, which introduces the art and science of economic analysis.

You have been reading and hearing about economic issues for years—unemployment, inflation, poverty, the federal budget, tuition, air fares, the stock market, computer prices, gas prices. When the explanations of these issues go into any depth, your eyes may glaze over and you may tune out the same way you do when a weather forecaster tries to provide an in-depth analysis of high-pressure fronts colliding with moisture carried in from the coast.

What many people fail to realize is that economics is much more lively than the dry accounts offered by the news media. Economics is about making choices, and you make economic choices every day—choices about whether to get a part-time job or focus on your studies, to live in a dorm or off-campus, to take a course in accounting or one in history, to pack a lunch or buy a Big Mac. You already know much more about economics than you realize. You bring to the subject a rich personal experience, an experience that we will tap throughout the book, to reinforce your understanding of the basic ideas. Topics discussed in this chapter include:

- The economic problem
- Marginal analysis
- Rational self-interest
- Scientific method
- Normative versus positive analysis
- Pitfalls of economic thinking

THE ECONOMIC PROBLEM: SCARCE RESOURCES BUT UNLIMITED WANTS

Would you like a new car, a nicer home, better meals, more free time, a more interesting social life, more spending money, more sleep? Who wouldn't? But even if you can satisfy some of these desires, others will pop up. *The problem is that, although your wants, or desires, are virtually unlimited, the resources available to satisfy these wants are scarce.* A resource is *scarce* when it is not freely available—that is, when its price exceeds zero. Because resources are scarce, you must choose from among your many wants and, whenever you choose, you must forgo satisfying some other wants. The problem of scarce resources but unlimited wants exists to a greater or lesser extent for each of the six billion people around the world. Everybody—taxicab drivers, farmers, brain surgeons, shepherds, students, politicians—faces the problem.

Economics examines how people use their scarce resources in an attempt to satisfy their unlimited wants. The taxicab driver uses the cab and other scarce resources, such as knowledge of the city, driving skills, and time, to earn income. The income, in turn, can be exchanged for housing, groceries, clothing, trips to Disney World, and thousands of other goods and services that help satisfy some of the driver's unlimited wants.

Let's pick apart the definition of economics, beginning with resources, next examining goods and services, and finally focusing on the heart of the matter: economic choice, which arises from scarcity.

Resources
Resources are the inputs, or factors of production, used to produce the goods and services that humans want. *Goods and services are scarce because resources are scarce.* We can divide resources into four general categories: labor, capital, land, and entrepreneurial ability. **Labor** is the broad category of human effort, both physical and mental. It includes the effort of the cab driver and the brain surgeon. Labor itself comes from a more fundamental resource: *time.* Without time we can accomplish nothing. We allocate our time to alternative uses: we can *sell* our time as labor, or we can *spend* our time doing other things such as sleeping, reading, or watching TV.

Economics The study of how people use their scarce resources to satisfy their unlimited wants

Resources The inputs, or factors of production, used to produce the goods and services that humans want; they consist of labor, capital, land, and entrepreneurial ability

Labor The physical and mental effort of humans used to produce goods and services

Capital includes human creations used to produce goods and services. We often distinguish between physical capital and human capital. *Physical capital* consists of factories, machines, tools, buildings, airports, highways, and other manufactured items employed to produce goods and services. Physical capital includes the driver's cab, the surgeon's scalpel, the farmer's tractor, the interstate highway system, and the building where your economics class meets. *Human capital* consists of the knowledge and skill people acquire to enhance their labor productivity, such as the taxi driver's knowledge of the city's streets and the surgeon's knowledge of human biology.

Land includes not only land in the conventional sense of plots of ground, but all other natural resources—all so-called *gifts of nature,* including bodies of water, trees, oil reserves, minerals, even animals.

A special kind of human skill called **entrepreneurial ability** is the talent required to dream up a new product or find a better way to produce an existing one. The entrepreneur tries to discover and act on profitable opportunities by hiring resources and assuming the risk of business success or failure. The largest firms in the world today, such as Ford, IBM, and Microsoft, each began as an idea in the mind of an individual entrepreneur.

Resource owners are paid **wages** for their labor, **interest** for the use of their capital, and **rent** for the use of their land. The entrepreneur's effort is rewarded by **profit,** which is the difference between *total revenue* from sales and the *total cost* of the resources employed. The entrepreneur claims what is left over after paying other resource suppliers. Sometimes the entrepreneur suffers a loss. Resource owners are usually paid for the *time* their resources are employed by entrepreneurs. Resource payments therefore have a time dimension, as in a wage of $10 *per hour,* interest of 6 percent *per year,* rent of $600 *per month,* or profit of $10,000 *per year.*

Goods and Services

Resources are combined in a variety of ways to produce goods and services. A farmer, a tractor, fifty acres of land, seeds, and fertilizer produce a good: corn. One hundred musicians, musical instruments, some chairs, a conductor, a musical score, and a music hall combine to produce a service: Beethoven's Fifth Symphony. Corn is a **good** because it is something we can see, feel, and touch; it requires scarce resources to produce; and it is used to satisfy human wants. The book you are now holding, the chair you are sitting in, the clothes you are wearing, and your next meal are all goods. The performance of the Fifth Symphony is a **service** because it is intangible, yet it uses scarce resources to satisfy human wants. Lectures, movies, concerts, phone calls, on-line computer services, piano lessons, dry cleaning, and haircuts are all services.

Because goods and services are produced using scarce resources, they are themselves scarce. A good or service is scarce if the amount people desire exceeds the amount that is available at a zero price. Since we cannot have all the goods and services we would like, we must continually choose among them. We must choose among more pleasant living quarters, better meals, nicer clothes, more reliable transportation, faster computers, and so on. Making choices in a world of **scarcity** means we must pass up some goods and services.

A few goods and services seem *free* because the amount freely available (that is, available at a zero price) exceeds the amount people desire. For example, air and seawater often seem free because we can breathe all the air we want and have

Capital The buildings, equipment, and human skill used to produce goods and services

Land Plots of ground as well as other natural resources used to produce goods and services

Entrepreneurial ability Managerial and organizational skills, combined with the willingness to take risks

Wages The payment that resource owners receive for their labor

Interest The payment that resource owners receive for the use of their capital

Rent The payment that resource owners receive for the use of their land

Profit The payment resource owners receive for their entrepreneurial ability; the total revenue from sales minus the total cost of resources employed by the entrepreneur

Good A tangible item that is used to satisfy human wants

Service An activity that is used to satisfy human wants

Scarcity When the amount people desire exceeds the amount available at a zero price

all the seawater we can haul away. Yet, despite the old saying that "The best things in life are free," most goods and services are scarce, not free, and even those that appear to be free come with strings attached. For example, *clean* air and *clean* seawater have become scarce. *Goods and services that are truly free are not the subject matter of economics. Without scarcity, there would be no economic problem and no need for prices.*

Sometimes we mistakenly think of certain goods as free because they involve no apparent cost to us. Those subscription cards that fall out of magazines appear to be free. At least it seems we would have little difficulty rounding up about three thousand of them if necessary! Producing the cards, however, absorbs scarce resources, resources drawn away from competing uses, such as producing higher-quality magazines. You may have heard the expression "There is no such thing as a free lunch." There is no free lunch because all goods and services involve a cost to someone. The lunch may seem free to us, but it draws scarce resources away from the production of other goods and services, and whoever provides a free lunch likely expects something in return. A Russian proverb makes a similar point, but with a bit more bite: "The only place you find free cheese is in a mousetrap." Albert Einstein said, "Sometimes one pays the most for things one gets for nothing."

Economic Decision Makers

There are four types of decision makers, or participants, in the economy: households, firms, governments, and the rest of the world. The interaction between these decision makers determines how an economy's resources are allocated. *Households* play the leading role. As consumers, households demand the goods and services produced. As resource owners, households supply labor, capital, land, and entrepreneurial ability to firms, to governments, and to the rest of the world. *Firms, governments,* and *the rest of the world* demand the resources that households supply and use them to produce and supply the goods and services that households demand. The rest of the world includes foreign households, firms, and governments, which supply resources and products to U.S. markets and demand resources and products from U.S. markets.

Market A set of arrangements through which buyers and sellers carry out exchange at mutually agreeable terms

Markets are the means by which buyers and sellers carry out exchange; markets bring together the two sides of exchange—supply and demand—to determine price and quantity. Markets are often physical places, such as a supermarket, department store, shopping mall, or flea market. But markets also include the mechanisms by which buyers and sellers communicate, such as classified ads, radio and television ads, telephones, bulletin boards, the Internet, and face-to-face bargaining. These market mechanisms provide information about the quantity, quality, and price of products offered for sale. Goods and services are bought and sold in **product markets;** resources are bought and sold in **resource markets.** The most important resource market is the labor, or job, market. Think of your own experience looking for a job, and you get some idea of this market.

Product market A market in which a good or service is bought and sold

Resource market A market in which resources are bought and sold

Microeconomics and Macroeconomics

Although you have made thousands of economic choices, you probably have seldom thought about your own economic behavior. For example, why did you choose to spend your scarce resource—*time*—reading this book right now rather than doing something else?

Microeconomics The study of the economic behavior in particular markets, such as that for computers or for unskilled labor

Microeconomics is the study of your economic behavior and the economic behavior of others who make choices about such matters as what to buy and what to sell, how much to work and how much to play, how much to borrow and how much to save. Microeconomics examines the factors that influence individual economic choices and how the choices of various decision makers are coordinated by markets. For example, microeconomics explains how price and output are determined in individual markets, such as that for breakfast cereal, for sports equipment, or for Beanie Babies.

You have probably given little thought to the factors that influence your own economic choices. You have likely given even less thought to how your choices link up with those made by hundreds of millions of others in the U.S. economy to determine economy-wide sums such as total production, employment, and economic growth. **Macroeconomics** studies the performance of the economy as a whole. Whereas microeconomics studies the individual pieces of the economic puzzle, as reflected in particular markets, macroeconomics puts all the pieces together to focus on the big picture.

Macroeconomics The study of the economic behavior of entire economies

THE ART OF ECONOMIC ANALYSIS

An economy results from the choices that millions of individuals make in attempting to satisfy their unlimited wants. Because these choices lie at the very heart of the economic problem—coping with scarce resources but unlimited wants—they deserve a closer look. Developing an understanding of the forces that shape economic choice is the first step toward mastering the art of economic analysis.

Rational Self-Interest

A key economic assumption is that individuals, in making choices, rationally select alternatives they perceive to be in their best interests. By *rational,* economists mean simply that people try to make the best choices they can, given the available information. People may not know with certainty which alternative will turn out to be the best. They simply select the alternatives they *expect* will yield them the most satisfaction and happiness. *In general, rational self-interest means that individuals try to minimize the expected cost of achieving a given benefit or maximize the expected benefit achieved with a given cost.*

Rational self-interest should not be viewed as blind materialism, pure selfishness, or greed. We all know people who are tuned in to radio station WIIFM (What's In It For Me?). For most of us, however, self-interest often includes the welfare of our family, our friends, and perhaps the poor of the world. Even so, our concern for others is influenced by economic considerations. We may readily volunteer to drive a friend to the airport on Saturday afternoon, but we are less likely to offer a ride if the plane leaves at 6:00 A.M. We are more likely to donate old clothes rather than new ones to organizations such as Goodwill Industries. We tend to give more to our favorite charities if our contributions are tax deductible. TV stations are more likely to donate air time for public-service announcements during the dead of night than during prime time (in fact, 80 percent of such announcements air between 11:00 P.M. and 7:00 A.M.[1]). *The notion of self-interest does not rule out concern for others; it simply means that concern for others is to*

---

1 As reported in Sally Goll Beatty, "Media and Agencies Brawl Over Do-Good Advertising," *Wall Street Journal,*
29 September 1997.

some extent influenced by the same economic forces that affect other economic choices. The lower the personal cost of helping others, the more help we offer.

Economic Analysis Is Marginal Analysis

Economic choice usually involves some adjustment to the existing situation, or status quo. The software producer must decide whether to revise a word processing program. The town manager must decide whether to hire another worker for street maintenance. Your favorite jeans are on sale, and you must decide whether to buy another pair. You are wondering whether you should carry an extra course next term. You have just finished dinner and are deciding whether to have dessert.

Marginal Incremental, additional, or extra; used to describe the result of a change in an economic variable

Economic choice is based on a comparison of the *expected marginal cost* and the *expected marginal benefit* of the action under consideration. **Marginal** means incremental, additional, or extra. Marginal refers to a change in an economic variable, a change in the status quo. *You, as a rational decision maker, will change the status quo as long as your expected marginal benefit from the change exceeds your expected marginal cost.* For example, you compare the marginal benefit you expect from eating dessert (the added pleasure and satisfaction) with its marginal cost (the added money, time, and calories). Likewise, the software producer compares the marginal benefit expected from revising a software program (the added sales revenue) with the marginal cost (the added cost of the resources required).

Typically the change under consideration is small, but a marginal choice can involve a major economic adjustment, as in the decision to quit school and get a job. For a firm, a marginal choice might mean introducing a new product, building a plant in Mexico, or even filing for bankruptcy. By focusing on the effect of a marginal adjustment to the status quo, the economist is able to cut the analysis of economic choice down to manageable size. Rather than confront a bewildering economic reality head-on, the economist can begin with a marginal choice and then see how this choice affects a particular market and shapes the economic system as a whole. Incidentally, to the noneconomist, "marginal" usually means relatively inferior, as in "restaurant meals of marginal quality." Forget that meaning for this course and instead think of marginal as meaning incremental, additional, or extra.

Choice Requires Time and Information

Rational choice takes time and requires information, but time and information are scarce and valuable. If you have any doubts about the time and information required to make choices, talk to someone who recently purchased a home, a car, or a personal computer. Talk to a corporate official deciding whether to introduce a new product, build a new factory, or acquire another firm. Or think back to your own experience in selecting a college. You probably talked to friends, relatives, teachers, and guidance counselors. You likely looked at school catalogs and college guides. You may have visited campuses to meet with the admissions staff and anyone else willing to talk. The decision took time and money, and it probably involved aggravation and anxiety.

Because information is costly to acquire, we are often willing to pay others to gather and digest it for us. The existence of markets for college guidebooks, stock analysts, travel agents, real-estate brokers, career counselors, restaurant guidebooks, and *Consumer Reports* magazine indicates our willingness to pay for information that will improve our economic choices. *Rational decision makers will continue to acquire information as long as the expected marginal benefit from the information exceeds its expected marginal cost.*

Normative Versus Positive

Economists usually try to explain how the economy works. Sometimes they concern themselves not with how the economy *does* work but how it *should* work. Compare these two statements: "The U.S. unemployment rate is 5.1 percent" and "The U.S. unemployment rate should be lower." The first is called a **positive economic statement** because it is an assertion about economic reality that can be supported or rejected by reference to the facts. The second is called a **normative economic statement** because it reflects an opinion. And an opinion is merely that—it cannot be shown to be true or false by reference to the facts. Positive statements concern what *is;* normative statements concern what, in someone's opinion, *should be.* Positive statements need not necessarily be true, but they must be subject to verification or refutation by reference to the facts.

Theories are expressed as positive statements such as "If the price increases, then the quantity demanded will decrease." Most of the disagreement among economists involves normative debates—for example, the appropriate role of government—rather than statements of positive analysis. To be sure, many theoretical issues remain unresolved, but economists largely agree on most fundamental theoretical principles—that is, about positive economic analysis. For example, in a survey of 464 U.S. economists, only 6.5 percent disagreed with the statement "A ceiling on rents reduces the quantity and quality of housing available." This is a positive statement because it can be shown to be consistent or inconsistent with the evidence. In contrast, there was much less agreement on normative statements such as "The distribution of income in the United States should be more equal." Half the economists surveyed "generally agreed," a quarter "generally disagreed," and a quarter "agreed with provisos."[2]

Normative statements, or value judgments, have a place in policy debates about the proper role of government, provided that statements of fact are distinguished from statements of opinion. It's been said that "You are entitled to your own opinion, but you are not entitled to your own facts."

To review: The art of economic analysis focuses on how individuals use their scarce resources in an attempt to satisfy their unlimited wants. Rational self-interest guides individual choice. Choice involves a comparison of the marginal cost and marginal benefit of alternative actions, a comparison that requires time and information. Care must be taken to distinguish between positive statements, which focus on how the economy works, and normative statements, which represent people's opinions about how the economy should work.

THE SCIENCE OF ECONOMIC ANALYSIS

Economists use scientific analysis to develop theories, or models, that help explain how economic choices are made and how the economy works. An **economic theory,** or **economic model,** is a simplification of economic reality that *is used to make predictions about the real world.* A theory, or model, captures

Positive economic statement A statement that can be proved or disproved by reference to facts

Normative economic statement A statement that represents an opinion, which cannot be proved or disproved

Economic theory, economic model A simplification of reality used to make predictions about the real world

---

2 Richard M. Alston, et al., "Is There a Consensus Among Economists in the 1990s?," *American Economic Review* 82 (May 1992): pp. 203–209, Table 1.

the important elements of the problem under study; it need not spell out every detail and interrelation. In fact, the more details a theory contains, the more unwieldy it becomes and the less useful it may be. The world we live in is so complex that we must simplify if we want to make any sense of things. Similarly, comic strips simplify characters; most are missing fingers, and some lack other features (Dilbert has no mouth). You might think of economic theory as a stripped-down version of economic reality.

The Role of Theory

People often don't understand the role of theory. Perhaps you have heard "Oh, that's fine in theory, but in practice it's another matter." The implication is that the theory provides little aid in practical matters. People who say this fail to realize that they are merely substituting their own theory for a theory they either do not believe or do not understand. They are really saying "I have my own theory, which works better."

All of us employ theories, however poorly defined or understood. Someone who pounds on the Pepsi machine that just ate a quarter has a crude theory about how that machine works and what went wrong. One version of that theory might be "The quarter drops through a series of whatchamacallits, but sometimes the quarter gets stuck. *If* I pound on the machine, *then* I can free up the quarter and send it on its way." Evidently this theory is so prevalent that many people continue to pound on machines that fail to perform (a real problem for the vending machine industry and a reason why newer machines are fronted with glass). Yet, if you asked this mad pounder to explain the "theory" about how the machine operates, he or she would look at you as if you were crazy.

The Scientific Method

To study economic problems, economists employ a process of theoretical investigation called the *scientific method,* which consists of four steps.

Step One: Identify the Question and Define Relevant Variables. The first step is to identify the economic question and define the variables that are relevant to the solution. For example, the question might be "What is the relationship between the *price* of Pepsi and the *quantity* of Pepsi purchased." In this case the relevant variables are price and quantity. A **variable** is a measure that can take on different values. The variables of concern become the elements of the theory, so they must be selected with care.

Variable A measure, such as price or quantity, that can take on different possible values

Step Two: Specify Assumptions. The second step is to specify the assumptions under which the theory is to apply. One major category of assumptions is the **other-things-constant assumption**—in Latin, the *ceteris paribus* assumption. The idea is to identify the variables of interest, then to focus exclusively on the relations among them, assuming that nothing else of importance will change—that other things will remain constant. Again, suppose we are interested in how the price of Pepsi influences the amount purchased. To isolate the relation between the price of Pepsi and the quantity purchased, we assume that there are no changes in other relevant variables such as consumer income, the price of Coke, and the average temperature.

Other-things-constant assumption The assumption, when focusing on key economic variables, that other variables remain unchanged

We also make assumptions about how people will behave; these are called **behavioral assumptions.** Perhaps the most fundamental behavioral assumption

Behavioral assumption An assumption that describes the expected behavior of economic decision makers

is rational self-interest. Earlier we assumed that individual decision makers pursue their self-interest rationally and make choices accordingly. Rationality implies that each consumer buys the products expected to maximize his or her level of satisfaction. Rationality also implies that each firm supplies the products expected to maximize that firm's profit. These kinds of assumptions are called behavioral assumptions because they specify how we expect economic decision makers to behave—what makes them tick, so to speak.

Step Three. The third step is to formulate a **hypothesis,** a theory about how key variables relate to each other. For example, one hypothesis holds that *if* the price of Pepsi goes up, other things constant, *then* the quantity purchased will decline. The hypothesis becomes a prediction of what will happen to the quantity purchased if the price goes up. The purpose of this hypothesis, like that of any theory, is to help make predictions about the real world.

Hypothesis A statement about relationships among key variables

Step Four. The validity of a theory is tested by comparing its predictions with evidence. To test a hypothesis, we must focus attention on the variables in question, while at the same time carefully controlling for other effects, which are assumed not to change. The test will lead us either to reject the theory as inconsistent with the evidence or to continue using the theory until a better one comes along. Even though a particular theory may not predict well at all times, it may still predict better than competing theories.

Economists Tell Stories

Despite economists' reliance on the scientific method for developing and evaluating theories, economic analysis is perhaps as much art as science. Formulating a question, isolating the key variables, specifying the assumptions, proposing a theory to answer the question, and devising a way to test the predictions all involve more than simply an understanding of economics and the scientific method.

Carrying out these steps requires good intuition and the imagination of a storyteller. Economists explain their theories by telling stories about how they think the economy works. To tell a compelling story, an economist relies on case studies, anecdotes, parables, and the personal experience of the listener. Throughout this book you will hear stories that bring you closer to the ideas under consideration. The story about the Pepsi machine mentioned earlier is one of those stories that help breathe life into economic theory and help you personalize abstract ideas. As an example, here is a case study about the popularity of vending machines in Japan.

A Yen for Vending Machines

In recent decades, the rate of unemployment has usually been lower in Japan than in other countries. Because of a declining birth rate, negligible immigration, and an aging population, Japan faces a steady drop in the number of people of working age. Because labor is relatively scarce in Japan, it is relatively costly. To sell products, Japanese retailers rely more on capital, particularly vending machines. Vending machines eliminate the need for a sales clerk.

CaseStudy

Other Times, Other Places

Speaking of storytelling, could an economist explain the arrangement of letters on your computer's keyboard? One story is told by David Tenenbaum in "Dvorak Keyboards" in *Technology Review* at http://www.techreview.com/articles/july96/trends.html.

Japan has more vending machines per capita than any other country in the world—more than twice as many as the United States and nearly ten times as many as Europe. Also vending machines in Japan are more sophisticated. For example, through a phone link, some vending machines tell vendors when more product or more change is needed, thereby eliminating unnecessary trips to restock the machines. Vending machines that sell cigarettes or alcohol now have a device that can verify a driver's license to check whether the customer is old enough to purchase these products legally. Robo Shop Super 24, a convenience store in Tokyo, is completely automated. After browsing long display cases, customers can make selections by punching product numbers on a keyboard. A bucket whirs around the store, rounding up the selections. Robo Shop is a giant vending machine.

A relatively low unemployment rate is not the only reason that vending machines are so popular in Japan. We already discussed how it is common practice in the United States to shake down vending machines that perform poorly. Such abuse increases the probability that the machines will malfunction in the future, leading to yet more abuse. In Japan, however, vending machines get more respect, in part because they are more sophisticated and more reliable and in part because of Japan's lower crime rate and greater respect for property. (For example, the automobile theft rate in Japan is only one-twentieth the U.S. rate.)

Japanese consumers use vending machines with great frequency. Sales per machine in Japan are double the U.S. level. Vending machines in Japan also sell a wider range of products, including videos, boxer shorts, stuffed animals, whisky, hot pizza, and even dating services. Some vending machines look like robots, which may seem natural in gadget-crazy Japan, where many childhood heroes are robotic characters. Despite the relative abundance of vending machines in Japan, their use is expected to grow even more, spurred on in part by technological innovations and a shrinking labor pool.

Sources: Nicholas Kristof, "In Japan, Chicken Little Lays the Golden Egg," *New York Times*, 30 July 1995; "The Coke Machine is Calling Again On Line 1," *The Nikkei Weekly*, 1 September 1997; "Economic Indicators," *The Economist*, 3 October 1997; and Serv-o-matic International, a worldwide seller of vending machines at http://www.ecity.net/~servom/.

This case study makes two points. First, producers combine resources in a way that conserves, or economizes on, the resource that is more costly, in this case labor. Second, the customs and conventions of the marketplace may differ across countries, and this may result in different types of economic arrangements, such as the more extensive use of vending machines in Japan.

Predicting Average Behavior

The task of an economic theory is to predict the impact of an economic event on economic choices and, in turn, the effect of these choices on particular markets or on the economy as a whole. Does this mean that economists try to predict the behavior of particular consumers or producers? Not necessarily, because any particular individual may behave in an unpredictable way. But the unpredictable actions of numerous individuals tend to cancel one another out, so the *average behavior* of groups can be predicted more accurately. For example, if the federal government cuts personal income taxes, certain households may decide to save the entire tax cut. On average, however, household spending in the economy will increase. Likewise, if Burger King cuts the price of Whoppers, the manager can better predict how much Whopper sales will increase than how a given customer will respond. *The random actions of individuals tend to offset one another, so the average behavior of a large group can be predicted more accurately than the behavior of a particular individual.* Consequently, economists tend to focus on the average, or typical, behavior of people in groups—for example, as average taxpayers or Whopper consumers—rather than on the specific behavior of a particular individual.

Some Pitfalls of Faulty Economic Analysis

Economic analysis, like other forms of scientific inquiry, is subject to common mistakes in reasoning that can lead to faulty conclusions. We will discuss three possible sources of confusion.

The Fallacy That Association Is Causation. Does something like this sound familiar: "The stock market was up today as traders reacted favorably to higher profits reported by Intel"? Although stock market analysts typically claim that millions of stock market transactions spring from a single event, such simplifications are often misleading and even wrong. To assume that event *A* caused event *B* simply because *B* followed *A* in time is to commit the **association-is-causation fallacy,** a common error. The fact that one event precedes another or that the two occur simultaneously does not necessarily mean that one causes the other. Remember: *Association is not necessarily causation.*

The Fallacy of Composition. Standing up at a football game to get a better view does not work if others stand as well. Arriving early to get in line for concert tickets does not work if many others have the same idea. Selling shares of stock before the price drops will not work if many others also try to sell. These are examples of the **fallacy of composition,** which is an erroneous belief that what is true for the individual or the part is also true for the group or the whole.

The Mistake of Ignoring the Secondary Effects. In many cities, public officials, out of concern about rising rents, have imposed rent controls on apartments. The *primary effect* of this policy, the effect on which policy makers focus, is to keep rents from rising. Over time, however, fewer new apartments get built because the rental business becomes less profitable. Moreover, existing rental units deteriorate because owners have no incentive to pay for maintenance. Thus, the quantity and quality of housing may well decline as a result of what appears to be a reasonable measure to control rents. The policy makers' mistake was to ignore the **secondary effects,** or the *unintended consequences,* of their policy. Economic actions have secondary effects that often turn out to be more important than the primary effects. Secondary effects may develop more slowly and may not be obvious, but good economic analysis takes them into account.

Association-is-causation fallacy The incorrect idea that if two variables are associated in time, one must necessarily cause the other

Fallacy of composition The incorrect belief that what is true for the individual or part must necessarily be true for the group or whole

Secondary effects Unintended consequences of economic actions that may develop slowly over time as people react to events

If Economists Are So Smart, Why Aren't They Rich?

Why aren't economists rich? Well, some of them are. Until his death, Taikichiro Mori, of Japan, a former economics professor, was reportedly the richest person in the world. Some economists earn as much as $25,000 per appearance on the lecture circuit. Others earn thousands of dollars a day as consultants. Economists have been appointed to the cabinet positions of Secretaries of Commerce, Defense, Labor, State, and Treasury. Economics is the only social science and the only

QUESTIONS FOR REVIEW

1. *(Definition of Economics)* What determines whether or not a resource is scarce? Why is the concept of scarcity important to the definition of economics?

2. *(Resources)* To which category of resources does each of the following belong?
   a. A taxicab
   b. Computer software
   c. One hour of legal counsel
   d. A parking lot
   e. A forest
   f. The Mississippi River
   g. An individual introducing a new way to market products on the Internet

3. *(Goods and Services)* Explain why each of the following would *not* be considered "free" for the economy as a whole:
   a. Food stamps
   b. U.S. aid to developing countries
   c. Corporate charitable contributions
   d. Noncable television programs
   e. Public high school education

4. *(Economic Decision Makers)* Which group of economic decision makers plays the leading role in the economic system? Which groups play supporting roles? In what sense are they supporting actors?

5. *(Micro versus Macro)* Determine whether each of the following is primarily a microeconomic or a macroeconomic issue:

   a. Determining the price to charge for an automobile
   b. Measuring the impact of tax policies on total consumption spending in the economy
   c. A household's decisions about how to allocate its disposable income among various goods and services
   d. A worker's decision regarding how many hours to work each week
   e. Designing a government policy to affect the level of employment

6. *(Micro versus Macro)* Some economists believe that in order to really understand macroeconomics, you must fully understand microeconomics. How does microeconomics relate to macroeconomics?

7. *(Normative versus Positive Analysis)* Determine whether each of the following statements is normative or positive:
   a. The U.S. unemployment rate was below 5 percent in 1998.
   b. The inflation rate in the United States is too high.
   c. The U.S. government should increase the minimum wage.
   d. U.S. trade restrictions cost consumers $19 billion annually.

8. *(Role of Theory)* What good is economic theory if it cannot predict an individual's behavior?

PROBLEMS AND EXERCISES

9. *(Rational Self-Interest)* Discuss the impact of rational self-interest on each of the following decisions:
   a. Whether to attend college full time or enter the full-time workforce
   b. Whether to buy a new or a used textbook
   c. Whether to attend a local college or an out-of-town college

10. *(Rational Self-Interest)* If behavior is governed by rational self-interest, why do people make contributions to charity?

11. *(Marginal Analysis)* The owner of a small pizzeria is deciding whether to increase the radius of its delivery area by one mile. What considerations must be taken into account if such a decision is to contribute to profitability?

12. *(Time and Information)* It is often costly to obtain information necessary to make good decisions. Yet your own interests can be best served by rationally weighing all options available to you. This requires completely informed decision making. Does this mean that making uninformed decisions is irrational? How do you determine what amount of information is the right amount?

13. *(CaseStudy: A Yen for Vending Machines)* Do vending machines conserve on any resources other than labor? Does your answer offer any additional insight into the widespread use of vending machines in Japan?

14. *(CaseStudy: A Yen for Vending Machines)* Suppose you had the choice of purchasing identically priced lunches

from a vending machine or at a cafeteria. Which would you choose? Why?

15. *(Pitfalls of Economic Analysis)* Review the discussion of pitfalls in economic thinking in this chapter. Then identify the fallacy or mistake in thinking in each of the following statements:
    a. Raising taxes will always increase government revenues.
    b. Whenever there is a recession, imports decrease. Therefore, to stop a recession, we should increase imports.

    c. Raising the tariff on imported steel will help the U.S. steel industry. Therefore, the entire economy will be helped.
    d. Gold sells for about $300 per ounce. Therefore, the U.S. government could sell all of the gold in Fort Knox at $300 per ounce and eliminate the national debt.

16. *(Association versus Causation)* Suppose I observe that communities with lots of doctors tend to have relatively high rates of illness. I conclude that doctors cause illness. What's wrong with this reasoning?

EXPERIENTIAL EXERCISES

17. *(Microeconomics and Macroeconomics)* Go to the Bank of Sweden's page on the Nobel Prize in economic science at http://www.ee.nobel.se/prize/memorial.html. Review the descriptions of some recent awards and try to determine whether those particular awards were primarily for work in macroeconomics or in microeconomics.

18. *(CaseStudy: College Major and Career Earnings)* The Bureau of Labor Statistics maintains online copies of articles from their *Monthly Labor Review*. Go to the site http://stats.bls.gov/opub/mlr/mlrhome.htm, click on "Archives" and find the article by Daniel Hecker entitled "Earnings of College Graduates: Women versus Men" (March, 1998). What can you learn about the payoff to college education for both women and men? (Note: You will need an Adobe Acrobat reader to get the full text of this article. You can download a copy of the reader at http://www.adobe.com/prodindex/acrobat/.

19. *(Wall Street Journal)* Detecting economic fallacies is a key skill. Review the section titled "Some Pitfalls of Economic Analysis" in this chapter. Then use the *Wall Street Journal* to find at least one example of faulty reasoning. (Hint: Begin with the "Markets Diary" column in the "Money & Investing" section.)

Appendix

UNDERSTANDING GRAPHS

Take out a pencil, a ruler, and a blank piece of paper. Go ahead, do it. Put a point in the middle of the paper. This is our point of departure, called the **origin.** With your pencil at the origin, draw a three-inch straight line off to the right. This line is called the **horizontal axis.** The value of the variable *x* measured along the horizontal axis increases as you move to the right of the origin. Now mark off this line into increments of 5 units each, from 0 to 20. Returning to the origin, draw another three-inch line straight up. This line is called the **vertical axis.** The value of the variable *y* measured along the vertical axis increases as you move upward. Now mark off this line into increments of 5 units each, from 0 to 20.

Within the space framed by the axes, you can plot possible combinations of the variables measured along each axis. Each point identifies a value measured along the horizontal, or *x,* axis *and* a value measured along the vertical, or *y,* axis. For example, place point *a* in your graph to reflect the combination where *x* equals 5 units and *y* equals 15 units. Likewise, place point *b* in your graph to reflect 10 units of *x* and 5 units of *y.* Now compare your results with those shown in Exhibit 2.

A **graph** is a picture showing how variables relate, and a picture can be worth a thousand words. Take a look at Exhibit 3, which shows the U.S. annual unemployment rate since 1900. The year is measured along the horizontal axis and the unemployment rate along the vertical axis. Exhibit 3 is a **time-series graph** because it shows the value of a variable, in this case the unemployment rate, over time. If you had to describe the information presented in Exhibit 3 in words, the explanation could take pages and would be mind-numbing. The picture shows not only how one year compares to the next, but also how one decade compares to another and how the rate has trended over time. Your eyes can wander over the hills and valleys to observe patterns that would be hard to convey in words. The sharply higher unemployment rate during the Great Depression of the 1930s is unmistakable. *Graphs convey information in a compact and efficient way.*

This appendix shows how graphs express a variety of possible relations among variables. Most of the graphs of interest in this book reflect the relationship between two economic variables, such as the year and the unemployment rate, the price of a product and the quantity demanded, or the cost of production and the quantity supplied. Because we focus on just two variables at a time, we usually assume that other relevant variables remain constant.

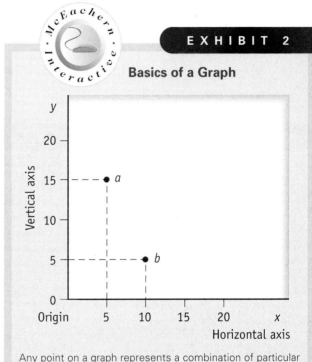

EXHIBIT 2

Basics of a Graph

Any point on a graph represents a combination of particular values of two variables. Here point *a* represents the combination of 5 units of variable *x* (measured on the horizontal axis) and 15 units of variable *y* (measured on the vertical axis). Point *b* represents 10 units of *x* and 5 units of *y.*

We often observe that one variable appears to depend on another. The time it takes you to drive home depends on your average speed. Your weight depends on how much you eat. The amount of Pepsi purchased depends on its price. A *functional relation* exists between two variables when the value of one variable *depends* on the value of another variable. The value of the **independent variable** determines the value of the **dependent variable**.

The task of the economist is to isolate economic relations and determine the direction of causality, if any. Recall that one of the pitfalls of economic thinking is the erroneous belief that association is causation. We cannot conclude, simply because two events are related in time, that the first event causes the second. There may be no relation between the two events.

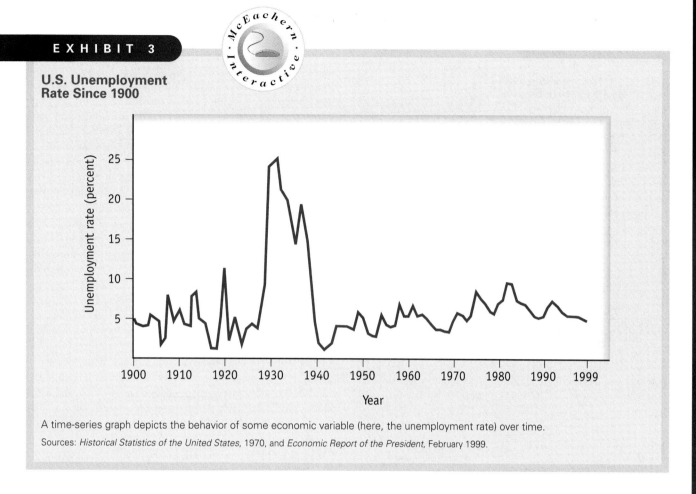

EXHIBIT 3

U.S. Unemployment Rate Since 1900

A time-series graph depicts the behavior of some economic variable (here, the unemployment rate) over time.

Sources: *Historical Statistics of the United States*, 1970, and *Economic Report of the President*, February 1999.

DRAWING GRAPHS

Let's begin with a simple relation. Suppose you are planning to drive across country and want to determine how far you will travel each day. You estimate that your speed will average 50 miles per hour. Possible combinations of driving time and distance traveled appear in Exhibit 4. One column lists the hours driven per day, and the next column gives the number of miles traveled per day, assuming an average speed of 50 miles per hour. The distance traveled, the dependent variable, depends on the number of hours driven, the independent variable. We identify combinations of hours driven and distance traveled as *a, b, c,* and so on. We can plot these combinations as a graph in Exhibit 5, with hours driven per day measured along the horizontal axis and total distance traveled along the vertical axis. Each combination of hours driven and distance traveled is represented by a point in Exhibit 5. For example, point *a* shows that when you drive for only 1 hour, you travel only 50 miles. Point *b* indicates that when you drive for 2 hours, you travel 100 miles. By connecting the points, or combinations, we create a line running upward and

to the right. This makes sense because the longer you drive, the farther you travel. Held constant along this line is the average speed of 50 miles per hour.

EXHIBIT 4

Schedule Relating Distance Traveled to Hours Driven

	Hours Driven per Day	Distance Traveled per Day (miles)
a	1	50
b	2	100
c	3	150
d	4	200
e	5	250

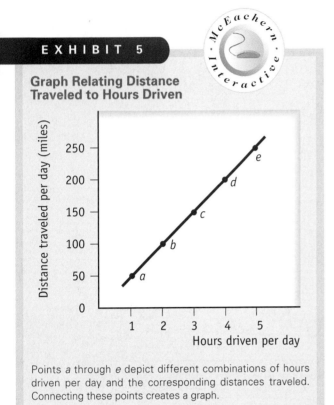

EXHIBIT 5

Graph Relating Distance Traveled to Hours Driven

Points *a* through *e* depict different combinations of hours driven per day and the corresponding distances traveled. Connecting these points creates a graph.

Each of the four panels in Exhibit 6 indicates a vertical change, given a 10-unit increase in the horizontal variable. In panel (a), the vertical distance increases by 5 units when the horizontal distance increases by 10 units. The slope of the line in panel (a) is therefore 5/10, or 0.5. Notice that the slope in this case is a positive number because the relation between the two variables is positive, or direct. This slope indicates that for every 1-unit increase in the horizontal variable, the vertical variable increases by 0.5 units. The slope, incidentally, does not imply causality; the increase in the horizontal variable does not necessarily *cause* the increase in the vertical variable. The slope simply indicates in a uniform way the relation between an increase in the horizontal variable and the associated change in the vertical variable.

In panel (b), the vertical distance declines by 7 units when the horizontal distance increases by 10 units, so the slope equals −7/10, or −0.7. The slope in this case is a negative number because the two variables have a negative, or inverse, relation. In panel (c), the vertical variable remains unchanged as the horizontal variable increases by 10, so the slope equals 0/10, or 0. These two variables are unrelated. Finally, in panel (d), the vertical variable can take on any value, although the horizontal variable remains unchanged. In this case any change in the vertical measure, for example a 10-unit change, is divided by 0, since the horizontal value does not change. Any change divided by 0 is infinitely large, so we say that the slope of a vertical line is infinite. Again, the two variables are unrelated.

Types of relations between variables include the following: (1) As one variable increases, the other increases, too—as in Exhibit 5; in this case there is a **positive, or direct, relation** between the variables; (2) as one variable increases, the other decreases; in this case there is a **negative, or inverse, relation;** and (3) as one variable increases, the other remains unchanged; in this case the two variables are said to be *independent, or unrelated.* One of the advantages of graphs is that they easily convey the relation between variables. We do not need to examine the particular combinations of numbers; we need only focus on the shape of the curve.

THE SLOPES OF STRAIGHT LINES

A more precise way to describe the shape of a curve is to measure its slope. The **slope** of a line indicates how much the vertical variable changes for a given increase in the horizontal variable. Specifically, the slope between any two points along any straight line is the vertical change between these two points divided by the horizontal increase, or

$$\text{Slope} = \frac{\text{Change in the vertical distance}}{\text{Increase in the horizontal distance}}$$

THE SLOPE, UNITS OF MEASUREMENT, AND MARGINAL ANALYSIS

The mathematical value of the slope depends on the units of measurement on the graph. For example, suppose copper tubing costs $1 a foot to produce. Graphs depicting the relation between output and total cost are shown in Exhibit 7. In panel (a), total cost of production increases by $1 for each 1-foot increase in the amount of tubing produced. Thus, the slope in panel (a) equals 1/1, or 1. If the cost remains the same but the unit of measurement is not *feet* but *yards,* the relation between output and total cost is as depicted in panel (b). Now, total cost increases by $3 for each 1-yard increase in output, so the slope equals 3/1, or 3. Because of differences in the units used to measure copper tubing, the two panels reflect different slopes, even though the cost of tubing is $1 per foot in each panel. Keep in mind that *the slope will depend in part on the units of measurement.*

Economic analysis usually involves *marginal analysis,* such as the marginal cost of producing one more unit of output. The slope is a convenient device for measuring marginal effects because it reflects the change in total cost along the vertical axis for each 1-unit change along the horizontal axis. For example, in panel (a) of Exhibit 7, the marginal cost of

EXHIBIT 6

**Alternative Slopes
for Straight Lines**

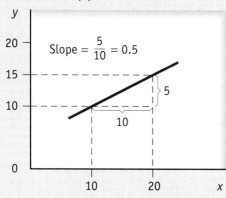

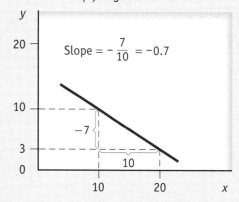

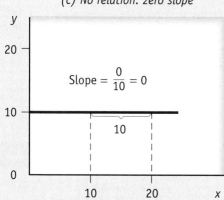

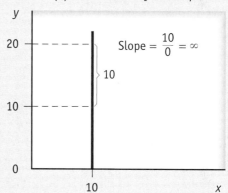

The slope of a line indicates how much the vertically measured variable changes for a given increase in the variable measured on the horizontal axis. Panel (a) shows a positive relation between two variables; the slope is 0.5, a positive number. Panel (b) depicts a negative, or inverse, relation. When the *x* variable increases, the *y* variable decreases; the slope is –0.7, a negative number. Panels (c) and (d) represent situations in which two variables are unrelated. In panel (c), the *y* variable always takes on the same value; the slope is 0. In panel (d), the *x* variable always takes on the same value; the slope is infinite.

another *foot* of copper tubing is $1, which also equals the slope of the line. In panel (b), the marginal cost of another *yard* of tubing is $3, which again is the slope of that line. Because of its applicability to marginal analysis, the slope has special significance in economics.

THE SLOPES OF CURVED LINES

The slope of a straight line is the same everywhere along that line, but the slope of a curved line varies at different points along the curve, as in Exhibit 8. To find the slope of that curved line at a particular point, draw a straight line that just touches the curve at that point but does not cut or cross the curve. Such a line is called a **tangent** to the curve at that point. The slope of the tangent is the slope of the curve at that point. Look at the line *AA*, which is tangent to the curve at point *a*. As the horizontal value increases from 0 to 10, the vertical value drops along *AA* from 40 to 0. Thus, the vertical change divided by the horizontal change equals –40/10, or –4, which is the slope of the curve at point *a*. This slope is negative because the curve slopes downward at that point. Along *BB*, a line drawn tangent to the curve at point *b*, the

EXHIBIT 7

Slope Depends on the Unit of Measure

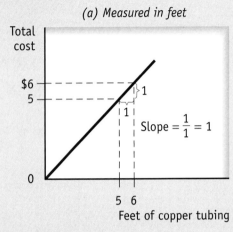

(a) Measured in feet

Total cost

$6
5

Slope $= \frac{1}{1} = 1$

1
1

0

5 6
Feet of copper tubing

(b) Measured in yards

Total cost

$6

3

Slope $= \frac{3}{1} = 3$

3
1

0

1 2
Yards of copper tubing

The value of the slope depends on the units of measure. In panel (a), output is measured in feet of copper tubing; in panel (b), output is measured in yards. Although the cost of production is $1 per foot in each panel, the slope is different in the two panels because copper tubing is measured using different units.

slope again is the change in the vertical divided by the change in the horizontal, or −10/30, which equals −0.33. As you can see, the curve depicted in Exhibit 8 gets flatter as the horizontal variable increases, so the value of its slope approaches zero.

Other curves, of course, will reflect different slopes as well as different changes in the slope along the curve. Downward-sloping curves have a negative slope, and upward-sloping curves, a positive slope. Sometimes curves are more complex, having both positive and negative ranges, such as in the hill-shaped curve in Exhibit 9. For relatively small values of *x*, there is a positive relation between *x* and *y*, so the slope is positive. As the value of *x* increases, however, the slope declines and eventually becomes negative. We can divide the curve into two segments: (1) the segment between the origin and point *a*, where the slope is positive, and (2) the segment of the curve to the right of point *a*, where the slope is negative. The slope of the curve at point *a* is 0. The U-shaped curve in Exhibit 9 represents the opposite relation: *x* and *y* are negatively related until point *b* is reached; thereafter they are positively related. The slope equals 0 at point *b*.

CURVE SHIFTS

Let's go back to your cross country trip, where we were trying to determine how many miles you traveled per day. Re-

EXHIBIT 8

Slopes at Different Points on a Curved Line

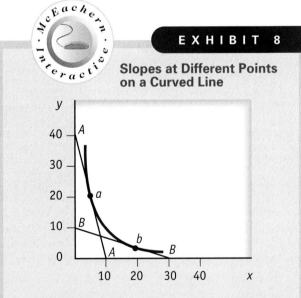

The slope of a curved line varies from point to point. At a given point, such as *a* or *b*, the slope of the curve is equal to the slope of the straight line that is tangent to the curve at that point.

EXHIBIT 9

Curves with Both Positive and Negative Ranges

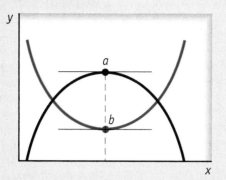

Some curves have both positive and negative slopes. The hill-shaped curve has a positive slope to the left of point *a*, a slope of 0 at point *a*, and a negative slope to the right of that point. The U-shaped curve starts off with a negative slope, has a slope of 0 at point *b*, and has a positive slope to the right of that point.

EXHIBIT 10

Shift in Curve Relating Distance Traveled to Hours Driven

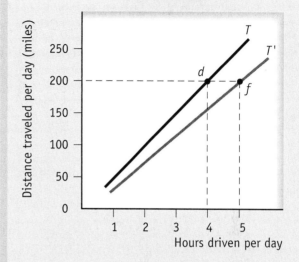

Curve *T* appeared originally in Exhibit 5 to show the relation between hours driven per day and distance traveled per day, assuming an average speed of 50 miles per hour. If the average speed is only 40 miles per hour, the entire relation shifts to the right to *T'*, indicating that each distance traveled requires more driving time. For example, 200 miles traveled takes 4 hours of driving at 50 miles per hour, but that distance takes 5 hours at 40 miles per hour.

call that we measured hours driven per day on the horizontal axis and distance traveled per day on the vertical axis, assuming an average speed of 50 miles per hour. That same relation is shown as curve *T* in Exhibit 10. What if the average speed is not 50 miles per hour, but instead is 40 miles per hour? The entire relation between hours driven and distance traveled would change, as shown by the shift to the right in the curve to *T'*. With a slower average speed, any distance traveled per day now requires more driving time. For example, 4 hours of driving result in 200 miles traveled when the average speed is 50 miles per hour (as shown by point *d* on curve *T*), but that distance takes five hours when the speed averages 40 miles per hour (as shown by point *f* on curve

T'). Thus, *a change in the assumption about average speed changes the relationship between the two variables observed.* This changed relationship is expressed by a shift in the curve that shows how the two variables relate.

With this we close our once-over of graphs. Return to this appendix when you feel you need to review.

APPENDIX QUESTIONS

1. *(Understanding Graphs)* Look at Exhibit 3 and answer the following questions:
    a. In what year (approximately) was the unemployment rate the highest? In what year was it the lowest?
    b. In what decade, on average, was the unemployment rate highest? In what decade was it lowest?
    c. Between 1950 and 1980, did the unemployment rate *generally* increase, decrease, or remain about the same?

2. *(Drawing Graphs)* Sketch a graph to illustrate your idea of each of the following relationships. Be sure to label both axes appropriately. In each case, explain under what circumstances, if any, the curve could shift:
    a. The relationship between a person's age and height
    b. Average monthly temperature over the course of a year
    c. A person's income and the number of hamburgers consumed per month
    d. The amount of fertilizer added to an acre of land and the amount of corn grown on that land in one growing season
    e. An automobile's horsepower and its gasoline mileage (in miles per gallon)

3. *(Slope)* Suppose you are given the following data on wage rates and number of hours worked:

Point	Hourly Wage	Hours Worked Per Week
A	$ 0	0
B	5	0
C	10	30
D	15	35
E	20	45
F	25	50

   a. Construct and label a set of axes and plot these six points. Label each point. What variable do you think should be measured on the vertical axis, and which variable should be measured on the horizontal axis?
   b. Connect the points. Describe the curve you find. Does it make sense to you?
   c. Compute the slope of the curve between points A and B. Between points B and C. Between points C and D. Between points D and E. Between points E and F. What happens to the slope as you move from point A to point F?

Some Tools of Economic Analysis

Visit the McEachern
Interactive Study Center
for this chapter at
ttp://mcisc.swcollege.com

Why are you reading this book right now rather than doing something else? What does college attendance cost you? Why will you eventually major in one discipline rather than take courses in many different disciplines? Why is fast food so fast? Why is there no sense crying over spilt milk? These and other questions are addressed in this chapter, which introduces some tools of economics—some tools of the trade.

The first chapter introduced the idea that scarcity forces us to make economic choices, but the chapter said little about how to make good choices. In this chapter we develop a framework for evaluating economic alternatives. First, we think about the cost involved in selecting one alternative over others. Next, we develop tools to explore the production choices available to individuals and to the economy as a whole. Finally, we examine the questions that different economies must answer—questions about what goods and services to produce, how to produce them and for whom. Topics discussed in this chapter include:

- Opportunity cost
- Division of labor
- Comparative advantage
- Specialization

- Production possibilities frontier
- Three economic questions
- Economic systems

CHOICE AND OPPORTUNITY COST

Think about a decision you just made: the decision to read this chapter right now rather than use the time to study for another course, play sports, watch TV, get some sleep, or do something else. Suppose your best alternative to reading right now is getting some sleep. The cost of reading is passing up the opportunity to sleep. Because of scarcity, whenever you make a choice, you must pass up another opportunity; you must incur an *opportunity cost*.

Opportunity Cost

Opportunity cost The value of the best alternative forgone when an item or activity is chosen

What do we mean when we talk about the cost of something? Isn't it what we have to give up—to sacrifice—to get that thing? The **opportunity cost** of the chosen item or activity is *the value of the best alternative that is forgone*. You might think of opportunity cost as the *opportunity lost*. Sometimes opportunity cost can be measured in terms of money, although, as we shall see, money is usually only part of the opportunity cost.

How many times have you heard people say they did something because they "had nothing better to do"? They actually mean they had no alternatives as attractive as the choice they selected. Yet, according to the idea of opportunity cost, people *always* do what they do because they have nothing better to do. The choice selected seems, at the time, preferable to any other possible choice. You are reading this chapter right now because you have nothing better to do. In fact, you are attending college for the same reason: College appears more attractive than your best alternative. In the following case study, consider the opportunity cost of attending college.

The Opportunity Cost of College

What is your opportunity cost of attending college full time this year? What was the most valued alternative you gave up to attend college? If you had a job, you have a good idea of the income you gave up to attend college. Suppose you expected to earn $16,000 a year, after taxes, from a full-time job. As a college student, you can work part time during the school year and full time during the summer. Suppose you can earn a total of $7,000 throughout the year after taxes. Thus, by attending college this year you are giving up net earnings of $9,000 (= $16,000 − $7,000).

There is also the direct cost of college itself. Suppose you are paying $5,000 this year for tuition, fees, and books at a public college. This money is unavailable to you (or your family) to spend elsewhere. So the opportunity cost of paying for tuition, fees, and books is the value of the goods and services that money could have purchased. Tuition, fees, and books would be much higher at a private college—more like $15,000 to $20,000.

Expenses for room and board are not necessarily opportunity costs because, even if you were not attending college, you would still need to live somewhere and eat something (though these costs could be higher at college). Likewise, whether or not you attended college, you would still incur outlays for items such as entertainment, clothes, toiletries, and laundry. Such expenses do not represent an opportunity cost of attending college. They are personal upkeep costs that arise regardless of what you are doing. For simplicity, let's assume that room, board, and personal expenses are the same whether or not you attend college; so they are not an opportunity cost of college. Thus, the forgone earnings of $9,000 plus the $5,000 for tuition, fees, and books yield an opportunity cost of $14,000 for attending college this year at a public college (at a private college, your opportunity cost could be double that amount).

This analysis assumes that other things are constant. If, in your view, attending college is more of a pain than you expected the most valued alternative to be, the opportunity cost of attending college is even higher. In other words, if you are one of those people who find college difficult, often boring, and in most ways more unpleasant than a full-time job, then the cost in money terms understates your true opportunity cost. Not only are you incurring the expense of college, but you are forgoing a more pleasant quality of life. If, on the contrary, you think the wild and crazy life of a college student is more enjoyable than a full-time job, then $14,000 overstates your true opportunity cost, because the best alternative involves a less satisfying quality of life.

Evidently, you view college as a wise investment in your future, even though it is costly and perhaps even painful. In fact, a growing fraction of college students are willing to go into debt to finance their education. Some students, even those who attend public universities, graduate with debts exceeding $20,000.

Still, college is not for everyone. Some people find college less attractive than alternatives. Tiger Woods, once an economics major at Stanford, dropped out after two years to earn millions in professional golf. Some high school seniors who believe they are ready for professional basketball skip college altogether, as do most pro tennis players and many actors. (Tom Cruise even dropped out of high school.)

Sources: "Debt Load—Class of '96," *America's Best Colleges: 1998, U.S. News & World Report,* pp. 63–64; Ellen Graham, "Study Now, Pay Later: Students Pile on Debt," *Wall Street Journal,* 11 August 1995; and CollegeNET, the "Internet Guide to Colleges and Universities" at http://www.collegenet.com.

Opportunity Cost Is Subjective

Opportunity cost is subjective. Only the individual chooser can select the most attractive alternative. And the chooser seldom knows the actual value of the best alternative forgone, since that alternative is "the road not taken." (Incidentally, focusing on only the best alternative forgone makes all other alternatives irrelevant.) Thus, if you give up an evening of pizza and conversation with friends to work on a term paper, you will never know the exact value of what you gave up. You know only what you *expected*. Evidently you expected the value of working on that paper to exceed the value of the best alternative.

Calculating Opportunity Cost Requires Time and Information. We have assumed that people rationally choose the most valued alternative. This does not mean they exhaustively calculate the value of all possible alternatives. Since acquiring information about alternatives is costly and time consuming, people usually make choices based on limited or even incorrect information. Indeed, some choices may turn out to be poor ones (as examples, you went on a picnic and it rained; the movie you rented was boring; the shoes you bought gave you blisters). At the time you made the choice, however, you thought you were making the best use of all your scarce resources, including the time required to gather and evaluate information about your alternatives.

Time Is the Ultimate Constraint. The Sultan of Brunei is among the world's richest people, based on the huge oil revenues that flow into his tiny country. His palace has 2,000 rooms, with walls of fine Italian marble. His throne room is the size of a football field. He owns 150 Rolls Royces.[1] Supported by such wealth, he appears to have overcome the economic problem caused by scarce resources but unlimited wants. But even though the Sultan can buy whatever he wants, the *time* he has to enjoy his acquisitions is limited. If he pursues one activity, he cannot at the same time do something else, so each activity he undertakes has an opportunity cost. Consequently, the Sultan must choose from among the competing uses of his scarcest resource, time. Though your alternatives are not as exotic as the Sultan's, you, too, face a time constraint, especially toward the end of the college term.

Opportunity Cost May Vary with Circumstance. Opportunity cost depends on the value of your alternatives. This is why you are more likely to study on a Tuesday night than on a Saturday night. On a Tuesday night, the opportunity cost of studying is lower because you have fewer attractive alternatives than on a Saturday night, when more is happening. Suppose you choose a movie for Saturday night. The opportunity cost of the movie is the value forgone from your best alternative, which might be attending a sporting event. For some of you, studying on Saturday night may be well down the list of alternatives—perhaps ahead of reorganizing your closet, but certainly behind watching trucks being unloaded at the supermarket.

Opportunity cost is subjective, but in some circumstances money paid for goods and services is a good approximation of their opportunity cost. For example, the opportunity cost of the new CD player you bought is the value of spending that $300 on the best forgone alternative. However, sometimes the monetary-cost definition may leave out some important elements, particularly the time involved. For example, watching a video costs you not only the rental fee but also the time and travel expense to get it, watch it, and return it.

---

1 These figures are reported by Kieran Cooke in "Sultan's Swing to Reform," *London Financial Times*, 4 August 1995.

Sunk Cost and Choice

Suppose you have just finished shopping for groceries and are wheeling your grocery cart toward the row of checkout counters. How do you decide which line to join? You pick the line you think will involve the least time. Suppose, after waiting for 10 minutes in a line that barely moves, you notice that a cashier has opened another register and invites you to check out. Do you switch to the new line, or do you think, "Since I have already spent 10 minutes in this line, I'm going to stay here"? The 10 minutes you already waited represents a *sunk cost*, which is a cost that you cannot recover regardless of what you do. **Sunk costs** are costs that cannot be avoided, regardless of what you do in the future, because they have already been incurred. You should ignore sunk costs in making economic choices, because your choice has no impact on something that has already happened. Therefore, you should switch to the newly opened line.

Economic decision makers should consider only those costs that are affected by the choice. Sunk costs have already been incurred and thus are not affected by the choice, so they are irrelevant. Likewise, you should walk out on a boring movie even if the admission cost you $8. The irrelevance of sunk costs is underscored by the proverb is "There is no sense crying over spilt milk." Remember, you should ignore sunk costs because they have already been incurred; the milk has already spilled, so whatever you do now has no impact on those costs.

Sunk cost A cost that has already been incurred in the past and, hence, a cost that is irrelevant to present and future economic decisions

SPECIALIZATION, COMPARATIVE ADVANTAGE, AND EXCHANGE

Suppose you live in a dormitory. You and your roommate have such busy schedules that you each can spare only about an hour per week for such mundane tasks as typing and ironing. Each of you must turn in a three-page typed paper every week, and you each prefer to have your shirts ironed if you have the time. Suppose it takes you a half hour to type the three-page paper. Your roommate is from the hunt-and-peck school and takes about an hour to type the paper. But your roommate is talented at ironing and can iron a shirt in 5 minutes flat (or should that be, iron it flat in 5 minutes). You take about twice as long, or 10 minutes, to iron a shirt.

During the hour available each week for typing and ironing, the typing takes priority. If you each do your own typing and ironing, your roommate takes the entire hour to type the paper and so has no time left for ironing. You type your paper in a half hour and iron three shirts in the remaining half hour. Thus, with each of you performing your own tasks, the combined output is two typed papers and three ironed shirts.

The Law of Comparative Advantage

Before long, you each realize that total output would increase if you did all the typing and your roommate did all the ironing. In the hour available for these tasks, you type both papers and your roommate irons twelve shirts. As a result of specialization, total output increases by nine shirts! You strike a deal to exchange your typing for your roommate's ironing, so you each end up with a typed paper and six ironed shirts. Thus, *each of you is better off as a result of specialization*

Law of comparative advantage The individual, firm, region, or country with the lowest opportunity cost of producing a particular good should specialize in producing that good.

Absolute advantage The ability to produce something using fewer resources than other producers use

Comparative advantage The ability to produce something at a lower opportunity cost than other producers face

and exchange. By specializing in the task that you each do best, you both employ the **law of comparative advantage,** which states that the individual with the lower opportunity cost of producing a particular output should specialize in producing that output.

Absolute and Comparative Advantage

The gains from specialization and exchange in the previous example seem obvious. A more interesting case arises if you are not only a faster typist but also a faster ironer. Suppose we change the example so that your roommate takes 12 minutes to iron a shirt, compared to your 10 minutes. You now have an *absolute advantage* in both tasks, meaning each task takes you less time than it does your roommate. More generally, having an **absolute advantage** means being able to produce a product using fewer resources than other producers require.

Does your absolute advantage in both activities mean specialization is no longer a good idea? Recall that the law of comparative advantage states that the individual with *the lower opportunity cost* of producing a particular good should specialize in producing that good. You still take 30 minutes to type a paper and 10 minutes to iron a shirt, so your opportunity cost of typing a paper is ironing 3 shirts. Your roommate takes an hour to type a paper and 12 minutes to iron a shirt, so your roommate could iron 5 shirts in the time taken to type a paper. Hence your opportunity cost of typing a paper is ironing 3 shirts, and your roommate's opportunity cost is ironing 5 shirts. *Because your opportunity cost of typing is lower than your roommate's, you have a comparative advantage in typing.* Since you have a comparative advantage in typing, your roommate must have a comparative advantage in ironing (try working this out to your satisfaction). Hence you should do all the typing and your roommate, all the ironing. Although you have an absolute advantage in both tasks, your **comparative advantage** calls for specializing in the task for which you have the lower opportunity cost—in this case, typing.

If neither of you specialized, you could type one paper and iron three shirts; your roommate could still type just the one paper. Your combined output would be two papers and three shirts. If you each specialized according to comparative advantage, in an hour you could type both papers and your roommate could iron five shirts. Thus, specialization increases total output by two ironed shirts. Exhibit 1 summarizes this example. Even though you are better at both tasks than your roommate, you are comparatively better at typing. Put another way, your roommate, although worse at both tasks, is not quite as poor at ironing as at typing.

Don't think this is simply common sense. Common sense would lead you to do your own ironing and typing, since you are more skilled at both. *Absolute advantage focuses on who uses the fewest resources, but comparative advantage focuses on what else those resources could have been used to produce—that is, on the opportunity cost of those resources.* Comparative advantage is the better guide to who should do what.

The law of comparative advantage applies not only to individuals but also to firms, regions of a country, and entire nations. Those individuals, firms, regions, or countries with the lowest opportunity cost of producing a particular good should specialize in producing that good. Because of such factors as climate, the skills of the workforce, plus the capital and natural resources available,

EXHIBIT 1

CASE 1: You are a faster typist and your roommate is a faster ironer.

	Output per Hour				
	Each Does Own			Each Specializes	
	Typed Papers	Ironed Shirts		Typed Papers	Ironed Shirts
You	1	3		2	0
Roommate	1	0		0	12
Total	2	3		2	12

CASE 2: You are a faster typist and a faster ironer, but you are a comparatively faster typist.

	Output per Hour				
	Each Does Own			Each Specializes	
	Typed Papers	Ironed Shirts		Typed Papers	Ironed Shirts
You	1	3		2	0
Roommate	1	0		0	5
Total	2	3		2	5

Comparative Advantage: Maximizing Output

Cases 1 and 2 both show gains from specialization and exchange for you and your roommate. In both cases it takes you half an hour to type the paper and 10 minutes to iron one shirt. In both cases your roommate takes 1 hour to type the paper. But, whereas in Case 1 it takes your roommate only 5 minutes to iron a shirt, in Case 2 it takes 12 minutes to iron a shirt. In Case 1 you have an absolute advantage and a comparative advantage in typing, so total output is greater if you do all the typing and your roommate does all the ironing. In Case 2 you have an absolute advantage in both typing and ironing. But you have a comparative advantage only in typing because you have a lower opportunity cost of typing than does your roommate. So in Case 2 output is maximized if you do all the typing and your roommate does all the ironing.

certain parts of the country and certain parts of the world have a comparative advantage in producing particular goods. From Apple computers in California's Silicon Valley to oranges in sunny Florida, from VCRs in Korea to bananas in Honduras—*resources are allocated most efficiently across the country and around the world when production and trade conform to the law of comparative advantage.*

Specialization and Exchange

In the previous example, you and your roommate specialized and then exchanged your output. No money was involved. In other words, you engaged in barter. **Barter** is a system of exchange in which products are traded directly for other products. Barter works satisfactorily in very simple economies where there is little specialization and few different goods to trade. But for economies with greater specialization, *money* plays an important role in facilitating exchange. Money—coins, bills, and checks—serves as a *medium of exchange* because it is the one thing that everyone is willing to accept in return for all goods and services.

Barter The direct exchange of one good for another without the use of money

Because of specialization and comparative advantage, most people consume little of what they produce and produce little of what they consume. People specialize in particular activities, such as plumbing or carpentry, and they exchange their products for money, which in turn is exchanged for goods and services produced by others. Did you make any article of the clothing you are wearing? Probably not. Think about the degree of specialization that goes into your cotton shirt. Some farmer in a warm climate grew the cotton and sold it to someone who spun it into thread, who sold it to someone who wove it into fabric, who sold it to someone who sewed the shirt, who sold it to a wholesaler, who sold it to a retailer, who sold it to you. Your shirt was produced by many specialists.

Division of Labor and Gains from Specialization

Picture a visit to McDonald's: "Let's see, I'll have a Big Mac, an order of fries, and a chocolate shake." About a minute later your order is ready. It would take you about an hour to make a homemade version of this meal. Why is the McDonald's meal faster, cheaper, and—for some people—better tasting than one you could make yourself? Why is fast food so fast?

Division of labor Organizing production of a good into its separate tasks

McDonald's is taking advantage of the gains resulting from the **division of labor.** Rather than have each worker prepare an entire individual meal, McDonald's breaks down meal preparation into various tasks and has individuals specialize in these separate tasks. This division of labor allows the group to produce much more than it could if each person tried to prepare an entire meal. Instead of each of 10 workers doing it all and making a total of, say, 50 complete meals in an hour, workers specialize and produce more like 500 meals per hour.

How is this increase in productivity possible? First, the manager can assign tasks according to *individual preferences and abilities*—according to comparative advantage. The employee with the toothy smile and pleasant personality can handle the customers up front; the employee with the strong back but few social graces can do the heavy lifting out back. Second, a worker who performs the same task again and again gets better at it. Experience is a good teacher. The employee filling orders at the drive-through window, for example, becomes better at handling the special problems that arise in dealing with customers. Third, there is no time lost in moving from one task to another. Finally, and perhaps most important, the **specialization of labor** allows for the introduction of more sophisticated production techniques, techniques that would not make economic sense on a smaller scale. For example, McDonald's large shake machine would be impractical in the home. The specialization of labor allows for the introduction of specialized machines, and these machines make each worker more productive.

Specialization of labor Focusing an individual's efforts on a particular product or a single task

To review: The specialization of labor takes advantage of individual preferences and natural abilities, allows workers to develop more experience at a particular task, reduces the time required to shift between different tasks, and permits the introduction of labor-saving machinery. Specialization and the division of labor occur not only among individuals but also among firms, regions, and indeed entire countries. The clothing production mentioned earlier might involve growing cotton in one country, turning the cotton into cloth in another, sewing the clothing in a third country, and marketing that clothing in a fourth country.

We should also note that specialization can create problems, since doing the same thing all day often becomes tedious. Consider, for example, the assembly line worker whose task is to tighten a particular bolt. Such a job could drive that worker nuts. Repetitive motion can also lead to injury. Thus, the gains from breaking production down into individual tasks must be weighed against the problems caused by assigning workers to repetitive and tedious jobs. Specialization is discussed in the following case study.

Evidence of Specialization

Evidence of specialization is all around us. Dozens of "specialty stores" at the mall focus on products ranging from luggage to party supplies to pet products. Restaurants specialize in cuisine from soup to sushi. Let your fingers do the walking through the Yellow Pages, and you will find thousands of separate specializations. Listings under "Physicians" alone offer dozens of medical specialties. Without moving a muscle, you can witness the division of labor within a single industry; watch the credits roll at the end of a movie, and you will see dozens and sometimes hundreds of specialists are listed—everyone from the gaffer (lighting electrician) to the assistant location scout.

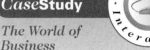

CaseStudy

The World of Business

Economics is a subject that has benefited from specialization and the division of labor. To get a feel for the many different subjects that economists investigate, take a look at the *Journal of Economic Literature's* classification system at http://www.econlit.org/elclasbk.htm.

Perhaps the easiest way to explore specialization and the division of labor is on the Internet, where millions of individual sites offer specialized products or activities. For example, Cyberian Outpost sells computers around the world; its Web site takes orders in more than a dozen languages. BigBook, a huge on-line phone directly offering over 16 million business listings allows you to look up any specialty listing for any U.S. state or city. For example, South Carolina has only one tattoo parlor, whereas Oregon, a state with a smaller population, has 43.

With a search engine such as Lycos, you can identify the number of Web sites that reference any specialty. For example, at last count, "economist" yielded about 13,000 sites, compared to 11,000 for "accountant," 7,000 for "physicist," and 2,000 for "sociologist." "Economics" turns up about 100,000 sites. "Entrepreneurs" are found at over 12,000 sites. From "aardvark" to "zucchini," the Internet identifies more specialties than any other reference source in the world.

Sources: Lycos technology is developed and marketed by Lycos, Inc., an independent operating company of CMG Information Services; BigBook's address is http://www.bigbook.com.

THE ECONOMY'S PRODUCTION POSSIBILITIES

The focus to this point has been on how individuals choose to use their scarce resources to satisfy their unlimited wants or, more specifically, how they specialize based on comparative advantage. This emphasis on the individual has been appropriate because the economy is shaped by the choices of individual decision makers, whether they are consumers, producers, or public officials. Just as resources are scarce for the individual, they are also scarce for the economy as a whole (no fallacy of composition here). An economy has millions of different resources that can be combined in all kinds of ways to produce millions of possible goods and services. In this section, we step back from the immense complexity of the real economy to develop our first model, which presents the economy's production options.

Efficiency and the Production Possibilities Frontier

Let's develop a model to get some idea how much can be produced in the economy with the resources available. What is the economy's production capabilities? Here are the model's simplifying assumptions:

1. To reduce the analysis to manageable proportions, we limit the output to just two broad classes of products. In our example they are consumer goods, such as pizzas and haircuts, and capital goods, which includes physical capital such as tractors, and human capital, such as college education.
2. The focus is on production during a given time period—in this case, a year.
3. The resources available in the economy are fixed in both quantity and quality during the time period.
4. Society's knowledge about how these resources can be combined to produce output—that is, the available *technology*—does not change during the year.

The point of these assumptions is to freeze the economy in time and to focus on the economy's production alternatives based on the resources and technology available during that time.

Given the resources and the technology available in the economy, the **production possibilities frontier,** or **PPF,** identifies the various possible combinations of the two types of goods that can be produced when all available resources are employed efficiently. *Resources are said to be employed efficiently when there is no change in the way the resources are combined that could increase the production of one type of good without decreasing the production of the other type of good.* **Efficiency** involves getting the maximum possible output from available resources.

The economy's PPF for consumer goods and capital goods is shown by the curve *AF* in Exhibit 2. Point *A* identifies the amount of consumer goods produced per year if all the economy's resources are used efficiently to produce consumer goods, and *F* identifies the amount of capital goods produced per year if all the economy's resources are used efficiently to produce capital goods. Points along the curve between *A* and *F* identify possible combinations of the two types of goods that can be produced when all the economy's resources are used *efficiently*.

Inefficient and Unattainable Production

Points inside the PPF, including *G* in Exhibit 2, represent combinations that either do not employ resources fully or employ them inefficiently. Note that point *C* yields more consumer goods and no fewer capital goods than *G*. And point *E* yields more capital goods and no fewer consumer goods than *G*.

Production possibilities frontier (PPF) A curve showing alternative combinations of goods that can be produced when available resources are used efficiently

Efficiency The condition that exists when there is no way resources can be reallocated to increase the production of one good without decreasing the production of another

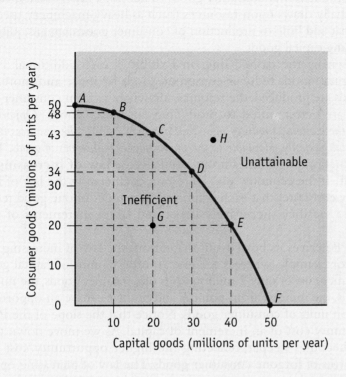

The Economy's Production Possibilities Frontier

If the economy uses its available resources and technology fully and efficiently in producing consumer goods and capital goods, it will be on its production possibilities frontier curve *AF*. The PPF is bowed out to illustrate the law of increasing opportunity cost: additional units of capital goods require the economy to sacrifice more and more units of consumer goods. Note that more consumer goods must be given up in moving from *D* to *E* than in moving from *A* to *B*, although in each case the gain in capital goods is 10 million units. Points inside the PPF, such as *G*, represent inefficient use of resources. Points outside the PPF, such as *H*, represent unattainable combinations.

Indeed, any point along the PPF between *C* and *E*, such as point *D*, yields both more consumer goods and more capital goods than *G*. Hence, point *G* is *inefficient*; by using resources more efficiently or by using previously idle resources, the economy can produce more of at least one good without reducing the production of the other good.

Points outside the PPF, such as *H* in Exhibit 2, represent *unattainable* combinations, given the resources and the technology available. Thus *the PPF not only reflects efficient combinations of production but also identifies the border between inefficient combinations inside the frontier and unattainable combinations outside the frontier.*

Shape of the Production Possibilities Frontier

Focus again on point *A* in Exhibit 2. Any movement along the PPF involves giving up some of one good to get more of the other. Movements down along the curve indicate that the opportunity cost of more capital goods is fewer consumer goods. For example, moving from point *A* to point *B* *increases* the amount of capital goods produced from none to 10 million units and *reduces* production of consumer goods from 50 million to 48 million units, a decline of

The new PPFs in both panels (a) and (b) appear to be parallel to the original PPF, indicating that the resource that changed could produce either good. For example, an increased supply of electrical power can be used in the production of both consumer goods and capital goods. If, however, a resource (such as farmland, for example) is suited only to the production of consumer goods, then an increase in the supply of that resource will shift the PPF more along the consumer goods axis than along the capital goods axis, as shown in panel (c). Panel (d) shows the effect of an increase in the supply of a resource (such as construction equipment) that is suited only to capital goods.

Increases in the Capital Stock. An economy's production possibilities frontier depends in part on the stock of human and physical capital. The more capital an economy accumulates during one period, the more output can be produced in the next period. Thus, increased production of capital goods this period (for example, by more machines in the case of physical capital or better education in the case of human capital) will shift out the economy's PPF next period.

Technological Change. Another type of change that could shift the economy's PPF outward is a technological discovery that employs available resources more efficiently. Some discoveries enhance the production of both products, such as an innovation that manages resources more efficiently. This is shown in panel (a) of Exhibit 3. The effect of a technological advance in the production of consumer goods, such as genetically altered seeds that double crop production, is reflected by a shift outward of the PPF along the consumer goods axis, as shown in panel (c) of Exhibit 3 (note that point *F* remains unchanged since the technological breakthrough does not affect the production of capital goods). Panel (d) shows the result of a technological advance in the production of capital goods, such as the development of improved software that reduces the cost of designing and manufacturing heavy machinery.

What We Can Learn from the PPF

The production possibilities frontier demonstrates several ideas introduced so far. The first is *efficiency*: The PPF describes the efficient combinations of output that are possible, given the economy's resources and technology. The second is *scarcity*: Given the resources and the technology, the economy can produce only so much. The PPF slopes downward, indicating that, as the economy produces more of one good, it produces less of the other good. This tradeoff demonstrates *opportunity cost*. The bowed-out shape of the PPF reflects the *law of increasing opportunity cost;* it arises because not all resources are perfectly adaptable to the production of each good. And a shift outward in the PPF reflects *economic growth*. Finally, because society must somehow choose a specific combination of output—a single point—along the PPF, the PPF also underscores the need for *choice*. That choice will determine not only current consumption but also the capital stock available next period. One thing the PPF does not tell us is which combination to choose; the PPF tells us only about the costs, not the benefits, of the two goods. To make a selection, we need information on both costs *and* benefits. How society goes about choosing a particular combination will depend upon the nature of the economic system, as we will see in the next section.

Three Questions Every Economic System Must Answer

Each point along the economy's production possibilities frontier is an efficient combination of output. Whether the economy produces efficiently and how the economy selects the most preferred combination will depend on the decision-making rules employed. Regardless of how decisions are made, each economy must answer three fundamental questions: What goods and services will be produced? How will they be produced? For whom will they be produced? An **economic system** is the set of mechanisms and institutions that resolve the *what, how,* and *for whom* questions. Some criteria used to distinguish among economic systems are (1) who owns the resources, (2) what decision-making process is used to allocate resources and products, and (3) what types of incentives guide the economic decision makers.

Economic system The set of mechanisms and institutions that resolve the what, how, and for whom questions

What Goods and Services Will Be Produced? Most of us take for granted the incredible number of choices that go into deciding what gets produced—everything from which new kitchen appliances are introduced and which aspiring novelists get published to which roads get built. Although different economies resolve these and millions of other questions using different decision-making rules and mechanisms, all economies must somehow make such choices.

How Will Goods and Services Be Produced? The economic system must determine how output is to be produced. Which resources should be used, and how should they be combined to produce each product? How much labor should be used, and at what skill levels? What kinds of machines should be used? What type of fertilizer should be applied to grow the best strawberries? Should the factory be built in the city or closer to the interstate highway? Millions of individual decisions determine which resources are employed and how these resources are combined.

For Whom Will Goods and Services Be Produced? Who will actually consume the goods and services produced? The economic system must determine how to allocate the fruits of production among the population. Should equal amounts be provided to everyone? Should the weak and the sick get more? Should those willing to wait in line the longest receive more? Should goods be allocated according to height? Weight? Religion? Age? Gender? Race? Looks? Strength? Political connections? The value of resources supplied? The question "For whom will goods and services be produced?" is often referred to as the *distribution question*.

ECONOMIC SYSTEMS

Although we discussed the three economic questions separately, they are closely interwoven. The answer to one depends very much on the answers to the others. For example, an economy that distributes goods and services in uniform amounts to all will, no doubt, answer the what-is-to-be-produced question differently than an economy that somehow allows each person to choose a unique mix of goods and services. Laws about resource ownership and the extent to which the government attempts to coordinate economic activity determine the "rules of the game"—the set of conditions that shape individual incentives and constraints. Along a spectrum ranging from the most free to the most regimented type of economic system, the *market system* would be at one end and the *command system* would be at the other end.

Pure Market System

Under the **pure market system,** the rules of the game include the private ownership of all resources and the coordination of economic activity based on the price signals generated in free, unrestricted markets. Any income derived from supplying labor, capital, land, or entrepreneurial ability goes exclusively to the individual owners of those resources. Owners have *property rights* to the use of their resources and are therefore free to supply those resources to the highest bidder. Producers are free to make and sell whatever they think will be profitable. Consumers are free to buy whatever goods they can afford. All this voluntary buying and selling is coordinated by unrestricted markets, where buyers and sellers make their wishes known. Market prices guide resources to their highest-valued use and channel goods and services to consumers who value them the most.

Under the market system, markets answer the what, how, and for whom questions. Markets transmit information about relative scarcity, provide individual incentives, and distribute income among resource suppliers. No single individual or small group coordinates these activities. Rather, it is the voluntary choices of many buyers and sellers responding only to their individual incentives and constraints that direct resources and products to those who value them the most. According to Adam Smith (1723–1790), one of the first to explain the allocative role of markets, market forces coordinate as if by an "invisible hand"—an unseen force that harnesses the pursuit of self-interest to direct resources where they earn the greatest payoff. According to Smith, *although each individual pursues his or her self-interest, the "invisible hand" of markets promotes the general welfare.* The market system is sometimes called laissez-faire; translated from the French, this phrase means "to let do," or to let people do as they choose without government intervention. Thus, under the market system, voluntary choices based on rational self-interest are made in unrestricted markets to answer the questions what, how, and for whom.

As we shall see in later chapters, a pure market system has its flaws. The most notable market failures are the following:

1. There is no central authority that can protect property rights, enforce contracts, and otherwise ensure that the rules of the game are followed.
2. People with no resources to sell may starve.
3. Some producers may try to monopolize markets by eliminating the competition.
4. The production or consumption of some goods generates byproducts, such as pollution, that affect those not involved in the market transaction.
5. So-called *public goods*, such as national defense, will not be produced by private firms because private firms cannot prevent nonpayers from enjoying the benefits of public goods.

Because of these limitations, countries have modified the pure market system to allow a role for government. Even Adam Smith believed government should play a role. Hong Kong is perhaps the most market-oriented economy in the world today.

Pure market system An economic system characterized by private ownership of resources and the use of prices to coordinate economic activity in unregulated markets

*Net*Bookmark

The Center for International Comparisons at the University of Pennsylvania at http://pwt.econ.upenn.edu/ is a good source of information on the performance of economies around the world.

Pure Command System

In a **pure command system,** resources are directed and production is coordinated based on the "command," or central plan, of government rather than by markets. At least in theory, there is public—communal—ownership of property. Government planners, as representatives of all the people, answer such questions as how much steel, how many cars, how many homes, and how many loaves of bread to produce. They also decide how to produce these goods and how to allocate them.

In theory, the pure command system incorporates individual choices into collective choices, which, in turn, are reflected in central planning decisions. In practice, the pure command system also has flaws. Most notably:

1. Running an economy is so complicated that some resources are used inefficiently.
2. Since nobody in particular owns resources, people have less incentive to employ them in their highest-valued use; so some resources are wasted.
3. Central plans may reflect more the preferences of central planners than those of society.
4. Since the central government is responsible for all production, the variety of products is much more limited than what is available in a competitive economy.
5. Each individual has less personal freedom in making economic choices.

Because of these limitations, countries have modified the pure command system to allow a role for markets. North Korea is perhaps the most centrally planned economy in the world today.

Pure command system An economic system characterized by public ownership of resources and centralized economic planning

Mixed and Transitional Economies

No country on earth exemplifies either type of economic system in its pure form. Economic systems have grown more alike over time, with the role of government increasing in market economies and the role of markets increasing in command economies. The United States represents a **mixed system,** with government directly accounting for about one-third of all economic activity. What's more, government regulates the private sector in a variety of ways. For example, local zoning boards determine lot sizes, home sizes, and the types of industries allowed. Federal bodies regulate workplace safety, environmental quality, competitive fairness, and many other activities.

Nearly all countries around the world have mixed economies. Countries with command systems are currently introducing more market incentives. For example, about 20 percent of the world's population live in the People's Republic of China, which grows more market oriented each day. The former Soviet Union dissolved into 15 independent republics; most are trying to privatize what had been state-owned enterprises. From Hungary to Mongolia, the transition to mixed economies now under way in former command economies will shape the 21st century.

Mixed system An economic system characterized by private ownership of some resources and public ownership of other resources; some markets are unregulated and others are regulated.

Economies Based on Custom or Religion

Finally, some economic systems are molded largely by custom or religion. For example, caste systems in India and elsewhere restrict occupational choice.

Family relations also play important roles in organizing and coordinating economic activity. Your own pattern of consumption and choice of occupation may be influenced by some of these factors.

CONCLUSION

Although economies can answer the three economic questions in a variety of ways, this book will focus primarily on the mixed market system found in the United States. This type of economy blends *private choice*, guided by the price system in competitive markets, with *public choice*, guided by democracy in political markets. The study of mixed market systems grows more relevant as former command economies try to develop market economies.

If you were to stop reading right now, you would already know more economics than most people. But to understand market economies, you must learn how markets work. You will do so in the next chapter, which introduces the market interaction of demand and supply.

SUMMARY

1. Resources are scarce, but human wants are unlimited. Since we cannot satisfy all wants, we must choose, and choice always involves an opportunity cost. The opportunity cost of the selected option is the value of the best alternative forgone.

2. The law of comparative advantage states that the individual, firm, region, or country with the lowest opportunity cost of producing a particular good should specialize in the production of that good. Specialization according to the law of comparative advantage promotes the most efficient use of resources.

3. The specialization of labor increases efficiency by (1) taking advantage of individual preferences and natural abilities, (2) allowing each worker to develop more experience at a particular task, (3) reducing the time required to move between different tasks, and (4) allowing for the introduction of more specialized capital and production techniques.

4. The production possibilities frontier shows the productive capabilities of an economy when all resources are used efficiently. The frontier's bowed-out shape reflects the law of increasing opportunity cost, which arises because some resources are not perfectly adaptable to the production of different goods. Over time, the frontier can shift in or out as a result of changes in the availability of resources or in technology. The frontier demonstrates several economic concepts, including efficiency, scarcity, opportunity cost, the law of increasing opportunity cost, economic growth, and the need for choice.

5. All economic systems, regardless of their decision-making processes, must answer three fundamental questions: What is to be produced? How is it to be produced? For whom is it to be produced? Economies answer the questions differently, depending on who owns their resources and how economic activity is coordinated.

QUESTIONS FOR REVIEW

1. (Opportunity Costs) Discuss the ways in which the following conditions might affect the opportunity cost of going to a movie tonight:
   a. You have a final exam tomorrow.
   b. School will be out for one month starting tomorrow.
   c. The same movie will be shown on TV next week.

2. (Opportunity Costs) Determine whether each of the following statements is true, false, or uncertain. Explain your answers:
   a. The opportunity cost of an activity is the total value of all the alternatives passed up.
   b. Opportunity cost is an objective measure of cost.

c. When making choices, people gather all available information about the costs and benefits of alternative choices.

d. A decision maker seldom knows the actual value of a forgone alternative and must base decisions on expected values.

3. *(Law of Comparative Advantage)* "You should never buy precooked frozen foods because you are paying for the labor costs of preparing food." Is this conclusion always valid, or can it be invalidated by the principle of comparative advantage?

4. *(Specialization and Exchange)* Explain how the specialization of labor can lead to increased productivity.

5. *(Production Possibilities)* Under what conditions is it possible to increase production of one good without decreasing production of another good?

6. *(Production Possibilities)* Under what conditions would an economy be operating inside its PPF? Outside its PPF?

7. *(Shifting Production Possibilities)* In response to an influx of illegal aliens, Congress made it a federal offense to hire them. How do you think this measure affected the U.S. production possibilities frontier? Do you think all industries were affected equally?

8. *(Production Possibilities)* "If society decides to use its resources fully (that is, to produce *on* its production possibilities frontier), then future generations will be worse off because they will not be able to use these resources." If this assertion is true, full employment of resources may not be a good thing. Comment on the validity of this assertion.

9. *(Economic Questions)* What basic economic questions must be answered in a barter economy? In a primitive economy? In a pure capitalist economy? In a command economy?

10. *(Economic Systems)* What are the major differences between a pure market system and a pure command system? Is the United States more like a pure market system or more like a pure command system?

PROBLEMS AND EXERCISES

11. **(CaseStudy:** *The Opportunity Cost of College)* During the Vietnam War, colleges and universities were overflowing with students. Was this bumper crop of students caused by a greater expected return on a college education or by a change in the opportunity cost of attending college? Explain.

12. *(Sunk Cost and Choice)* You go to a restaurant and buy an expensive meal. Halfway through, in spite of feeling full, you decide to clean your plate. After all, you think, you paid for the meal, so you are going to eat all of it. What's wrong with this thinking?

13. *(Comparative and Absolute Advantage)* You have the following information concerning the production of wheat and cloth in the United States and England:

Labor Hours Required to Produce One Unit

	England	United States
Wheat	2	1
Cloth	6	5

a. What is the opportunity cost of producing a unit of wheat in England? In the United States?

b. Which country has an absolute advantage in producing wheat? In producing cloth?

c. Which country has a comparative advantage in producing wheat? In producing cloth?

d. Which country should specialize in producing wheat? In producing cloth?

14. **(CaseStudy:** *Evidence of Specialization)* Provide some examples of specialized markets or retail outlets. What makes a medium like the World Wide Web conducive to specialization?

15. *(Shape of the PPF)* Suppose a production possibilities frontier includes the following data points:

Cars	Washing Machines
0	1,000
100	600
200	0

a. Graph the production possibilities frontier, assuming that it has no curved segments.

b. What is the cost of producing an additional car when 50 cars are being produced?

c. What is the cost of producing an additional car when 150 cars are being produced?

d. What is the cost of producing an additional washing machine when 50 cars are being produced? When 150 cars are being produced?

e. What do your answers tell you about opportunity costs?

16. *(Production Possibilities)* Suppose that there are two resources in the economy (labor and capital) that are used to produce two goods (wheat and cloth). Capital is relatively more useful in producing cloth, and labor is relatively more useful in producing wheat. If the supply of capital falls by 10 percent and the supply of labor increases by 10 percent, how will the PPF for wheat and cloth change?

17. *(Production Possibilities)* There's no reason why a production possibilities frontier could not be used to represent the situation facing an individual. Imagine your own PPF. Right now—today—you have certain resources—your time, your skills, perhaps some capital. And you can produce various outputs. Suppose you can produce combinations of two outputs, call them studying and partying.
    a. Draw your PPF for studying and partying. Be sure to label the axes of the diagram appropriately. Label the points where the PPF intersects the axes, as well as several other points along the frontier.
    b. Explain what it would mean for you to move upward and to the left along your personal PPF. What kinds of adjustments would you have to make in your life to make such a movement along the frontier?
    c. Under what circumstances would your personal PPF shift outward? Do you think the shift would be a "parallel" one? Why, or why not?

18. *(Shifting Production Possibilities)* Determine whether each of the following would cause the economy's PPF to shift inward, outward, or not at all:
    a. An increase in average length of annual vacations.
    b. An increase in immigration.
    c. A decrease in the average retirement age.
    d. The migration of skilled workers to other countries.

19. *(Economic Systems)* The United States is best described as having a "mixed" economic system. What are some elements of command in the U.S. economy? What are some elements of tradition?

EXPERIENTIAL EXERCISES

20. *(Production Possibilities Frontier)* Here are some data on the U.S. economy taken from the *Economic Report of the President* at http://www.access.gpo.gov/eop/.

Year	Unemployment Rate	Real Government Spending (billions)	Real Civilian Spending (billions)
1982	9.7%	$ 947.7	$3,672.6
1983	9.6	960.1	3,843.6
1996	5.4	1,257.9	5,670.5
1997	4.9	1,270.6	5,920.8

   a. Sketch a production possibilities frontier for the years 1982 and 1983, showing the tradeoff between public-sector (government) and private-sector (civilian) spending. Assume that resource availability and technology were the same in both years, but notice that the unemployment rate was relatively high.
   b. Sketch a PPF for the years 1996 and 1997. Assume that resource availability and technology were the same in both years, but higher than in 1982 and 1983. Note that the unemployment rate in the late 1990s was much lower than in the early 1980s.
   c. What lessons did you learn about the U.S. economy during the past 20 years?

21. *(Economic Systems)* The transitional economies of Eastern Europe are frequently in the news since they provide testing grounds for the transition from socialist central planning to freer, more market-oriented economies. Take a look at the World Bank's *Transition Newsletter* at http://www.worldbank.org/html/prddr/trans/WEB/trans.htm. Choose a particular economy and try to determine how smoothly the transition is proceeding. What problems is that nation encountering?

22. *(Wall Street Journal)* The ability to measure the true (opportunity) cost of a choice is a skill that will pay you great dividends. Use any issue of the *Wall Street Journal*, and find an article that discusses a decision some firm has made. (Try the "Business Bulletin" column on the front page of Thursday's issue.) Then review this chapter's section titled "Choice and Opportunity Cost." Finally, make a list of the kinds of opportunity costs involved in the firm's decision.

The Market System

Why do roses cost more on Valentine's Day than during the rest of the year? Why does TV advertising time cost more during the Super Bowl ($1.2 million for 30 seconds) than during *Nick-at-Nite* reruns. Why do hotel rooms in Phoenix cost more in February than in August? Why do surgeons earn more than butchers? Why do pro basketball players earn more than pro hockey players? Why do economics majors earn more than most other majors? Answers to these and most economic questions boil down to the workings of demand and supply, which will be examined in this chapter.

This chapter will introduce you to the underpinnings of demand and supply and show you how they interact in competitive markets. *Demand and supply are the most fundamental and the most powerful of all economic tools—important enough to warrant their own chapter.* Indeed, some believe that if you programmed a computer to respond "demand and supply" to every economic question, you could put many economists out of work. An understanding of the two concepts will take you far in mastering the art and science of economic analysis. As you will see, the correct analysis of demand and supply takes skill and care. This chapter uses graphs extensively, so you may want to refer to the Appendix of Chapter 1 for a refresher. Topics discussed in this chapter include:

- Demand and quantity demanded
- Supply and quantity supplied
- Markets

- Equilibrium price and quantity
- Changes in demand and in supply
- Disequilibrium

DEMAND

Demand A relation showing the quantities of a good that consumers are willing and able to buy at various prices during a given period of time, other things constant

How much Pepsi will consumers buy each week if the price is $3 per six-pack? If the price is $2? If it's $4? The answers reveal the relationship between the price of Pepsi and the quantity purchased. Such a relationship is called the *demand* for Pepsi. **Demand** indicates the quantity of a product that consumers are both *willing* and *able* to buy at each possible price during a given period of time, other things constant. Because demand pertains to a specific period of time, such as a day, a week, or a month, think of demand as the desired *rate of purchase* per time period at each possible price. Also, note the emphasis on *willing* and *able*. You may be *able* to buy a motorcycle at a price of $4,000 because you can afford one, but you may not be *willing* to buy one if motorcycles don't interest you.

The Law of Demand

In a remote region of western Pennsylvania is a poorly lit, run-down yellow building known as Pechin's Mart. The aisles are unmarked and strewn with half-empty boxes arranged in no apparent design. The sagging roof leaks when it rains. Why do shoppers come from as far away as Maryland and put up with the chaos and the grubbiness of Pechin's Mart to buy as many groceries as they can haul away? The store has violated nearly all the traditional rules of retailing, yet it thrives, with annual sales more than four times the national average. The store thrives because it reflects a rule merchants have known for thousands of years: Its prices are the lowest around.

As a consumer, you have little trouble understanding that people will buy more of a product at a lower price than at a higher price. Sell the product for less, and the world will beat a path to your door. This relation between the price of a product and the quantity demanded is an economic law. The **law of demand** states that the quantity of a product demanded during a given time period varies inversely with its price, other things constant. Thus, the higher the price, the smaller the quantity demanded; the lower the price, the greater the quantity demanded.

Law of demand The quantity of a good demanded in a given time period is inversely related to its price, other things constant

Demand, Wants, and Needs. Consumer *demand* and consumer *wants* are not the same thing. As we have seen, wants are unlimited. You may *want* a Mercedes-Benz 500-SL, but the $130,000 price is likely beyond your budget (that is, the quantity you demand at that price is zero). Nor is *demand* the same as *need*. You may *need* a new muffler for your car, but if the price is $200, you may decide

"I am not going to pay a lot for this muffler." Apparently, you have better ways to spend your money. If, however, the price of mufflers drops enough—say, to $90—then you become both willing and able to buy one.

The Substitution Effect of a Price Change. What explains the law of demand? Why, for example, is more demanded when the price is lower? The explanation begins with unlimited wants confronting scarce resources. Many goods and services are capable of satisfying particular wants. For example, you can satisfy your hunger with pizza, tacos, burgers, chicken, or dozens of other dishes. Similarly, you can satisfy your desire for warmth in the winter with warm clothing, a home-heating system, a trip to Hawaii, or many other ways. Clearly, some ways of satisfying your wants will be more appealing than others (a trip to Hawaii is more fun than warmer clothing). In a world without scarcity, everything would be free, so you would always choose the most attractive alternative. Scarcity, however, is a reality, and the degree of scarcity of one good relative to another helps determine each good's *relative* price.

Notice that the definition of demand includes the "other-things-constant" assumption. Among "other things" assumed to remain constant are the prices of other goods. When the price of pizza declines and other prices remain constant, pizza becomes relatively cheaper. Consumers are then more *willing* to purchase pizza when its relative price falls; they tend to substitute pizza for other goods. This is called the **substitution effect** of a price change. On the other hand, an increase in the price of pizza, other things constant, causes consumers to substitute other goods for the now higher-priced pizza. Remember, *it is the change in the relative price—the price of one good relative to the prices of other goods—that causes the substitution effect.* If all prices changed by the same percentage, there would be no change in relative prices and no substitution effect.

The Income Effect of a Price Change. A fall in the price of a product increases the quantity demanded for a second reason. Suppose you earn $30 a week from a part-time job and spend all your income on pizza, buying three a week at $10 per pizza. What if the price drops to $6? At that price you can now afford five pizzas a week with your income. The decrease in the price of pizza has increased your **real income**—that is, your income measured in terms of what it can buy. The price reduction, other things constant, increases the *purchasing power* of your income, thereby increasing your *ability* to purchase pizza. The quantity of pizza you demand will likely increase because of this **income effect** of a price decrease. You may not increase your quantity demanded to five pizzas, but you could. If you purchase four pizzas per week when the price drops to $6, you would have $6 left over to buy other goods. Thus, the income effect of a lower price increases your real income and thereby increases your ability to purchase all goods.

More generally, because of the income effect of a price decrease, other things constant, consumers typically increase their quantity demanded. Conversely, an increase in the price of a good, other things constant, reduces real income, thereby reducing the *ability* to purchase all goods. Because of the income effect of a price increase, consumers typically reduce their quantity demanded.

The Demand Schedule and Demand Curve

Demand can be expressed as a *demand schedule* or as a *demand curve*. Panel (a) of Exhibit 1 shows a hypothetical demand schedule for milk. When we describe

Substitution effect When the price of a good falls, consumers will substitute that good for other goods, which are now relatively more expensive

Real income Income measured in terms of the goods and services it can buy

Income effect A fall in the price of a good increases consumers' real income, making the consumers more able to purchase all goods; for normal goods, the quantity demanded increases

EXHIBIT 9

Effects of Changes in Both Supply and Demand

When the supply and demand curves shift in the same direction, equilibrium quantity also shifts in that direction; the effect on equilibrium price depends on which curve shifts more. If the curves shift in opposite directions, equilibrium price will move in the same direction as demand; the effect on equilibrium quantity depends on which curve shifts more.

	Change in Demand	
	Demand increases	**Demand decreases**
Supply increases	Equilibrium price change is indeterminate. Equilibrium quantity increases.	Equilibrium price falls. Equilibrium quantity change is indeterminate.
Supply decreases	Equilibrium price rises. Equilibrium quantity change is indeterminate.	Equilibrium price change is indeterminate. Equilibrium quantity decreases.

(Change in Supply — labeled along the vertical axis)

CaseStudy

The World of Business

The Busine$$ of Sport$ is a Web page devoted to economic issues surrounding (mainly) professional sports at http://www.bizsports.com/index.html. What is the latest on the market for pro basketball?

The Market for Professional Basketball

Toward the end of the 1970s, the National Basketball Association (NBA) seemed on the verge of collapse. Game attendance had sunk to only 58 percent of capacity. One-fifth of the teams were nearly bankrupt. The NBA championship game did not even merit prime-time television coverage.

During the 1980s, however, three superstars turned the league around. Michael Jordan, Larry Bird, and Magic Johnson brought new life to the sagging game and attracted millions of new fans. Since 1980, total attendance has doubled, the number of NBA teams has increased from 22 to 29 (with new franchises selling for record amounts), and the value of television broadcast rights has jumped *35*-fold from $76 million in 1978–1982 to $2.64 billion in 1998–2002.

The NBA is more popular than ever, though a labor dispute during what would have been the 1998–99 season took some luster off that popularity. Celebrities such as Jack Nicholson and Spike Lee have become fixtures in court-side seats (seats that sell for as much as $500 per game). Basketball's popularity has also increased around the world. The NBA formed global marketing alliances with Coca-Cola, McDonald's, and IBM; and the 1998 NBA finals were televised in more than 165 countries.

The players are the key resource in the production of NBA games. The growth in demand for pro basketball, coupled with a collective bargaining agreement that gave players more than half of total revenue (in 1997–98 players were paid 57 percent of total league revenues), jacked up average player salaries from $170 thousand in 1980 to $2.5 million in 1997–98. Basketball players are now the highest-paid team professionals in the world; their average pay is more than double that in pro football and pro hockey.

The primary source of talent for the NBA is college basketball. College games, especially the NCAA tournament nicknamed "March Madness," serve to heighten interest in the NBA, because fans can follow top collegiate players into the professional ranks. Top college prospects sign multimillion-dollar contracts. Such numbers attract talented players earlier and earlier in their academic years, since top players who remain in school risk a costly injury. In 1997, Kevin Garnett, who entered the NBA right out of high school in 1995, signed a seven-year contract worth $121 million. Because of basketball's worldwide popularity, talented players who fail to make the NBA often can sign attractive contracts overseas.

The high pay earned by the top players stems from the limited supply of those with such talent, combined with a large and growing demand for that talent. But rare talent alone is not enough. For example, top rodeo riders, top bowlers, and top women basketball players also possess rare talent, but the demand for their talent is not great enough to support pay anywhere close to NBA levels. Both supply *and* demand determine the average pay level.

Sources: "Garnett Accepts $121 Million," *Hartford Courant*, 2 Oct. 1997; Anthony Bianco, "David Stern: This Time It's Personal," *Business Week*, 13 July 1998, pp. 114–118; *The American Almanac: Statistical Abstract of the United States: 1996–1997*, Bureau of the Census (Austin, Texas: Hoover's Business Press, 1996).

DISEQUILIBRIUM PRICES

A surplus exerts downward pressure on the price; a shortage exerts upward pressure on the price. Markets, however, do not always attain equilibrium quickly. During the time required for adjustment, the market is said to be in disequilibrium. **Disequilibrium** is usually a temporary phase when the market gropes for equilibrium. For example, popular toys, best-selling books, and chartbusting compact discs often sell out and are temporarily unavailable. On the other hand, some new products attract few customers and pile up unsold on store shelves, awaiting a "clearance sale." Sometimes, however, often as a result of government intervention in markets, disequilibrium can last a long time, as we will see next.

Disequilibrium A mismatch between quantity supplied and quantity demanded as the market seeks equilibrium

Price Floors

Sometimes public officials set prices above their equilibrium values. For example, the federal government often regulates the prices of some agricultural commodities in an attempt to ensure farmers a higher and more stable income than they would otherwise earn. To achieve higher prices, the federal government sets a **price floor,** or a *minimum* selling price above the equilibrium price. Panel (a) of Exhibit 10 shows the effect of a $1.00 per quart price floor for milk. At that price, farmers supply 24 million quarts of milk per month, but

Price floor A minimum legal price below which a good or service cannot be sold; to be effective, a price floor must be set above the equilibrium price

EXHIBIT 10

Effects of a Price Floor and a Price Ceiling

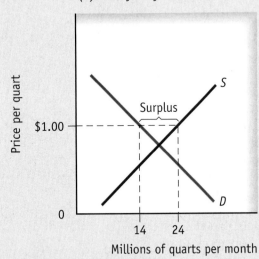

(a) Price floor for milk

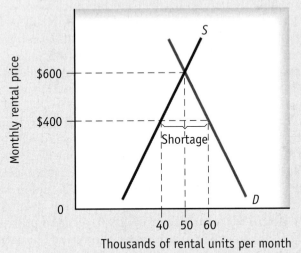

(b) Price ceiling for rent

If a price floor is established above the equilibrium price, a permanent surplus will result. A price floor established at or below the equilibrium price will have no effect. If a price ceiling is established below the equilibrium price, a permanent shortage will result. A price ceiling established at or above the equilibrium price will have no effect.

consumers demand only 14 million quarts. Thus the price floor results in a surplus of 10 million quarts. This surplus, unless somehow eliminated, will force the price down. So, as part of the price support program, the government usually agrees to buy the surplus milk to take it off the market. The federal government, in fact, has spent billions buying and storing surplus agricultural products.

Price Ceilings

Sometimes public officials try to keep prices below their equilibrium values by establishing a **price ceiling,** or a *maximum* selling price. For example, concern about the rising cost of rental housing in some cities prompted legislation to impose rent ceilings. Panel (b) depicts the demand and supply for rental housing in a hypothetical city; the vertical axis shows the monthly rent, and the horizontal axis shows the quantity of rental units. The equilibrium, or market-clearing, rent is $600 per month, and the equilibrium quantity is 50,000 housing units.

Suppose the government sets a maximum rent of $400 per month. At that ceiling price, 60,000 rental units are demanded, but only 40,000 are supplied, resulting in a housing shortage of 20,000 units. Because of such excess demand, the rental price no longer rations housing to those who value it the most. Other devices emerge to ration housing, such as waiting lists, political connections, and the willingness to pay under-the-table charges, such as "key fees," "finder's fees," higher security deposits, and the like.

Price ceiling A maximum legal price above which a good or service cannot be sold; to be effective, a price ceiling must be set below the equilibrium price

To have an impact, a price floor must be set above the equilibrium price. A price ceiling, to have an impact, must be set below the equilibrium price.[1] Effective price floors and ceilings distort market forces. Price floors above the equilibrium price create surpluses, and price ceilings below the equilibrium price create shortages. Various nonprice allocation devices emerge to cope with the disequilibrium resulting from the market interference.

Government intervention in the market is not the only source of disequilibrium, as shown in the following case study.

Toys Are Serious Business

U.S. toy sales exceed $25 billion a year, but the business is not much fun for toy makers. Most toys don't make it from one season to the next, turning out to be costly duds. A few have staying power; for example, G.I. Joe could retire after more than 30 years of military service, Barbie is over 35 years old, and the Wiffle Ball is still a hit after 40 years.

Store buyers must order in February for Christmas delivery. Can you imagine the uncertainty of this market? Who, for example, could have anticipated the phenomenal success of Tickle-Me-Elmo, Beanie Babies, Teletubbies, or Furbies? How about the Cabbage Patch Kids frenzy that some of you experienced as toddlers? Over 20 million Kids were sold for about $30 each, and there was still a shortage at that price. The shortage attracted boatloads of counterfeit dolls from overseas. Some of these illegal aliens were detained at the border, but many more made it through.

A few years ago, the Mighty Morphin Power Rangers were the hot toy. Between 1993 and 1994, the manufacturer expanded production tenfold, with 11 new factories churning out nearly $1 billion worth of Rangers. Still, at a selling price of $13, the quantity demanded exceeded quantity supplied. A more recent hit toy was Tomagotchi, a virtual pet. The manufacturer had nine plants around the world turning them out.

Why didn't toy manufacturers simply allow the price to seek its market-clearing level? Suppose, for example, that the market-clearing price of Cabbage Patch Kids was $60, twice the actual price. Consumers may have resented paying such a high price for a doll, and Coleco, a producer of a variety of toys, may not have wanted to risk criticism for being opportunist, a "price gouger." After all, a firm's reputation is important. Suppliers who hope to retain customers over the long haul will often avoid appearing greedy. That's why the local hardware store doesn't raise the price of snow shovels after the first winter storm, why Wal-Mart doesn't jack up prices of air conditioners during the dog days of summer, and why Mercedes-Benz prefers long waiting lists to raising prices still higher for its new utility vehicle.

Eventually, market equilibrium is achieved. But in the meantime, disequilibrium prevails. Uncertainty abounds in the market for new products such as

CaseStudy

The World of Business

If you are interested in learning more about the serious business of toys, you can find a wealth of information at ToySource http://www.toysource.com/faq1.htm.

---

1 Note that the terms "price floor" and "price ceiling" are used to describe situations in a way that is opposite from the way we usually think of the floor and ceiling of a room. A price floor is up high, where we find a room's ceiling, and a price ceiling is down low, where we find a room's floor.

toys. Suppliers can only guess what the demand will be, so they must feel their way in deciding how much to produce and what price to charge.

Sources: Patrice Apodaca, "Chicken Boom: Bandai Basks in Digital Pet Success," *Los Angeles Times*, 22 August 1997; Gretchen Morgenson, "Saturation Barbie?" *Forbes*, 20 Oct. 1997; and "Cabbage Patch Comeback Kids," *Business Week*, 14 August 1995;. Visit the Virtual Toy Store Directory at http://www.halcyon.com/uncomyn/home.html; or visit FAO Schwarz at http://www.faoschwarz.com/.

CONCLUSION

Although a market usually involves the interaction of many buyers and sellers, few markets are consciously designed. Just as the law of gravity works whether or not we understand Newton's principles, market forces operate whether or not market participants understand demand and supply. These forces arise naturally, much the way car dealers cluster on the outskirts of town. Demand and supply are the foundation of a market economy.

Markets have their critics. Some observers are troubled, for example, that U.S. consumers spend billions each year on pet food, when some people do not have enough to eat. On your next trip to the supermarket, notice how much shelf space is devoted to pet products—often an entire aisle. Petsmart, a chain store for pet products, sells over 12,000 different items. Veterinarians charge up to $10,000 for cancer treatment, cataract removal, and other high-tech medical care for pets. Pet owners can even buy pet health insurance.[2] In the next chapter we'll discuss some limitations of market economies and introduce the role of government.

[2] See Pamela Sebastian, "Canine Oncology and Other Advances Propel Costs and Insurance," *Wall Street Journal*, 23 October 1997.

SUMMARY

1. Demand is a relationship between the price of a good and the quantity consumers are willing and able to buy per time period, other things constant. According to the law of demand, the price of a good varies inversely with the quantity demanded, so the demand curve slopes downward.

2. A demand curve slopes downward for two reasons. A decrease in the price of a good (1) makes consumers more willing to substitute this good for other goods and (2) increases the real income of consumers, making them more able to buy the good.

3. Assumed to be constant along a demand curve are (1) consumer incomes, (2) the prices of related goods, (3) consumer expectations, (4) the number and composition of consumers in the market, and (5) consumer tastes. A change in any one of these could shift the demand curve.

4. Supply is a relationship between the price of a good and the quantity producers are willing and able to sell per period, other things constant. According to the law of

supply, price and quantity supplied are usually directly related, so the supply curve typically slopes upward. The supply curve slopes upward because higher prices (1) make producers more willing to supply this good rather than alternative goods and (2) make producers better able to cover the higher marginal cost associated with greater output rates.

5. Assumed to be constant along a supply curve are (1) the state of technology, (2) the prices of relevant resources, (3) the prices of alternative goods, (4) producer expectations, and (5) the number of producers. A change in any one of these could shift the supply curve.

6. Demand and supply come together in the market for a given product. Markets provide information about the price, quantity, and quality of the product for sale. They also reduce the transaction costs of exchange—the costs of time and information required to undertake exchange. The interaction of demand and supply guides resources and products to their highest-valued use.

7. Impersonal market forces reconcile the personal and independent intentions of buyers and sellers. Market equilibrium, once established, will continue unless there is a change in one of the determinants of demand or supply. Disequilibrium is usually a temporary phase while markets seek equilibrium, but sometimes it lasts a while.

QUESTIONS FOR REVIEW

1. *(Law of Demand)* What is the law of demand? Give two examples of how you have observed the law of demand at work in the "real world." How is the law of demand related to the demand curve?

2. *(Changes in Demand)* What variables influence the demand for a normal good? Explain why a reduction in the price of a normal good does not increase the demand for that good.

3. *(Substitution and Income Effects)* Distinguish between the substitution and income effects of a price change. If a good's price increases, does each effect have a positive or a negative impact on the quantity demanded?

4. *(Demand)* Explain the effect of an increase in consumer income on demand for a good.

5. *(Income Effects)* When moving along the demand curve, income must be assumed constant. Yet one factor that can cause a change in the quantity demanded is the "income effect." Reconcile these seemingly contradictory facts.

6. *(Supply)* What is the law of supply? Give an example of how you have observed the law of supply at work. What is the relationship between the law of supply and the supply curve?

7. *(Changes in Supply)* What kinds of changes in underlying conditions can cause the supply curve to shift? Give some examples and explain the direction in which the curve shifts.

8. *(Markets)* How do markets coordinate the independent decisions of buyers and sellers

9. *(Case**Study:** The Market for Professional Basketball)* In what sense can we speak of a market for professional basketball? Who are the demanders and who are the suppliers? What are some examples of how changes in supply or demand conditions have affected this market? (If you are interested in learning more about the economics of sports, visit the Busine$$ of Sport$ page at http://www.bizsports.com/index.html.

PROBLEMS AND EXERCISES

10. *(Shifting Demand)* Using supply and demand curves, show the effect of each of the following events on the market for cigarettes:
    a. A cure for lung cancer is found.
    b. The price of cigars increases.
    c. Wages increase substantially in states that grow tobacco.
    d. A fertilizer that increases the yield per acre of tobacco is discovered.
    e. There is a substantial increase in the price of matches and lighter fluid.
    f. More states pass laws restricting smoking in public places.

11. *(Substitutes and Complements)* For each of the following pairs, determine whether the goods are substitutes, complements, or unrelated:
    a. Peanut butter and jelly
    b. Private and public transportation
    c. Coke and Pepsi
    d. Alarm clocks and automobiles
    e. Golf clubs and golf balls

12. *(Equilibrium)* "If a price is not an equilibrium price, there is a tendency for it to move to its equilibrium value. Regardless of whether the price is too high or too low to begin with, the adjustment process will increase the quantity of the good purchased." Explain, using a supply and demand diagram.

13. *(Market Equilibrium)* Determine whether each of the following statements is true, false, or uncertain. Then provide a short explanation for your answer.
    a. In equilibrium, all sellers can find buyers.
    b. In equilibrium, there is no pressure on the market to produce or consume more than is being sold.
    c. At prices above equilibrium, the quantity exchanged exceeds the quantity demanded.
    d. At prices below equilibrium, the quantity exchanged is equal to the quantity supplied.

14. *(Supply and Demand)* How do you think each of the following affected the world price of oil? (Use basic supply and demand analysis.)

a. Tax credits were offered for expenditures on home insulation.
b. The Alaskan oil pipeline was completed.
c. The ceiling on the price of oil was removed.
d. Oil was discovered in Mexico and the North Sea.
e. Sport utility vehicles and minivans became popular.
f. The use of nuclear power decreased.

15. *(Equilibrium)* Consider the following graph in which demand and supply are initially D and S, respectively. What are the equilibrium price and quantity? If demand increases to D', what are the new equilibrium price and quantity? What happens if the government does not allow the price to change when demand increases?

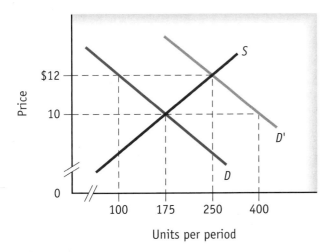

16. *(Demand and Supply)* What happens to the equilibrium price and quantity of ice cream in response to each of the following? Explain your answers.
a. The price of dairy cow fodder increases.
b. The price of beef decreases.
c. Concerns arise about the fat content of ice cream. Simultaneously, the price of sugar (used to produce ice cream) increases.

17. *(Changes in Equilibrium)* What are the effects on the equilibrium price and quantity of steel if the wages of steelworkers rise and, simultaneously, the price of aluminum rises?

18. *(Price Floor)* There is considerable interest in whether the minimum wage rate contributes to teenage unemployment. Draw a supply and demand diagram for the unskilled labor market, and discuss the effects of a minimum wage. Who is helped and who is hurt by the minimum wage?

19. *(Price Ceilings)* Suppose the supply and demand curves for rental housing units have the typical shapes and that the rental housing market is in equilibrium. Then, government establishes a rent ceiling below the equilibrium level.
a. What happens to the quantity of housing consumed?
b. Who gains from rent control?
c. Who loses from rent control?

20. *(CaseStudy: Toys Are Serious Business)* Use a supply and demand graph to describe developments in the market for Mighty Morphin Power Rangers toys. Keep in mind the shortage at the $13 selling price, the development of new factories, and the continued shortage.

EXPERIENTIAL EXERCISES

21. *(Market Demand)* Together with some other students in your class, determine your market demand for gasoline. Make up a chart listing a variety of prices per gallon of gasoline—$1.00, $1.25, $1.50, $1.75, $2.00, $2.25. Ask each student—and yourself—how many gallons *per week* they would purchase at each possible price. Then
a. Plot each student's demand curve. Check to see whether each student's responses are consistent with the law of demand.
b. Derive the "market" demand curve by adding up the quantities demanded by *all* students at each possible price.
c. What do you think will happen to that market demand curve after your class graduates and your incomes rise?

22. *(Price Floors)* The minimum wage is a price floor in a market for labor. The government sets a minimum price per hour of labor in certain markets and no employer is permitted to pay a wage lower than that. Go to the Department of Labor's minimum wage page to learn more about the mechanics of the program http://www.dol.gov/dol/esa/public/minwage/main.htm. Then use a supply and demand diagram to illustrate the effect of imposing an above-equilibrium minimum wage on a particular labor market. What happens to quantity demanded and quantity supplied as a result of the minimum wage?

23. *(Wall Street Journal)* After reading this chapter, you have a basic understanding of how supply and demand determine market price and quantity. Find an article in the "first section" of today's *Wall Street Journal* and interpret the article, using a supply and demand diagram. Explain at least one case in which a curve shifts. What caused the shift, and how did it affect price and quantity?

Economic Decision Makers: Households, Firms, Governments, and the Rest of the World

I f we live in the age of specialization, then why haven't specialists taken over all production—that is, why do most of you still do your own laundry and perform dozens of other tasks for yourself? If the "invisible hand" of competitive markets is such an efficient allocator of resources, why did government get into the act? Finally, how can it be said in economics that "what goes around comes around"? Answers to these and other questions are addressed in this chapter, which examines the four economic decision makers: households, firms, governments, and the rest of the world.

To develop a better understanding of how the economy works, you must become more acquainted with these key players in the economy. You already know more about them than you realize. You grew up in a household. You

EXHIBIT 1

**Sources of U.S.
Personal Income
in 1998**

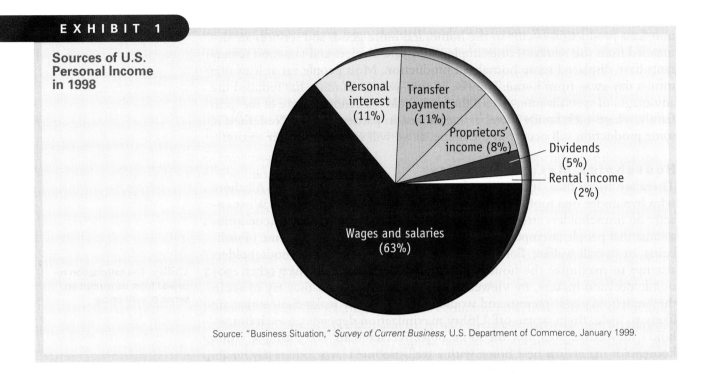

Source: "Business Situation," *Survey of Current Business,* U.S. Department of Commerce, January 1999.

Households as Demanders of Goods and Services

What happens to personal income, once it comes into the household? Personal income is allocated among personal consumption, saving, and taxes. On average, about 80 percent of U.S. personal income goes to personal consumption, about 5 percent is saved, and about 15 percent goes to taxes. Personal consumption sorts into three broad spending categories: (1) *durable goods*, such as automobiles and refrigerators, which are designed to last three years or more; (2) *nondurable goods*, such as food, clothing, and gasoline; and (3) *services*, such as haircuts, plane trips, and medical care. Durable goods make up 13 percent of U.S. personal consumption, nondurables make up 30 percent, and services make up 57 percent. The service sector is the fastest growing, because many activities—such as meal preparation and child care—that formerly were produced in the household are now often purchased in the market.

THE FIRM

Members of households once built their own homes, made their own clothes and furniture, grew their own food, and amused themselves. Over time, however, the efficiency arising from comparative advantage resulted in a greater specialization among resource suppliers. In this section, we take a look at firms, beginning with their evolution.

The Evolution of the Firm

For about 200 years, profit-seeking entrepreneurs relied on "putting out" raw material, such as wool and cotton, to rural households that turned this raw material into finished goods, such as woolen goods made from yarn. The system developed in the British Isles, where workers' cottages served as tiny factories. This approach to production, which came to be known as the *cottage industry system*, still exists in some parts of the world.

As the British economy expanded in the 18th century, entrepreneurs began to organize the various stages of production under one roof. Technological developments increased the productivity of each worker and contributed to the shift of employment from rural areas to urban factories. *Work, therefore, became organized in large, centrally powered factories that (1) promoted a more efficient division of labor, (2) allowed for the direct supervision of production, (3) reduced transportation costs, and (4) facilitated the use of machines far bigger than anything that had been used in the home.* The development of large-scale factory production, known as the **Industrial Revolution,** began in Great Britain around 1750 and spread to the rest of Europe, North America, and Australia.

Production, then, evolved from self-sufficient rural households, through the cottage industry system, where specialized production occurred in the household, to the current system of handling much production under one roof. Today, entrepreneurs combine resources in firms such as factories, mills, offices, stores, and restaurants. **Firms** are economic units formed by profit-seeking entrepreneurs who combine labor, capital, and land to produce goods and services. Just as we assume that householders attempt to maximize utility, we assume that firms attempt to *maximize profit*. Profit, the entrepreneur's reward, is total revenue minus the total cost of production.

Industrial Revolution Development of large-scale factory production that began in Great Britain around 1750 and spread to the rest of Europe, North America, and Australia

Firms Economic units, formed by profit-seeking entrepreneurs who employ resources to produce goods and services for sale

Why Does Household Production Still Exist?

Why are such activities as house cleaning and meal preparation still undertaken primarily by households, not by firms? Some people fix their own cars, paint their own homes, and perform many other tasks that are also performed by firms. Why hasn't all production shifted to firms?

If a householder's opportunity cost of performing a task is below the market price of the task, then the householder usually performs that task. Thus, householders with a lower opportunity cost of time will tend to do more for themselves. For example, janitors typically mow their own lawns; physicians do not. Let's look at some reasons for household production.

No Skills or Specialized Resources Are Required. Some activities require so few skills or specialized resources that households find it cheaper to do these jobs themselves. Sweeping the floor requires only a broom and time, and so this job is usually performed by household members. Sanding the floor, however, involves costly machinery and special skills, so this service is usually purchased in the market. Similarly, although you wouldn't hire someone to brush your teeth each morning and evening, dental work is another matter. *Households usually perform tasks that demand neither particular skills nor specialized machinery.*

Household Production Avoids Taxes. Governments tax income, sales, and other market transactions. Suppose you are trying to decide whether to paint your home or hire a painter. If the income tax rate is one-third, a painter who requires $2,000 net of taxes to do the job must charge you $3,000 to net $2,000 after paying $1,000 in taxes. You must earn $4,500 before taxes in order to have $3,000 after taxes to pay the painter. Thus, you must earn $4,500 so that the painter can net

$2,000 after taxes. If you paint the house yourself, no taxes are imposed. *The tax-free nature of do-it-yourself activity favors household production over market purchases.*

Household Production Reduces Transaction Costs. Lining up bids from painting contractors, hiring a contractor, negotiating terms, and monitoring job performance all take time and require information. Doing the job yourself reduces these *transaction costs*. Household production also allows for more personal control over the final product than is usually available through the market. For example, some people prefer home-cooked meals to restaurant food, in part because home-cooked meals can be prepared according to individual tastes.

Technological Advances Increase Household Productivity. Technological breakthroughs are not confined to market production. Vacuum cleaners, dishwashers, microwave ovens, and other modern appliances reduce the time and often the skill required to perform household tasks. Also, modern technologies such as VCRs, CD players, cable TV, and computer games produce home entertainment. In fact, microchip-based technologies have shifted some production from the firm back to the household, as discussed in the following case study.

The Electronic Cottage

CaseStudy

The Information Economy

Economists have begun to study the economic implications of the virtual office and other virtual phenomena. Visit Yahoo! (http://www.yahoo.com/) and Excite (http://www.excite.com/) and search for the words "virtual" and "economics." Try it, and see what you find.

The Industrial Revolution shifted production from rural cottages to large urban factories. But the *Information Revolution* spawned by the invention of the microchip is decentralizing the acquisition, analysis, and transmission of information. These days people who say they work at a home office are often referring not to corporate headquarters, but to the room just off their kitchen. There are an estimated 8 to 11 million telecommuters in the United States, including nearly half the white-collar work force at AT&T. Merrill Lynch's Telecommuting Simulation Lab helps people learn how to work at home.

People with a personal computer, a modem, a fax machine, a cellular phone, and Internet access are ready for business. They can send a memo via fax or e-mail to colleagues around the corner, around the country, or around the globe. With the right software, they can write a document with coworkers scattered throughout the world. They can also buy or sell thousands of products from securities to hot sauce. And they can do all this without leaving home. An entire industry has sprung up to serve those who work at home, including magazines, newsletters, Web pages, even national conferences, such as the Telecommuting & Home Office Conference in San Francisco.

In fact, an office need not even be in a specific place. With chip-based technology, some people now work in a *virtual office*, which has no permanent location—"deals on wheels," so to speak. For example, accountants at Ernst & Young spend most of their time in the field. When workers need to return to company headquarters, they call a few hours ahead to reserve an office.

Newly developed software such as Netscape Virtual Office®, Virtual File Cabinet®, or Netopia Virtual Office® allows thousands of employees to share electronic files. When Anderson Consulting moved its headquarters from Boston to a suburb, the company got rid of 120 tons of paper, replacing it with a huge on-line data base accessible any time of the day or night from anywhere in the world. Computers have changed the world of work.

Sources: Gene Marcial, "Netopia: An Internet Sleeper," *Business Week*, 27 July 1998; "A Connected World," *The Economist*, 13 September 1997; Mark Davis, "Consulting Firm Puts Office Space Up for Grabs as Day-by-Day Commodity," *Kansas City Star*, 26 September 1997; Godfrey Nolan, "A Good Day at the Virtual Office," *The Irish Times*, 27 July 1997; and as an example of sales over the Internet, visit Hot Hot Hot, "the Net's coolest hot sauce shop" http://www.hot.presence.com/g/p/H3/.

Kinds of Firms

There are about 22 million for-profit businesses in the United States. Two-thirds of these are small retail businesses, small service operations, part-time home-based businesses, and small farms. Each year more than a million new businesses are started, many of which fail. Entrepreneurs organize firms in one of three ways: as a sole proprietorship, as a partnership, or as a corporation. Let's examine the advantages and disadvantages of each.

Sole Proprietorships. The simplest form of business organization is the **sole proprietorship,** a single-owner firm. Examples are a self-employed plumber, electrician, farmer, or family physician. To organize a sole proprietorship, the proprietor simply opens for business by, for example, taking out a classified ad announcing availability for carpentry, snow plowing, or lawn mowing. The owner is in complete control. But he or she faces *unlimited liability* for any business debts and could lose everything, including a home and other assets, as a result of a debt or claim against the business. Also, since the sole proprietor has no partners or other financial backers, raising enough money to get the business up and running can be difficult. One final disadvantage is that sole proprietorships usually go out of business upon the death of the proprietor. Still, they are the most common form of business organization, accounting most recently for 73 percent of all U.S. businesses. Because this type of firm is typically small, proprietorships generate a small portion of all U.S. business sales—only 6 percent.

Sole proprietorship A firm with a single owner who has the right to all profits and who bears unlimited liability for the firm's debts

Partnerships. A more complicated form of business organization is the **partnership,** which involves two or more individuals who agree to contribute resources to the business in return for a share of the profit or loss. Law, accounting, and medical partnerships typify this business form. Partners have strength in numbers and often find it easier than the sole proprietor to raise sufficient funds to get the business going. But the partners may not always agree. Also, each partner usually faces unlimited liability for all the debts and claims against the partnership, so one partner could lose everything because of another's foolish mistake. Finally, the death or departure of one partner may disrupt the firm's continuity and could require a complete reorganization. The partnership is the least common form of U.S. business organization, making up only 7 percent of all firms and accounting for just 5 percent of all business sales.

Partnership A firm with multiple owners who share the firm's profits and each of whom bears unlimited liability for the firm's debts

Corporations. By far the most important form of business organization is the corporation. The **corporation** is a legal entity established through articles of incorporation. The owners of a corporation are issued shares of stock entitling them to corporate profits in proportion to their stock ownership. A major advantage of the corporate form is that many individuals—hundreds, thousands,

Corporation A legal entity owned by stockholders whose liability is limited to the value of their stock

even millions—can pool their money, so incorporating represents the easiest way to amass large sums of money to finance the firm. Also, stockholders have *limited liability*, meaning their liability for any losses is limited to the value of their stock. A final advantage of this form of organization is that the corporation has a life apart from those of the owners. The corporation continues to exist even if ownership changes hands, and it can be taxed and sued as if it were a person.

The corporate form has some disadvantages as well. A stockholder's ability to influence corporate policy is limited to voting for a board of directors, which oversees the operation of the firm. Each share of stock usually carries with it one vote; the typical stockholder of a large corporation owns only a tiny fraction of the shares and thus has little say. Whereas the income from sole proprietorships and partnerships is taxed only once, corporate income is taxed twice: first as corporate profits and second as stockholder income, either as corporate dividends or as realized capital gains. A *realized capital gain* is any increase in the market value of a share that occurs between the time the share is purchased and the time it is sold.

A hybrid type of corporation has evolved to take advantage of the limited liability feature of the corporate structure, while reducing the impact of double taxation. The *S corporation* provides owners with limited liability, but profits are taxed only once—as income on each shareholder's personal income tax return. To qualify as an S corporation, a firm must have no more than 35 stockholders and must have no foreign or corporate stockholders.

Corporations make up only 20 percent of all U.S. businesses, but because they tend to be much larger than the other two forms of business, corporate sales represent 89 percent of all business sales. Exhibit 2 shows, by type of U.S. firm, the percentage of firms and the percentage of total sales. *The sole proprietorship is the most important form in terms of total numbers, but the corporation is the most important in terms of total sales.*

Nonprofit Institutions

To this point we have considered firms that maximize profit. Some institutions, such as museums, ballet companies, nonprofit hospitals, the Red Cross, the Salvation Army, churches, synagogues, mosques, and perhaps the college you attend, are private organizations that do not have profit as an explicit objective. Yet even nonprofit institutions must somehow pay for the resources they employ. Revenue sources typically include some combination of voluntary contributions and service charges, such as college tuition and hospital bills. Although there are millions of nonprofit institutions, when we talk about firms in this book, we will be referring to for-profit firms.

THE GOVERNMENT

You might think that production by firms and by households could satisfy all consumer demands. Why must yet another economic decision maker get into the act?

The Role of Government

Market failure A condition that arises when unrestrained operation of markets yields socially undesirable results

Sometimes the unrestrained operation of markets has undesirable results. Too many of some goods and too few of other goods may be produced. In this section we discuss the sources of **market failure** and how society's overall welfare could at times be improved through government intervention.

EXHIBIT 2

Number and Sales of Each Type of Firm

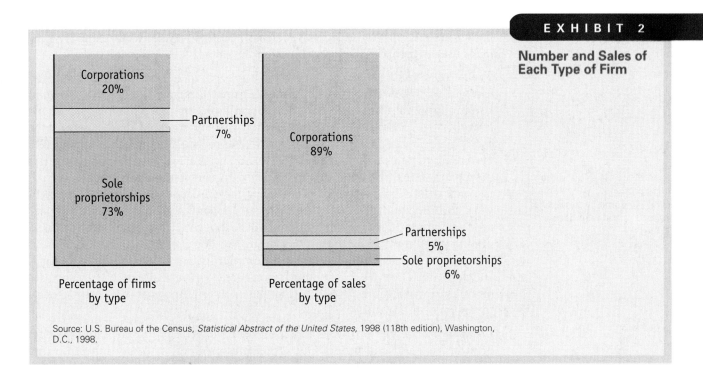

Source: U.S. Bureau of the Census, *Statistical Abstract of the United States*, 1998 (118th edition), Washington, D.C., 1998.

Establishing and Enforcing the Rules of the Game. Market efficiency depends on people like you using your resources to maximize your utility. But what if you were repeatedly robbed of your paycheck on your way home from work? Or what if, after you worked a month, your employer said you would not get paid? Why bother working? The system of private markets would break down if you could not safeguard your private property or if you could not enforce contracts. Governments play a role in *safeguarding private property* through police protection and in *enforcing contracts* through a judicial system. More generally, governments try to make sure that market participants play fair and abide by the "rules of the game." These rules are established through laws and through the customs and conventions of the market.

Promoting Competition. Although the "invisible hand" of competition usually promotes an efficient allocation of resources, some firms try to avoid competition through *collusion*, which is an agreement among firms to divide the market or to fix the market price. An individual firm may try to eliminate the competition by using unfair business practices. For example, to drive out local competitors, a large firm may temporarily sell at a price below its cost. *Government antitrust laws try to promote competition by prohibiting collusion and other anticompetitive practices.*

Regulating Natural Monopolies. Competition usually keeps the product price lower than it is when the product is sold by a **monopoly,** a sole supplier to the market. In rare instances, however, a monopoly can produce and sell the product for less than could several competing firms. For example, electricity is delivered more efficiently by a single firm that wires the community than by competing firms stringing their own wires. When it is cheaper for one firm to serve the market than for two or more firms to do so, that firm is called a **natural monopoly.**

Monopoly A sole producer of a product for which there are no close substitutes

Natural monopoly One firm that can serve the entire market at a lower per-unit cost than can two or more firms

Since a natural monopoly faces no competition, it maximizes profit by charging a higher price than is optimal from society's point of view. Therefore, the government usually regulates the natural monopoly, forcing it to lower the price.

Providing Public Goods. So far in this book, we have been talking about private goods, which have two important features. First, private goods are *rival* in consumption, meaning that the amount consumed by one person is unavailable for others to consume. For example, when you and a friend share a pizza, each slice your friend eats is one less slice available to you. Second, the supplier of a private good can easily exclude those who fail to pay. Only paying customers get a pizza. Thus, private goods are *exclusive*. In contrast, **public goods,** such as national defense and a system of justice, are *nonrival* in consumption. One person's consumption does not diminish the amount available to others. What's more, once produced, public goods are available to all. Suppliers cannot easily prevent consumption by those who fail to pay. For example, national defense is *nonexclusive*. It is available to all in the community, regardless of who pays for it and who does not. Because public goods are *nonrival* and *nonexclusive*, private firms cannot sell them profitably. The government, however, has the authority to collect taxes for public goods.

Dealing with Externalities. Market prices reflect the *private* costs and benefits of producers and consumers. But sometimes production or consumption imposes costs or benefits on third parties—on those who are neither suppliers nor demanders in a market transaction. For example, a paper mill fouls the air breathed by nearby residents, but the price of paper, as determined in the private market, fails to reflect the cost such pollution imposes on society. Since these pollution costs are outside, or *external* to, the market activity, they are called *externalities*. An **externality** is a cost or a benefit that falls on third parties. A *negative externality* imposes on third parties a cost such as factory pollution, jet noise, or auto emissions. A *positive externality* confers on third parties an external benefit, such as getting a flu shot so you will not contract and transmit the disease, observing traffic signs and speed limits so you don't hit other cars, and planting a flower garden in your front yard, where it beautifies the neighborhood.

Because market prices do not reflect externalities, governments often employ taxes, subsidies, and regulations to discourage negative externalities and to encourage positive externalities. For example, because education generates positive externalities (educated people are more apt to be able to read road signs and are less likely to resort to violent crime for income), government tries to encourage people to get more education. One approach is to pass laws requiring students to stay in school until they are 16 years old. Another approach is for taxpayers to fund education so the cost to students is minimal, as with free public schools, or to subsidize education, as with public higher education.

A More Equal Distribution of Income. As mentioned earlier, some people—because of a lack of education, mental or physical disabilities, or perhaps the need to care for small children—may be unable to earn enough to support themselves and their family. Since resource markets do not guarantee each household even a minimum level of income, transfer payments reflect society's attempt to provide a basic standard of living to all households. Nearly all citizens agree that, through government transfer payments, society should alter some of the results of the market by redistributing income to the poor. (Notice

---

Public good A good that, once produced, is available for all to consume, regardless of who pays and who does not

Externality A cost or a benefit that falls on third parties and is therefore ignored by the two parties to the market transaction

NetBookmark

The annual *Economic Report of the President* is an invaluable source of information on current economic policy. It also contains many useful data tables. You can find it on-line at http://www. access.gpo.gov/eop/.

the normative nature of this statement.) But differences of opinion arise in deciding just how much redistribution should occur, what form it should take, who should receive the benefits, and how long those benefits should continue.

Full Employment, Price Stability, and Economic Growth. The government, through its ability to tax and spend and its control of the money supply, attempts to promote full employment, price stability, and an adequate rate of growth in the economy. The government's pursuit of these objectives through taxing and spending is called **fiscal policy** and pursuing them by regulating the money supply is called **monetary policy.** The study of macroeconomics examines these policies.

Government's Structure and Objectives

The United States has a *federal system* of government, meaning that responsibilities are shared across levels of government. State governments grant some powers to local governments and surrender some powers to the national, or federal, government. As the system has evolved, the federal government has assumed primary responsibility for national security and the stability of the economy. State governments fund public higher education, prisons and, with aid from the federal government, highways and welfare. Local government responsibilities include primary and secondary education, plus police and fire protection.

Difficulty in Defining Government Objectives. We assume that households maximize utility and firms maximize profit, but what about governments—or, more specifically, what about government decision makers? What do they maximize? One problem is that the federal system consists of many governments—more than 80,000 separate jurisdictions in all. What's more, because the federal government relies on offsetting, or countervailing, powers among the *executive, legislative,* and *judicial* branches, government does not act as a single, consistent decision maker. Even within the federal executive branch, there are so many agencies and bureaus that at times they seem to work at cross purposes. For example, at the same time as the U.S. Surgeon General requires health warnings on cigarettes, the U.S. Department of Agriculture subsidizes tobacco farmers. Given this thicket of jurisdictions, branches, and bureaus, one useful theory of government behavior is that elected officials try to maximize the number of votes they will get in the next election. Thus, we can assume that elected officials *maximize votes.* In this theory, vote maximization guides the decisions of elected officials who, in turn, control government employees.

Voluntary Exchange Versus Coercion. Market exchange relies on the voluntary behavior of buyers and sellers. If you don't like tofu, no problem—just don't buy any. But in political markets the situation is different. Any voting rule except unanimous consent will involve some government coercion. Public choices are enforced by the police power of the state. Those who fail to pay their taxes could go to jail, even though they may object to programs those taxes support.

Absence of Market Prices. Another distinguishing feature of governments is that the selling price of public output is usually either zero or some amount below its cost. If you are now attending a state college or university, your tuition probably covers less than half of the total cost of providing your education. Since the revenue side of the government budget is usually separate from the expenditure side, there is no necessary link between the cost and benefit of a

Fiscal policy The use of government purchases, transfer payments, taxes, and borrowing to influence aggregate economic activity

Monetary policy Regulation of the money supply in order to influence aggregate economic activity

PROBLEMS AND EXERCISES

15. *(Evolution of the Household)* Determine whether each of the following would increase or decrease the opportunity costs for mothers who choose not to accept paid employment outside the home. Explain your answers.
    a. Higher levels of education for women
    b. Higher unemployment rates for women
    c. Higher average pay levels for women
    d. Lower demand for labor in industries that traditionally employ large numbers of women

16. *(Household Production)* Many households supplement their food budget by cultivating small vegetable gardens. Explain how each of the following might influence this kind of household production:
    a. Both husband and wife are professionals who earn high salaries.
    b. The household is located in a city rather than in a rural area.
    c. The household is located in a region where there is a high sales tax on food.
    d. The household is located in a region that has a high property tax rate.

17. *(Government)* Complete each of the following sentences:
    a. When the private operation of a market leads to overproduction or underproduction of some good, this is known as a(n) _____ .

    b. Goods that are nonrival and nonexcludable are known as _____ .
    c. _____ are cash or in-kind benefits given to individuals as outright grants from the government.
    d. A(n) _____ confers an external benefit on third parties that are not directly involved in a market transaction.
    e. _____ refers to the government's pursuit of full employment and price stability through variations in taxes and government spending.

18. *(Tax Rates)* Suppose taxes are related to income level as follows:

Income	Taxes
$1,000	$200
$2,000	$350
$3,000	$450

    a. What percent of income is paid in taxes at each level?
    b. Is the tax rate progressive, proportional, or regressive?
    c. What is the marginal tax rate on the first $1,000 of income? The second $1,000? The third $1,000?

EXPERIENTIAL EXERCISES

19. *(The Evolution of the Firm)* Get a library copy of *The Wealth and Poverty of Nations* by David Landes and read pages 207–210. How would you interpret Landes' story about mechanization using the ideas developed in this chapter?

20. *(The Evolution of the Firm)* The Center for Research on Contracts and the Structure of Enterprise at the University of Pittsburgh http://crcse. business.pitt.edu/ maintains lots of interesting information about the evolution of the firm. Visit that site to familiarize yourself with the kinds of issues economists are studying.

21. *(International Trade)* Visit McEachern Interactive Web Site http://mceachern.swcollege.com and click on EconDebates Online. Review the materials on "Does the U.S. Economy Benefit from Foreign Trade?" What are some of the benefits of international trade—not just to the U.S., but to all nations?

22. *(Wall Street Journal)* The household is the most important decision-making unit in our economy. Look through the rotating columns (e.g., "Work and Family," and "Personal Technology") in the *Wall Street Journal* this week. Find a description of some technological change that might affect household production. Explain how production would be affected.

Introduction to Macroeconomics

What's the big deal with macroeconomics? Why is the focus of macroeconomics typically the national economy? What are the similarities and differences between the economy and the human body? How do we measure the performance of an economy over time? Answers to these and related questions are provided in this chapter, which introduces macroeconomics.

In macroeconomics we think big—not about the demand and supply for apples but the demand and supply for everything produced in the economy; not about the price of computers but the average price of all goods and services produced in the economy; not about consumption by the Jackson household but consumption by all households; not about the investment by Intel but the investment by all firms in the economy.

Macroeconomists develop and test theories about how the economy as a whole works—theories they can use to predict the consequences of economic policies and events. They are concerned not only with what determines such big-picture measures as the level of the economy's prices, employment, and production but also with understanding how these variables fluctuate over time.

Macroeconomists are especially interested in what makes an economy grow over time, because a growing economy usually means more job opportunities and more goods and services—in short, growth means a rising standard of living. What determines the economy's ability to use resources productively, to adapt, to grow? In this chapter, we will begin to explore these questions; then in Chapter 6 we will introduce a major concern of the day—economic growth. Topics discussed in this chapter include:

- The national economy
- Economic fluctuations
- Aggregate demand and aggregate supply
- Short history of the U.S. economy
- Demand-side economics
- Supply-side economics

THE NATIONAL ECONOMY

Economy The structure of economic life or economic activity in a community, a region, a country, a group of countries, or the world

Macroeconomics concerns the overall performance of the *economy*. The term **economy** describes the structure of economic life, or economic activity, in a community, a region, a country, a group of countries, or the world. We could talk about the Chicago economy, the Illinois economy, the Midwest economy, the U.S. economy, the North American economy, or the world economy. We measure an economy's performance in different ways, such as the number of workers employed, their average earnings, the amount produced, or the size and number of firms. The most commonly used measure of an economy's performance is the *gross product,* which measures the market value of final goods and services produced in a particular geographical region during a given time period, usually one year. If the focus is the Illinois economy, we consider the *gross state product*.

Gross domestic product, or GDP The market value of all final goods and services produced by resources located in the United States, regardless of who owns those resources

If the focus is the U.S. economy, we consider the **gross domestic product, or GDP,** which measures the market value of all final goods and services produced in the United States during a given time period, usually a year. GDP helps federal statisticians keep track of the economy's incredible variety of goods and services, from trail bikes to pedicures. We can use the gross product to track the same economy over time or to compare different economies at the same time.

What's Special About the National Economy

The national economy deserves special attention. Here's why. If you were to drive west on Interstate 10 in Texas, you would hardly notice crossing the state line into New Mexico. If, however, you took the Juarez exit off I-10 south into Mexico, you would be stopped at the border, asked for identification, and possibly searched. You would be quite aware that you were crossing an international border. Like most countries, the United States and Mexico usually allow freer movement of people and goods *within* their borders than *across* their borders.

The differences between the United States and Mexico are far greater than the differences between Texas and New Mexico. For example, each country has its own culture and language, its own communication and transportation systems, its own system of government, its own currency, and, most importantly, its own "rules of the game"—that is, its own laws, regulations, customs, and conventions for conducting economic activity both within and across its borders.

Macroeconomics typically focuses on the performance of the national economy, including how the national economy interacts with other economies around the world. To get some idea of the complex nature of the U.S. economy, consider this profile of households, firms, governments, and the rest of the world. In the United States, there are more than 100 million households, about 22 million for-profit businesses, and about 80,000 separate units of government. And there are more than 200 sovereign countries throughout the world, ranging from tiny Liechtenstein, with a population of only 30,000, to immense China, with 1.3 billion people. These numbers offer snapshots of economic decision makers, but the economy is a moving picture—too complex to describe in snapshots. This is why we use theoretical models to simplify the key relationships. Let's begin with an analogy.

The Human Body and the Economy

Consider the similarities and differences between the human body and the economy. The body consists of millions of cells, each performing particular functions yet each linked to the operation of the entire body. Similarly, the economy is composed of millions of economic units, each acting with some independence yet each connected with the economy as a whole. The economy, like the body, is continually renewing itself, with new households, new businesses, a changing set of public officials, and new foreign competitors.

Blood circulates throughout the body, facilitating the exchange of vital nutrients among cells. Similarly, **money** circulates throughout the economy, facilitating the exchange of resources and products among individual economic units. In fact, money is called a *medium of exchange*. In Chapter 4 we saw that the movement of money, products, and resources throughout the economy follows a *circular flow*, as does the movement of blood and nutrients throughout the body.

Money Something accepted as a medium of exchange

FLOWS AND STOCKS.   Just as the same blood circulates again and again in the body, the same money circulates again and again in the economy to finance transactions. The same dollars you spend on blueberry muffins are spent by the baker on butter, then spent by the dairy farmer on work boots. The dollars *flow* through the economy. To measure a flow, we use a **flow** variable, which is a measure per period of time, such as heartbeats per minute or your earnings per week. We distinguish between a *flow* variable and a *stock* variable. A **stock** variable represents an amount of something at a particular point in time, such as the volume of blood in your body or the number of dollars in your possession right now.

Flow A variable that measures the amount of something over an interval of time, such as the amount of money you spend on food per week

Stock A variable that measures the amount of something at a particular point in time, such as the amount of food in your refrigerator or the amount of money you have with you right now

ROLE OF EXPECTATIONS.   In both medicine and macroeconomics, *expectations* play an important role. For example, if the patient expects a medicine to work, it often does work, even if it is only a sugar pill, or placebo. A similar mechanism can operate in the economy. Suppose, for example, that all firms expect greater demand for their products. To expand output, firms buy more capital and hire more workers. As a result, households, as resource suppliers, earn more income and so increase their demand for goods and services. Thus, producers may help bring about the very prosperity they expect. Negative expectations can also be self-fulfilling. If firms expect demand to fall, they invest less and hire fewer workers. As a result, household incomes decline, reducing the demand for goods and services. As we will see later, the role of expectations is especially important in evaluating the appropriate role of government in the macroeconomy.

Differences of Opinion. Both in medicine and in macroeconomics, matters are subject to different interpretations. First, experts within each field may disagree about what ails the patient or the economy. In macroeconomics, experts may differ about the source of the problem. Second, even when experts agree about what's wrong, they may disagree over what to do about it. Medical researchers, however, have two big advantages over macroeconomists: They have collected vastly more information about their subject, and they can test their theories in a laboratory setting.

Testing New Theories

Physicians and other natural scientists can test theories using controlled experiments. Macroeconomists have no laboratory and little ability to run experiments of any kind. Granted, they can study different economies throughout the world, but each economy is unique, so comparisons across countries are tricky. Controlled experiments also provide scientists with something seldom available to macroeconomists—the chance, or serendipitous, discovery (such as penicillin). But with only one patient—the U.S. economy—the macroeconomist cannot introduce particular policies in a variety of ways. Cries of "Eureka!" are seldom heard from macroeconomists.

Knowledge and Performance

Throughout history, little was known about human biology, yet many people enjoyed good health. For example, the fact that blood circulates in our bodies was not discovered until 1638; it took scientists another 150 years to figure out why. Similarly, over the millennia various complex economies developed and flourished, although there was little understanding or even concern about how these economies worked.

The economy is much like the body: As long as it functions smoothly, policy makers need not understand its operation. But if a problem develops—severe unemployment, high inflation, or sluggish growth, for example—we must know how a healthy economy works before we can consider if and how the problem can be corrected. We need not know every detail of the economy, just as we need not know every detail of the body. But we must understand the essential relationships among key economic variables. For example, we would like to know the extent to which the economy is self-adjusting. Does the economy work well enough on its own, or does it often perform poorly? If the economy does perform poorly, what are the policy options and can we be sure that the proposed remedy won't do more harm than good?

When doctors did not understand how the body works, their cures were often worse than the disease. Much of the history of medicine describes misguided attempts to deal with maladies. As recently as the 19th century, for example, medical "remedies" included "bleeding, cupping, violent purging, the raising of blisters by vesicant ointments, the immersion of the body in either ice water or intolerably hot water, endless lists of botanical extracts evoked up and mixed together under nothing more than pure whim."[1] Even today, medical care is based on less scientific evidence than we think. According to one researcher, only one in seven medical interventions is supported by reliable scientific evidence.[2]

Likewise, national policy makers have sometimes implemented the wrong economic prescription because of a flawed theory about how the economy works. At one time, for example, a nation's economic vitality was thought to spring from the stock of precious metals accumulated in the public treasury. This theory spawned a policy called *mercantilism,* which held that, as a way of accumulating gold and silver, a nation should sell more output to foreigners than it bought from them. To achieve this, nations restricted imports by such devices as tariffs and quotas. But these restrictions reduced international trade, thereby reducing the gains from specialization that arise from trade. Another flawed economic theory prompted President Herbert Hoover to introduce a major tax *increase* while the nation was suffering through the Great Depression. We have since learned that such a policy does more harm than good.

Let's turn now to the performance of the U.S. economy over time.

ECONOMIC FLUCTUATIONS AND GROWTH

The U.S. economy and other industrial market economies historically have experienced alternating periods of expansion and contraction in the level of economic activity. **Economic fluctuations** are the rise and fall of economic activity relative to the long-term growth trend of the economy. These fluctuations, or *business cycles,* vary in length and intensity, yet some features appear common to all. The ups and downs usually involve the entire nation and often the world, and they affect nearly all dimensions of economic activity, not simply employment and production levels.

Economic Fluctuation Analysis

Perhaps the easiest way to understand economic fluctuations is to examine their components. During the 1920s and 1930s, Wesley C. Mitchell, director of the National Bureau of Economic Research (NBER), analyzed economic fluctuations. The economy, according to Mitchell, has two phases: periods of expansion and periods of contraction. Before World War II, some contractions were so severe that they were called *depressions.* Although there is no official definition, a **depression** is a sharp reduction in the nation's total production, accompanied by high unemployment that lasts more than a year. A milder contraction is called a **recession,** which the NBER identifies as a period of decline in total output and employment, usually lasting at least two consecutive quarters, or six months. Prior to World War II, the economy experienced both recessions and depressions. Since World War II, there have been recessions but no depressions.

Despite these ups and downs, the U.S. economy has grown dramatically over the long run. Measured by the amount of goods and services produced, the economy today is eight times larger than it was in 1940, reflecting an average

---

1 As described by Lewis Thomas in *The Youngest Science: Notes of a Medicine Watcher* (New York: Viking Press, 1983), p. 19.
2 See Sherwin Nuland, "Medical Fads: Bran, Midwives and Leeches," *New York Times,* 25 January 1995.

*Net*Bookmark

How long do economic expansions last? Why do they end? Find out by reading Joseph Haimowitz's "The Longevity of Expansions," which can be downloaded from http://www.kc.frb.org/publicat/econrev/er98q4.htm#expansions.

Economic fluctuations The rise and fall of economic activity relative to the long-term growth trend of the economy; also called business cycles

Depression A severe reduction in an economy's total production accompanied by high unemployment lasting more than a year

Recession A period of decline in total output usually lasting at least six months and marked by contractions in many sectors of the economy

EXHIBIT 1

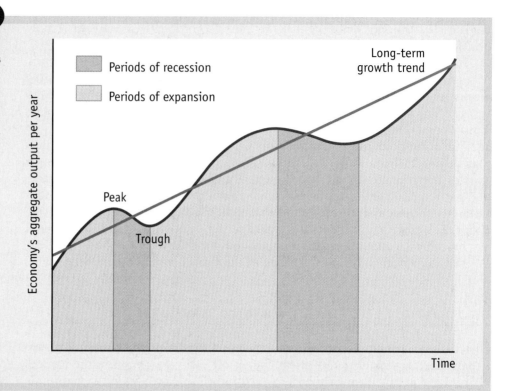

Hypothetical Business Fluctuations

Business fluctuations reflect movements of economic activity around a trend line that shows long-term growth. A recession (shown in pink) begins after a previous expansion (shown in gold) has reached its peak and continues until the economy reaches a trough. An expansion begins when economic activity starts to increase and continues until the economy reaches a peak.

EXHIBIT 2

Historical Business Fluctuations in the United States

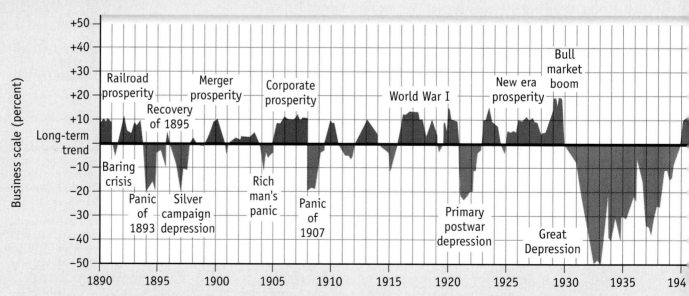

This historical chart shows the phases of business fluctuations since 1890. The vertical scale indicates the percentage by which the level of business activity exceeded or fell short of the long-term trend.

Source: "American Business Activity from 1790 to Today," Ameritrust Corporation, January 1988. Updated by author.

annual growth in production of 3.6 percent per year. Production tends to increase over the long run because of (1) increases in the amount and quality of resources, (2) better technology, and (3) improvements in the "rules of the game" that facilitate production and exchange, such as property rights, patent laws, the legal system, and customs of the market. Exhibit 1 shows such a long-term growth trend as an upward-sloping straight line. Economic fluctuations reflect movements around this growth trend. A recession begins after the previous expansion has reached its *peak* and continues until the economy reaches a *trough.* The period between the peak and the trough is a *recession,* and the period between the trough and the subsequent peak is an **expansion.** Note that expansions tend to last longer than recessions, and the length of the full cycle varies.

The U.S. economic record appears in Exhibit 2, which shows the annual percentage change in economic activity relative to the long-term trend during the last hundred years. As you can see, the fluctuations vary widely in duration and in rate of change. The big declines during the Great Depression of the 1930s and the sharp gains during World War II stand in stark contrast to one another. Analysts at NBER have been able to track the U.S. economy back to 1854. Since then, the country has experienced 31 full peak-to-trough fluctuations. No two have been exactly alike. The longest *peacetime* expansion began in the spring of 1991 and was eight years old by the spring of 1999. The longest contraction lasted five and a half years, from 1873 to 1879.

Since 1933, the U.S. economy has completed 11 cycles of peaks and troughs. During this period, peacetime expansions averaged about 5 years and

Expansion A phase of economic activity during which there is an increase in the economy's total production

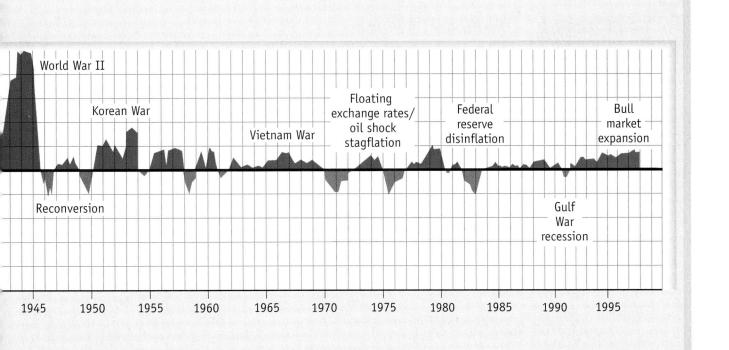

peacetime recessions about 1 year; wartime expansions were longer. The entire cycle lasts about 6 years on average. Again, despite the ups and downs, the economy has grown substantially over the long term, so the growth during expansions more than offsets the decline during recessions. As we will see in the next chapter, growth has not been uniform, but it has been nonetheless impressive: Since 1940 the U.S. economy has doubled its size every 20 years on average.

The intensity of the economic fluctuations varies from region to region across the United States. For example, a recession hits hardest those regions that produce durable goods, such as appliances, furniture, and automobiles; with the onset of a recession, the demand for these items falls more than the demand for nondurable goods, such as groceries, clothing, and gasoline.

Because of seasonal fluctuations and random disturbances, the economy does not move smoothly through phases of economic fluctuations. We cannot always distinguish between temporary setbacks in economic activity and the beginning of a downturn. The drop in production in a particular month may be the result of a snowstorm or a poor harvest rather than the onset of a recession. Turning points—peaks and troughs—are thus identified by the NBER only after the fact. Since a recession usually involves declining output for two consecutive quarters, a recession is not so designated until at least six months after it begins.

As noted earlier, the U.S. economy's ups and downs usually involve the entire nation; indeed, business fluctuations seem to be linked across economies around the world. The following case study compares the year-to-year change in production in the United States with another leading economy, the United Kingdom.

CaseStudy

Other Times, Other Places

The Foundation for International Business and Economic Research maintains a rich set of information regarding the international transmission of economic fluctuations. You can find their Web Site at http://www.global-trends.com/fiber2.htm.

The Global Economy

Though economic fluctuations are not perfectly synchronized across countries, a link is often apparent. Consider the recent experience in two leading economies—the United States and the United Kingdom, nations separated by the Atlantic Ocean. Exhibit 3 shows the year-to-year percentage change in their total output—their *real gross domestic product*, or *real GDP.* "Real" in this context means that the effects of inflation have been eliminated, so remaining changes are "real" changes (more on this later in this chapter).

If you spend a little time following the year-to-year changes in each country, you will begin to see similarities. For example, U.S. real GDP declined, or had a negative growth rate, in 1980, 1982, and 1991, reflecting recessions during those years. The deepest U.S. recession occurred in 1982, when output declined by 2.2 percent. The United Kingdom experienced recessions in roughly the same years, although in the early 1980s it had one long recession rather than the two shorter ones experienced in the United States.

EXHIBIT 3

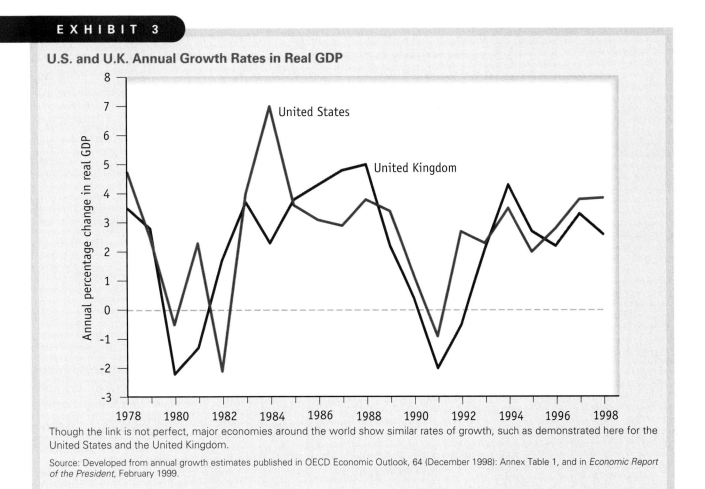

U.S. and U.K. Annual Growth Rates in Real GDP

Though the link is not perfect, major economies around the world show similar rates of growth, such as demonstrated here for the United States and the United Kingdom.

Source: Developed from annual growth estimates published in OECD *Economic Outlook*, 64 (December 1998): Annex Table 1, and in *Economic Report of the President*, February 1999.

One problem with this linkage of business activity across economies is that the swings tend to reinforce one another. For example, a slump of economies abroad could cause a recession in the United States, and vice-versa. Evidence of such ties can be found in the relationship between stock markets around the world. Recent troubles in Asia and Russia, for example, resounded in stock markets in Europe and the Americas.

Although year-to-year fluctuations in output are of interest, even more important is an economy's long-term growth trend in output. Between 1978 and 1998, for example, U.S. real GDP grew on average by 2.6 percent per year, compared to 2.3 percent in the United Kingdom. These growth rates may seem similar, but tiny differences compound over the years to make a big difference. For example, if U.S. real GDP had averaged only 2.3 percent growth, output in 1998 would have been $450 billion below that achieved by 2.6 percent growth. In per capita terms, the lower rate would have reduced U.S. production per capita in 1998 by about $1,700. That's enough to provide everyone in the nation a powerful computer plus Internet service for a year.

Sources: Annual growth data from *Economic Report of the President,* February 1998; "Farewell, Golden Goose, *The Economist,* 13–19 December 1997; and *OECD Economic Outlook,* 63 (June 1998).

Leading Economic Indicators

Certain events foreshadow a turning point in economic activity. Months before a recession is fully under way, changes in the leading economic indicators point to the coming storm. In the early stages of a recession, business slows down, orders for machinery and equipment slip, and the stock market, in anticipation of lower profits, turns down. The confidence consumers have in the economy also begins to sag, and households reduce their spending on big-ticket items, such as automobiles and new homes. All these activities are called *leading economic indicators* because they are the first variables to predict, or *lead to,* a downturn. Upturns in leading indicators point to an economic recovery. But leading indicators cannot predict precisely *when* turning points will occur.

Our introduction to economic fluctuations has been largely mechanical, focusing on the history and measurement of these fluctuations. We have not discussed the reasons behind the fluctuations, in part because such a discussion requires a firmer footing in macroeconomic theory and in part because the causes remain in dispute. In the next section we begin to build a macroeconomic framework by introducing a key model of analysis.

AGGREGATE DEMAND AND AGGREGATE SUPPLY

The economy is so complex that we need to simplify, or to abstract from the millions of relationships, in order to isolate the important elements under consideration. We must step back from all the individual economic transactions to survey the resulting mosaic. Let's begin with the tools of demand and supply.

Aggregate Output and the Price Level

The demand for food shows the relationship between the relative price of food and the quantity of food demanded. When we consider the demand for food, we must take into account a diverse array of products—milk, bread, fruit, seafood, vegetables, meat, and so on. Moving from the demand for a specific product, milk, to the demand for a general product, food, is not conceptually difficult. Likewise, we can make the transition from the demand for food, housing, clothing, entertainment, transportation, or medical care to the demand for all output produced in the economy—the demand for aggregate output. **Aggregate output** is the total quantity of goods and services produced in the economy during a given time period. A unit of aggregate output is a composite measure of all output in the same sense that a unit of food is a composite measure of all food.

Aggregate demand is the relationship between the average price level of *all* goods and services in the economy and the quantity of *all* goods and services demanded. The **price level** in the economy is a composite measure reflecting the average price of food, housing, clothing, entertainment, transportation, medical care, and all other production.

You are more familiar than you may think with these aggregate measures. Media reports of economic growth or an economic slowdown refer to changes in the *gross domestic product,* or *GDP,* the most common measure of aggregate output. As noted earlier, the gross domestic product measures the market value of all final goods and services produced in the United States during a given

Aggregate output A composite measure of all final goods and services produced in an economy during a given time period; real GDP

Aggregate demand The relationship between the price level in the economy and the quantity of aggregate output demanded, other things held constant

Price level A composite measure reflecting the prices of all goods and services in the economy relative to prices in a base year

time period, usually a year. And the economy's price level relates to the "cost of living" so often mentioned in news reports. Two common measures of the price level are (1) the *consumer price index,* which tracks the average price of a "basket" of goods and services consumed by the typical family, and (2) the *GDP price index,* which tracks the average price of all items in the gross domestic product.

In Chapter 8, you will learn how the economy's price level is computed. All you need to know now is that the economy's price level reflects the average price level in a particular year relative to the average level in some base, or reference, year. If we say that the price level is relatively high or low, we mean compared to the price level of some base year. In earlier chapters, we talked about the price of a particular product, such as milk, *relative to the prices of other products.* Here we talk about the *average price* of all goods and services produced in the economy compared to the price level in some base year.

The price level in the *base year* is set at a benchmark value of 100, and the price levels in other years are expressed relative to the base-year price level. For example, in 1998 the U.S. GDP price index averaged 113, indicating that the price level that year averaged 13 percent higher than its value of 100 in the base year of 1992.

Economists use the GDP *price index* to "deflate" the gross domestic product—that is, to eliminate any year-to-year changes in GDP due solely to changes in the average price level. After deflation, remaining changes are thus changes in real output—the amount of goods and services produced. After deflating GDP for price changes, we end up with what is called the *real* gross domestic product.

Aggregate Demand Curve

In Chapter 3 we learned about the demand for a particular product. Now let's talk about the demand for our composite measure of output—aggregate output. The **aggregate demand curve** shows the relationship between the price level in the economy and the amount of aggregate output demanded, other things constant. Exhibit 4 pictures a hypothetical aggregate demand curve, *AD.* The vertical axis measures an index of the economy's price level (relative to a 1992 base-year price level of 100). The horizontal axis measures aggregate output as real GDP, or real gross domestic product. Real GDP is measured by the dollar value of output, in this case using prices that prevailed in 1992.

The aggregate demand curve in Exhibit 4 reflects an inverse relationship between the price level in the economy and real GDP demanded. Aggregate demand reflects demand by households, firms, governments, and the rest of the world. As the price level falls, other things constant, households demand more Snapple and sneakers, firms demand more trucks and tools, governments demand more computer software and military hardware, and the rest of the world demands more U.S. grain and U.S. aircraft.

The reasons behind this inverse relationship will be examined more closely in later chapters. Here's a quick summary. The quantity of aggregate output demanded depends in part on household *wealth.* Some wealth is usually held in bank accounts and currency. An increase in the price level, other things constant, decreases the purchasing power of bank accounts and currency. Therefore, households are poorer when the price level increases, so the quantity of

Aggregate demand curve
A curve representing the relationship between the economy's price level and the amount of aggregate output demanded per period, other things held constant

EXHIBIT 4

Aggregate Demand Curve

The quantity of output demanded is inversely related to the price level, other things equal. This inverse relationship is reflected by the aggregate demand curve *AD*.

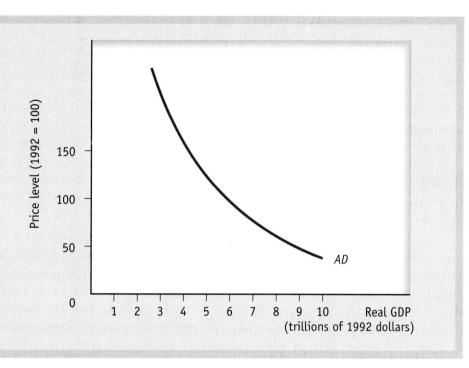

aggregate output they demand decreases. Conversely, a reduction in the price level increases the purchasing power of bank accounts and currency. Because households are richer as the price level decreases, the quantity of aggregate output they demand increases.

Among the factors held constant along a given aggregate demand curve are the price levels in other countries as well as the exchange rates between the U.S. dollar and foreign currencies. When the U.S. price level falls, U.S. products become cheaper relative to foreign products. Consequently, households, firms, and governments both here and abroad increase the quantity of U.S. output they demand. On the other hand, a higher U.S. price level makes U.S. goods relatively more costly compared to foreign goods, so the quantity of U.S. output demanded decreases.

Aggregate Supply Curve

Aggregate supply curve
A curve representing the relationship between the economy's price level and the amount of aggregate output supplied per period, other things held constant

The **aggregate supply curve** shows how much output U.S. producers are willing and able to supply at each price level, other things constant. How does the quantity supplied respond to changes in the price level? The shape of the aggregate supply curve and the reasons for that shape remain controversial issues among macroeconomists. This section bypasses the controversy to present a relatively simple approach.

The upward-sloping aggregate supply curve, *AS*, in Exhibit 5 depicts a positive relationship between the price level and the quantity of aggregate output that producers supply, other factors held constant. Held constant along an aggregate supply curve are (1) resource owners' willingness and ability to supply

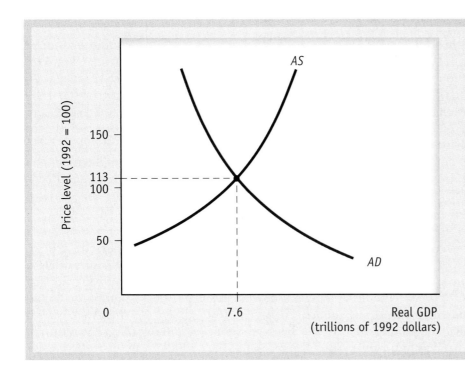

EXHIBIT 5

Aggregate Demand and Supply

The total output of the economy and its price level are determined at the intersection of the aggregate demand and aggregate supply curves. The equilibrium reflects real GDP and the price level for 1998, using 1992 as the base year.

resources, (2) the state of technology, and (3) the "rules of the game" that provide production incentives, such as patent and copyright laws. Wage rates are typically assumed to be constant along the aggregate supply curve. With wages constant, firms find a higher price level more profitable so they increase the quantity of output supplied. *Whenever the prices firms receive rise by more than the cost of production, firms find it profitable to expand output, so the aggregate output supplied varies directly with the economy's price level.*

Equilibrium

The intersection of the aggregate demand curve and aggregate supply curve determines the equilibrium levels of price and aggregate output in the economy. Exhibit 5 is a rough depiction of aggregate demand and supply in 1998; the equilibrium price level in 1998 was 113 (compared to a price level of 100 in the base year of 1992). The equilibrium real GDP in 1998 was $7.6 trillion (measured in dollars of 1992 purchasing power).

Incidentally, although employment is not measured directly along the horizontal axis, firms usually must hire more workers to produce more output. So higher levels of real GDP are beneficial because (1) more people in the economy are employed and fewer are unemployed, and (2) more goods and services are available in the economy.

Perhaps the best way to understand aggregate demand and aggregate supply is to apply these tools to the U.S. economy. In the following section we simplify U.S. economic history to review changes in the price and output levels over time.

A SHORT HISTORY OF THE U.S. ECONOMY

The history of the U.S. economy can be crudely divided into four economic eras: (1) prior to and including the Great Depression, (2) after the Great Depression to the early 1970s, (3) from the early 1970s to the early 1980s, and (4) since the early 1980s. The first era was marked by a series of recessions and depressions, culminating in the Great Depression of the 1930s. These depressions were often accompanied by a falling price level. The second era was one of generally strong economic growth, with only moderate increases in the price level. The third era was characterized by episodes of both high unemployment and high inflation. And the fourth era was more like the second, with good economic growth and moderate increases in the price level.

The Great Depression and Before

Prior to World War II, the U.S. economy alternated between periods of prosperity and sharp economic declines. As noted earlier, the longest contraction on record occurred between 1873 and 1879, when 80 railroads went bankrupt and most of the steel industry was shut down. During the depression of the 1890s, the unemployment rate topped 18 percent. In October 1929 the stock market crashed, beginning what was to become the deepest economic contraction in our nation's history, the Great Depression of the 1930s.

In terms of aggregate demand and aggregate supply, the Great Depression can be viewed as a shift to the left in the aggregate demand curve, as shown in Exhibit 6. AD_{1929} is the aggregate demand curve in 1929, before the onset of the depression. Real GDP in 1929 was $791 billion (measured in dollars of 1992 purchasing power) and the price level was 13.1, relative to a base-year (1992) price level of 100. By 1933, aggregate demand had decreased to AD_{1933}.[3] Why did aggregate demand fall so sharply? Though the causes are still debated, grim business expectations, a drop in consumer spending, a sharp decline in the nation's money supply, and restrictions on world trade each contributed to the drop in aggregate demand.

Because of this decline in aggregate demand, both the price level and real GDP declined. Between 1929 and 1933, the price level decreased by 25 percent, from 13.1 to 9.8, and real GDP fell by 27 percent, from $791 billion to $577 billion. As aggregate output declined, the unemployment rate jumped, climbing from about 3 percent in 1929 to 25 percent in 1933, the highest U.S. rate ever recorded.

Prior to the Great Depression, macroeconomic policy was based primarily on the *laissez-faire* philosophy of Adam Smith. Smith, you may recall, argued in his book *The Wealth of Nations* that if people were allowed to pursue their self-interest in free markets, resources would be guided as if by an "invisible hand" to produce the greatest, most efficient level of aggregate output. Although the U.S. economy had suffered several sharp contractions since the beginning of the 19th century, most economists of the day viewed these as a natural phase of the economy—unfortunate but therapeutic and essentially *self-correcting*.

---

3 The aggregate supply curve probably also shifted somewhat during this period, but for simplicity we assume it was unchanged. Most economists agree that the shift in the aggregate demand curve was the dominant factor.

EXHIBIT 6

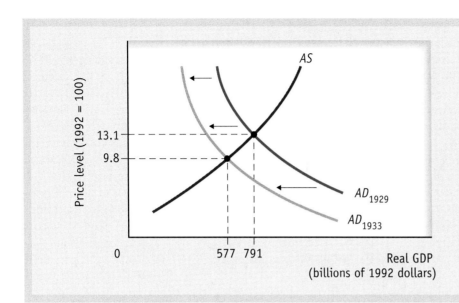

The Decrease in Aggregate Demand Between 1929 and 1933

The Great Depression of the 1930s can be represented by a shift to the left of the aggregate demand curve, from AD_{1929} to AD_{1933}. In the resulting depression, real GDP fell from $791 billion to $577 billion, and the price level dropped from 13.1 to 9.8.

The Age of Keynes: After the Great Depression to the Early 1970s

The Great Depression was so severe that it stimulated new thinking about how the economy worked (or didn't work). In 1936, John Maynard Keynes (1883–1946) published *The General Theory of Employment, Interest, and Money,* perhaps the most famous economics book of the 20th century. In it, Keynes argued that aggregate demand was inherently unstable, in part because investment decisions were often guided by the unpredictable "animal spirits" of business expectations. Thus, if businesses grew pessimistic about the economy, they would cut back on their demand for investment, which would reduce aggregate demand, output, and employment. Keynes saw no natural forces operating to ensure that the economy, even if allowed a reasonable time to adjust, would return to a higher level of output and employment.

Keynes proposed that the government jolt the economy out of its depression by increasing aggregate demand. He recommended an *expansionary fiscal policy* to deal with contractions. The government could achieve this directly by increasing its spending, or indirectly by cutting taxes to stimulate the primary components of private-sector demand, consumption and investment. Either action would likely result in a government budget deficit. A **government budget deficit** is a flow variable that measures, for a particular period, the amount by which total government outlays exceed total government revenues.

To understand what Keynes had in mind, imagine federal budget policies that increase aggregate demand in Exhibit 6, shifting the aggregate demand curve to the right, back to its original position. Such a shift would raise the equilibrium level of aggregate output and employment. According to the Keynesian prescription, the miracle drug of government fiscal policy—changes in government spending and taxes—was needed to compensate for what he viewed as the inherent instability of private spending, especially investment. If

Government budget deficit A flow variable that measures the amount by which total government outlays exceed total government revenues in a particular period

Demand-side economics
Macroeconomic policy that focuses on changing aggregate demand as a way of promoting full employment and price stability

Inflation A sustained increase in the economy's average price level

demand in the private sector declined, Keynes said the government should pick up the slack. We can think of the Keynesian approach as **demand-side economics** because it focused on how changes in aggregate demand could promote full employment. Keynes argued that government spending could be just the tonic to shock the economy out of its depression and back to health.

The U.S. economy languished during the 1930s, but when World War II broke out, huge federal budget deficits financed the war. War-related demand for tanks, ships, aircraft, and the like stimulated output and employment, seeming to confirm the powerful impact that government spending could have on the economy. Immediately after the war, memories of the Great Depression were still vivid. Trying to avoid another depression, Congress approved the *Employment Act of 1946,* which imposed a clear responsibility on the federal government to foster, in the language of the act, "maximum employment, production, and purchasing power." The act also required the president to report annually on the state of the economy and to appoint a *Council of Economic Advisers,* a three-member group with a professional staff, to provide the president with economic advice.

The economy seemed to prosper during the 1950s largely without the added stimulus of fiscal policy. The 1960s, however, proved to be the *golden age of Keynesian economics,* a period when fiscal policy makers thought they could "fine-tune" the economy to avoid recessions—just as a mechanic fine-tunes a race car to achieve high performance.

During the 1960s, nearly all developed economies of the world enjoyed low unemployment and healthy growth in output with only modest **inflation,** which is a sustained increase in the price level. In short, the world economy was booming, and the U.S. economy was on top of the world.

The economy was on such a roll that toward the end of the 1960s some economists began to think economic fluctuations were a thing of the past. As a sign of the times, the federal government changed the name of their publication *Business Cycle Developments* to *Business Conditions Digest.* In the early 1970s, however, fluctuations returned with a fury. Worse yet, the problem of recession was compounded by inflation, which increased during the recessions of 1974–1975 and 1979–1980. Until then, inflation was limited primarily to periods of expansion. Confidence in demand-side policies was shaken, and the expression "fine-tuning" passed from economists' vocabularies. What ended the golden age of Keynesian economics?

The Great Stagflation: 1973–1980

During the late 1960s, the federal government escalated the war in Vietnam and increased spending on social programs at home. These efforts stimulated aggregate demand enough that in 1968 the *inflation rate,* the annual percentage increase in the price level, jumped to 4.4 percent, after averaging only 2.0 percent during the previous decade. Inflation climbed to 4.7 percent in 1969 and to 5.3 percent in 1970. These rates were so alarming that in 1971 President Richard Nixon introduced measures to freeze prices and wages.

The freeze was eliminated in 1973, about the time that crop failures around the world caused grain prices to soar. To compound these problems, the Organization of Petroleum Exporting Countries (OPEC) pushed up the world price of oil. The resulting reduction in aggregate supply, shown in Exhibit 7 by the shift to the left in the aggregate supply curve from AS_{1973} to AS_{1975}, created the **stagflation** of the 1970s, meaning a *stag*nation, or contraction, in the economy's aggregate output combined with in*flation*, or a rise, in the economy's price level. Between 1973 and 1975, real GDP declined by about $50 billion, while the price level jumped nearly 20 percent. The percent of the labor force unemployed jumped from 4.9 percent in 1973 to 8.5 percent in 1975.

Stagflation appeared again at the end of the 1970s, partly as a result of another boost in oil prices. Between 1979 and 1980, real GDP declined; at the same time, the price level increased by 9.2 percent. Macroeconomics has not been the same since. Because the problem of stagflation was primarily on the supply side, not on the demand side, the demand-management prescriptions of Keynes seemed ineffective. If government stimulated aggregate demand, this might reduce unemployment but would worsen inflation.

Stagflation A contraction, or *stag*nation, of a nation's output accompanied by in*flation* in the price level

Experience Since 1980

Increasing aggregate supply seemed an appropriate way to combat stagflation, for such a move would both lower inflation and increase output and employment. Attention therefore turned from aggregate demand to aggregate supply. A key idea behind **supply-side economics** was that the federal government, by lowering tax rates, would increase after-tax earnings and thereby provide resource owners with incentives to increase their supply of labor and other resources. This greater resource supply would increase aggregate supply. According to advocates of the supply-side approach, the increase in aggregate supply would achieve the happy result of increasing real GDP and reducing the price level. But this was easier said than done.

Supply-side economics Macroeconomic policy that focuses on increasing aggregate supply through tax cuts or other changes to increase production incentives

EXHIBIT 7

Stagflation Between 1973 and 1975

The stagflation of the mid-1970s can be represented as a reduction in aggregate supply from AS_{1973} to AS_{1975}. Aggregate output fell from $3.92 trillion to $3.87 trillion (stagnation), and the price level rose from 35.3 to 42.1 (inflation).

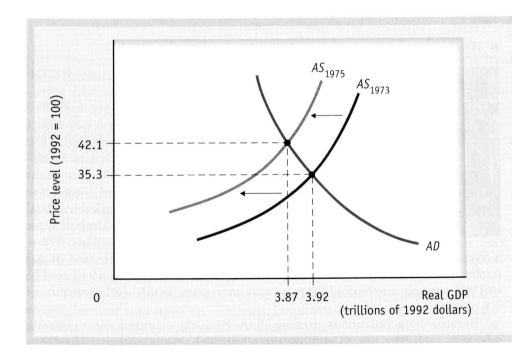

Unemployment and Inflation

Who among the following would be counted as unemployed: a college student who is not working, a bank teller displaced by an automatic teller machine, Julia Roberts between movies, or baseball slugger Mark McGwire in the off-season? What type of unemployment might be healthy for the economy? What's so bad about inflation? Why is anticipated inflation better than unanticipated inflation? These and other questions are answered in this chapter, where we explore two macroeconomic problems: unemployment and inflation.

To be sure, unemployment and inflation are not the only problems an economy could face. Sluggish growth, rising poverty, and a huge federal debt are some others. But low unemployment and low inflation go a long way toward helping diminish the effects of other economic problems. Although unemployment and inflation are often related, we will initially describe each separately. Our focus will be more on the extent and consequences of these problems than on their causes. The causes of each and the relationship between the two will become clearer in later chapters, as you learn more about how the economy works.

As this chapter will show, not all unemployment nor all inflation harms the economy. Even in a healthy economy, a certain amount of unemployment reflects the voluntary choices of workers and employers seeking their best opportunities. And inflation that is fully anticipated creates fewer distortions than does unanticipated inflation. Topics discussed in this chapter include:

- Measuring unemployment
- Frictional, structural, seasonal, and cyclical unemployment
- Meaning of full employment
- Sources and consequences of inflation
- Relative price changes
- Nominal and real interest rates

UNEMPLOYMENT

"They scampered about looking for work . . . . They swarmed on the highways. The movement changed them; the highways, the camps along the road, the fear of hunger and the hunger itself, changed them. The children without dinner changed them, the endless moving changed them."[1] There is no question, as John Steinbeck wrote in *The Grapes of Wrath*, that a long stretch of unemployment can have a profound effect on the individual and the family. The most obvious loss is a steady paycheck, but those who are unemployed often suffer a loss of self-esteem, as well. Moreover, unemployment appears to be linked to a greater incidence of crime and to a variety of afflictions including heart disease, suicide, and mental illness. However much people complain about their jobs, they rely on those same jobs not only for income but also for part of their personal identity. When strangers meet, the "What-do-you-do" question is usually one of the first to come up. The loss of a long-held job usually involves some loss of that identity.

In addition to these personal costs, unemployment imposes a cost on the economy as a whole, because fewer goods and services are produced. When the economy does not generate enough jobs to employ all those who are willing and able to work, that unemployed labor service is lost forever. *This lost output coupled with the economic and psychological damage to unemployed workers and their families represents the true cost of unemployment.* As we begin our analysis, keep in mind that unemployment statistics reflect millions of individuals with their own stories. As President Harry Truman said, "It's a recession when your neighbor loses his job; it's a depression when you lose your own." For some people, unemployment is a brief break between jobs. For others, a long stretch of unemployment can have a lasting effect on self-esteem, on family stability, and on economic welfare.

Measuring Unemployment
The unemployment rate is perhaps the most widely reported measure of the nation's economic health. What does the unemployment rate measure, what are the sources of unemployment, and how does unemployment change over time?

---

1 John Steinbeck, *The Grapes of Wrath* (New York: Viking Press, 1939), p. 392.

Labor force Individuals 16 years of age and older who are either working or actively looking for work

Unemployment rate The number of unemployed individuals expressed as a percentage of the labor force

Discouraged worker A person who has dropped out of the labor force because of lack of success in finding a job

Labor force participation rate The ratio of the number in the labor force to the adult population

These are some of the questions explored in this section. Let's start by considering how unemployment is measured.

We begin with the U.S. *civilian noninstitutional adult population,* which consists of all civilians 16 years of age and older, except those who are institutionalized in prisons or mental hospitals. The adjective *civilian* means that the definition excludes those in the military. In this chapter, when we refer to the *adult population,* we will mean the civilian noninstitutional adult population. The **labor force** consists of those in the adult population who are either working or looking for work. *Those looking for work are considered unemployed.* More specifically, the Bureau of Labor Statistics surveys 50,000 households monthly and counts people as unemployed if they have no job but have looked for work at least once during the preceding four weeks. Thus, the college student, displaced bank teller, Julia Roberts, and Mark McGwire would all be counted as unemployed if they looked for work in the previous month but could not find a suitable job. The unemployment rate measures the percentage of those in the labor force who are unemployed. Hence, the **unemployment rate,** which is reported monthly, equals the number unemployed—that is, those without jobs who are looking for work—divided by the number in the labor force.

Only a fraction of adults who are not working are considered unemployed. The others may have retired, may have chosen to remain at home to care for small children, may be full-time students, or may simply not want to work. Others may be unable to work because of long-term illness or disability. Some people may have become so discouraged by a long, unfruitful job search that they have given up their search in frustration. These **discouraged workers** have, in effect, dropped out of the labor force, so they are not counted as unemployed. Finally, about one-third of those who are working part time would prefer to work full time, yet all part-time workers are counted as employed. Because the official unemployment rate does not include discouraged workers and counts all part-time workers as employed, it may underestimate the true extent of unemployment in the economy. Later we will consider some factors that could cause the official rate to exceed the true rate.

These definitions are illustrated in Exhibit 1, where circles represent the various groups and subgroups, and the number (in millions) of individuals in each category and subcategory is listed in parentheses. The circle on the left depicts the entire U.S. labor force, including both those who are employed and those who are unemployed. The circle on the right represents those in the adult population who, for whatever reason, are not working. These two circles reflect the entire adult population. The overlapping area identifies the number of *unemployed* workers—that is, the number in the labor force who aren't working.

The unemployment rate is found by dividing the number unemployed by the number in the labor force; in 1998, the unemployment rate averaged 4.5 percent.

The productive capability of any economy depends in part on the proportion of adults who are in the labor force, called the *labor force participation rate.* Let's step back from the unemployment rate to bring into the picture this more fundamental measure. In Exhibit 1, the U.S. adult population equals those in the labor force (137.7 million) plus those not in the labor force (67.5 million)—a total of 205.2 million. The **labor force participation rate** therefore equals the number in the labor force divided by the adult population, or

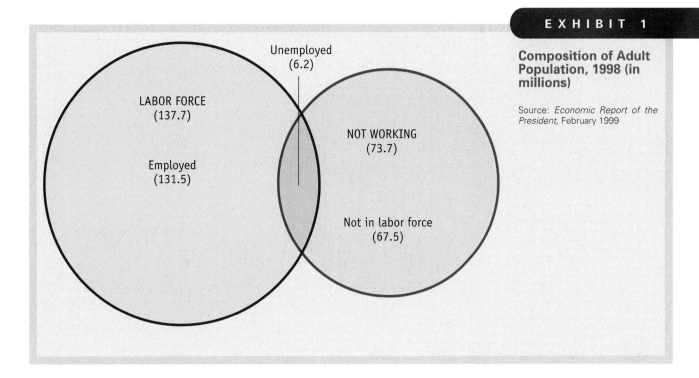

EXHIBIT 1

Composition of Adult Population, 1998 (in millions)

Source: *Economic Report of the President*, February 1999

67.1 percent (137.7/205.2). So, on average, about two out of three adults are in the labor force. The labor force participation rate increased from about 60 percent in 1970 to about 67 percent in 1990, and it has remained relatively constant since then.

Changes over Time in Unemployment Statistics

The noninstitutional adult population changes slowly over time. The only way to join that group is to become 16 years of age, get released from prison or a mental hospital, or immigrate to the United States. The only way to leave the adult population is to die, become institutionalized, or emigrate from the United States to another country. Since 1950, the adult population in the United States has grown by an average of 1.4 percent per year.

The labor force participation rate can change more quickly than the adult population, because moving in and out of the labor force is easier than moving in and out of the adult population. One striking development since World War II has been the convergence in the labor force participation rates of men and women. In 1950, only 34 percent of adult women were in the labor force; today that rate is 60 percent, with the largest increase among younger women. The labor force participation rate among men has declined from 86 percent in 1950 to about 75 percent today, primarily because of earlier retirement. The participation rate is slightly higher among white males than black males, but higher among black females than white females.

But, over time, what changes even more quickly than the labor force participation rate or the adult population is the unemployment rate. Exhibit 2 depicts the U.S. unemployment rate since 1900, with shading to indicate years of recession or depression. As you can see, the rate rises during recessions and falls

*Net*Bookmark

The Bureau of Labor Statistics provides abundant data on labor market conditions, including unemployment rates, labor force estimates, and earnings data. Visit their Web site at http://stats.bls.gov:80/blshome.html. Click on "Economy at a Glance" for easy access to the latest data.

EXHIBIT 2

The U.S. Unemployment Rate Since 1900

Since 1900 the unemployment rate has fluctuated widely, rising during recessions and falling during expansions. During the Great Depression of the 1930s, the rate rose as high as 25.2 percent.

Sources: *Historical Statistics of the United States*, 1970; and *Economic Report of the President*, February 1996.

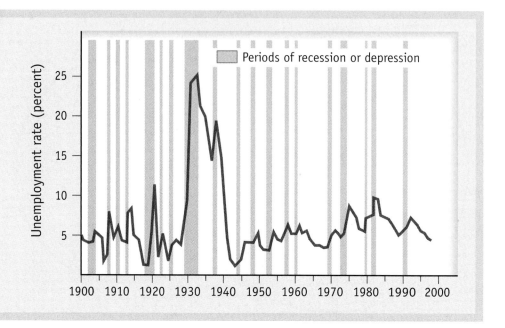

during expansions. Perhaps the most striking feature of the graph is the dramatic jump that occurred during the Great Depression, when the unemployment rate peaked at 25 percent. Note that since the end of World War II the unemployment rate trended upward until the early 1980s, and then came back down.

Since 1970, the entry of baby boomers—coupled with a rising female labor force participation rate—boosted U.S. employment by well over 50 million workers. In fact, since 1970 the United States has been called an incredible job machine and is the envy of the world. At the same time that the U.S. economy was creating over 50 million jobs, the industrialized countries of Western Europe experienced only modest employment growth.

Unemployment in Various Groups

The overall unemployment rate says nothing about who is unemployed or for how long. Even a low overall rate often hides wide differences in unemployment rates across age, race, gender, and geographical area. Unemployment rates since 1972 for different groups appear in Exhibit 3. Each panel presents the unemployment rate by race and by gender. Panel (a) considers those 20 years of age and older, and panel (b) those 16 to 19 years old. Years of recession are shaded. As you can see, rates are higher among blacks than among whites, and rates are higher among teenagers than among those aged 20 and older. During recessions, the rates of all groups climbed. For all groups, rates peaked during the recession of 1982. The unemployment rate among blacks aged 20 and older fell below double digits in 1995 for the first time in two decades.

Why are unemployment rates among teenagers about twice as high as among older workers? Young workers enter the job market with little training and so are usually employed in relatively unskilled positions, where they are

E X H I B I T   3

Unemployment Rates Among Various Groups Since 1972

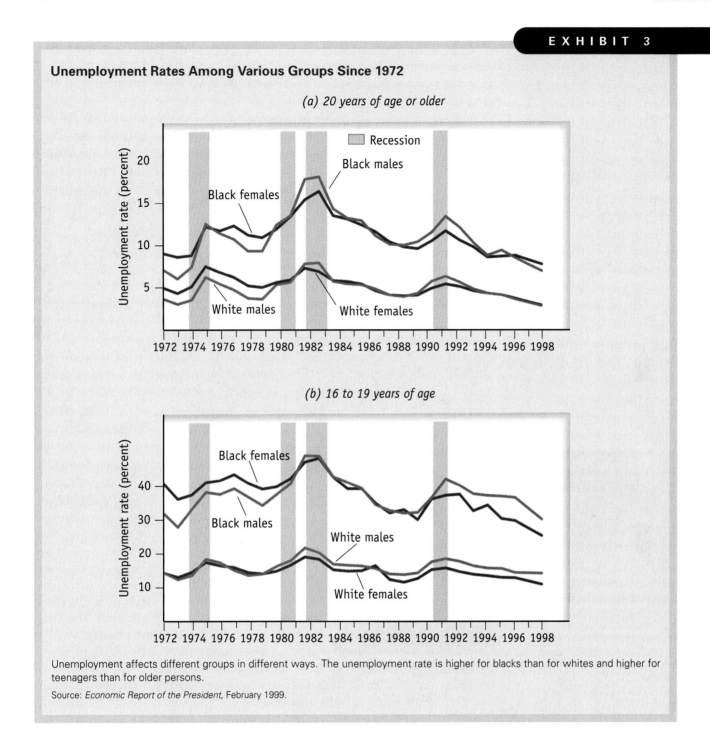

(a) 20 years of age or older

(b) 16 to 19 years of age

Unemployment affects different groups in different ways. The unemployment rate is higher for blacks than for whites and higher for teenagers than for older persons.

Source: *Economic Report of the President*, February 1999.

among the first dismissed if the economy stalls. Young workers also move in and out of the job market frequently during the year as they juggle school demands. Even those who have left school often shop around more than older workers, quitting one job and searching for another that suits them better.

Unemployment also varies by occupational group. Professional and technical workers experience lower unemployment rates than blue-collar workers. Construction workers experience the highest average unemployment rate because that business is seasonal and is subject to swings over the business cycle.

Duration of Unemployment

Any given unemployment rate says little about how long people have been unemployed—that is, the *average duration of unemployment*. The average duration of unemployment rises during recessions and starts to fall soon after a recovery begins. The average duration of unemployment in 1998 was 14.5 weeks. Some were unemployed longer than others: 42 percent were unemployed fewer than 5 weeks; 31 percent from 5 to 14 weeks; 13 percent from 15 to 26 weeks; and 14 percent 27 weeks or longer. Typically, a rise in the unemployment rate reflects both a larger number of unemployed and a longer average duration of unemployment. The duration of unemployment varies across countries. For example, only 6 percent of the U.S. jobless in 1997 were out of work for more than a year, compared to 37 percent in France and 51 percent in Spain.

Unemployment Differences Across the Country

The national unemployment rate masks much variation in rates across the country. For example, in 1998, the unemployment rates in Alaska, New Mexico, and West Virginia were more than double the rates in Nebraska, North Dakota, and South Dakota. To look behind the numbers, let's consider the experience of one troubled county in West Virginia, in the following case study.

Poor King Coal

CaseStudy

Public Policy

Carolyn Sherwood-Call of the Federal Reserve Bank of San Francisco has written "The 1980s divergence in state personal incomes: What does it tell us?" Download her article at http://www.frbsf.org/econrsrch/econrev/96-1/14-25.pdf to learn more about the shifting fortunes of various U.S. regions—your own included.

For decades, McDowell County, West Virginia, prospered by supplying the coal that fired the nation's steel mills. Mining jobs were abundant and wages attractive. Many miners earned over $40,000 a year in 1980, which would exceed the purchasing power of $75,000 in today's dollars. Most young people, rather than finish their education, became miners (more than half of those over age 25 are high school dropouts). The mining companies dominated the county, owning most of the property.

But between 1980 and 1985, the value of the dollar rose relative to foreign currencies, so American steel became more expensive overseas and foreign steel became cheaper in the United States. Steel imports increased by 56 percent between 1980 and 1985. As the world's demand for U.S. steel fell, so did the demand for the coal needed to produce that steel. Coal mines in McDowell County shut down, and by the end of the decade, the official unemployment rate for the county was more than double the national average. Local officials claimed the actual rate was much higher because of discouraged workers. According to the 1990 census, half those under 18 lived in poverty, as did 36 percent of those 18 to 64 years of age.

The county tried to attract new industry—even a nuclear-waste dump—but met with little success. The county's poor roads and bridges and a labor force trained only for mining scared off potential employers. By 1995, transfer payments exceeded all earnings as a source of income; the largest employer in the county was state and local government. In short, the county had all its eggs in one basket—mining—but that basket fell.

Sources: Walter Adams, "Steel," *The Structure of American Industry,* Walter Adams and James Brock, eds. (Englewood Cliffs, N.J.: Prentice Hall, 1995), pp. 93–118. Recent employment and income figures for McDowell County can be found at Internet site http://musom.mu.wvnet.edu/0u:/wvvhs/root.html.

Types of Unemployment

Pick up any metropolitan newspaper and thumb through the classified pages. The "Help Wanted" section may run more than 40 pages and include thousands of jobs, from accountants to x-ray technicians. Why, when millions are unemployed, are so many jobs unfilled? To understand this paradox, we must take a closer look at the reasons behind unemployment.

Think about all the ways people can become unemployed. They may quit or get fired from their jobs. They may be looking for a first job, or they may be reentering the labor force after an absence. An examination of the reasons behind unemployment during 1998 indicates that 45 percent of the unemployed lost their previous jobs, 12 percent quit their previous jobs, 9 percent were entering the labor market for the first time, and 34 percent were reentering the market. *Thus, 55 percent were unemployed either because they quit their jobs or because they were just joining or rejoining the labor force.*

We distinguish four types of unemployment, based on the source: frictional, structural, seasonal, and cyclical.

Frictional Unemployment. Just as employers do not always hire the first applicant who comes through the door, workers do not always accept their first job offer. Both employers and job applicants need time to explore the job market. Employers need time to learn about the talent available, and job seekers need time to learn about employment opportunities. The time required to bring together labor suppliers and labor demanders results in **frictional unemployment.** Although unemployment often creates economic and psychological hardships, not all unemployment is necessarily bad. Frictional unemployment does not usually last long and results in a better match-up between workers and jobs, so the entire economy becomes more efficient.

Frictional unemployment
Unemployment that arises because of the time needed to match qualified job seekers with available job openings

Structural Unemployment. A second reason job vacancies and unemployment coexist is that unemployed workers often do not have the skills demanded by employers or do not live in the area where their skills are in demand. For example, the Lincoln Electric Company in Euclid, Ohio, could not fill 200 job openings because few of the thousands who applied could operate computer-controlled machines. Unemployment arising from a mismatch of skills or geographic location is called **structural unemployment.** *Structural unemployment occurs because changes in tastes, technology, taxes, or competition reduce the demand for certain skills and increase the demand for other skills.* In our dynamic economy, some

Structural unemployment
Unemployment that arises because (1) the skills demanded by employers do not match the skills of the unemployed, or (2) the unemployed do not live where the jobs are located

workers, such as the coal miners in West Virginia, are stuck with skills that are no longer demanded. Likewise, golf carts replaced caddies and ATMs put many bank tellers out of work.

Whereas most frictional unemployment is short-term and voluntary, structural unemployment poses more of a problem because workers must seek jobs elsewhere or must develop the skills that are in demand. For example, unemployed coal miners and bank tellers must seek work in other industries or in other regions. But moving to where the jobs are is easier said than done. People prefer to remain near friends and relatives. Those laid off from high-wage jobs may be reluctant to leave an area because they hope to be rehired. Families in which one spouse is still employed may not want to give up one job to seek two jobs elsewhere. Finally, available jobs may be in areas where the cost of living is much higher. So the unemployed often stay put, remaining structurally unemployed.

Seasonal unemployment
Unemployment caused by seasonal shifts in labor supply and demand

Seasonal Unemployment. Unemployment caused by seasonal changes in labor supply and demand during the year is called **seasonal unemployment.** During cold winter months, demand for farm hands, lifeguards, golf instructors, and lawn-care specialists shrinks, as it does for dozens of other seasonal occupations. Likewise, the tourist trade in places such as Miami and Phoenix melts in the summer heat. The Christmas season increases the demand for sales clerks, postal workers, and Santa Clauses. Those with seasonal jobs know they will probably be unemployed in the off-season. Some may even have chosen a seasonal occupation to complement their lifestyle or academic schedule. To eliminate seasonal unemployment, we might have to outlaw winter and abolish Christmas. Monthly employment statistics are usually "seasonally adjusted" to smooth out the bulges that result from seasonal factors.

Cyclical unemployment
Unemployment that fluctuates with the business cycle, increasing during recessions and decreasing during expansions

Cyclical Unemployment. As production declines during recessions, many firms reduce their demand for inputs, including labor. **Cyclical unemployment** is the fluctuation in unemployment that is caused by the business cycle. Cyclical unemployment increases during recessions and decreases during expansions. Between 1932 and 1934, when unemployment averaged about 24 percent, there was clearly much cyclical unemployment. Between 1942 and 1945, when the unemployment rate averaged only 1.6 percent, there was no cyclical unemployment. Government policies that stimulate aggregate demand during recessions are aimed at reducing cyclical unemployment.

The Meaning of Full Employment

In an ever-changing economy such as ours, changes in product demand and changes in technology continually alter the supply and demand for particular types of labor. Thus, even in a healthy economy, there will be some frictional, structural, and seasonal unemployment. The economy is viewed as operating at *full employment* if there is no cyclical unemployment. When economists talk about "full employment," they do not mean zero unemployment, but relatively low unemployment, with estimates ranging from 4 to 6 percent. Even when the economy is at **full employment,** there will be some frictional, structural, and seasonal unemployment. After all, more than half of those unemployed have quit their last job or are new entrants or reentrants into the labor force. A large proportion of this group could be counted among the frictionally unemployed.

Full employment The level of employment when there is no cyclical unemployment

Unemployment Compensation

We know that unemployment often imposes an economic and psychological hardship on those unemployed. For a variety of reasons, however, the burden of unemployment on the individual and the family may not be as severe today as it was during the Great Depression. Today, a large proportion of households have two workers in the labor force, so if one becomes unemployed, another is likely to have a job, a job that often provides health insurance and other benefits. When a household has more than one person in the labor force, the economic shock of unemployment is cushioned to some extent.

Moreover, workers who lose their jobs now often receive unemployment benefits. In response to the massive unemployment of the Great Depression, Congress passed the Social Security Act of 1935, which provided unemployment insurance financed by a tax on employers. Unemployed workers who meet certain qualifications can receive **unemployment benefits** for up to six months, provided they actively seek work. During recessions, benefits are often extended beyond six months in states with especially high unemployment rates. The insurance is aimed primarily at those who have lost jobs. Not covered are those just entering or reentering the labor force, those who quit their last job, or those fired for just cause such as excessive absenteeism or theft. Because of these restrictions, only about half of all unemployed workers receive unemployment benefits.

Unemployment insurance usually replaces more than half of a person's take-home pay. In 1998, for example, an average of $200 per week was paid to the unemployed who received benefits. Because unemployment benefits reduce the opportunity cost of remaining unemployed, they may reduce incentives to find work. For example, if you faced the choice of washing dishes for a take-home pay of $200 per week or collecting $150 per week in unemployment benefits, which would you choose? Evidence suggests that unemployed workers who receive insurance benefits tend to search less actively than those without such benefits. Therefore, although unemployment insurance provides a safety net for the unemployed, it may also reduce the urgency of finding work, thereby increasing the average duration of unemployment and the unemployment rate. On the plus side, unemployment insurance may allow for a higher-quality search, since the insured job seeker has walking-around money and need not take the first job that comes along. As a result of a better search, there is a better match between job skills and job requirements; and this promotes economic efficiency in the economy.

Unemployment benefits
Cash transfers provided to unemployed workers who actively seek employment and who meet other qualifications

International Comparisons of Unemployment

How do U.S. unemployment rates compare with those around the world? In January 1999, when the civilian unemployment rate was 4.3 percent in the U.S., it was 7.8 percent in Canada, 10.6 percent in Germany, 11.4 percent in France, 6.2 percent in the United Kingdom, 12.3 percent in Italy, and 4.4 percent in Japan. Unemployment rates in Europe tend to be higher than in the United States. The ratio of unemployment benefits to average pay tends to be higher in Europe, and unemployment insurance tends to last longer, sometimes for years.

We should view international comparisons carefully, however, because the definitions of unemployment differ across countries with respect to age limits, the criteria used to determine whether a person is looking for work, the way layoffs are treated, how those in the military are counted, and in other subtle ways.

These differences can affect estimates of unemployment. For example, most countries in North and South America and some European countries base their unemployment estimates on periodic surveys of the labor force. Each month the U.S. Bureau of Labor Statistics surveys 50,000 households around the nation. Experts believe that such extensive surveys yield the most reliable results.

But most other countries, including Germany, the United Kingdom, and a majority of less-developed countries, base official estimates on registrations with government employment offices. Reliance on such self-reporting tends to underestimate the actual level of unemployment, particularly in less-developed countries where there are few jobs, no unemployment benefits, and hence no real reason to bother registering with the government as unemployed. Command economies, such as North Korea and Cuba, usually do not publish unemployment rates.

Employment practices differ across countries. For example, Germany imposes penalties on firms for "socially unjustified" layoffs, and Swedish law makes it harder to lay off Swedish citizens than foreign workers. In Japan, many firms have offered job security for life. As a result, some employees there who do little or no work are still carried on the company's payroll. Layoffs in Japan are limited by both labor laws and social norms. Unemployment has increased there lately only because many firms are going bankrupt and have no alternative but to lay off workers.

Problems with Official Unemployment Figures

Official unemployment statistics are not without their problems. As we saw earlier, not counting discouraged workers in the official labor force understates unemployment. Official employment data also ignore the problem of **underemployment**, which arises because people are counted as employed even if they can find only part-time jobs or are vastly overqualified for their job, as when someone with a Ph.D. in English can find employment only as a bookstore clerk. Counting overqualified and part-time workers as employed tends to understate the actual amount of unemployment.

On the other hand, because unemployment insurance and most welfare programs require recipients to seek employment, some people may act as if they are looking for work just to qualify for such programs. If these people do not in fact want to find a job, their inclusion among the unemployed tends to overstate the official unemployment figures. Also, people working in the underground economy may not readily acknowledge employment on a government survey since their intent is to evade taxes or skirt the law. *On net, however, most experts believe that official U.S. unemployment figures tend to underestimate unemployment because of the exclusion of discouraged workers and because underemployed workers are counted as employed.* Despite several qualifications and limitations, the unemployment rate is a useful measure of unemployment trends over time.

We turn next to the second major concern in today's economy: inflation.

Underemployment A situation in which workers are overqualified for their jobs or work fewer hours than they would prefer

INFLATION

Let's begin our discussion of inflation with a case study that highlights the cost of high inflation by focusing on the recent experience of Brazil.

Hyperinflation in Brazil

CaseStudy

*Other Times,
Other Places*

What's happening in Brazil?
The Brazilian Ministry of
Finance maintains a comprehensive Web page devoted
to economic developments
there. You can find it at
http://www.brasil.emb.nw.dc.
us/econmenu.htm.

Between 1988 and 1994, year-to-year infla-tion rates in Brazil were 1,300 percent, 2,900 percent, 440 percent, 1,000 percent, 1,260 percent, and 1,740 percent. Six years of such in-flation meant that prices on average were about *4 million* times higher in 1994 than in 1988! To put this in perspective, if that inflation rate had prevailed in the United States, the price of a gal-lon of gasoline would have climbed from $1.25 in 1988 to $5 million in 1994. A pair of jeans that sold for $35 in 1988 would have cost $140 million in 1994!

With the value of the Brazilian cruzeiro cheapening by the hour, people understandably did not want to hold cruzeiros. As soon as workers got paid, they tried either to buy goods and services before prices increased or to ex-change cruzeiros for a more stable currency, such as the U.S. dollar. With such wild inflation, everyone, including merchants, had difficulty keeping track of prices. Price differences among sellers of the same product increased, prompting shoppers to incur the "shoe-leather cost" of looking for the lowest price.

The huge increase in the average price level meant that wads of money were needed to carry out even the simplest transactions. Think again in terms of dollars. To carry in 1994 the equivalent of $20 in preinflated spending power for pizza and a movie, you would have to load yourself down with $80 million. Even in $100 bills, this amount of currency would weigh nearly a ton. That's one fat wallet! Because carrying even small amounts of purchasing power be-came physically impossible, Brazilian officials issued currencies in larger and larger denominations. Between the mid-1980s and 1994, new currency denom-inations were issued on five separate occasions. Each new currency was worth a large multiple of the previous one. For example, the 1994 issue of the new *cruzeiro real* (now called simply the *real*) exchanged for 2,750 of the cruzeiro it replaced. New currency issues made transactions easier.

Lugging money around, shopping for the lowest price, and constant preoc-cupation with money matters all take time and energy away from production. Thus, high and unpredictable inflation leads to wasteful activity, such as imme-diately converting each day's pay into another currency or into goods and services. Such activity is rational for each individual but unproductive for the economy as a whole. Inflation in Brazil dropped from the runaway levels of the early 1990s to only 5 percent in 1997, though inflation was starting to heat up again in 1998.

Sources: "Latin America Seeks Shelter," *The Economist,* 29 August 1998, pp. 63–65; Thomas Vogel and Pamela Druckerman, "Brazil Appears to Thwart Speculative Attack on Real," *Wall Street Journal,* 30 Oct. 1997; "Brazil: An-other Try," *The Economist* 9 July 1994, p. 44; and "Brazil," *Britannica Book of the Year* (Encyclopaedia Britannica: Chicago, 1994), pp. 570–571.

We have already discussed inflation in different contexts. *Inflation* is a sus-tained increase in the average level of prices. If the price level bounces around—moving up one month, falling back another—any particular increase in the price

other things constant. The supply curve for the amount people are willing to lend, *loanable funds*, therefore slopes upward, as indicated by line *S* in Exhibit 7.

These funds are demanded by households, firms, and governments to finance purchases, such as homes, buildings, and machinery, and in the case of governments, to finance deficits. The higher the interest rate, other things constant, the higher the opportunity cost of borrowing funds. Hence, the quantity of loanable funds demanded decreases as the interest rate rises, other things constant. That is, the interest rate and the quantity of loanable funds demanded are inversely related. The demand curve for loans therefore slopes downward, as indicated by curve *D* in Exhibit 7. The downward-sloping demand curve for loanable funds and the upward-sloping supply curve intersect at the equilibrium point to yield the equilibrium nominal rate of interest, *i*.

The **nominal rate of interest** measures interest in terms of the current dollars paid. The nominal rate of interest is the rate that appears on the borrowing agreement; it is the rate discussed in the news media and is often of political significance. The **real rate of interest** is the nominal rate of interest minus the inflation rate:

Nominal rate of interest The interest rate expressed in current dollars as a percentage of the amount loaned; the interest rate on the loan agreement

Real rate of interest The interest rate expressed in dollars of constant purchasing power as a percentage of the amount loaned; the nominal rate of interest minus the inflation rate

Real interest rate = nominal interest rate − inflation rate

For example, if the nominal interest rate is 5 percent and the annual rate of inflation is 3 percent, the real interest rate is 2 percent. If there were no inflation, the nominal interest rate and the real interest rate would be identical. But with inflation, the real interest rate will be less than the nominal interest rate. Lenders and borrowers are concerned more about the real interest rate than the nominal interest rate. The real rate of interest, however, is known only after the fact—that is, only after inflation actually occurs. The nominal rate of interest is always positive; the real rate could turn out to be negative.

Because the future is uncertain, lenders and borrowers must form expectations about inflation, and base their willingness to lend and to borrow on these expectations. Other things constant, the higher the *expected* rate of inflation, the higher the nominal rate of interest that lenders require and that borrowers are

EXHIBIT 7

The Market for Loanable Funds

The upward-sloping supply curve, *S*, shows that more funds are supplied to financial markets at higher interest rates. The downward-sloping demand curve, *D*, shows that the quantity of loanable funds demanded is greater at lower interest rates. The two curves intersect to determine the equilibrium interest rate, *i*.

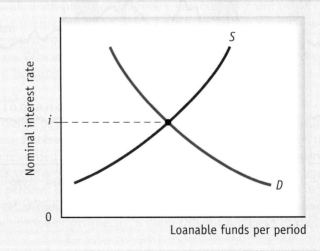

willing to pay. Lenders and borrowers base their decisions on the *expected* real interest rate, which equals the nominal rate of interest minus the expected inflation rate.[3]

Why Is Inflation So Unpopular?

Whenever the price level increases, more money must be spent to buy the same goods and services. If you think of inflation only in terms of spending, you consider only the problem of paying those higher prices. But if you think of inflation in terms of the higher money incomes that result, you see that higher prices mean higher receipts for resource suppliers. When viewed from the income side, inflation is not so bad.

If every higher price is received by some resource supplier, why are people so troubled by inflation? Whereas people view their higher incomes as well-deserved rewards for their labor, they see inflation as a penalty that unjustly robs them of purchasing power. Most people do not stop to realize that, unless their labor productivity increases, higher wages *must* result in higher prices. Prices and wages are simply two sides of the same coin. To the extent that nominal wages on average keep up with inflation, most workers do not suffer a loss of real income as a result of inflation. In a recent survey of 1,000 adults, more than two-thirds believed that price increases are due to companies trying to manipulate their prices to increase profits.[4] Fewer than one-third attributed price increases to the workings of supply and demand.

Presidents Ford and Carter could not control inflation and were turned out of office. Inflation slowed significantly during the Reagan administration, and President Reagan was reelected in a landslide, even though the level of unemployment was higher during his first term than during President Carter's tenure. During the 1988 presidential election, George Bush won in part by reminding voters what the rate of inflation was in 1980, the last time a Democrat had been president. Since then, inflation has been so low that it has not been a campaign issue.

Although inflation affects everyone, it hits hardest those whose incomes are fixed in nominal terms. For example, pensions are often fixed and are eroded by inflation, although the benefits paid by the largest pension program, Social Security, are adjusted annually for changes in the CPI. Retirees who rely on fixed nominal interest income also see their incomes eroded by inflation.

In summary, to the extent that the level and composition of inflation are fully anticipated by all market participants, inflation is of less concern in macroeconomic analysis than unanticipated inflation. *Unanticipated inflation arbitrarily redistributes income and wealth from one group to another, reduces the ability to make long-term plans, and forces buyers and sellers to pay more attention to prices.* The more variable and unpredictable inflation is, the greater the difficulty of negotiating long-term contracts. The overall productivity of the economy falls, because people must spend more time coping with the uncertainty created by inflation, leaving less time for production or consumption.

---

3 Although the discussion has implied that there is only one rate of interest, there are actually many rates. Rates differ depending on such factors as the risk, the maturity of different loans, and tax treatment of the interest.
4 As reported in Robert J. Blendon, et al., "Bridging the Gap Between the Public's and Economists' Views of the Economy," *Journal of Economic Perspectives,* Vol. 11 (Summer 1997), p. 116.

CONCLUSION

This chapter has focused on two macroeconomic problems: unemployment and inflation. Although we have discussed them separately, they are related in a variety of ways, as we will see in later chapters. Politicians sometimes add the unemployment rate to the rate of inflation to come up with what they refer to as the "misery index." In 1980, for example, an unemployment rate of 7.1 percent combined with a CPI increase of 13.6 percent to yield a misery index of 20.6—a number that explains why President Carter was not reelected that year. By 1984 the misery index had dropped to 11.8, and by 1988 to 9.6; Republicans retained the White House in both elections. In 1992, the index climbed slightly to 10.4 percent, an increase that spelled trouble for President Bush. And in 1996, the index fell back to 8.4 percent, assuring President Clinton's reelection.

In Chapter 8, we will address how to measure economic activity and how to adjust data for inflation. In later chapters, we will develop aggregate demand and aggregate supply curves to build a model of the economy. Once we have some idea how a healthy economy works, we can consider the policy options in the face of high unemployment, high inflation, or both.

SUMMARY

1. The unemployment rate equals the number of people looking for work divided by the number in the labor force. The overall unemployment rate masks differences in rates among particular groups. The lowest rate is among white adults; the highest rate is among black teenagers.

2. There are four types of unemployment. Frictional unemployment arises because employers and qualified job seekers need time to find one another. Structural unemployment arises because changes in taste, technology, taxes, and competition reduce the demand for certain skills. Seasonal unemployment stems from the effects of the weather and the calendar on certain industries, such as construction and agriculture. Cyclical unemployment results from the fluctuations in employment over the business cycle. Full employment occurs when cyclical unemployment is zero.

3. Unemployment imposes both an economic and a psychological burden on the unemployed. For some people, this burden is reduced by an employed spouse and by unemployment insurance, which typically replaces more than half of their take-home pay. Unemployment insurance provides a safety net for some people who are unemployed, but it also may reduce their incentive to find work.

4. Inflation is a sustained rise in the average level of prices. Demand-pull inflation results from an increase in aggre-gate demand. Cost-push inflation results from a decrease in aggregate supply. Until World War II, both increases and decreases in the price level were common; but since then the price level has steadily increased.

5. Anticipated inflation causes fewer distortions in the economy than does unanticipated inflation. Unanticipated inflation arbitrarily creates winners and losers, and forces people to spend more time and energy coping with the effects of inflation. The negative effects of high and variable inflation on an economy's productivity can be observed in countries that have experienced hyper-inflation, such as Brazil.

6. Because not all prices change by the same amount during inflationary periods, people have difficulty keeping track of relative prices. Inflation fuels uncertainty about relative prices, making long-term planning more costly and more risky.

7. The intersection of the supply curve and demand curve for loanable funds indicates the equilibrium interest rate. The nominal rate of interest equals the real rate of interest plus the rate of inflation. The higher the expected inflation rate, the higher the nominal rate of interest. Borrowers and lenders base decisions on the expected real rate of interest.

QUESTIONS FOR REVIEW

1. *(Labor Force)* Refer to Exhibit 1 in the chapter to determine whether the following statements are true or false.
    a. Some people who are officially unemployed are not in the labor force.
    b. Some people in the labor force are not working.
    c. Everyone who is not unemployed is in the labor force.
    d. Some people who are not working are not unemployed.

2. *(Unemployment in Various Groups)* Does the overall unemployment rate provide an accurate picture of the impact of unemployment on all U.S. population groups?

3. *(Case**Study:** Poor King Coal)* Is the unemployment in McDowell County primarily frictional, seasonal, structural, or cyclical? Explain your answer, using the text definitions for these categories of unemployment.

4. *(The Meaning of Full Employment)* When the economy is at full employment, is the unemployment rate at 0 percent? Why or why not? How would a more generous unemployment insurance system affect the full employment figure?

5. *(International Comparisons of Unemployment)* In recent years how has the U.S. unemployment rate compared with unemployment rates in other industrial economies? Why should we be careful in comparing unemployment across countries? (If you wish to look at the latest data, refer to the Bureau of Labor Statistics' Web page on International Comparisons of Foreign Labor Statistics at http://stats.bls.gov/flsdata.htm.

6. *(Official Unemployment Figures)* Explain why most experts believe that official U.S. data underestimate the actual rate of unemployment. What factors could make the official rate overstate the actual unemployment rate?

7. *(Case**Study:** Wild Inflation in Brazil)* In countries such as Brazil and Russia, which have had problems with high inflation, the increased use of another country's currency (such as the U.S. dollar) is common. Why do you suppose this occurs?

8. *(Source of Inflation)* What are the two sources of inflation? How would you illustrate them graphically?

9. *(Anticipated versus Unanticipated Inflation)* If actual inflation exceeds anticipated inflation, who will lose purchasing power and who will gain?

10. *(Inflation and Relative Price Changes)* What does the consumer price index measure? Does the index measure changes in relative prices? Why, or why not?

11. *(Inflation and Interest Rates)* For much of 1998, the spread between short- and long-term interest rates on U.S. government debt was at a record low. What does this say about expectations of inflation in the near term versus expectations for the distant future?

12. *(Inflation and Interest Rates)* Explain as carefully as you can why borrowers would be willing to pay a higher rate of interest if they expected the inflation rate to increase in the future.

13. *(Inflation)* Why is a relatively constant inflation rate less harmful to an economy than a rate that fluctuates a lot?

PROBLEMS AND EXERCISES

14. *(Measuring Unemployment)* Determine the impact on each of the following if 2 million formerly unemployed workers decide to return to school full time and stop looking for work:
    a. The labor force participation rate
    b. The size of the labor force
    c. The unemployment rate

15. *(Measuring Unemployment)* Suppose that the U.S. noninstitutional adult population is 206 million and the labor force participation rate is 67 percent.

    a. What is the size of the U.S. labor force?
    b. If 74 million adults are not working, what is the unemployment rate?

16. *(Types of Unemployment)* Determine whether each of the following would be considered frictional, structural, seasonal, or cyclical unemployment:
    a. A UPS employee who was hired for the Christmas season is laid off after Christmas.
    b. A worker is laid off due to reduced aggregate demand in the economy.

c. A worker in the audiocassette manufacturing industry becomes unemployed as compact disks replace cassettes.

d. A new college graduate is looking for employment during the summer after graduation.

17. *(Inflation)* Here are some recent data on the U.S. consumer price index:

Year	CPI	Year	CPI	Year	CPI
1985	107.6	1990	130.7	1995	152.4
1986	109.6	1991	136.2	1996	156.9
1987	113.6	1992	140.3	1997	160.5
1988	118.3	1993	144.5	1998	163.0
1989	124.0	1994	148.2		

Compute the inflation rate for each year 1986–1998 and determine which years were years of inflation. In which years did deflation occur? In which years did disinflation occur? Was there hyperinflation in any year?

18. *(Sources of Inflation)* Using the concepts of aggregate supply and aggregate demand, explain why inflation usually accelerates during wartime.

19. *(Inflation and Interest Rates)* Using a supply-demand diagram for loanable funds (like Exhibit 7), show what happens to the nominal interest rate and the equilibrium quantity of loans when both borrowers and lenders increase their estimates of the expected inflation rate from 5 percent to 10 percent.

EXPERIENTIAL EXERCISES

20. *(Measuring Unemployment)* The chapter explains the definitions the government employs in measuring unemployment. Interview 10 members of your class to determine their labor market status—employed, unemployed, or not in the labor force. Include yourself, and then compute the unemployment rate and the labor force participation rate for these 11 people.

21. *(International Comparisons of Inflation)* In recent years how has the U.S. inflation rate compared with rates in other industrial economies? Why should we be careful in comparing inflation rates across countries? The Federal Reserve Bank of St. Louis maintains a

page devoted to international economic trends: http://www.stls.frb.org/publications/iet/. Choose two countries and compare their recent inflation experiences. (If you have an Adobe Acrobat reader, you can look at bar charts of the data.)

22. *(Wall Street Journal)* Scan the "Economy" page in the First Section of today's *Wall Street Journal.* You are almost sure to find a discussion of a policy proposal that will affect unemployment, inflation, or both. Use the aggregate demand and supply model to describe the effect of the proposal—if enacted—on the U.S. unemployment and inflation rates.

Measuring Economic Aggregates and the Circular Flow of Income

Visit the McEachern
Interactive Study Center
for this chapter at
http://mcisc.swcollege.com

How do we keep score of the most complex economy in the history of the world? What's gross about the gross domestic product? What's domestic about it? If you make yourself a tuna sandwich, how much does your effort add to the gross domestic product? Since prices change over time, how can we compare the economy's production in one year with that in other years? Answers to these and other questions are addressed in this chapter, which introduces an economic scorecard for tracking an $8 trillion economy.

Although Americans account for only 5 percent of the world's population, they produce 20 percent of the world's output. In this chapter you will learn how economists keep track of the billions of economic transactions that constitute the U.S. economy. The scorecard is the national income accounting system, which reflects the performance of the economy as a whole by reducing a huge network of economic activity to a few aggregate measures. This chapter focuses on the most important measure of economic activity: gross domestic product, or GDP, a term already introduced.

As you shall see, the value of total output can be measured either from the total spending on aggregate output or from the total income derived from producing that output. We will examine both approaches, see why they are equivalent, and learn how to adjust for the effects of inflation over time. The major components and important equalities built into the national income accounts are offered here as another way of understanding how the economy works—not as a foreign language to be mastered before the next exam. The emphasis is more on economic intuition than on accounting precision. The main part of this chapter provides the background sufficient for later chapters. More details about the national income accounts are offered in the appendix to this chapter. Topics discussed in this chapter include:

- Gross domestic product
- National income accounts
- Expenditure and income approaches
- Circular flow of income and expenditure

- Leakages and injections
- Limitations of national income accounting
- Consumer price index
- GDP price index

THE PRODUCT OF A NATION

How do we measure the economy's performance? During much of the 17th and 18th centuries, when the dominant economic policy was mercantilism, many thought that economic prosperity was best measured by the *stock* of precious metals a nation accumulated. This policy of mercantilism led to tariffs and quotas aimed at restricting imports, which had the unintended consequence of limiting the gains from comparative advantage and trade.

In the latter half of the 18th century, Francois Quesnay became the first to measure economic activity as a *flow*. In 1758 he published his *Tableau Économique*, which described the *circular flow* of output and income among different sectors of the economy. His insight was probably inspired by his knowledge of the circular flow of blood in the body—Quesnay was the court physician to King Louis XV of France.

Rough measures of national income were developed in England some two centuries ago, but detailed calculations built up from microeconomic data were refined in the United States during the Great Depression. The resulting *national income accounting system* organizes huge quantities of data collected from a variety of sources around the country. These data are summarized, assembled into a coherent framework, and reported periodically by the federal government. The U.S. national income accounts are the most widely reported and among the most highly regarded in the world and have earned their developer, Simon Kuznets, a Nobel prize.

National Income Accounts

How do the national income accounts keep track of the economy's incredible variety of goods and services, from hiking boots to guitar lessons? As you learned earlier, the *gross domestic product*, or GDP, measures the market value of all final goods and services produced during a year by resources located in the United States, regardless of who owns those resources. For example, GDP includes U.S. production by foreign firms, but excludes foreign production by U.S. firms.[1]

The national income accounts are based on the idea that *one person's spending is another person's receipts.* This idea that spending equals receipts is expressed in a double-entry bookkeeping system in which spending on aggregate output is recorded on one side of the ledger and resource income is recorded on the other side. GDP can be measured either by total spending on U.S. production or by total income received from that production. The **expenditure approach** involves adding up the aggregate expenditure on all final goods and services produced during the year. The **income approach** involves adding up the aggregate income earned during the year by those who produce that output.

Gross domestic product includes only **final goods and services,** which are goods and services sold to the final, or ultimate, user. A toothbrush, a pair of contact lenses, and a bus ride are examples of final goods and services. Whether a sale is to the final user often depends on who buys the product. Your purchase of chicken from a grocer is reflected in GDP. When a KFC franchise purchases chicken, however, this transaction is not directly recorded in GDP because the franchise is not the final consumer. Only after the chicken is prepared, deep fried, and sold to consumers is a sale recorded as part of GDP.

Intermediate goods and services are those purchased for additional processing and resale, such as the chicken purchased by KFC. This additional processing may be imperceptible, as when a grocer buys canned goods to stock the shelves. Or the intermediate goods can be dramatically altered, as when an artist transforms paint and canvas into a work of beauty.

Sales of intermediate goods and services are excluded from GDP to avoid the problem of **double counting,** which is counting an item's value more than once. For example, suppose the grocer buys a can of tuna for $0.60 and sells it for $1.00. If GDP included both the intermediate transaction of $0.60 and the final transaction of $1.00, that can of tuna would be counted twice in GDP, and its recorded value of $1.60 would exceed its final value by $0.60. Hence, the gross domestic product counts only the final value of the product. GDP also ignores the secondhand value of used cars, existing homes, and used textbooks. These goods were counted in GDP the year they were produced. (But just as the value of services provided by the grocer is included in GDP, so is the value of services provided by used-car dealers, realtors, and booksellers.)

GDP Based on the Expenditure Approach

As noted already, one way to measure the value of GDP is to add up all spending on final goods and services produced in the economy during the year. The easiest way to understand the spending approach to GDP is to divide aggregate expenditure into its four components: consumption, investment, government purchases, and net exports. We will discuss each in turn.

Consumption, or more specifically, *personal consumption expenditures,* consists of purchases of final goods and services by households during the year.

Expenditure approach to GDP A method of calculating GDP by adding up spending on all final goods and services produced during the year

Income approach to GDP A method of calculating GDP by adding up all payments to owners of resources used to produce output during the year

Final goods and services Goods and services sold to final, or ultimate, users

Intermediate goods and services Goods and services purchased for further reprocessing and resale

Double counting The mistake of including the value of intermediate goods plus the value of final goods in gross domestic product; counting the value of the same good more than once

Consumption All household purchases of final goods and services

---

1 Prior to 1992, the federal government's measure of output was gross national product, or GNP, which measures the market value of all goods and services produced by resources supplied by U.S. residents and firms, regardless of the location of the resources.

Consumption is the easiest to understand and the largest spending category, accounting during the 1990s for about two-thirds of U.S. GDP. Along with services such as dry cleaning, haircuts, and air travel, consumption includes purchases of nondurable goods, such as soap and soup, and durable goods, such as televisions and furniture. Durable goods are those expected to last at least three years.

Investment, or more specifically, *gross private domestic investment*, consists of spending on new capital goods and additions to inventories. More generally, investment consists of spending on current production that is not used for current consumption. The most important category of investment is new **physical capital,** such as new buildings and new machinery purchased by firms and used to produce goods and services. Investment also includes purchases of new **residential construction.** Although investment fluctuates from year to year, on average it accounted for about one-seventh of U.S. GDP during the 1990s.

Changes in firms' inventories are another category of investment. **Inventories** are stocks of goods in process, such as computer parts, and stocks of finished goods, such as new computers awaiting sale. Inventories help manufacturers deal with unexpected changes in the supply of their resources or in the demand for their products. A *net* increase in inventories during the year counts as investment, since inventories are not used for current consumption. Conversely, a net decrease in inventories during the year counts as negative investment, or *disinvestment*, since net inventory reductions represent the sale of output already credited to a prior year's GDP. Disinvestment reduces investment.

Investment excludes household purchases of durable goods, such as furniture and major appliances (which are counted as consumption). Investment also excludes purchases of *existing* buildings, machines, and financial assets, such as stocks and bonds. Existing buildings and machines were counted in GDP when they were built. Purchases of stocks and bonds sometimes provide firms the funds to invest, but stocks and bonds are not themselves investments.

Government purchases, or more specifically, *government consumption and gross investment*, include spending by all levels of government for goods and services—from clearing snowy roads to clearing court dockets, from library books to the librarian's pay. Government purchases accounted for a little less than one-fifth of U.S. GDP during the 1990s. Government purchases, and therefore GDP, do not include transfer payments, such as Social Security, welfare benefits, and unemployment insurance. Such payments reflect an outright grant from the government to recipients and are not true purchases by the government or true earnings by the recipients.

The final component of aggregate expenditure results from the interaction between the U.S. economy and the rest of the world. **Net exports** equal the value of U.S. exports of goods and services minus the value of U.S. imports of goods and services. Net exports include the value of not only *merchandise* trade—that is, goods, or stuff you can drop on your feet—but also services, or so-called *invisibles*, such as tourism, insurance, accounting, and consulting. Since spending on consumption, investment, and government purchases includes purchases of foreign goods and services, that spending does not count as part of U.S. GDP, so we subtract imports from exports to get the net effect of the rest of the world on GDP. The value of U.S. imports has exceeded the value of our

---

Investment The purchase of new plants, new equipment, new buildings, new residences, and net additions to inventories

Physical capital Manufactured items used to produce goods and services

Residential construction Building new permanent homes or dwelling places

Inventories Producers' stocks of finished or in-process goods

Government purchases Spending for goods and services by all levels of government; government outlays minus transfer payments

Net exports The value of a country's exports minus the value of its imports

exports nearly every year for the last several decades, meaning U.S. net exports have been negative.

With the expenditure approach, the nation's **aggregate expenditure** equals the sum of consumption, C, investment, I, government purchases, G, and net exports, which is the value of exports, X, minus the value of imports, M, or $(X - M)$. Summing these spending components yields aggregate expenditure, or GDP:

Aggregate expenditure Total spending on final goods and services during a given time period, usually a year

$$C + I + G + (X - M) = \text{Aggregate expenditure} = \text{GDP}$$

GDP Based on the Income Approach

The expenditure approach sums, or aggregates, spending on production. The income approach sums, or aggregates, income arising from that production. Again, double-entry bookkeeping ensures that the value of aggregate output equals the aggregate income paid for resources used to produce that output: the wages, interest, rent, and profit arising from production. The price of a Hershey Bar® reflects income earned by all resource suppliers who bring the candy bar to the grocer's shelf. **Aggregate income** equals the sum of all the income earned by resource suppliers in the economy. Thus, we can say that

Aggregate income The sum of all income earned by resource suppliers in an economy during a given time period

$$\text{Aggregate expenditure} = \text{GDP} = \text{Aggregate income}$$

A finished product is usually processed by several firms on its way to the consumer. A wooden desk, for example, starts as raw timber, which is usually cut by one firm, milled by another, made into a desk by a third, and retailed by a fourth. Double counting is avoided either by including only the market value of the desk when it is sold to the final user or by *calculating the value added at each stage of production*. The **value added** by each firm equals that firm's selling price minus the amount paid for inputs from other firms. The value added at each stage represents income to resource suppliers at that stage. *The sum of the value added at all stages equals the market value of the final good, and the sum of the value added for all final goods and services equals the GDP based on the income approach.* For example, suppose you buy a wooden desk for $200, which is the final market value added directly into GDP. Consider the history of that desk. Suppose the tree that gave its life for your studies was cut into a log that was sold to a miller for $20. That log was milled into lumber and sold for $50 to a manufacturer, who assembled your desk and sold it for $120 to a retailer, who sold it to you for $200.

Value added The difference at each stage of production between the value of a product and cost of intermediate goods bought from other firms

Column (1) of Exhibit 1 lists the selling price at each stage of production. If all of these transactions were added together, the desk would add a total of $390 to GDP. To avoid double counting, we include only the value added at each stage of production, listed in column (3) as the difference between the purchase price and the selling price. Again, *the value added at each stage equals the income to all who supplied resources at that stage*. For example, the $80 in value added by the retailer represents income to all who contribute resources at that final stage, from the newspaper that carries the retailer's advertising and the electric utility that lights the store showroom to the trucker who provides "free delivery" of your desk. The value added at all stages totals $200, which is both the final market value of the desk and the total income earned by all resource suppliers along the way.

Disposable income (DI)
The income households have
available to spend or save after
paying taxes and receiving
transfer payments

income into **disposable income,** or **DI,** which flows to households at juncture (4). Disposable income is take-home pay, which households can spend or save.

The bottom half of this circular flow is the *income half* because it focuses on what happens to the income arising from production. Aggregate income is the total income from producing GDP, and disposable income is the income remaining after taxes are subtracted and transfers added. To simplify the discussion, we define **net taxes,** or **NT,** as taxes minus transfer payments. So *disposable income equals GDP minus net taxes.* To put it another way, we can say that aggregate income equals disposable income plus net taxes:

Net taxes (NT) Taxes minus
transfer payments

$$GDP = \text{Aggregate income} = DI + NT$$

At juncture (4), firms have produced output and have paid resource suppliers; governments have collected taxes and made transfer payments. Households, with disposable income in hand, must now decide how much to spend and how much to save. Since firms have already produced the output and have paid resource suppliers, firms await to see how much consumers want to spend. Should any output go unsold, suppliers will be stuck with it; unsold goods must become unplanned additions to firm inventories.

The Expenditure Half of the Circular Flow

Disposable income splits at juncture (5). Part flows to consumption, *C*, and the remainder to saving, *S*. Thus,

$$DI = C + S$$

Spending on consumption remains in the circular flow and represents the most important source of aggregate expenditure, about two-thirds of the total. Household saving flows to **financial markets,** which consist of banks and other financial institutions that provide a link between savers and borrowers. For simplicity, Exhibit 2 shows households as the only savers, although governments, firms, and the rest of the world could be savers too. The primary borrowers are firms and governments, but households borrow as well, particularly for new homes, and the rest of the world also borrows. In reality, financial markets should be connected to all four economic decision makers, but we have simplified the flows to keep the exhibit from looking like a plate of spaghetti.

Financial markets Banks
and other institutions that facilitate the flow of loanable funds
from savers to borrowers

Since firms in our simplified model pay resource suppliers an amount equal to the entire value of output, firms have no revenue left for investment. They must borrow in financial markets to finance purchases of physical capital plus any increases in their inventories. Households also borrow from financial markets to purchase new homes. Therefore, investment, *I*, consists of spending on new capital by firms, including inventory changes, plus spending on residential construction. Investment spending enters the circular flow at juncture (6), so aggregate spending at that point totals *C + I*.

Governments must also borrow whenever they incur deficits, that is, whenever their total outlays—transfer payments plus purchases of goods and services—exceed their revenues. Government purchases of goods and services, represented by *G*, enter the spending stream in the upper half of the circular flow at juncture (7). Remember that G *excludes* transfer payments, which already entered the income stream at juncture (3).

Some spending by households, firms, and governments goes for imports. Since spending on imports, M, flows to foreign producers, not U.S. producers, import spending leaks from the circular flow at juncture (8). But the rest of the world also buys U.S. products, so foreign spending on U.S. exports, X, enters the circular flow at juncture (9). The net impact of the *rest of the world* on aggregate expenditure equals exports minus imports, or net exports, $X - M$, which can be positive, negative, or zero.

The upper half of the circular flow can be viewed as the *expenditure half* because it focuses on the components that make up aggregate expenditure: consumption, C, investment, I, government purchases, G, and net exports, $X - M$. Aggregate expenditure flows into firms at juncture (10). Total spending on U.S. output equals the market value of aggregate output in the economy, or GDP. In other words,

$$C + I + G + (X - M) = \text{Aggregate expenditure} = \text{GDP}$$

Leakages Equal Injections

Let's step back now to grasp the big picture. In the lower half of the circular flow, aggregate income equals disposable income plus net taxes. In the upper half, aggregate expenditure equals the total spending on U.S. output. *The aggregate income arising from production equals the aggregate expenditure on that production.* This is the first accounting identity. Thus, aggregate income (disposable income plus net taxes) equals aggregate expenditure (spending by each sector), or

$$DI + NT = C + I + G + (X - M)$$
$$\text{Aggregate income} = \text{Aggregate expenditure}$$

Since disposable income equals consumption plus saving, we can substitute $C + S$ for DI in the above equation to yield

$$C + S + NT = C + I + G + (X - M)$$

After subtracting C from both sides and adding M to both sides, the equation reduces to

$$S + NT + M = I + G + X$$

Note that at various points around the circular flow, some of the flow leaks from the main stream. Saving, S, net taxes, NT, and imports, M, are **leakages** from the circular flow. **Injections** into the main stream also occur at various points around the circular flow. Investment, I, government purchases, G, and exports, X, are *injections* of spending into the circular flow. As you can see from the preceding equation, *leakages from the circular flow equal injections into that flow.* This leakages–injections equation demonstrates a second accounting identity based on the principles of double-entry bookkeeping.

Leakage Any diversion of income from the domestic spending stream; includes saving, taxes, and imports

Injection Any payment of income other than by firms or any spending other than by domestic households; includes investment, government purchases, transfer payments, and exports

Planned Investment Versus Actual Investment

As we have learned already, at juncture (1) in the circular flow, firms produce the aggregate output expected to meet the demand. But aggregate expenditure may not match production. Suppose, for example, that firms produce $8.0 trillion in output, but the spending components add up to only $7.8 trillion. Firms will end up with $0.2 trillion in unsold products, which must be added to their inventories. Since increases in inventories are counted as investment, *actual* investment turns out to be $0.2 trillion greater than firms had *planned*.

Planned investment The amount of investment firms plan to undertake during a year

Note the distinction here between **planned investment,** the amount firms plan to invest before they know how much output will be sold, and **actual investment,** which includes both planned investment and any unplanned changes in inventories. Unplanned increases in inventories will cause firms to smarten up and decrease their production next time around so as not to get stuck with more unsold goods. Only when there are no unplanned changes in inventories will the level of GDP be at what we will call an *equilibrium level—* that is, *a level that can be sustained period after period.* Only in equilibrium will planned investment equal actual investment.

Actual investment The amount of investment actually undertaken during a year; equals planned investment plus unplanned changes in inventories

The relationship between actual and planned investment will be examined more closely in Chapter 10. For now, you need only understand that the national income accounting system reflects *actual* investment, not necessarily *planned* investment. *The national income accounts always look at economic activity after transactions have occurred—after the dust has settled.* Although planned leakages may differ from planned injections, actual leakages must always equal actual injections.

LIMITATIONS OF NATIONAL INCOME ACCOUNTING

Imagine the difficulty of developing an accounting system that must capture the subtleties of a complex and dynamic economy, such as the United States'. In the interest of clarity and simplicity, some features of the economy are neglected; others receive perhaps too much weight. In this section, we examine some limitations of the national income accounting system, beginning with productive activity that is not captured by GDP.

Some Production Is Not Included in GDP

With some minor exceptions, GDP includes only those products that are sold in markets, thereby neglecting all "do-it-yourself" household production. Household services not purchased in the market are excluded from GDP—child care, meal preparation, house cleaning, and do-it-yourself home repair. Thus an economy in which householders are largely self-sufficient will have a lower GDP than will an otherwise similar economy in which households specialize and sell goods and services to one another.

During the 1950s, more than 80 percent of mothers with small children stayed at home caring for the family, but all this care added not one whit to GDP. Today more than half of mothers with small children are in the work force, where their market labor is captured in GDP. What's more, GDP has increased because household services, such as meals and child care, are now more frequently purchased in markets rather than provided by householders. In less developed economies, more economic activity is do-it-yourself or provided by the extended family. *Because official GDP figures ignore most home production, these figures understate the household goods and services produced in less-developed countries.*

Underground economy An expression used to describe all market exchange that goes unreported either because it is illegal or because those involved want to evade taxes

GDP also ignores production for which no official records are kept. The **underground economy** is an expression used to describe all market exchange that goes unreported either because the activity itself is illegal or because those involved want to evade taxes on otherwise legal activity. Although there are no official estimates on the extent of the underground economy, most economists agree that it is substantial. Recent estimates range from 5 percent to 15 percent of GDP.[2] A Census Bureau study suggests that the nation's underground economy amounts to about 7.5 percent of GDP, or about $625 billion in 1999.

Even though some production is not reflected in GDP, the *imputed income* from certain activities that do not pass across recorded markets is included. Income must be imputed, or estimated, because market exchange does not occur. For example, included in GDP is an *imputed rental income* that homeowners receive from home ownership, even though no rent is actually paid or received. (This imputed income is discussed in the appendix to this chapter.) Also included in GDP is an imputed dollar amount for (1) wages paid *in kind*, such as employers' payments for employees' medical insurance, and (2) food produced on the farm for that farm family's own consumption. The national income accounts therefore reflect some economic production that does not involve market exchange.

Leisure, Quality, and Variety

The average U.S. work week is much shorter now than it was at the turn of the century, so people work less to produce today's output. People also retire now at a much earlier age. The increase over the years in the amount of leisure available has resulted in a higher quality of life. But leisure time is not reflected in GDP because leisure is not explicitly bought and sold in a market. The quality and variety of products available have on average also improved over the years, as a result of technological advances and competition, yet most of these improvements are not reflected in GDP. For example, improvements have occurred in recording systems, computers, tires, running shoes, and hundreds of other products. Also, new products are getting introduced all the time, such as digital videodisks and high-definition television. *The gross domestic product fails to reflect changes in the availability of leisure time and sometimes fails to reflect changes in the quality of existing products as well as changes in the availability of new products.* The special problem of measuring production in an economy shaped by changing technology is discussed in the following case study.

Tracking an $8 Trillion Economy

How does the government keep track of this, the most sophisticated economy in the history of the world? Ever since Article I of the U.S. Constitution required a decennial population census, the federal government has been gathering data. The three main data-gathering agencies are the Bureau of the Census, the Bureau of Economic Analysis, and the Bureau of Labor Statistics. Since 1980, real GDP has increased by more than two-thirds, employment has increased by more than 30 million, and real foreign trade has tripled. Yet the federal budget

CaseStudy

The Information Economy

The Bureau of Economic Analysis is charged with estimating GDP and its components. At http://www.bea.doc.gov/bea/dn/niptbl-d.htm you can find recent data on real GDP (in Table 1) and the sources of change in GDP (in Table 2). Review Table 2 and find the components of spending that have been most important in the GDP growth of the mid to late 1990s. You can compare current real GDP to previous years from 1929 on at http://www.bea.doc.gov/bea/dn/0898nip3/tab2a.htm. What was real GDP during the year you were born? How many times larger is it today?

---

2 See Joel F. Houston, "The Underground Economy: A Troubling Issue for Policymakers," *Federal Reserve Bank of Philadelphia Business Review* (September–October 1987): 3–12.

for data-gathering agencies has declined in real terms. Only 0.2 percent of the federal budget goes toward keeping track of the economy.

Federal budget cuts have eliminated some data-collection efforts and have slowed down others. For example, computations of monthly international trade statistics have become so overwhelming that as many as half of the imports counted for a particular month reflect a "carryover" from previous months. And the monthly household sample used to track unemployment has been cut from 60,000 to 50,000. Some agencies must do more with the same staff. For example, in 1980 the Bureau of Labor Statistics had 18 analysts to monitor productivity in 95 different industries. The number of industries they track now has quadrupled, but the number of analysts has hardly changed.

The traditional ways of monitoring economic activity were originally developed in the 1930s and 1940s, when manufacturing dominated. Manufacturing output is relatively easy to measure because the output is tangible, such as automobiles, toasters, or in-line skates. But service output, such as financial advice, physical therapy, or on-line services, is intangible, and is therefore more difficult to measure.

Because services are intangible, measures for the service sector tend to be less reliable than those for the manufacturing sector. Measures of service output often fail to reflect improvements in the speed or quality of services. For example, computerized checkout systems not only save time and provide customers with detailed receipts but also allow retailers to track inventory and order new supplies. Likewise, speedier modems cut the time of using on-line services. Or consider the Wisconsin trucking firm that uses onboard computers in its vehicles to map the most efficient routes and remap the routes should priorities change. The firm has become so efficient that the number of ton-miles (tonnage times miles) carried per month has declined. Yet, according to Government statisticians, these truck drivers are less productive because ton-miles is how output is measured.

Government statisticians have no way of measuring output in a wide range of industries, including banking, medicine, software, legal services, wholesale trade, and communications. For example, productivity measures do not reflect the benefits of new surgical procedures that are safer and require less recuperation time, such as microsurgical techniques that remove cataracts and arthroscopic surgery that repairs torn knee ligaments.

There are indications that output and productivity in the service sector may be rising faster than official estimates show. For example, capital investment in the service sector has grown more in recent years than has investment in the manufacturing sector. And the United States has experienced a growing trade surplus in services, suggesting that the U.S. service sector is competitive and relatively productive, at least when compared to services produced abroad. In contrast, the trade balance on goods has been in deficit, and this deficit has been growing.

Sources: Robert D. Hersey, "Concern Is Voiced Over Quality of Economic Data," *New York Times*, 24 November 1996; "The Real Truth about the Economy," *Business Week* (7 November 1994): 110–118; and Leonard Nakamura, "Is the U.S. Economy Really Growing Too Slowly? Maybe We're Measuring Growth Wrong," *Federal Reserve Bank of Philadelphia Business Review* (March–April 1997): 1–12.

Gross Domestic Product Ignores Depreciation

In the course of producing GDP, some capital wears out, such as the delivery truck that finally dies, and some capital becomes obsolete, such as an aging computer that can't keep up with the latest software. A new truck that logs

100,000 miles its first year has been subject to wear and tear, and therefore has a diminished value as a resource. A truer picture of the *net* production that actually occurs during a year is found by subtracting this *depreciation* from GDP. **Depreciation** measures the value of the capital stock that is used up or grows obsolete in the production process. The gross domestic product is called "gross" because it fails to take into account this depreciation. **Net domestic product** equals gross domestic product minus depreciation—the value of the capital stock used up in the production process.

We can now distinguish between two definitions of investment. *Gross investment* measures the value of all investment during a year. Gross investment is used in computing GDP. *Net investment* equals gross investment minus depreciation. The economy's production possibilities depend on what happens to net investment. If net investment is negative—that is, if depreciation exceeds gross investment—the capital stock declines, so its contribution to output will decline as well. If net investment is zero, the capital stock remains constant, as does its contribution to output. And if net investment is positive, the capital stock grows, as does its contribution to output.

As the names imply, *gross* domestic product (GDP) reflects gross investment and the *net* domestic product (NDP) reflects net investment. But developing a figure for depreciation involves much guesswork. For example, what is the appropriate measure of depreciation for the roller coasters at Busch Gardens, the metal display shelves at Wal-Mart, the 5,000-gallon casks used to age wine in the Napa Valley, the parking lots at Disney World, or the Library of Congress building in Washington, D.C.?

Depreciation The value of capital stock used up during a year in producing GDP

Net domestic product Gross domestic product minus depreciation

GDP Does Not Reflect All Costs

Some production and consumption degrades the quality of our environment. Trucks and automobiles pump carbon monoxide into the atmosphere. Housing developments displace forests. Most paper mills foul the lungs and burn the eyes. These negative externalities—costs that fall on those not directly involved in the transactions—are largely ignored in GDP accounting, even though they diminish the quality of life and may limit future production. To the extent that growth in GDP also involves growth in such negative externalities, a rising GDP may not be as attractive as it would first appear.

Although the national income accounts reflect the depreciation of buildings, machinery, vehicles, and other manufactured capital, this accounting ignores the depletion of natural resources, such as standing timber, fish stocks, and soil fertility. So national income accounts reflect depreciation of the manufactured capital stock but not the natural capital stock. For example, suppose intensive farming raises farm productivity temporarily but depletes the fertility of the soil. The additional farm production adds to GDP but subtracts from the soil's fertility. And some economic development may cause the extinction of certain plants and animals. The U.S. Commerce Department is now in the process of developing so-called "green" accounting to reflect the impact of production on air pollution, water pollution, lost trees, soil depletion, and the loss of other natural resources.

GDP and Economic Welfare

In computing GDP, the market price of output is the measure of its value. Therefore, each dollar spent on handguns or cigarettes is counted in GDP the

16. *(Expenditure Approach to GDP)* You have the following annual information about a hypothetical country:

	Billions of Dollars
Personal consumption expenditures	$200
Personal taxes	50
Exports	30
Depreciation	10
Government purchases	50
Gross private domestic investment	40
Imports	40
Government transfer payments	20

  a. What is the value of GDP?
  b. What is the value of net domestic product?
  c. What is the value of net investment?
  d. What is the value of net exports?

17. *(Investment)* Answer these questions using these data:

	Billions of Dollars
New residential construction	$500
Purchases of existing homes	250
Sales value of newly issued stocks and bonds	600
New physical capital	800
Depreciation	200
Household purchases of new furniture	50
Net change in firms' inventories	100
Production of new intermediate goods	700

  a. What is the value of gross private domestic investment?
  b. What is the value of net investment?
  c. Are any intermediate goods counted in gross investment?

18. *(Consumer Price Index)* Calculate a new consumer price index for the data in Exhibit 4 in this chapter. Assume that current-year prices of Twinkies, fuel oil, and cable TV are $0.89/package, $1.25/gallon, and $15.00/month, respectively. Calculate the current year's cost of the market basket and the value of the current year's price index. What is this year's percent change in the price level compared to the base year?

19. *(Consumer Price Index)* Given the following data, what was the value of the consumer price index in the base year? Calculate the annual rate of consumer price inflation in 2000 in each of the following situations:
  a. The CPI equals 200 in 1999 and 240 in 2000.
  b. The CPI equals 150 in 1999 and 175 in 2000.
  c. The CPI equals 325 in 1999 and 340 in 2000.
  d. The CPI equals 325 in 1999 and 315 in 2000.

EXPERIENTIAL EXERCISES

20. *(Limitations of National Income Accounting)* One often-heard criticism of the U.S. national income accounts is that they ignore the effect of environmental pollution. The World Bank's group on Environmental Economics and Indicators has been investigating ways of assessing environmental degradation. Take a look at their work on "green accounting" at http://www-esd.worldbank.org/eei/text/greenacc.html. What kinds of problems have they identified, and what proposals have they made to deal with those problems?

21. *(Problems with the CPI)* A Web site devoted to issues of bias in the Consumer Price Index can be found at http://www.geocities.com/CapitolHill/2394/. Take a look, and determine what are some of the criticisms of the CPI as presently calculated.

22. *(Wall Street Journal)* Data on the Consumer Price Index are released near the middle of each month. (You can find the exact date by consulting the on-line calendar at http://www.leggmason.com/CAL/calendar.html. Data on GDP are released on the last Friday of each month (in preliminary, revised, and then final form). Analysis of these data releases appears in the first section of the following weekday's *Wall Street Journal*. Look in the "Economy" section to find the story. What do the latest available data tell you about the current rate of inflation and the current rate of GDP growth? Is the economy in a recession or an expansion?

Appendix

NATIONAL INCOME ACCOUNTS

This chapter has focused on gross domestic product, or GDP, the measure of output that will be of most interest in subsequent chapters. Other economic aggregates also convey useful information and receive media attention. One of these, *net domestic product*, has already been introduced. Exhibit 6 shows that net domestic product equals gross domestic product minus depreciation. In this appendix we examine other aggregate measures.

NATIONAL INCOME

Thus far we have been talking about the value of production from resources located in the United States, regardless of who owns the resources. Sometimes we want to know how much American resource suppliers earn for their labor, capital, land, and entrepreneurial ability. **National income** captures all income earned by American-owned resources, whether those resources are located in the United States or abroad. *National income* results from several adjustments to net domestic product. First, the net value of production from American-owned resources abroad, and hence the net income earned from that production, must be added to net domestic product. To get the net value of production, we add income earned by American resources abroad and subtract income earned by foreign-owned resources in the United States.

Second, the value of final goods and services is computed at market prices, but, because of **government subsidies,** such as payments to suppliers of low-income housing, some products sell for less than resource suppliers receive.

Since subsidies are received as income, they should be included in national income, even though they are not part of the selling price.

Third, because of **indirect business taxes,** such as sales, excise, and property taxes, some products sell for more than resource suppliers receive. For example, a gallon of gasoline may sell for $1.25, but about $0.25 in taxes must be paid to the government before any resource supplier earns a penny. Since indirect business taxes are not received as income by any individual, they should not be included in national income, even though they are part of the selling price. Since indirect business taxes are about 20 times greater than government subsidies, we simplify the reporting by computing *indirect business taxes net of subsidies*.

National income therefore equals net domestic product plus net earnings from American resources abroad minus indirect business taxes (net of subsidies). Exhibit 6 shows how to go from net domestic product to national income. We have now moved from gross domestic product to net domestic product to national income. Next we peel back another layer to arrive at personal income, the income people actually receive.

PERSONAL INCOME

Some of the income received this year was not earned this year, and some of the income earned this year was not actually received this year by those who earned it. By adding to national income the income received but not earned and subtracting the income earned but not received, we convert national income into all income *received* by individuals, which is termed **personal income.** Personal income, a widely reported measure of economic welfare, is computed by the federal government monthly.

The adjustment from national income to personal income is shown in Exhibit 7. Income *earned but not received* includes the employer's share of Social Security taxes, corporate income taxes, and undistributed corporate profits, which are profits the firm retains rather than pays as dividends. Income *received but not earned* in the current period includes government transfer payments, receipts from private pension plans, and interest paid by government and by consumers.

DISPOSABLE INCOME

Although several taxes have been considered so far, we have not yet discussed personal taxes. Personal taxes consist primarily of federal, state, and local personal income taxes and the employee's share of the Social Security tax. Subtracting

---

EXHIBIT 6

Deriving Net Domestic Product and National Income Using 1998 Data (in trillions of dollars)

Gross domestic product (GDP)	$8.51
Minus depreciation	–0.91
Net domestic product	7.60
Plus net earnings of American resources abroad minus indirect business taxes (net of subsidies)	–0.60
National income	$7.00

Source: *Economic Report of the President,* February 1999, and *Survey of Current Business* 79 (February 1999).

EXHIBIT 7

Deriving Personal Income and Disposable Income Using 1998 Data (in trillions of dollars)

National income	$7.00
Minus income earned but not received (Social Security taxes, corporate income taxes, undistributed corporate profits)	–2.06
Plus income received but not earned (government and business transfers, net personal interest income)	2.18
Personal income	7.12
Minus personal tax and nontax charges	–1.10
Disposable income	$6.02

Source: *Economic Report of the President*, February 1999, and *Survey of Current Business* 79 (February 1999).

personal taxes and other government charges from personal income yields *disposable income*, which is the amount available for spending or saving—the amount that can be "disposed of" by the household. Think of disposable income as take-home pay. Exhibit 7 shows that personal income minus personal taxes and other government charges yields disposable income.

SUMMARY OF NATIONAL INCOME ACCOUNTS

The income side of national income accounts can be summarized as follows. We begin with *gross domestic product*, or *GDP*, the market value of final goods and services produced during the year by resources located in the United States. We subtract depreciation from GDP to yield the *net domestic product*. To net domestic product we add net earnings from American resources abroad and subtract indirect business taxes (net of subsidies) to yield *national income*. We obtain *personal income* by subtracting from national income all income earned but not received (e.g., undistributed corporate profits) and by adding all income received but not earned (e.g., transfer payments). By subtracting personal taxes and other government charges from personal income, we arrive at the bottom line: *disposable income*, the amount people are actually free either to save or to spend.

SUMMARY INCOME STATEMENT OF THE ECONOMY

Exhibit 8 presents an annual income statement for the entire economy. The upper portion lists aggregate expenditure, which consists of consumption, gross investment, govern-

ment purchases, and net exports. Because imports exceeded exports, net exports are negative. You might think of aggregate expenditure as the revenue of a giant firm. The income from this expenditure is broken down in the lower portion of Exhibit 8. After subtracting both depreciation and net indirect business taxes, and adding net earnings from American resources abroad to the remaining forms of income, we get national income. National income, which is the sum of all earnings from resources supplied by U.S. residents and firms, can be divided into its five components: employee compensation, proprietors' income, corporate profits, net interest, and rental income of persons.

Employee compensation, which is by far the largest source of income, includes both money wages and employer contributions to cover Social Security taxes, medical insurance, and other fringe benefits. **Proprietors' income** includes the earnings of unincorporated businesses. **Corporate profits** are the net revenues received by incorporated businesses before subtracting corporate income taxes.

EXHIBIT 8

Expenditure and Income Statement for the U.S. Economy Using 1998 Data (in trillions of dollars)

Aggregate Expenditure

Consumption (*C*)	$5.81
Gross investment (*I*)	1.37
Government purchases (*G*)	1.49
Net exports (*X* – *M*)	–0.16
GDP	$8.51

Allocation of Income

Depreciation	$0.91
Net earnings of American resources abroad	–0.02
Net indirect business taxes	0.62
Compensation of employees	4.98
Proprietors' income	0.58
Corporate profits	0.83
Net interest	0.45
Rental income of persons	0.16
GDP	$8.51

Source: *Economic Report of the President*, February 1999, and *Survey of Current Business* 79 (February 1999).

Net interest is the interest received by individuals, excluding interest paid by consumers to businesses and interest paid by government.

Each family that owns its own home is viewed as a tiny firm that rents its home to itself. Since homeowners do not, in fact, rent homes to themselves, an imputed rental value is estimated based on what the market rent would be. **Rental** **income of persons** consists primarily of the imputed rental value of owner-occupied housing minus the cost of owning that property (such as property taxes, insurance, depreciation, and interest paid on the mortgage). From the totals in Exhibit 8, you can see that aggregate spending in the economy equals the income generated by that spending.

APPENDIX QUESTIONS

1. *(National Income Accounting)* Use the following data to answer the questions below:

	Billions of Dollars
Net investment	$110
Depreciation	30
Exports	50
Imports	30
Government purchases	150
Consumption	400
Indirect business taxes (net of subsidies)	35
Income earned but not received	60
Income received but not earned	70
Personal income taxes	50
Employee compensation	455
Corporate profits	60
Rental income	20
Net interest	30
Proprietor's income	40
Net earnings of U.S. resources abroad	40

a. Calculate GDP using the income and the expenditure methods.
b. Calculate gross investment.
c. Calculate net domestic product, national income, personal income, and disposable income.

2. *(National Income Accounting)* According to Exhibit 8 in this chapter, GDP can be calculated either by adding up expenditures on final goods or by adding up the allocations of these expenditures to the resources used to produce these goods. Why do you suppose the portion of final goods expenditures that goes to pay for intermediate goods or raw materials is excluded from the income method of calculation?

Aggregate Expenditure: Consumption, Investment, Government Purchases, and Net Exports

W hen driving through a neighborhood new to you, how can you figure out

the income status of residents? What's the most predictable and useful relation-

ship in macroeconomics? Why is so much attention paid to consumer confi-

dence and business confidence? Answers to these and other questions are

addressed in this chapter, which focuses on the components of aggregate

expenditure. Consumption is the most important spending component, account-

ing for about two-thirds of all spending, but in this relatively short chapter we also

discuss investment, government purchases, and net exports. You will learn whether

and how each component relates to the level of income in the economy.

Let's preview where this leads. In Chapter 10, we will combine these spend-

ing components to show the link between aggregate spending and income, then derive the aggregate demand curve. In Chapter 11 we will develop the aggregate supply curve and see how it interacts with the aggregate demand curve to determine the economy's equilibrium levels of price and output. The role of government will be examined in Chapter 12. Topics discussed in this chapter include:

- Consumption and income
- Marginal propensities to consume and to save
- Changes in consumption and saving

- Investment
- Government purchases
- Net exports
- Composition of spending

CONSUMPTION

Suppose a new college friend invited you home for the weekend. One thing you would learn from your visit is how well off the family is—you would get an impression of their standard of living. Is their home something you might see on *Lifestyles of the Rich and Famous*, or is it more modest? Do they drive a new BMW or take the bus? What do they eat? What do they wear? The simple fact is that consumption tends to reflect income.

You can usually tell much about a family's economic status by observing their consumption pattern. Although you sometimes come across people who live well beyond their means and others who still have the first nickel they ever earned, by and large consumption and income tend to be highly correlated. *The positive and stable relationship between consumption and income, both for the household and for the economy as a whole, is the main point of this chapter.* Got it?

A key decision in the circular flow model developed in the previous chapter is how much households spend on consumption. Consumption depends primarily on income and income depends on how much is produced. Although this seems obvious, the link between income and consumption is fundamental to an understanding of how the economy works. Let's look at this income-consumption link over time in the U.S. economy.

An Initial Look at Income and Consumption

The red line in Exhibit 1 depicts disposable income in the United States for the last four decades, and the blue line depicts consumer spending. (Data have been adjusted for inflation so that dollars are of constant purchasing power, in this case 1992 dollars.) *Disposable income*, remember, is the income actually available for spending and saving.

Note in Exhibit 1 that consumer spending and disposable income tend to move together over time. Both are measured along the vertical axis in 1992 dollars. Consumer saving is the difference between disposable income and consumer spending; saving is indicated in Exhibit 1 by the vertical distance between the two lines. Both consumer spending and disposable income increased nearly every year, and the relationship between consumption and income has been relatively stable. Specifically, consumer spending averaged 90 percent of disposable income during the 1960s, 89 percent during the 1970s, 90 percent during the 1980s, and 92 percent during the 1990s. Put another way, saving averaged 10 percent of disposable income during the 1960s, 11 percent during the 1970s, 10 percent during the 1980s, and 8 percent during the 1990s.

EXHIBIT 1

Consumer Spending and Disposable Income in the United States

Income and consumer spending move together over time. Saving is the difference between disposable income and consumer spending.

Source: *Economic Report of the President,* February 1999.

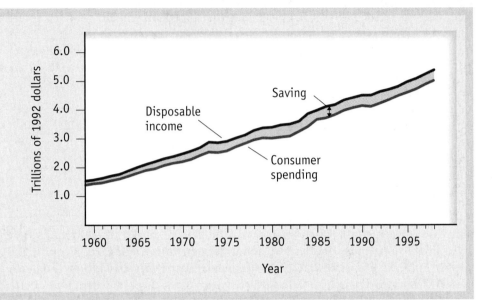

Another way to graph the relationship between income and consumption over time is shown in Exhibit 2, where U.S. disposable income is measured along the horizontal axis and U.S. consumption along the vertical axis. Notice that each axis measures the same units: trillions of dollars of 1992 purchasing power. Each year is depicted by a point that reflects two values: disposable income and consumption. In 1976, for example, disposable income (read from the horizontal axis) was $3.0 trillion, and consumption (read from the vertical axis) was $2.7 trillion.

As you can see, there is a clear and direct relationship between consumption and disposable income, a relationship that should come as no surprise after Exhibit 1. You need little imagination to see that by connecting the points on the graph in Exhibit 2, you could trace a line relating consumption to income. That relationship has special significance in macroeconomics.

The Consumption Function

So far we have examined the link between consumption and income and have found it to be quite stable. Given their level of disposable income, households decide how much to consume and how much to save. So consumption depends on disposable income. *Disposable income is the independent variable, and consumption the dependent variable.*

Because consumption depends on income, we say that consumption is a *function* of income. Exhibit 3 presents a hypothetical **consumption function,** which shows a positive relationship between the level of disposable income in the economy and the amount spent on consumption, with other determinants of consumption held constant. Again, both disposable income and consumption are measured in real terms, or in inflation-adjusted dollars. Notice that our hypothetical consumption function in Exhibit 3 looks similar to the actual historical relationship between consumption and disposable income, shown in Exhibit 2.

Consumption function
The relationship between the level of income in an economy and the amount households plan to spend on consumption, other things constant

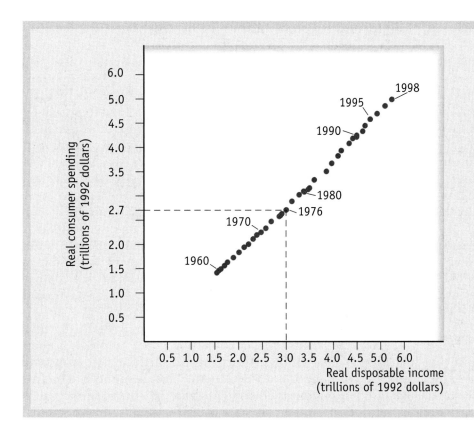

EXHIBIT 2

Dependence of Consumer Spending on Disposable Income

Source: Developed based on estimates found in *Economic Report of the President*, February 1999.

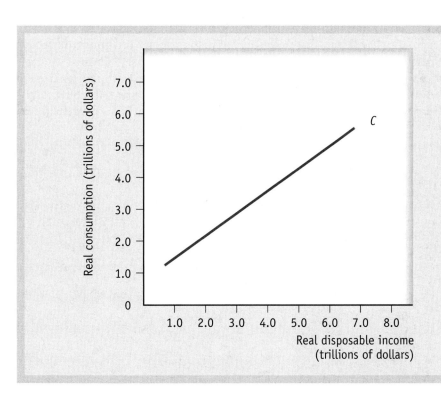

EXHIBIT 3

The Consumption Function

The consumption function, *C*, shows the relationship between consumption expenditure and disposable income, other things constant.

Marginal propensity to consume (MPC) The fraction of a change in income that is spent on consumption; the change in consumption spending divided by the change in income that caused it

Marginal propensity to save (MPS) The fraction of a change in income that is saved; the change in saving divided by the change in income that caused it

Marginal Propensities to Consume and to Save

In Chapter 1, you learned that economic analysis focuses on activity at the margin. For example, what happens to consumption if income changes by a certain amount? To study such changes, we must apply marginal analysis to the relationship between changes in disposable income and changes in consumption. Suppose U.S. households receive another billion dollars in disposable income. Some of this additional income will be spent on consumption and some will be saved. The fraction of the additional income that is consumed is called the marginal propensity to consume. More precisely, the **marginal propensity to consume,** or **MPC,** equals the change in consumption divided by the change in income. Likewise, the fraction of that additional income that is saved is called the marginal propensity to save. More precisely, the **marginal propensity to save,** or **MPS,** equals the change in saving divided by the change in income.

These propensities can be best understood by reference to Exhibit 4, which presents the hypothetical data underlying the consumption function of Exhibit 3. The table shows, for a range of possible incomes, how much consumers would like to spend and how much they would like to save. The first column presents alternative levels of disposable income, *DI,* beginning with $6.0 trillion and ranging up to $8.0 trillion in increments of $0.5 trillion.

As you can see from the table, if income increases from $6.0 trillion to $6.5 trillion, an increase of $0.5 trillion, consumption increases by $0.4 trillion and saving increases by $0.1 trillion. The marginal propensity to consume equals the change in consumption divided by the change in income. In this case, the change in consumption is $0.4 trillion and the change in income is $0.5 trillion, so the marginal propensity to consume is 0.4/0.5, or 4/5. Notice that each time income increases by $0.5 trillion, as indicated in column (2), consumption increases by $0.4 trillion, as indicated in column (4). Therefore the MPC, listed in column (7), is 4/5 at all levels of income shown.

At each income level, disposable income not spent on consumption is saved. Notice from column (6) that saving increases by $0.1 trillion with each $0.5 trillion increase in disposable income, so the marginal propensity to save equals 0.1/0.5, or 1/5, at all levels of income. The MPS is listed in column (8). Since disposable income is either spent or saved, the marginal propensity to

EXHIBIT 4

Marginal Propensity to Consume and Marginal Propensity to Save (trillions of dollars)

Income (Real *DI*) (1)	Change in Income (Δ*DI*) (2)	Consumption (*C*) (3)	Change in *C* (Δ*C*) (4)	Saving (*S*) (5)	Change in Saving (Δ*S*) (6)	MPC = (4) ÷ (2) (Δ*C*/Δ*DI*) (7)	MPS = (6) ÷ (2) (Δ*S*/Δ*DI*) (8)
6.0		5.7		0.3		0.4/0.5 = 4/5	0.1/0.5 = 1/5
	0.5		0.4		0.1		
6.5		6.1		0.4		4/5	1/5
	0.5		0.4		0.1		
7.0		6.5		0.5		4/5	1/5
	0.5		0.4		0.1		
7.5		6.9		0.6		4/5	1/5
	0.5		0.4		0.1		
8.0		7.3		0.7			

consume plus the marginal propensity to save must add up to 1. In our example, 4/5 + 1/5 = 1. We can say more generally that MPC + MPS = 1.

MPC, MPS, and the Slope of the Consumption and Saving Functions

You may recall from the appendix to Chapter 1 that the slope of a straight line is equal to the vertical distance between any two points divided by the horizontal distance between those points. Consider, for example, the slope between points *a* and *b* on the consumption function in panel (a) of Exhibit 5. The horizontal distance between these points shows the change in disposable income (denoted ΔDI)—in this case, $0.5 trillion. The vertical distance shows the change in consumption (denoted ΔC)—in this case, $0.4 trillion. The slope equals the vertical distance divided by the horizontal distance, or 0.4/0.5, which equals the marginal propensity to consume of 4/5.

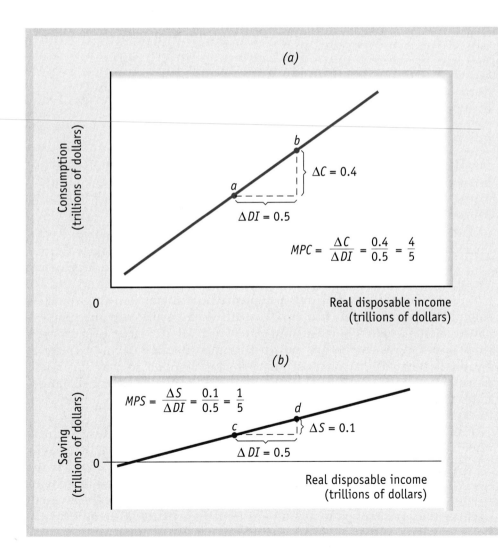

EXHIBIT 5

Marginal Propensities to Consume and to Save

The slope of the consumption function equals the marginal propensity to consume. For the straight-line consumption function of panel (a), the slope is the same at all levels of income and is given by the change in consumption divided by the change in disposable income that causes it. Hence, the marginal propensity to consume equals $\Delta C/\Delta DI$, or 0.4/0.5 = 4/5. The slope of the saving function equals the marginal propensity to save, $\Delta S/\Delta DI$, or 0.1/0.5 = 1/5.

Thus, *the marginal propensity to consume is measured graphically by the slope of the consumption function.* After all, the slope is nothing more than the increase in consumption divided by the increase in income. *Because the slope of any straight line is constant everywhere along the line, the MPC for any linear, or straight-line, consumption function will be constant at all levels of income.* We are assuming for convenience that the consumption function is a straight line, though it need not be.

Panel (b) of Exhibit 5 presents the **saving function,** *S,* which relates saving to the level of income, reflecting the hypothetical data presented in Exhibit 4. The saving function can be subjected to the same sort of graphical analysis as the consumption function. The slope between any two points on the saving function measures the change in saving divided by the change in income. For example, between points *c* and *d* in panel (b) of Exhibit 5, the change in income is $0.5 trillion and the resulting change in saving is $0.1 trillion. The slope between these two points therefore equals 0.1/0.5, or 1/5, which by definition equals the marginal propensity to save. Since the marginal propensity to consume and the marginal propensity to save are simply different sides of the same coin, from here on we focus mostly on the marginal propensity to consume.

Nonincome Determinants of Consumption

Along a given consumption function, consumer spending depends on the level of disposable income in the economy, other things constant. Now let's see what factors are held constant and how changes in these factors could cause the entire consumption function to shift.

Net Wealth and Consumption. Given the level of income in the economy, an important factor influencing consumption is each household's **net wealth**—that is, the value of all assets that each household owns minus any liabilities, or debts owed. Consider your own family. Your family's assets may include a home, cars, furniture, bank accounts, cash, and the value of stocks, bonds, and pension funds. Your family's liabilities, or debt, may include a mortgage, car loans, student loans, credit card balances, and the like. To increase net wealth, your family can save or can pay off debts.

Total household net wealth is assumed to be constant along a given consumption function. A decrease in net wealth would make consumers less inclined to spend and more inclined to save at each level of income. To see why, suppose prices fall sharply on the stock market. Because of the decrease in wealth, households that own corporate stock are poorer so they spend less. Hence, a decrease in net wealth, other things held constant, encourages households to save more and spend less at each level of income. For example, when stock market prices fell sharply in October of 1987, the decrease in stockholders' net wealth prompted them to reduce consumption and increase saving at each level of income. Household saving as a percent of disposable income increased from 3.9 percent in the quarter before the crash to 5.7 percent in the quarter following the crash. Spending on new homes and cars declined. Our original consumption function is depicted as line *C* in Exhibit 6. If net wealth declines, the consumption function shifts from *C* down to *C'*, because households now want to spend less and save more at every level of income.

Conversely, suppose stock prices on average increase sharply. This increase in net wealth increases the desire to spend. For example, stock prices surged in

Saving function The relationship between saving and the level of income in the economy, other things constant

Net wealth The value of a household's assets minus its liabilities

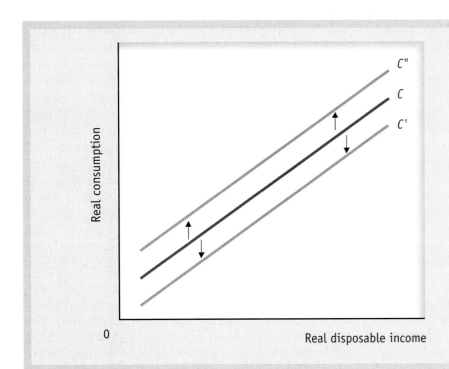

EXHIBIT 6

Shifts in the Consumption Function

A downward shift in the consumption function, such as from *C* to *C'*, can be caused by a decrease in wealth, an increase in the price level, an unfavorable change in consumer expectations, or an increase in the interest rate. An upward shift, such as that from *C* to *C"*, can be caused by an increase in wealth, a decrease in the price level, a favorable change in expectations, or a decrease in the interest rate.

1995, 1996, and 1997, and in the first half of 1998, increasing stockholders' net wealth. Consumption averaged 93 percent of disposable income during these three years, compared to an average of about 90 percent between 1960 and 1990. Sales of homes and cars took off. According to the *Economist,* a highly regarded publication, the strong stock market "made consumers feel richer, and as a result, they saved less and consumed more. In the second quarter [of 1998] America's personal saving rate fell to a historic low."[1]

As a result of an increase in net wealth, the consumption function shifts from *C* up to *C"*, reflecting households' desire to spend more at every level of income. Again, *it is a change in net wealth, not a change in disposable income, that shifts the consumption function. A change in disposable income, other things held constant, is reflected by a movement along a given consumption function, not a shift in that function.* Be mindful of the difference between a *movement along* the consumption function, which results from a change in income, and a *shift in* the consumption function, which results from a change in one of the nonincome determinants of consumption, such as net wealth.

The Price Level. Another variable that can affect the consumption function is the price level prevailing in the economy. As we have seen, households' net wealth is an important determinant of consumption. The greater the net wealth, other things constant, the greater consumption will be at each level of income. Some household wealth is held in dollar-denominated assets, such as bank accounts and cash. When the price level changes, so does the real value of bank accounts, cash, and other dollar-denominated financial assets.

---

1 "On the Edge," *Economist* (5 September 1998): 20.

For example, suppose your stock of wealth consists of $20,000 in a bank account. If the price level increases by 5 percent, your bank account will purchase about 5 percent fewer real goods and services. You feel poorer because you are poorer. The real value of your wealth has declined. To rebuild your wealth to some desired level, you decide to spend less and save more. An increase in the price level reduces the purchasing power of wealth held in fixed-dollar assets and, as a consequence, causes households to consume less and save more at each level of income. So the consumption function shifts down from C to C', as shown in Exhibit 6.

Conversely, should the price level ever fall, that would increase the real value of dollar-denominated assets. Since households would be wealthier, they would be willing and able to consume more at each level of income. For example, if the price level declined by 5 percent, your $20,000 bank account would then buy about 5 percent more real goods and services. A drop in the price level is reflected by a shift in the consumption function from C up to C''. *At each level of income, a change in the price level influences consumption by affecting the real value of net wealth.*

The Interest Rate. Interest is the reward paid to savers for deferring consumption and the amount paid by borrowers for current spending power. When graphing the consumption function, we assume a given interest rate. If the rate of interest increases, other things constant, savers, or lenders, are rewarded more, and borrowers are charged more. The higher the interest rate, the less is spent on those items typically purchased on credit, such as homes and cars. Thus at a higher rate of interest, households will save more, borrow less, and spend less. Greater saving at each level of income means less consumption. Simply put, *a rise in the interest rate, other things constant, will shift the consumption function downward.* Conversely, *a drop in the interest rate, other things constant, will shift the consumption function upward.*

Expectations. As we've seen, expectations influence economic behavior in a variety of ways. For example, suppose you are a senior in college and you land a high-paying job that starts upon graduation. Your consumption will probably jump long before the job actually begins. Conversely, a worker who receives a layoff notice to take effect at the end of the year will likely reduce consumption immediately, well before the actual date of the layoff. More generally, if people grow concerned about job security, they will reduce the amount consumed at each level of income.

Changing expectations about price levels and interest rates also affect consumption. For example, a change that leads householders to expect higher car prices or higher interest rates in the future will prompt some to purchase new cars now. On the other hand, a change leading householders to expect lower prices or lower interest rates in the future will cause some to defer car purchases. Thus expectations affect spending at each level of income, and a change in expectations can shift the consumption function. This is why consumer confidence is monitored so closely by economic forecasters.

Again, keep in mind the distinction between *movements along a given consumption function* as a result of a change in income and *shifts in the consumption function* as a result of a change in another variable. We conclude our introduction to consumption with the following case study, which discusses consumption and saving patterns over people's lifetimes.

The Life-Cycle Hypothesis

Do people who earn a high income save a larger fraction of their incomes than do those with low income? Both theory and evidence suggest that they do. The easier it is to make ends meet, the more likely it is that income will be left over for saving. Does it follow from this that richer economies save more than poorer ones—that economies save a larger fraction of total disposable income as they grow? In his famous book, *The General Theory*, published in 1936, John Maynard Keynes drew that conclusion. But as later economists studied the data—such as that presented in Exhibit 2—it became clear that Keynes was wrong. *For societies, the fraction of total disposable income saved seems to stay constant as the economy grows.*

CaseStudy

Public Policy

The Japanese government has been trying various changes in government spending and tax policies to encourage more consumer spending. However, the Japanese public often just puts any extra income into savings. How can they be persuaded to spend more? A new, innovative policy is to issue purchase vouchers. The Japanese Information Agency reports on these at http://jin.jcic.or.jp/trends/honbun/ntj981201.html. To whom does the government intend to distribute these coupons? Why? Would receiving 20,000 yen in vouchers ensure that spending would increase by that amount?

So how can it be that richer individuals save more than poorer individuals, yet richer countries do not necessarily save more than poorer countries? By the early 1950s, several answers had been proposed. One of the most important of these was the *life-cycle model of consumption*. According to this model, people tend to borrow when they are young to finance education and home purchases; in middle age, they pay off their debts and save more; in old age, they draw down their savings, or dissave. Some people still have substantial wealth at death, because they are not sure when death will occur and because some parents want to pass wealth to their children. But net savings over a person's entire lifetime tend to be relatively small.

The life-cycle hypothesis suggests that the saving rate for an economy as a whole depends on, among other things, the relative number of savers and dissavers in the population. Other factors that influence the saving rate across countries include the manner in which saving is taxed, the convenience and reliability of saving institutions, and the relative cost of each household's major purchase—housing. In Japan, for example, about 25,000 post offices nationwide offer convenient savings accounts, and more than half the country's population hold accounts. In fact, Japan's postal savings system, with over $2 trillion in savings deposits, is the world's largest financial institution. Also, a home buyer in Japan must come up with a substantial down payment that represents a relatively large fraction of the home's purchase price, and housing there is more expensive than in the United States. All this calls for substantial savings. Since saving in Japan is both necessary and convenient, the country has one of the highest saving rates in the world. In 1998, the Japanese saved a much higher percentage of their disposable income than did Americans.

Sources: Stephanie Strom, "Minister Hopes to Privatize Japan's Postal System, but Faces Uphill Battle," *New York Times* (18 November 1997); Malcolm Fisher, "Life Cycle Hypothesis," *The New Palgrave: A Dictionary of Economics* 3 (London: Macmillan Press, 1987), pp. 177–179; and *OECD Economic Outlook* 63 (June 1998), Annex Table 26.

We next consider the second component of aggregate expenditure: investment. Our ultimate objective is to understand the relationship between the total spending in the economy and the level of income.

INVESTMENT

The second component of aggregate expenditure is investment, or, more precisely, *gross private domestic investment*. By investment, we do not mean buying stocks, bonds, or other financial assets. Investment consists of spending on (1) new factories and new equipment such as computers, (2) new housing, and (3) net increases in inventories.

Business investment involves buying capital goods now in the expectation of a future return. Since the return is in the future, a would-be investor must estimate how much a particular investment will yield this year, next year, the year after, and in all future years covered by the productive life of the investment. *Firms buy new capital goods only if they expect this investment to yield a greater return than other possible uses of their funds.*

The Demand for Investment

To understand the investment decision, let's study a simple example. The operators of the Hacker Haven Golf Club are contemplating buying solar-powered golf carts to rent to golfers. The model under consideration, called the Weekend Warrior, sells for $2,000, requires no maintenance or operating expenses, and is expected to last indefinitely. *The expected rate of return equals the annual dollar earnings expected from the investment divided by the purchase price.* The first cart purchased is expected to earn a rental income of $400 per year. This income, divided by the cost of the cart, yields an expected rate of return on the investment of 400/2,000, or 20 percent per year. Additional carts will be used less. A second cart is expected to generate $300 per year in rental income, yielding a rate of return of 300/2,000, or 15 percent; a third cart, $200 per year, or 10 percent; and a fourth cart, $100 per year, or 5 percent. A fifth cart would not be used at all, so it has a zero expected rate of return.

Should the operators of Hacker Haven purchase any carts, and if so, how many? Suppose they plan to borrow the money to buy the carts. The number of carts they purchase will depend on the rate of interest they must pay to borrow money. If the market rate of interest exceeds 20 percent, their cost of borrowing exceeds the expected rate of return for even the first cart, so no carts will be purchased. What if the operators have enough money on hand to buy the carts? The market rate of interest also reflects what the club owners could earn on savings. If the interest rate paid on savings exceeds 20 percent, they could earn a higher rate of return by saving any funds on hand than by investing these funds in golf carts, so no carts would be purchased. *The market rate of interest represents the opportunity cost of investing in capital.*

Suppose the market rate of interest is 8 percent per year. At that rate, the first three carts, with expected rates of return exceeding 8 percent, would more than pay for themselves. A fourth cart would lose money, since its expected rate of return is only 5 percent. Exhibit 7 measures the nominal interest rate along the vertical axis and the amount invested in golf carts along the horizontal axis. The step-like relationship shows the expected rate of return earned on additional dollars invested in golf carts. This relationship also indicates the amount invested in golf carts at each interest rate, so you can view this step-like relationship as Hacker Haven's demand curve for this type of investment. For example, the first cart costs $2,000 and earns a rate of return of 20 percent. A firm

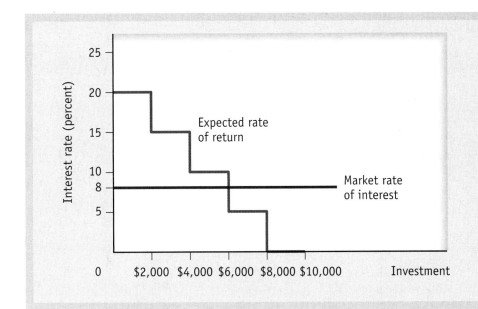

EXHIBIT 7

Rate of Return on Golf Carts and the Opportunity Cost of Funds

An individual firm will invest in any project whose rate of return exceeds the market interest rate. At an interest rate of 8 percent, Hacker Haven would purchase three golf carts, which represents investment spending of $6,000.

should reject any investment opportunity for which the expected rate of return falls below the market rate of interest.

The horizontal line at 8 percent indicates the market rate of interest, which represents Hacker Haven's opportunity cost of investing. Recall that the course operators' objective is to choose an investment strategy that maximizes profit. Profit is maximized when $6,000 is invested in the carts—that is, when three carts are purchased. The expected return from a fourth cart is 5 percent, which is below the opportunity cost of funds. Therefore, investing in four or more carts would lower total profit.

From Micro to Macro

So far we have examined the investment decision for a single golf course, but there are about 13,000 golf courses in the United States. The industry demand for golf carts shows the relationship between the amount all course operators invest and the expected rate of return. Like the step-like relationship in Exhibit 7, the investment demand curve for the golf industry slopes downward.

Let's move beyond golf carts and consider the investment decisions in all industries: publishing, hog farming, fast foods, apparel, and hundreds more. Individual industries generally have downward-sloping demand curves for investment. More is invested when the opportunity cost of borrowing is lower, other things equal. A downward-sloping investment demand curve for the entire economy can be derived, with some qualifications, from a horizontal summation of all industries' downward-sloping investment demand curves. The economy's *investment demand curve* is represented as *D* in Exhibit 8, which shows the inverse relationship between the quantity of investment demanded and the market rate of interest, other things—including business expectations—held constant. For example, in Exhibit 8, when the market rate of interest is 8 percent, the

EXHIBIT 8

Investment Demand Curve for the Economy

The investment demand curve for the economy is obtained by summing the amount of investment undertaken by each firm at each interest rate. At lower interest rates, more investment projects become profitable for individual firms, so the total investment spending in the economy increases.

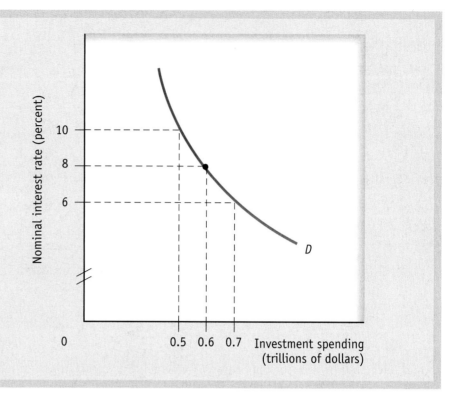

quantity of investment demanded is $0.6 trillion. If the interest rate rises to 10 percent, investment spending declines to $0.5 trillion, and if the interest rate falls to 6 percent, investment increases to $0.7 trillion. Held constant along the investment demand curve are business expectations about the economy. If firms grow more optimistic about profit prospects, the demand for investment increases, and the entire curve shifts to the right.

Planned Investment and the Economy's Level of Income

To integrate the discussion of investment with our earlier analysis of consumption, we need to know if and how investment varies with the level of income in the economy. Whereas we were able to present empirical evidence relating consumption to disposable income over time, the link between investment and disposable income is much weaker. Over the last dozen years, for example, investment shows little relation to the level of income. *Investment depends more on interest rates and on business expectations than on the prevailing level of income.* One reason investment is less related to the current level of income is that some investments, such as a new electric power plant, take years to complete. And once investment is in place, it is expected to last for years, even decades. The investment decision is thus said to be "forward looking," based more on expected profit than on current levels of income and output.

So how does planned investment relate to disposable income? The simplest **investment function** assumes that planned investment is unrelated to the cur-

Investment function The relationship between the amount businesses plan to invest and the level of income in the economy, other things constant

rent level of disposable income; investment is assumed to be **autonomous** with respect to income. For example, suppose that, given current business expectations and an interest rate of 8 percent, firms plan to invest $0.6 trillion, regardless of the economy's income level. Exhibit 9 measures disposable income on the horizontal axis and planned investment on the vertical axis. Investment of $0.6 trillion is shown by the flat investment function, *I*. As you can see, along investment function *I,* planned investment does not vary even though real disposable income does.

Nonincome Determinants of Investment

The investment function isolates the relationship between the level of income in the economy and *planned investment*—the amount firms would like to invest, other things constant. We have already mentioned two important determinants that are held constant: the interest rate and business expectations. Now let's look at the effect of changes in these factors on investment.

Market Interest Rate. Exhibit 8 showed that if the interest rate were 8 percent, desired, or planned, investment would be $0.6 trillion. This level of investment is shown as *I* in Exhibit 9. If the interest rate increases because of, say, a change in the nation's monetary policy that reduces the supply of loanable funds in the economy (as happened in 1994), the cost of borrowing increases and this increases the opportunity cost of investment. For example, if the interest rate increases from 8 percent to 10 percent, planned investment drops from $0.6 trillion to $0.5 trillion; this decrease is reflected in Exhibit 9 by a downward shift of the investment function from *I* to *I'*. Conversely, a drop in the rate of interest from 8 percent to 6 percent, other things held constant, will reduce the cost of borrowing and increase planned investment from $0.6 trillion to

Autonomous A term that means "independent"; autonomous investment is independent of the level of income

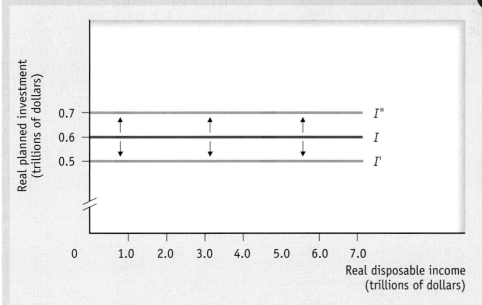

EXHIBIT 9

Autonomous Investment Function

Autonomous investment spending is assumed to be independent of income, as shown by the horizontal lines. An increase in the interest rate or declining business expectations can decrease autonomous investment, as shown by the downward shift from *I* to *I'*. A decrease in the interest rate or upbeat business expectations can shift the investment function up to *I"*.

CaseStudy

Public Policy

Visit the Web site for the Research Seminar in Quantitative Economics at the University of Michigan at http://rsqe.econ.lsa.umich.edu/index.html. RSQE is "an economic modeling and forecasting unit which has been in operation at the University of Michigan since 1952. RSQE provides forecasts of the economic outlook for the U.S. and Michigan economies, based on quarterly econometric models." Read the latest Executive Summary for their U.S. forecast. What are the "seeds" or sources of the predicted trend? How, specifically, do the forecasters believe that the types of consumption and investment spending cited in the text will change and affect real GDP?

$0.7 trillion, as reflected by the upward shift of the investment function from I to I''. Notice that the shifts in Exhibit 9 mirror interest-rate movements along the investment demand curve in Exhibit 8.

Business Expectations. As we saw in Chapter 5, investment depends primarily on business expectations, or on what Keynes called the "animal spirits" of business. Suppose planned investment initially is $0.6 trillion, as depicted by I in Exhibit 9. If most firms now become more pessimistic about profit prospects, perhaps expecting a recession, their planned investment will decrease at every level of income, as reflected in Exhibit 9 by a shift of the investment function from I down to I'. On the other hand, if profit expectations become rosier, firms will be more willing to invest, thereby increasing the investment function from I up to I''. *Examples of factors that could affect business expectations, and hence investment plans, include wars, technological change, changes in the tax structure, and financial crises around the world, such as occurred in Asia and Russia in 1998.* Changes in business expectations also shift the investment demand curve in Exhibit 8.

Now that we have examined consumption and investment individually, let's take a look at their year-to-year variability in the following case study.

Variability of Consumption and Investment

We already know that consumption makes up about two-thirds of GDP and that investment spending varies from year to year, averaging about one-seventh of GDP in the last decade. Now let's compare the year-to-year variability in consumption, investment, and GDP. Exhibit 10 shows the annual percentage changes since 1960 in consumption, investment, and GDP, all measured in real terms.

Two points are obvious. First, fluctuations in consumption and in GDP are similar, although consumption varies slightly less than GDP. Second, investment fluctuates much more than either consumption or GDP. For example, in the recession year of 1982, GDP declined by 2.1 percent but investment declined by 14.4 percent; consumption actually increased by 1.2 percent. In 1984, GDP increased by 7.0 percent, investment increased 29.8 percent, and consumption increased 5.2 percent. The recession that stretched into the first quarter of 1991 reduced GDP that year by 0.9 percent; investment declined by 9.4 percent, and consumption declined by 0.6 percent

During the 38 years since 1960, GDP declined during five recession years, with the decline averaging 0.9 percent annually. Investment during those five years declined an average of 12.2 percent. On average, consumption increased 0.3 percent during the five recession years. So *while consumption is the largest spending component, investment varies much more than consumption and accounts for most of the variability in real GDP.* This is why economic forecasters pay special attention to business expectations and investment plans.

Sources: *Economic Report of the President,* February 1999; U.S. Department of Commerce, *Survey of Current Business* 78 (December 1998); and *OECD Economic Outlook* 64 (December 1998).

EXHIBIT 10

Annual Percentage Changes in U.S. Real GDP, Real Consumption, and Real Investment

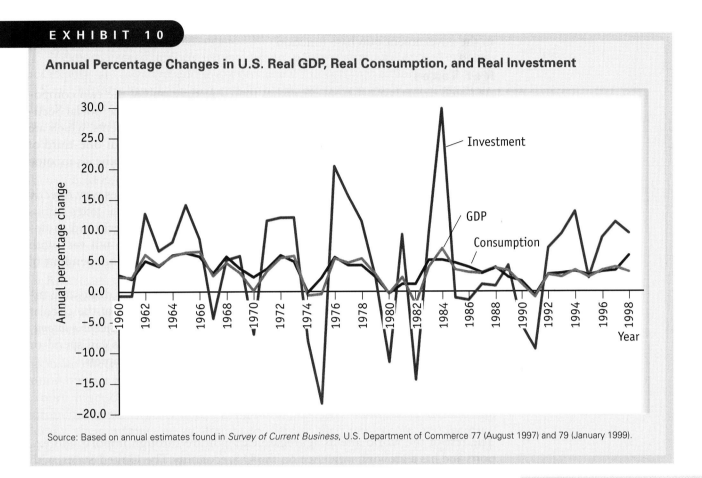

Source: Based on annual estimates found in *Survey of Current Business*, U.S. Department of Commerce 77 (August 1997) and 79 (January 1999).

GOVERNMENT

The third component of aggregate expenditure is government purchases of goods and services. Federal, state, and local governments purchase thousands of goods and services, ranging from weapon systems to road signs. In the United States, government purchases in 1998 accounted for about 17 percent of GDP—about one-third of which was by the federal government and about two-thirds by state and local governments.

Government Purchase Function

The **government purchase function** relates government purchases to the level of income in the economy, other things constant. Since decisions about government purchases are largely under the control of public officials, such as the decision to build an interstate highway system or to reduce military spending, these purchases do not depend directly on the level of income in the economy. We therefore assume that *government purchases, G,* are autonomous, or independent of the level of income. Such a function would relate to income as a flat line similar to the investment function shown in Exhibit 9. An increase in government purchases would result in a shift up in the government purchase

Government purchase function The relationship between government purchases and the level of income in the economy, other things constant

Government purchases are based on the public choices of elected officials and are assumed to be autonomous, or independent of the level of income in the economy. Net taxes, or taxes minus transfers, are also assumed for now to be unrelated to income.

6. Net exports equal the value of exports minus the value of imports. Exports are unrelated to the level of income

in this country. Imports tend to be positively related to income. Thus, net exports tend to decline as income increases. For simplicity, we initially assume that net exports are autonomous, or unrelated to domestic income. The appendix to this chapter deals with net exports that decline with income.

QUESTIONS FOR REVIEW

1. *(Consumption Function)* How would an increase in each of the following variables affect the consumption function? How would it affect the saving function?
   a. Autonomous net taxes
   b. The interest rate
   c. Consumer optimism, or confidence
   d. The price level
   e. Real wealth
   f. Disposable income

2. *(Consumption Function)* A number of factors can cause the consumption function to shift. What, if anything, happens to the saving function when the consumption function shifts? Explain.

3. *(CaseStudy: Life-Cycle Hypothesis)* According to the life-cycle hypothesis, what is the typical pattern of saving for an individual over his or her lifetime? What impact does this behavior have on an individual's lifetime consumption pattern? What impact does the behavior have on the saving rate in the overall economy?

4. *(Investment Spending)* What are the components of gross private domestic investment? What is the difference between the investment curve shown in Exhibit 7 and the one shown in Exhibit 8? Do these curves refer to actual or planned investment?

5. *(Investment)* Why would the following investment expenditures increase as the interest rate declines?
   a. Purchases of a new plant and equipment
   b. Construction of new housing
   c. Accumulation of planned inventories

6. *(Nonincome Determinants of Investment)* What are some factors that can cause the autonomous investment function to shift? What kinds of changes could cause investment spending to increase at each level of real disposable income?

7. *(CaseStudy: Variability of Consumption and Investment)* Why do economic forecasters pay special attention to investment plans? Take a look at the Conference Board's index of leading economic indictors at http://www.conferenceboard.org. Which of those indicators might affect investment plans?

8. *(Government Spending)* How do changes in disposable income affect government purchases and the government purchase function? How do changes in net taxes affect the consumption function?

9. *(Net Exports)* What factors are assumed constant along the net export function? What would be the impact on net exports of a change in real disposable income?

PROBLEMS AND EXERCISES

10. *(Consumption)* Use the following data to answer the questions below.

Real Disposable Income	Consumption Expenditures
$100	$150
200	200
300	250
400	300

a. Graph the consumption function with consumption spending on the vertical axis and disposable income on the horizontal axis.
b. If the consumption function is a straight line, what is its slope?
c. If investment is equal to $100, at what level of disposable income does saving equal investment?

11. *(MPC and MPS)* If consumption increases by $12 billion when real disposable income increases by $15 billion, what is the value of the MPC? What is the relationship between the MPC and the MPS? If the MPC rises, what must happen to the MPS? How is the MPC related to the consumption function? How is the MPS related to the saving function?

12. *(Consumption and Saving)* Suppose that consumption equals $500 billion when disposable income is $0 and that each increase of $100 billion in disposable income causes consumption to increase by $70 billion. Draw a graph of the saving function using this information.

13. *(Investment Spending)* Review Exhibit 7 in this chapter. If the owners of the golf course revised their revenue estimates so that each cart is expected to earn $100 less, how many carts would they buy at an interest rate of 8 percent? How many would they buy if the interest rate is 3 percent?

EXPERIENTIAL EXERCISES

14. *(Marginal Propensity to Consume)* Find some recent data on U.S. real disposable income and real consumption spending. (One possible source is the *Economic Report of the President* at http://www.access.gpo.gov/eop/, but there are many others.) Use the data to compute the marginal propensity to consume for each year, 1991 to 1998. Has the MPC been relatively constant?

15. *(Variability of Consumption and Investment)* Expectations and consumer confidence are important in determining fluctuations in aggregate spending. What is the present status of consumer confidence as measured by the Conference Board's index? You can find the data, with interpretation, at The Dismal Scientist at http://www.dismal.com/economy/releases/consumer.asp.

16. *(Wall Street Journal)* Business investment spending is an important component of aggregate expenditure. Review the "Business Bulletin" column on the front page of Thursday's *Wall Street Journal*. What are some recent trends in investment spending? Are they likely to increase or decrease aggregate expenditure? (Remember that purchases of stocks and bonds are *not* investment, in the sense described in this chapter!)

Appendix

VARIABLE NET EXPORTS

In this appendix, we examine more closely the relationship between net exports and the U.S. level of income. We first look at exports and imports separately and then consider exports minus imports, or net exports.

NET EXPORTS AND INCOME

As noted in the chapter, the amount of U.S. output purchased by foreigners depends not on the U.S. level of income but on income levels in their own countries. We therefore assume that U.S. exports do not vary with respect to the U.S. income level. Specifically, suppose the rest of the world spends $0.6 trillion per year on U.S. exports of goods and services; the export function, X, is as shown in panel (a) of Exhibit 13. On the other hand, when disposable income increases, U.S. consumers spend more on all goods and services, including imported goods and services. Thus, the relationship between imports and income is positive, as expressed by the upward-sloping import function, M, in panel (b) of Exhibit 13. Imports are assumed to be 10 percent of disposable income, so when disposable income is $6.0 trillion, imports are $0.6 trillion.

So far we have considered imports and exports as separate functions of income. What matters in terms of total spending on U.S. products are exports, X, minus imports, M, or net exports, $X - M$. Since money spent on imports goes to foreign producers, not U.S. producers, imports are subtracted from the circular flow of spending. By subtracting the import function depicted in panel (b) from the export function in panel (a), we derive the *net export function,* depicted as $X - M$ in panel (c) of Exhibit 13. Note that when income is $6.0 trillion, *imports* in panel (b) equal $0.6 trillion.

Since *exports* in panel (a) equal $0.6 trillion at all levels of income, net exports equal zero when U.S. disposable income equals $6.0 trillion. At levels of income below $6.0 trillion, net exports are positive because exports exceed imports. At levels of income greater than $6.0 trillion, net exports are negative because imports exceed exports. The United States has experienced negative net exports during most of the last four decades. Our high trade deficit in recent years traces in part to the economic expansion in the United States. The trade deficit shrank during the recession of the early 1990s, but then increased again as the U.S. economy recovered.

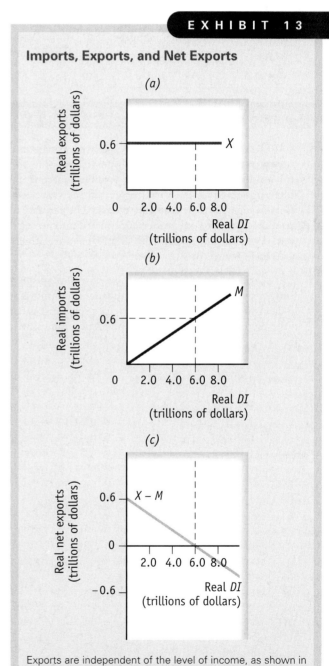

EXHIBIT 13

Imports, Exports, and Net Exports

Exports are independent of the level of income, as shown in panel (a). Imports are positively related to income, as shown in panel (b). Net exports equal exports minus imports; net exports are negatively related to income, as shown in panel (c).

SHIFTS IN NET EXPORTS

The net export function, $X - M$, shows the relationship between net exports and disposable income, other things constant. Suppose the value of the dollar increases relative to foreign currencies, as it did in 1998. With the dollar worth more on world markets, foreign products become cheaper for Americans and U.S. products become more expensive for foreigners. The impact of a rising dollar is to decrease exports but increase imports at each level of income. This decreases net exports, as shown in Exhibit 14 by the shift from $X - M$ down to $X' - M'$. A decline in the dollar's value will have the opposite effect, increasing exports and decreasing imports, as reflected in Exhibit 14 by an upward shift in the net export function from $X - M$ to $X'' - M''$.

In summary, in this appendix we assumed that *imports relate positively to the level of income, whereas exports are independent of the domestic level of income. Net exports, which equal exports minus imports, therefore vary inversely with the level of income. The net export function shifts upward if the value of the dollar falls and shifts downward if the value of the dollar rises.*

EXHIBIT 14

Shifts in Net Exports

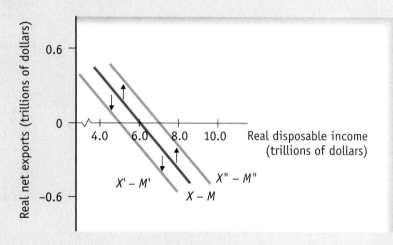

A rise in the value of the dollar, other things held constant, will decrease exports and increase imports, thereby contributing to a decrease in net exports, as shown by the shift from $X - M$ down to $X' - M'$. A decrease in the value of the dollar will increase exports and decrease imports, causing net exports to rise, as shown by the shift from $X - M$ up to $X'' - M''$.

APPENDIX QUESTION

(Rest of the World) Using a graph of net exports $(X - M)$ against disposable income, show the effects of the following:

a. An increase in foreign income
b. An increase in U.S. income
c. An increase in the U.S. interest rate
d. An increase in the value of the dollar against foreign currencies

Explain each of your answers.

Aggregate Expenditure and Aggregate Demand

How does aggregate spending in the economy relate to income? What is the effect of a change in the price level on aggregate spending? And what does all this have to do with aggregate demand? More fundamentally, what is the link between the economy's price level and the quantity of GDP demanded? Answers to these and other questions are covered in this chapter, which develops the aggregate demand curve.

Your economic success depends to a large extent on the overall performance of the economy. When the economy expands, jobs grow more abundant, so your chances of finding a good one increase. When the economy contracts, job opportunities shrink, as do job prospects. Thus, you should have a personal interest in the economy's level of output and the year-to-year changes in output. In this chapter we continue to build a model that will help us determine the economy's equilibrium level of output, or real GDP.

Chapter 9 discussed the components of aggregate spending—consumption, investment, government purchases, and net exports—showing how each relates to the level of income in the economy. In this chapter, these components are added up to show how total spending, or aggregate expenditure, relates to the level of income. We then use this information to derive the aggregate demand curve. Aggregate supply will be developed in Chapter 11; then, a fuller treatment of the effects of government spending and taxing will be examined in Chapter 12.

In Appendix A, you can see what happens when imports increase with income. An algebraic approach to the aggregate expenditure framework is developed in Appendix B. Topics discussed in this chapter include:

- Aggregate expenditure line
- Real GDP demanded
- Effect of changes in aggregate expenditure
- Simple spending multiplier
- Effect of changes in the price level
- Aggregate demand curve

AGGREGATE EXPENDITURE AND INCOME

In the previous chapter, the big idea was the link between income and consumption, a link that is the most stable in all of macroeconomics. In this section, we build on the income-consumption relationship to uncover the tie between total spending and income. If we try to confront the economy head-on, it soon becomes a bewildering maze, which is why we often make progress only by making simplifying assumptions. In this chapter, we continue to assume, as we did in developing the circular flow model, that there is no capital depreciation and no business saving. Hence, we can say that *each dollar spent on production translates directly into a dollar of aggregate income.* Therefore, gross domestic product, or GDP, equals aggregate income. We also continue to assume that net exports are autonomous, or independent of the level of income.

The Components of Aggregate Expenditure

Let's begin developing the aggregate demand curve by asking how much aggregate output would be demanded at a given price level. By finding the quantity demanded at a given price level, we'll identify a single point on the aggregate demand curve. We want to consider the relationship between aggregate spending in the economy and aggregate income, or real GDP. By *real* GDP, we mean GDP measured in terms of real goods and services produced.

To get us started, suppose the price level in the economy is 130, meaning that it is 30 percent higher than in the base year. We want to find out how much will be spent at various levels of real GDP, or real income. Exhibit 1 presents the hypothetical data that will serve as building blocks for constructing the relation between aggregate spending and income. This exhibit simply puts into tabular form relationships that were introduced in the previous chapter—consumption, saving, planned investment, government purchases, net taxes, and net exports. Although the entries are hypothetical, they bear some relation to levels observed in the U.S. economy.

EXHIBIT 1

Table for Real GDP, with Net Taxes and Government Purchases (trillions of dollars)

Real GDP (Y) (1)	Net Taxes (NT) (2)	Disposable Income (Y − NT) (3) = (1) − (2)	Consumption (C) (4)	Saving (S) (5)	Planned Investment (I) (6)	Government Purchases (G) (7)	Net Exports (X − M) (8)	Planned Aggregate Expenditure (AE) (9)	Unintended Inventory Adjustment (Y − AE) (10) = (1) − (9)
7.0	1.0	6.0	5.7	0.3	0.6	1.0	−0.1	7.2	−0.2
7.5	1.0	6.5	6.1	0.4	0.6	1.0	−0.1	7.6	−0.1
8.0	**1.0**	**7.0**	**6.5**	**0.5**	**0.6**	**1.0**	**−0.1**	**8.0**	**0.0**
8.5	1.0	7.5	6.9	0.6	0.6	1.0	−0.1	8.4	+0.1
9.0	1.0	8.0	7.3	0.7	0.6	1.0	−0.1	8.8	+0.2

The first column in Exhibit 1 lists a range of possible levels of real GDP in the economy, called *Y*. The second column shows *net taxes,* or *NT,* which are assumed to be $1.0 trillion at each level of real GDP. Subtracting net taxes from real GDP yields *disposable income,* listed in column (3) as *Y − NT*. Note that at all levels of real GDP, disposable income equals real GDP minus net taxes of $1.0 trillion. Since net taxes are assumed to be autonomous, each time real GDP increases by $0.5 trillion, disposable income also increases by $0.5 trillion.

Households have only two possible uses for disposable income: consumption and saving. Columns (4) and (5) show that the levels of *consumption, C,* and *saving, S,* increase with disposable income. Each time real GDP and disposable income increase by $0.5 trillion, consumption increases by $0.4 trillion and saving increases by $0.1 trillion. Thus, as in the previous chapter, the marginal propensity to consume is 4/5, or 0.8, and the marginal propensity to save is 1/5, or 0.2.

Columns (6), (7), and (8) list three now-familiar injections of spending into the circular flow: *planned investment* of $0.6 trillion, *government purchases* of $1.0 trillion, and *net exports* of − $0.1 trillion. In the table, government purchases equal net taxes, so the government budget is balanced. We want to see how a balanced budget works before we look at the effects of budget deficits or surpluses, which are discussed in Chapter 12. *The sum of consumption, C, planned investment, I, government purchases, G, and net exports, X − M, is listed in column (9) as planned aggregate expenditure, AE, which indicates the amount that households, firms, governments, and the rest of the world plan to spend on U.S. output at each level of real GDP.* Note that the only spending component that varies with the level of real GDP is consumption. As real GDP increases, so does disposable income, which increases the amount households spend on consumption.

The final column in Exhibit 1 lists any unplanned inventory adjustment, which equals real GDP minus planned aggregate expenditure, or *Y − AE*. For example, when real GDP is $7.0 trillion, planned aggregate expenditure is $7.2 trillion. Since planned spending exceeds the amount produced by $0.2 trillion, firms must reduce inventories by $0.2 trillion to make up the shortfall in output. So when real GDP is $7.0 trillion, the unplanned inventory adjustment in column (10) is –$0.2 trillion. Because firms cannot reduce inventories indefinitely, they respond to such reductions by increasing production, and they continue to do so until the amount they produce just matches planned spending.

If the amount produced exceeds planned spending, firms get stuck with unsold goods, which become unplanned increases in inventories. For example, if real GDP is $9.0 trillion, planned aggregate expenditure is only $8.8 trillion, so $0.2 trillion in output remains unsold. Hence, inventories increase by $0.2 trillion. Firms respond by reducing production and will do so until the amount produced just equals the amount people want to buy—that is, until real GDP equals planned aggregate expenditure.

When the amount people plan to spend equals the amount produced, there are no unplanned inventory adjustments. More precisely, *for a given price level, the quantity of real GDP demanded is found where real GDP equals planned aggregate expenditure.* In Exhibit 1, this occurs where planned aggregate expenditure and real GDP equal $8.0 trillion.

Quantity of Real GDP Demanded

Using a table, we have seen how firms adjust output until production just equals desired spending. You may find graphs easier to understand than tables. Graphs are also more general than tables and can show relationships between variables without focusing on specific numbers. The tabular relationship between real GDP and planned aggregate expenditure in Exhibit 1 can be expressed as an **aggregate expenditure line** in Exhibit 2. Like the aggregate expenditure amounts shown in column (9) of Exhibit 1, the aggregate expenditure line in Exhibit 2 reflects the sum of consumption, investment, government purchases, and net exports, or $C + I + G + (X - M)$. Planned aggregate expenditure is measured on the vertical axis.

Real GDP, measured along the horizontal axis in Exhibit 2, can be viewed in two ways—as the value of *aggregate output* and as the *aggregate income* generated by that level of output. Because real GDP, or income, is measured on the horizontal axis and aggregate expenditure is measured on the vertical axis, this graph is often called the **income-expenditure model.**[1]

To gain perspective on the relationship between income and expenditure, we use a handy analytical device: the 45-degree ray from the origin. The special feature of this line is that any point along it is exactly the same distance from both axes. Thus, the 45-degree line identifies all points where real GDP and planned expenditure are equal. *The quantity of aggregate output demanded at a given price level occurs where real GDP, measured along the horizontal axis, equals planned aggregate expenditure, measured along the vertical axis.* In Exhibit 2, this occurs at point *e,* where the aggregate expenditure line intersects the 45-degree line. At point *e,* the amount people plan to spend equals the amount produced. Keep in mind that this approach was based on a given price level.

Aggregate expenditure line A relationship showing, for a given price level, planned spending at each level of income; the total of $C + I + G + (X - M)$ at each level of income

Income-expenditure model A relationship between aggregate income and aggregate spending that determines, for a given price level, where income equals planned spending

---

1 Note that in Exhibit 2 the horizontal axis measures real GDP. In the previous chapter, the horizontal axis measured disposable income. There is not much of a difference because real GDP minus net taxes equals disposable income. Since net taxes in our example are $1.0 trillion, every level of real GDP implies a level of disposable income that is $1.0 trillion lower. The link between real GDP and each spending component was spelled out in Exhibit 1.

Deriving the Aggregate Output Demanded for a Given Price Level

The aggregate output de-manded, given the price level, is found where aggre-gate expenditure equals real GDP—that is, where desired spending equals the amount produced.

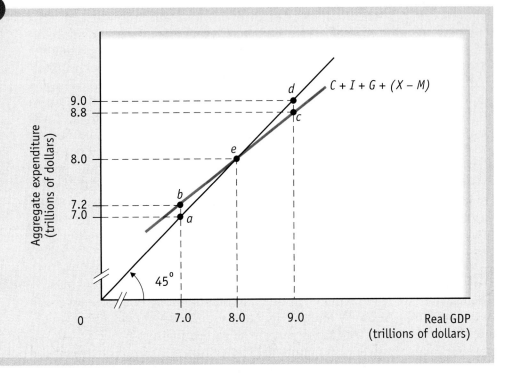

We conclude that, at the given price level, the quantity of real GDP demanded equals $8.0 trillion.

When Output and Planned Spending Differ

To find the quantity of real GDP demanded at the given price level, consider what happens when real GDP is initially less than $8.0 trillion. As you can see from Exhibit 2, at levels of real GDP less than $8.0 trillion, the planned aggre-gate expenditure line is above the 45-degree line, indicating that planned spending exceeds the amount produced. For example, if real GDP is $7.0 tril-lion, planned aggregate expenditure is $7.2 trillion, as indicated by point *b* on the aggregate expenditure line, so planned spending exceeds output by $0.2 trillion. When the amount people plan to spend exceeds the amount firms pro-duce, something has to give. Ordinarily what gives is the price level, but re-member that we are seeking the quantity of real GDP demanded for a given price level, so the price level is assumed to be constant, at least for now. What gives in this model are firms' *inventories*. Firms are forced to sell from invento-ries to make up the $0.2 trillion by which spending exceeds real GDP. Since firms cannot draw from inventories indefinitely, *unplanned inventory reductions* prompt firms to produce more output. That increases real GDP, which increases employment and consumer income, leading to more spending. As long as planned spending exceeds output, firms must increase production to make up the difference. This process of more output, more income, and more spending will continue until planned aggregate expenditure equals real GDP, an equality achieved at point *e*.

When output reaches $8.0 trillion, planned spending exactly matches output, so no unintended inventory adjustments occur. More importantly, when output reaches $8.0 trillion, planned spending equals the amount produced and equals the total income generated by that production. Earlier we assumed a price level of 130. Therefore, $8.0 trillion is the quantity of real GDP demanded at that given price level. In terms of the symbols introduced earlier, we say that *the quantity of real GDP demanded equals aggregate expenditure—the sum of consumption, C, plus planned investment, I, plus government purchases, G, plus net exports, X − M.*

To reinforce the logic of the model, consider what happens when real GDP exceeds $8.0 trillion—that is, when the aggregate expenditure line is below the 45-degree line. Note in Exhibit 2 that, along that portion of the aggregate expenditure line to the right of point *e*, planned spending falls short of production. For example, if the amount produced in the economy is $9.0 trillion, desired spending, as indicated by point *c* on the aggregate expenditure line, is $0.2 trillion less than real GDP, indicated by point *d* on the 45-degree line. Since real GDP exceeds the amount people want to spend, unsold goods accumulate. This swells inventories by $0.2 trillion more than firms wanted. Rather than allow inventories to pile up indefinitely, firms reduce production, which reduces employment and income. *Unplanned inventory buildups* cause firms to cut production until the amount they produce equals aggregate expenditure, which occurs, again, at a level of real GDP of $8.0 trillion.

Given the price level, the quantity of aggregate output demanded is found where the amount people plan to spend equals the amount produced. Hence, *for a given price level, there is only one point along the aggregate expenditure line at which planned spending equals real GDP.*

We have now discussed the forces that determine the quantity of real GDP demanded for a given price level. In the next section, we examine the impact of a shift in the aggregate expenditure line.

THE SIMPLE SPENDING MULTIPLIER

In the previous section, we employed the aggregate expenditure line to determine the quantity of aggregate output demanded for a particular price level. In this section, we continue to assume that the price level remains unchanged, as we trace the effects of changes in planned spending on the quantity of aggregate output demanded. Like a stone thrown into a still pond, the effect of any shift in planned spending ripples through the economy, generating changes in aggregate output that may far exceed the initial shift in planned spending.

Effects of an Increase in Aggregate Expenditure

We begin at point *e* in Exhibit 3, where planned spending equals real GDP at $8.0 trillion. Now let's consider the effect of an increase in one of the components of spending. Suppose that firms become more optimistic about future profit prospects and as a result increase their planned investment. Specifically, suppose planned investment increases from $0.6 trillion to $0.7 trillion per

*Net***Bookmark**

As mentioned in Chapter 1, economists are storytellers. One important storyteller is Alan Greenspan, Chair of the Board of Governors of the Federal Reserve. In a January 1998 speech he looked back at the economic events of 1997 and told stories about the forces influencing consumption and investment spending, two key aspects of aggregate demand. You can find the speech at http://www. federalreserve.gov/ BoardDocs/Speeches/ 1998/19980108.htm.

year, as reflected in Exhibit 3 by a change in the aggregate expenditure line, which shifts up by $0.1 trillion, from $C + I + G + (X - M)$ to $C + I' + G + (X - M)$.

What happens to real GDP demanded? An instinctive response is that real GDP demanded should increase by $0.1 trillion. In this case, however, instinct is a poor guide. As you can see, the new spending line intersects the 45-degree line at point e', where real GDP is $8.5 trillion. How can a $0.1 trillion increase in planned spending increase real GDP by $0.5 trillion? What's going on?

The idea of the circular flow is central to an understanding of the process of adjustment from one level of real GDP to another. As noted earlier, real GDP can be thought of as both the value of production and the income arising from that production. Recall that production yields income, which generates spending. We can think of each trip around the circular flow as a "round" of income and spending.

Round One. An upward shift of the aggregate expenditure line means that, at the initial real GDP level of $8.0 trillion, planned spending now exceeds output by $0.1 trillion, or $100 billion. This is shown in Exhibit 3 by the difference between point e and point a. Initially this increased spending may be satisfied by

Effect of an Increase in Autonomous Investment on Real GDP Demanded

The economy is initially at point e, where spending and real GDP both equal $8.0 trillion. A $0.1 trillion increase in autonomous investment shifts up the aggregate expenditure line vertically by $0.1 trillion from $C + I + G + (X - M)$ to $C + I' + G + (X - M)$. Real GDP rises until it equals spending at point e'. As a result of the $0.1 trillion increase in autonomous investment, real GDP demanded increases by $0.5 trillion, to $8.5 trillion.

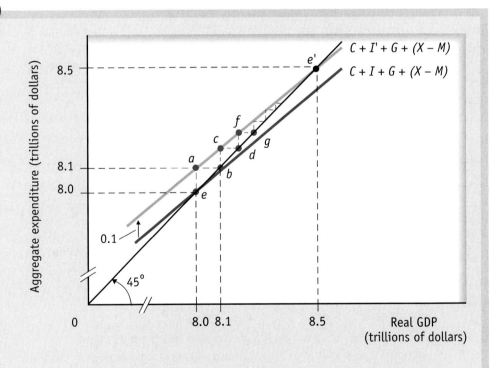

reducing inventories, but shrinking inventories prompt firms to expand production by $100 billion, as shown by the movement from point *a* to point *b*. This increased production generates $100 billion in increased income.

Thus output and income increase by $100 billion in the first round of new spending arising from the increase in planned investment of $100 billion. The movement from *e* to *b* represents the first round in the multiplier process. The income-generating process does not stop there, however, because those who receive this additional income spend some of it and save some of it, laying the basis for round two of spending and income.

Round Two. Given a marginal propensity to consume of 4/5, or 0.8, those who receive the $100 billion as income will spend a total of $80 billion on toasters, movies, backpacks, and thousands of other goods and services. The other $20 billion of that $100 billion will be saved. This $80 billion spending increase is reflected by the move from point *b* to point *c* in Exhibit 3. Firms respond by increasing their output by $80 billion, reflected by the movement from point *c* to point *d*. Thus the initial $100 billion in new income increases real GDP by $80 billion during the second round.

Round Three and Beyond. Focus now on the $80 billion that went toward consumption during round two. Production increases of $80 billion in the second round generate an equal amount of income for resource suppliers. Again, based on the marginal propensity to consume, we know that four-fifths of the additional income will be consumed and one-fifth will be saved. Thus, $64 billion will be spent on still more goods and services, as reflected by the movement from point *d* to point *f* (the remaining $16 billion will be saved). The additional spending causes firms to increase output by $64 billion, as shown by the movement from point *f* to point *g*. This increase in real GDP means that income also increases by $64 billion, laying the basis for subsequent rounds of spending, output, and income. *As long as planned spending exceeds output, production will increase, thereby creating more income, which will generate still more spending.*

Simple Spending Multiplier

When does the income-generating machine run out of fuel? At some point the new rounds of income and spending become so small that they disappear and the process stops. Looked at another way, saving leaks from the circular flow during every round. The more income that leaks as saving, the less that remains to fuel still more spending and income.

The initial increase of $0.1 trillion in autonomous investment has increased real GDP demanded from $8.0 trillion to $8.5 trillion, or by $0.5 trillion. Thus each dollar of increased investment spending has multiplied fivefold. The **simple spending multiplier** is the multiple by which real GDP changes for a given initial change in spending. The simple spending multiplier is computed as the ratio of the change in real GDP demanded to the initial expenditure change that caused it. In our example, the multiplier equals 0.5/0.1, or 5.

The quantity of real GDP demanded would have increased by the same amount if consumers had decided to spend $100 billion more at each level of income—that is, if the consumption function, rather than the investment function, had shifted up by $100 billion. Real GDP demanded would likewise have

Simple spending multiplier The ratio of a change in real GDP demanded to the initial change in expenditure that brought it about; the numerical value of the simple spending multiplier is $1/(1 - \text{MPC})$; called "simple" because consumption is the only component that varies with income

increased if government purchases or net exports had increased by $100 billion. *The change in the quantity of aggregate output demanded depends on how much the aggregate expenditure line shifts, not on which spending component causes the shift.*

Note that, in our example, planned investment increased by $100 billion, or $0.1 trillion, per year. *If this higher level of planned investment is not sustained in the following year, real GDP demanded will fall back.* For example, if planned investment returns to $0.6 trillion, other things constant, real GDP demanded will return to $8.0 trillion.

Numerical Value of the Simple Spending Multiplier

Tracing the rounds of spending is one way to determine the effects of a particular change in spending, but this process is slow and tedious. What we need is a quick way to translate changes in planned spending into changes in the level of real output demanded at a given price level. Recall that the expansion stemming from an increase in autonomous spending depends on the marginal propensity to consume. The spending multiplier and the marginal propensity to consume are related in a way that proves useful in formulating the multiplier. *The larger the fraction of an increase in income that is respent each round, the larger the spending multiplier.* The marginal propensity to consume and the multiplier are directly related; the larger the MPC, the larger the multiplier. Thus, we can define the simple spending multiplier in terms of the MPC as follows:

$$\text{Simple spending multiplier} = \frac{1}{1 - \text{MPC}}$$

Since the MPC is 4/5, the denominator equals $1 - 4/5$, or 1/5, and the simple spending multiplier equals the reciprocal of 1/5, which is 5. If the MPC were 3/4, the denominator would equal $1 - 3/4$, or 1/4, and the simple spending multiplier would equal the reciprocal of 1/4, which is 4.[2]

Recall from Chapter 9 that the MPC and the MPS add up to 1, so 1 minus the MPC equals the MPS. With this information, we can define the simple spending multiplier in terms of the MPS as follows:

$$\text{Simple spending multiplier} = \frac{1}{1 - \text{MPC}} = \frac{1}{\text{MPS}}$$

The simple spending multiplier is the reciprocal of the MPS. When we express the equation this way, we can see that the smaller the MPS, the larger the fraction of each fresh round of income that is spent and the less leaks out as saving, so the larger the multiplier. This spending multiplier is called *simple* because only consumption varies with the level of real GDP; the other spending components are assumed to be independent of real GDP.

---

2 A more formal way of deriving the spending multiplier is to total the additions to spending arising from each new round of income and spending. For example, a $1 increase in investment generates $1 in spending in the first round. In the second round, it generates $1 times the MPC. In the third round, the new spending equals the spending that arose in the second round ($1 × MPC) times the MPC. This goes on round after round, with each new round equal to the spending from the previous round times the MPC. Mathematicians have shown that the sum of an infinite series of rounds, each of which is a constant fraction of the previous round, is $1/(1 - \text{MPC})$ times the initial amount. In our context, $1/(1 - \text{MPC})$ is the spending multiplier.

The focus of the spending multiplier thus far has been the national economy. But the idea of the multiplier has some relevance for state and regional economies as well, as shown in the following case study.

Hard Times in Connecticut

Because of a cutback in federal defense spending and a fall in worldwide orders for commercial aircraft, the United Technologies Corporation (UTC), a major producer of jet engines, announced in January of 1993 that by the end of 1994 it would eliminate 10,000 manufacturing jobs in Connecticut. UTC also planned to reduce its orders from dozens of Connecticut firms that supplied the company with everything from precision parts to janitorial services, thereby causing several thousand more job losses in the state. The direct layoffs, as well as expected layoffs by subcontractors, reflected an initial payroll loss exceeding $1 billion.

In a state with an expanding economy, job losses in one sector can be made up at least in part by job expansions in other sectors. But such losses proved especially painful in Connecticut, where a long recession had already cut jobs sharply during the previous three years. Consequently, those who lost high-paying jobs making jet engines faced grim alternatives.

This loss in employment and payroll rippled through the Connecticut economy, reducing the demand for housing, clothing, entertainment, restaurant meals, and other goods and services. For example, the unemployed engine makers ate out less frequently, reducing the income of restaurant owners, workers, and suppliers. Those who lost restaurant jobs reduced their own demand for goods and services.

So reductions in jet production had a multiplier effect in Connecticut. But the effect spilled beyond the state's borders. For example, individuals who lost jobs demanded fewer automobiles, cutting the incomes of auto workers living in places such as Detroit and San Diego. Thus, the number of job losses resulting from UTC's job cuts was greater for the nation as a whole than for Connecticut alone. Therefore, the spending multiplier is greater for the nation as a whole than for Connecticut.

Sources: Michael Remez, "State Suppliers to Feel Big Sting from Pratt Cuts," *Hartford Courant* (28 January 1993); and William McEachern, "Picking Up the Pieces After Connecticut's Great Recession," *The Connecticut Economy: A University of Connecticut Quarterly Review* (April 1993).

CaseStudy

Public Policy

Check up on how the employment situation in Connecticut has fared since 1993 at http://www.state.ct.us/ecd/research/digest/articles/nov98art1.html. In this article, "Employment And Wages: Peak To Trough To Present," from the November 1998 on-line edition of *Connecticut Economic Digest,* Charles Joo reports on employment trends by industry. Which sectors have gained, and which have lost, jobs? How, in particular, has the economic recovery affected the manufacturing sector, which was hurt by the layoffs at UTC and other firms during the hard times in the state in 1992–93?

DERIVING THE AGGREGATE DEMAND CURVE

Thus far in this chapter we have used the aggregate expenditure line to find the quantity of real GDP demanded *for a given price level.* But, as we shall see, for each price level there is a specific aggregate expenditure line, which yields a unique quantity of real GDP demanded. By altering the price level, we can derive the aggregate demand curve.

A Higher Price Level

What is the effect of a higher price level on the economy's aggregate expenditure line and, in turn, on the quantity of real GDP demanded? Recall that consumers hold many assets that are fixed in dollar terms, such as currency and bank accounts. A higher price level decreases the real value of these dollar-denominated assets. Consumers therefore are poorer, so they are less willing to spend at each level of income. For reasons that will be more fully explained in a later chapter, a higher price level also tends to increase the market rate of interest, and a higher interest rate reduces investment. Finally, a higher U.S. price level means that foreign goods become relatively cheaper for U.S. consumers and U.S. goods become relatively more expensive abroad. So imports will rise and exports will fall, decreasing net exports. *A higher price level therefore reduces consumption, planned investment, and net exports, which all reduce aggregate spending.* This decrease in the aggregate expenditure line reduces the quantity of real GDP demanded.

The panels of Exhibit 4 represent different ways of expressing the effects of a change in the price level on the quantity of real GDP demanded. Panel (a) presents the income-expenditure model and panel (b) presents the aggregate demand curve, showing the inverse relationship between the price level and output demanded. The idea is to find, for a given price level, the quantity of aggregate output demanded in panel (a) and express that price-quantity combination as a point on the aggregate demand curve in panel (b).

The two panels are aligned so that levels of real GDP on the horizontal axes correspond. At the initial price level of 130 in panel (a), the aggregate expenditure line, now denoted by *AE*, intersects the 45-degree line at point *e* to yield $8.0 trillion, the quantity of real GDP demanded. Panel (b) shows more directly the link between the quantity of real GDP demanded and the price level. As you can see, when the price level is 130, the quantity demanded is $8.0 trillion. This combination of price level and real GDP is identified by point *e* on the aggregate demand curve.

What if the price level increases from 130 to, say, 140? An increase in the price level reduces consumption, investment, and net exports. This reduction in planned spending is reflected in panel (a) by a decrease in the aggregate expenditure line from *AE* down to *AE'*. As a result of this decrease in planned spending, the quantity of real GDP demanded declines from $8.0 trillion to, say, $7.5 trillion (we can't say exactly what this new level of real GDP demanded will be unless we know exactly how the component of aggregate expenditure respond to a higher price level). Panel (b) shows that an increase in the price level from 130 to 140 decreases the quantity of real GDP demanded from $8.0 trillion to $7.5 trillion, as reflected by point *e'*.

A Lower Price Level

The opposite holds if the price level falls. At a lower price level, the value of bank accounts, currency, and other dollar-denominated assets increases. Consumers on average are richer and are more inclined to spend on consumption at each level of real GDP. A lower price level also tends to decrease the market interest rate, which increases investment. Finally, a lower U.S. price level, other things constant, makes U.S. products relatively cheaper abroad and foreign prod-

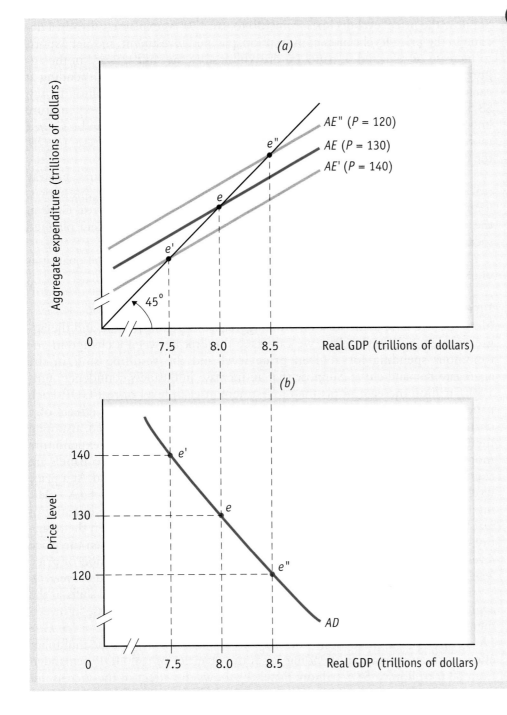

EXHIBIT 4

The Income-Expenditure Approach and the Aggregate Demand Curve

At the initial price level of 130, the aggregate expenditure line is *AE*, which identifies real GDP demanded of $8.0 trillion. Hence, this combination of a price level 130 and real GDP demanded of $8.0 trillion determine one point (point *e*) on the aggregate demand curve in panel (b).

At the higher price level of 140, the aggregate expenditure line is lower at *AE'* and real GDP demanded is less at $7.5 trillion. This price-output combination is plotted as point *e'* in panel (b).

At the lower price level of 120, the aggregate expenditure line is higher at *AE"* and so is real GDP demanded. That price-ouput combination is plotted as point *e"* in panel (b).

Connecting points *e*, *e'*, and *e"* gives us the downward-sloping aggregate demand curve that shows how much real GDP is demanded at each price level.

ucts relatively more expensive to Americans, so exports increase and imports decrease. Thus, *because of a decline in the price level, consumption, investment, and net exports increase at each level of real GDP.* A higher aggregate expenditure line leads to a higher quantity of real GDP demanded.

these frameworks, what do we assume about the price level? What do we assume about inventories?

5. *(Simple Spending Multiplier)* "A rise in planned investment spending in an economy will lead to a rise in the amount of desired spending." Use the concept of the spending multiplier to verify this statement.

6. *(CaseStudy: Hard Times in Connecticut)* How would cutbacks in defense spending, such as those described in the case study "Hard Times in Connecticut," affect the aggregate expenditure function and the aggregate demand curve? Explain fully.

7. *(Deriving the AD Curve)* What is the effect of a lower price level, other things constant, on the aggregate expenditure function and the level of real GDP demanded? How does the multiplier interact with the price change to determine the new level of real GDP demanded?

8. *(CaseStudy: Falling Consumption Triggers Japan's Recession)* What happened to consumption in Japan in 1998? Why did this happen? What was the impact on aggregate demand there?

PROBLEMS AND EXERCISES

9. *(Simple Spending Multiplier)* For each of the following values for the MPC, determine the size of the simple spending multiplier and the total change in real GDP demanded following a $10 billion decrease in autonomous spending:
    a. MPC = 0.9
    b. MPC = 0.75
    c. MPC = 0.6

10. *(Simple Spending Multiplier)* Suppose that the MPC is 0.8 and that $8 trillion of real GDP is currently being demanded. The government wants to increase real GDP demanded to $10 trillion. By how much would it have to increase government spending to achieve this goal?

11. *(Simple Spending Multiplier)* Suppose that the MPC is 0.8, while the sum of planned investment, government purchases, and net exports is $500 billion. Suppose also that the government budget is in balance.

    a. What is the sum of saving and net taxes when desired spending equals real GDP? Explain.
    b. What is the value of the multiplier?
    c. Explain why the multiplier is related to the slope of the consumption function.

12. *(Investment and the Multiplier)* This chapter assumes that all investment is autonomous. What would happen to the size of the multiplier if the amount of planned investment increased as real GDP increases? Explain.

13. *(Shifts in Aggregate Demand)* Assume the simple spending multiplier equals 10. Determine the size and direction of any shifts in the aggregate expenditure line, the level of real GDP demanded, and the aggregate demand curve for each of the following changes in autonomous spending:
    a. Autonomous spending rises by $8 billion.
    b. Autonomous spending falls by $5 billion.
    c. Autonomous spending rises by $20 billion.

EXPERIENTIAL EXERCISES

14. *(CaseStudy: Hard Times in Connecticut)* The Regional Economic Applications Laboratory at the University of Illinois http://www.uiuc.edu/unit/real/impact.html does economic impact analyses that measure the total impact of local and regional spending. Take a look at some of the examples they provide. Would you expect the multiplier effect of a dollar of spending at the local level to be larger or smaller than the effect at the national level?

15. *(CaseStudy: Falling Consumption Triggers Japan's Recession)* Professor Nouriel Roubini of New York University maintains an extensive Web page at

http://www.stern.nyu.edu/~nroubini/asia/AsiaHomepage.html devoted to global financial crises. Visit the page and determine what are the latest developments in Japan and around the world.

16. *(Wall Street Journal)* This chapter pointed out that net exports are an important influence on aggregate demand. Find a story in today's *Wall Street Journal* that describes an event that will affect U.S. imports or exports. A good place to look is the "International" page in the first section of the *Journal*. Analyze the story you have chosen, and illustrate the event using both the aggregate expenditure line and the aggregate demand curve.

Appendix A

VARIABLE NET EXPORTS

This chapter has assumed that net exports do not vary with the level of income. A more realistic approach allows net exports to vary inversely with income. Such a model of net exports was developed in the appendix to Chapter 9. The resulting net export function is presented in panel (a) of Exhibit 6. Recall that the higher the income level in the economy, the more is spent on imports, so the lower the net exports. (If necessary, review the appendix to Chapter 9.)

Panel (b) of Exhibit 6 shows what happens when variable net exports are added to consumption, government

EXHIBIT 6

Net Exports and the Aggregate Expenditure Line

(a) Variable net-export function

(b) Aggregate expenditure lines

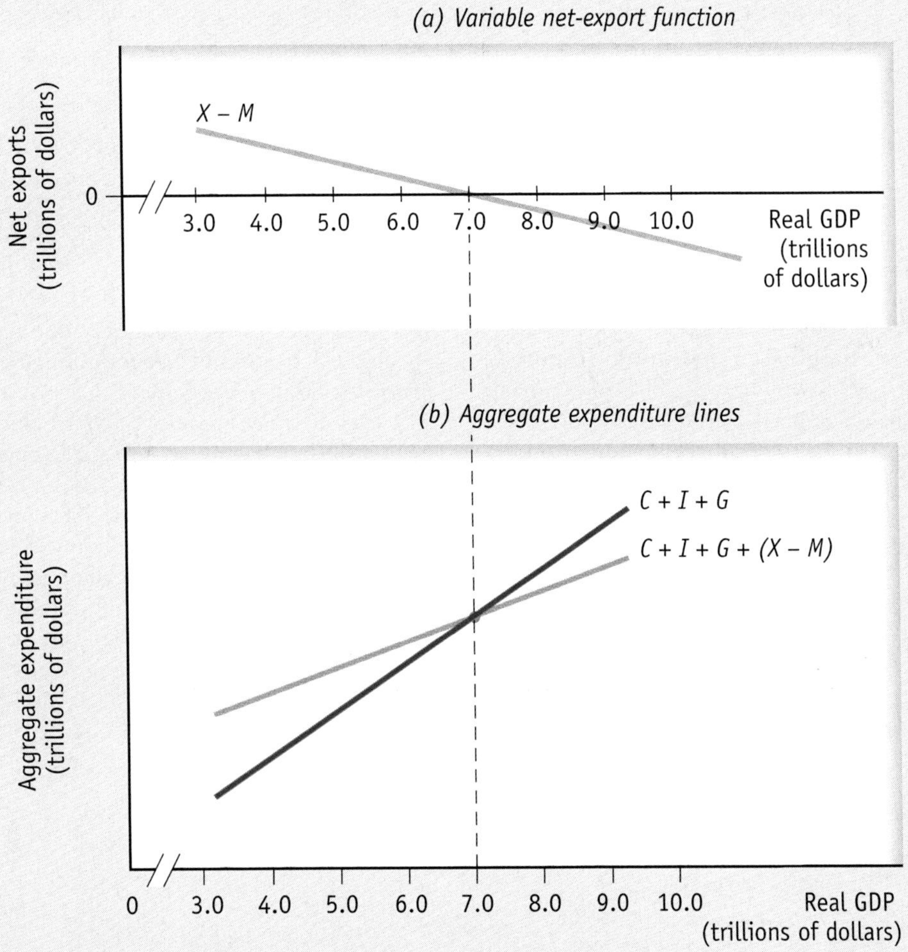

In panel (a), net exports, $X - M$, equal exports minus imports. Net exports are added to consumption, investment, and government purchases in panel (b) to yield $C + I + G + (X - M)$. The addition of net exports has the effect of rotating the spending line about the point where net exports are zero, which occurs where real GDP is $7.0 trillion.

purchases, and investment. We add the variable net export function to the $C + I + G$ spending function to derive the $C + I + G + (X - M)$ spending function. Perhaps the easiest way to see how the addition of net exports affects aggregate expenditure is to begin where real GDP equals $7.0 trillion. Since net exports equal zero when real GDP equals $7.0 trillion (which is also where disposable income equals $6.0 trillion, as shown in the appendix to Chapter 9), the addition of net exports has no effect on the aggregate expenditure line when real GDP is $7.0 trillion. Therefore, the $C + I + G$ and $C + I + G + (X - M)$ lines intersect where real GDP equals $7.0 trillion. At real GDP levels less than $7.0 trillion, net exports are positive, so the $C + I + G + (X - M)$ line is above the $C + I + G$ line. At income levels greater than $7.0 trillion, net exports are negative, so $C + I + G + (X - M)$ is below $C + I + G$. *Because variable net exports and real GDP are inversely related, the addition of variable net exports has the effect of flattening out, or reducing the slope of, the aggregate expenditure line.*

NET EXPORTS AND THE SPENDING MULTIPLIER

The inclusion of variable net exports makes the model more realistic but more complicated, and it requires a reformulation of the spending multiplier. If net exports are autonomous, only the marginal propensity to consume determines how much would be spent and how much would be saved as income increased. The inclusion of variable net exports means that as income increases, U.S. residents spend more on imports. The **marginal propensity to import**, or **MPM,** is the fraction of each additional dollar of disposable income that is spent on imported products. Imports are a leakage from the circular flow. Thus there are now two leakages that grow with income: saving and imports. The introduction of this additional leakage changes the value of the multiplier from 1/MPS to the

$$\text{spending multiplier with variable net exports} = \frac{1}{\text{MPS} + \text{MPM}}$$

The larger the marginal propensity to import, the greater the leakage during each round of spending and the smaller the resulting spending multiplier. Let's assume that the MPM equals about 1/10, or 0.1. If the marginal propensity to save is 0.2 and the marginal propensity to import is 0.1, then only 70 cents of each additional dollar of disposable income gets spent on output produced in the United States. We can compute the new multiplier as follows:

$$\text{spending multiplier with variable net exports} = \frac{1}{\text{MPS} + \text{MPM}} = \frac{1}{0.2 + 0.1} = \frac{1}{0.3} = 3.33$$

Thus the inclusion of net exports reduces the spending multiplier in our hypothetical example from 5 to 3.33. *Because some of each additional dollar of income is spent on imports, less is spent on U.S. products, so any given shift in the aggregate expenditure line has less of an impact on the quantity of output demanded.*

A CHANGE IN AUTONOMOUS SPENDING

What is the level of real GDP demanded, given the net export function described in the previous section, and how does income change when there is a change in autonomous spending? Let's begin in Exhibit 7 with an aggregate expenditure line of $C + I + G + (X - M)$, where net exports vary with income. This aggregate expenditure line intersects the 45-degree line at point e, determining real GDP demanded of $8.0 trillion. Suppose now that investment increases by $0.1 trillion at every level of income. This increase in investment will shift the entire aggregate expenditure line up by $0.1 trillion, from $C + I + G + (X - M)$ to $C + I' + G + (X - M)$, as shown in Exhibit 7. As you can see, output demanded increases from $8.0 trillion to $8.333 trillion, representing an increase of $0.333 trillion, or $333 billion, which is $0.1 trillion times the spending multiplier of 3.33. The derivation of the output level and the size of the multiplier are explained in Appendix B.

EXHIBIT 7

Effect of a Shift in Autonomous Spending on Real GDP Demanded

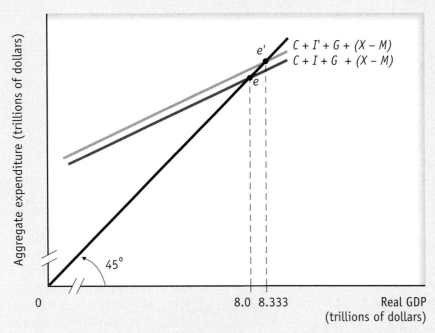

An increase in planned investment, other things constant, shifts the spending line up from $C + I + G + (X - M)$ to $C + I' + G + (X - M)$, increasing the quantity of real GDP demanded.

APPENDIX A QUESTIONS

1. *(Net Exports and the Spending Multiplier)* Suppose that the marginal propensity to consume (MPC) is 0.8 and the marginal propensity to import (MPM) is 0.05.
    a. What is the value of the multiplier?
    b. By how much would the equilibrium level of real GDP demanded change if investment increased by $100 billion?
    c. Using your answer to part (b), calculate the change in net exports caused by the change in aggregate output.

2. *(A Change in Autonomous Spending)* Suppose that when aggregate output equals zero, consumption equals $100 billion, autonomous investment equals $200 billion,

    government purchases equal $50 billion, and net exports equal $50 billion. Suppose also that MPC is 0.9 and MPM is 0.1.
    a. Construct a table showing the level of aggregate spending, net exports, and saving plus net taxes for aggregate output levels of zero, $500 billion, and $1,000 billion.
    b. Use autonomous spending and the multiplier to calculate the equilibrium level of real GDP demanded.
    c. What would be the new level of real GDP demanded if an increase in the U.S. interest rate caused net exports to change by $50 billion? Explain.

Appendix B

ALGEBRA OF INCOME AND EXPENDITURE

This appendix explains the algebra behind deriving aggregate output demanded. You should see some similarity between the presentation here and the circular-flow explanation of national income accounts.

THE AGGREGATE EXPENDITURE LINE

We first determine where aggregate expenditure equals real GDP and then derive the relevant spending multipliers, assuming a given price level. Initially let's assume net exports are autonomous. Then we'll incorporate variable net exports into the framework.

The quantity of aggregate output demanded occurs where aggregate expenditure equals real GDP. Aggregate expenditure is equal to the sum of consumption, C, investment, I, government purchases, G, and net exports, $X - M$. Algebraically, we can write the equality as

$$Y = C + I + G + (X - M)$$

where Y equals income, or real GDP demanded. To find where real GDP equals planned spending, we begin with the heart of the income-expenditure model: the consumption function. The consumption function used throughout this chapter was a straight line; the equation for this line can be written as

$$C = 0.9 + 0.8(Y - 1.0)$$

The marginal propensity to consume is 0.8, Y is income, or real GDP, and 1.0 is autonomous net taxes in trillions of dollars. Thus, $(Y - 1.0)$ is real GDP minus net taxes, which equals disposable income. The consumption function can be simplified to

$$C = 0.1 + 0.8Y$$

Consumption at each level of real GDP, therefore, equals $0.1 trillion (which could be called autonomous consumption) *plus* 0.8 times the level of real GDP, which is the marginal propensity to consume times income.

The second component of spending is investment, I, which we have assumed is autonomous and equal to $0.6 trillion. The third component of spending is autonomous government purchases, G, which we assumed to be $1.0 trillion. Net exports, $X - M$, the final spending component, we assumed to be –$0.1 trillion. Substituting the numerical val-

ues for each spending component in the aggregate expenditure line, we get

$$Y = 0.1 + 0.8Y + 0.6 + 1.0 - 0.1$$

Notice there is only one variable in this expression: Y. If we rewrite the expression as

$$Y - 0.8Y = 0.1 + 0.6 + 1.0 - 0.1$$
$$0.2Y = 1.6$$

we can solve for the level of real GDP demanded:

$$Y = \frac{1.6}{0.2}$$
$$Y = \$8.0 \text{ trillion}$$

A MORE GENERAL FORM OF INCOME AND EXPENDITURE

The advantage of algebra is that it allows us to derive the equilibrium quantity of real GDP demanded in a more general way. Let's begin with a consumption function of the general form

$$C = a + b(Y - NT)$$

where b is the marginal propensity to consume and NT is net taxes. Consumption can be rearranged to

$$C = a - bNT + bY$$

where $a - bNT$ is *autonomous* consumption—the portion of consumption that is independent of the level of income—and bY is *induced* consumption—that portion of consumption stimulated by the level of income in the economy. The quantity of GDP demanded equals the sum of consumption, C, autonomous investment, I, autonomous government purchases, G, and autonomous net exports, $X - M$, or

$$\text{income} = \text{expenditure}$$
$$Y = a - bNT + bY + I + G + (X - M)$$

Again, by rearranging terms and isolating Y on the lefthand side of the equation, we get

$$Y = \frac{1}{1 - b}(a - bNT + I + G + X - M)$$

The $(a - bNT + I + G + X - M)$ term represents autonomous spending—that is, the amount of spending that is independent of income. And $(1 - b)$ equals 1 minus the MPC. In the chapter we showed that $1/(1 - \text{MPC})$ equals the simple spending multiplier. One way of viewing what's going on is to keep in mind that autonomous spending is *multiplied* through the economy to arrive at the quantity of aggregate output demanded.

The formula that yields the quantity of aggregate output demanded can be used to focus on the origin of the spending multiplier. We can increase autonomous spending by, say, $1, to see what happens to real GDP demanded.

$$Y' = \frac{1}{1 - b}(a - bNT + I + G + X - M + \$1)$$

The difference between this expression and the initial one (that is, between Y' and Y) is $\$1/(1 - b)$. Since b equals the MPC, the simple multiplier equals $1/(1 - b)$. Thus, the change in equilibrium income equals the change in autonomous spending times the multiplier.

INTRODUCING VARIABLE NET EXPORTS

Here we explore the algebra behind variable net exports, first introduced in the appendix to Chapter 9. We begin with the equality

$$Y = C + I + G + (X - M)$$

Exports are assumed to equal $0.6 trillion at each level of income. Imports increase as disposable income increases, and the marginal propensity to import has been assumed to be 0.1. Therefore, net exports equal

$$X - M = 0.6 - 0.1(Y - 1.0)$$

After incorporating the values for C, I, and G presented earlier, we can express the equality as

$$Y = 0.1 + 0.8Y + 0.6 + 1.0 + 0.6 - 0.1(Y - 1.0)$$

which reduces to $0.3Y = \$2.4$ trillion, or $Y = \$8.0$ trillion. Algebra can be used to generalize these results. If m represents the marginal propensity to import, net exports become $X - m(Y - NT)$. The real GDP demanded can be found by solving for Y in the expression

$$Y = a + b(Y - NT) + I + G + X - m(Y - NT)$$

which yields

$$Y = \frac{1}{1 - b + m}(a - bNT + I + G + X + mNT)$$

The expression in parentheses represents autonomous spending. In the denominator, $1 - b$ is the marginal propensity to save and m is the marginal propensity to import. Appendix A demonstrates that $1/(\text{MPS} + \text{MPM})$ equals the spending multiplier when variable net exports are included. Thus aggregate output demanded equals the spending multiplier times autonomous spending. And an increase in autonomous spending times the multiplier gives us the resulting increase in aggregate output demanded.

APPENDIX B QUESTION

Suppose that $C = 100 + 0.75(Y - 100)$, $I = 50$, $G = 30$, and $X - M = -100$. What is the simple spending multiplier? What is the level of real GDP demanded? What would happen to real GDP demanded if government spending increased to 40?

Aggregate Supply

hat is your normal capacity for academic work and when do you usually exceed that effort? If the economy is already operating at full employment, how can it produce more? What valuable piece of information do firms and workers lack when they negotiate future wages? Why do workers and employers fail to agree on pay cuts that might save jobs? How might a long stretch of high unemployment reduce the economy's ability to produce in the future? These and other questions are answered in this chapter, which develops the aggregate supply curve in the short run and the long run.

Up to this point we have focused on the quantity of aggregate output demanded at a given price level. We have not yet introduced a theory of aggregate supply. Perhaps no other macroeconomic theory is subject to more debate. The debate involves the shape of the aggregate supply curve and the reasons for that shape. In this chapter, we will attempt to develop a single, coherent framework for aggregate supply.

Although our focus continues to be on economic aggregates, you should keep in mind that aggregate supply reflects billions of individual production decisions made by millions of individual resource suppliers and firms in the economy. Each firm operates in its own little world, dealing with its own suppliers and customers, and keeping a watchful eye on existing and potential competitors. Yet each firm also recognizes that success in part depends on the performance of the economy as a whole. The theory of aggregate supply we describe here must be consistent with both the microeconomic behavior of individual suppliers and the macroeconomic behavior of the economy. Topics discussed in this chapter include:

- Expected price level and long-term contracts
- Potential output
- Short-run aggregate supply
- Long-run aggregate supply
- Expansionary gaps and contractionary gaps
- Changes in aggregate supply

AGGREGATE SUPPLY IN THE SHORT RUN

As you know, *aggregate supply* is the relationship between the price level in the economy and the quantity of aggregate output firms are willing and able to supply, other things held constant. The other things held constant along a given aggregate supply curve include the supply of resources to firms, the state of technology, and the set of formal and informal institutions that structure production incentives, such as the system of property rights, patent laws, tax systems, and the customs and conventions of the market. The greater the supply of resources, the better the technology, and the more effective the production incentives provided by the economic institutions, the greater the aggregate supply. Let's begin by looking at the key resource: labor.

Labor Supply and Aggregate Supply

Labor is the most important resource, accounting for about 70 percent of production cost. The supply of labor in an economy depends on the size and abilities of the adult population and household preferences for work versus leisure. Along a given labor supply curve—that is, for a given adult population and given preferences for work versus leisure—the quantity of labor supplied depends on the wage rate. The higher the wage, other things constant, the more people are willing and able to work.

So far, so good. Things start getting complicated, however, once we recognize that the purchasing power of any given nominal wage depends on the economy's price level. *The higher the price level, the less any given dollar wage will purchase, so the less attractive that dollar wage is to workers.* Consider wages and the price level over time. Suppose a worker in 1970 was offered a job paying $20,000 per year. That salary may not impress you today, but, at the time, its real purchasing power was the equivalent of more than $75,000 in today's dollars.

Because the price level matters, we must distinguish between the **nominal wage**, which measures the wage in current dollars (the number of dollars on

Nominal wage The wage measured in terms of current dollars; the dollar amount on a paycheck

c. The higher the actual price level, the _____ is the real wage for a given nominal wage.
d. If nominal wages are growing at 2 percent per year while the annual inflation rate is 3 percent, then real wages change by _____ .

5. *(Contractionary Gaps)* After reviewing Exhibit 3 in this chapter, explain why contractionary gaps occur only in the short run and only when the actual price level is below what was expected.

6. *(Short-Run Aggregate Supply)* In interpreting the short-run aggregate supply curve, what does the adjective "short-run" mean? Explain the role of labor contracts along the SRAS curve.

7. *(Output Gaps and Wage Flexibility)* What are some reasons why nominal wages may not fall during a contractionary gap?

8. *(Contractionary Gap)* What does a contractionary gap imply about the actual rate of unemployment relative to the natural rate? What does it imply about the actual price level relative to the expected price level? What must happen to real and nominal wages in order to close a contractionary gap?

9. *(CaseStudy: Output Gaps and Wage Flexibility)* Unemployment is costly to employers, employees, and the economy as a whole. What are some explanations for the *coordination failures* that prevent workers and employers from reaching agreements?

10. *(Expansionary Gap)* How does an economy that is experiencing an expansionary gap adjust in the long run?

11. *(Long-Run Adjustment)* In the long run, why does an actual price level that exceeds the expected price level lead to changes in the nominal wage? Why do these changes cause shifts in the short-run aggregate supply curve?

12. *(Long-Run Aggregate Supply)* The long-run aggregate supply curve is vertical at the economy's potential output level. Why is the long-run aggregate supply curve located at this level of output rather than below or above the potential output level?

13. *(Long-Run Aggregate Supply)* Determine whether each of the following, other things held constant, would lead to an increase, a decrease, or no change in long-run aggregate supply.
a. An improvement in technology
b. A permanent decrease in the size of the capital stock
c. An increase in the actual price level
d. An increase in the expected price level
e. A permanent increase in the size of the labor force

14. *(Changes in Aggregate Supply)* What are supply shocks? Distinguish between beneficial and adverse supply shocks. Do such shocks affect the short-run supply curve, the long-run supply curve, or both? What is the resulting impact on potential GDP?

PROBLEMS AND EXERCISES

15. *(Real Wages)* In Exhibit 2 in this chapter, how does the real wage rate at point *c* compare with the real wage rate at point *a*? How do nominal wage rates compare at those two points? Explain your answers.

16. *(Natural Rate of Unemployment)* What is the relationship between potential output and the natural rate of unemployment?
a. If the economy currently has a frictional unemployment rate of 1 percent, structural unemployment of 2 percent, seasonal unemployment of 0.5 percent, and cyclical unemployment of 2 percent, what is the natural rate of unemployment? Where is the economy operating relative to its potential GDP?
b. What happens to the natural rate of unemployment and potential GDP if cyclical unemployment rises to 3 percent with other types of unemployment unchanged from part (a)?

c. What happens to the natural rate of unemployment and potential GDP if structural unemployment falls to 1.5 percent with other types of unemployment unchanged from part (a)?

17. *(Expansionary and Contractionary Gaps)* Answer the following questions on the basis of the following graph:
a. If the actual price level exceeds the expected price level reflected in long-term contracts, real GDP equals _____ and the actual price level equals _____ in the short run.
b. The situation described in part (a) results in a(n) _____ gap equal to _____ .
c. If the actual price level is lower than the expected price level reflected in long-term contracts, real GDP equals _____ and the actual price level equals _____ in the short run.

d. The situation described in part (c) results in a(n) _____ gap equal to _____.

e. If the actual price level equals the expected price level reflected in long-term contracts, real GDP equals _____ and the actual price level equals _____ in the short run.

f. The situation described in part (e) results in _____ gap equal to _____.

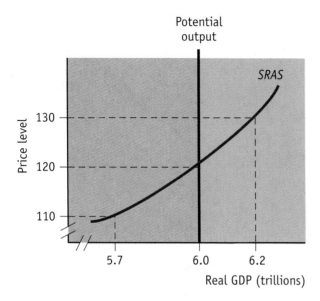

18. (*Long-Run Adjustment*) The ability of the economy to eliminate any imbalances between actual and potential output is sometimes called "self-correction." Using an aggregate supply and aggregate demand diagram, show why this self-correction process involves only temporary periods of inflation or deflation.

19. (*Changes in Aggregate Supply*) List three factors that can change the economy's potential output level. What is the impact of shifts in aggregate demand on potential output? Illustrate your answers with a diagram.

EXPERIENTIAL EXERCISES

20. (*Tracing Potential Output*) Although much of the theory is agreed upon, aggregate supply is still the most controversial topic in modern macroeconomics. To get a sense of some of the issues, read Stuart Weiner's brief article, "Challenges to the Natural Rate Framework," at http://www.kc.frb.org/publicat/econrev/er95q2.htm#Weiner. What are some of the challenges Weiner mentions and what evidence does he provide?

21. (*CaseStudy: Why is Unemployment So High in Europe?*) European unemployment is a hot topic. Use any Web browser (for example Alta Vista at http://www.altavist.com) to search for the words "European unemployment". Just by scanning the headlines, see how many possible explanations you can list. How do they compare to the explanations reviewed in the chapter case study?

22. (*Wall Street Journal*) In the short run, some workers' wages are determined by contracts, and some are not. The split between costs that change as production changes and those that do not is a key determinant of the shape of the short-run aggregate supply curve. To get a better feel for wage determination, look at the "Work Week" column in the first section of Tuesday's *Wall Street Journal*. Determine how some of the developments described there are likely to affect aggregate supply. Make sure that you distinguish between the short-run and the long-run effects. Draw a diagram to illustrate your conclusions.

Fiscal Policy

hat is the proper role of government taxing and spending in macroeconomic policy? How can fiscal policy curb swings in the business cycle? How might fiscal policy affect aggregate supply? Why has fiscal policy fallen on hard times in the last two decades? Why does introducing aggregate supply reduce the spending and tax multipliers? Under what circumstances are these multipliers zero? Answers to these and other questions are addressed in this chapter, which examines the theory and practice of fiscal policy.

During the 1992 presidential campaign, the candidates argued over the best way to revive the ailing economy, which at the time was barely recovering from the 1990–1991 recession. George Bush proposed tax cuts and a relatively smaller role for government. Bill Clinton proposed increases in government spending to be financed by tax increases on high-income earners. And Ross Perot wanted to reduce the huge federal budget deficits that had been a part of the fiscal landscape since the early 1980s. All three were talking about *fiscal policy*—the impact of government purchases, transfer payments, taxes, and borrowing on aggregate economic activity. In a more recent example of fiscal policy in practice, the Japanese government adopted a fiscal package in 1998 aimed at cutting taxes and increasing government purchases as a way to stimulate that troubled economy.

In this chapter, we first explore the effects of fiscal policy on aggregate demand. Next, we bring aggregate supply into the picture to consider the impact of taxes and government spending on the level of income and employment in the economy. We then examine the role of fiscal policy in moving the economy to its potential level of output. Finally, we review fiscal policy as it has been practiced since World War II.

Throughout the chapter, we use relatively simple tax and spending programs to explain fiscal policy. A more complex treatment, along with the algebra behind the numbers, appears in the appendix to this chapter. Topics discussed in this chapter include:

- Fiscal policy
- Discretionary fiscal policy
- Automatic stabilizers
- Lags in fiscal policy
- Limits of fiscal policy
- The supply-side experiment

THEORY OF FISCAL POLICY

Thus far, our macroeconomic model has viewed government as relatively passive. But U.S. government purchases and transfer payments at all levels today approach $3 trillion per year, making government an important player in the economy. From welfare reform to balancing the budget, fiscal policy affects the economy in myriad ways. We now move fiscal policy to center stage.

As introduced in Chapter 4, *fiscal policy* uses government purchases, transfer payments, taxes, and borrowing to affect macroeconomic variables such as employment, the price level, and the level of GDP. When economists study fiscal policy, they usually focus on the federal government, although governments at all levels have an impact on the economy.

The tools of fiscal policy can be divided into two categories: automatic stabilizers and discretionary fiscal policy. **Automatic stabilizers** are revenue and spending items in the federal budget that automatically change with the ups and downs of the economy so as to stabilize disposable income and, hence, consumption and real GDP. For example, the federal income tax is an automatic stabilizer because (1) it requires no congressional action to operate year after year and (2) it reduces the drop in income during recessions and reduces the jump in income during expansions. **Discretionary fiscal policy** requires ongoing decisions involving the deliberate manipulation of government purchases, taxation, and transfers to promote macroeconomic goals such as full employment, price stability, and economic growth.

Using the aggregate expenditure framework developed earlier, we will initially focus on the demand side to consider the effect of changes in government

Automatic stabilizers
Structural features of government spending and taxation that smooth fluctuations in disposable income, and hence consumption, over the business cycle

Discretionary fiscal policy
The deliberate manipulation of government purchases, taxation, and transfers in order to promote macroeconomic goals such as full employment, price stability, and economic growth

purchases, transfer payments, and taxes on the real quantity of GDP demanded. The short story is that *at any given price level, an increase in government purchases or transfer payments increases the amount of real GDP demanded, and an increase in taxes decreases the amount of real GDP demanded, other things constant.* In this section, we see how and why.

Changes in Government Purchases

Let's begin by looking at Exhibit 1, with real GDP demanded of $8.0 trillion, as reflected at point *a*, where the aggregate expenditure line crosses the 45-degree line. This equilibrium was determined in Chapter 10, where government purchases and net taxes each equaled $1.0 trillion and were assumed to be *autonomous*—that is, they did not vary with income. Since government purchases equal net taxes, the government budget is in balance at point *a*.

Now suppose government purchases increase by $0.1 trillion, or by $100 billion, assuming other things, including net taxes, remain constant. This additional spending shifts the aggregate expenditure line up by $0.1 trillion, to $C + I + G' + (X - M)$. Since, at real GDP of $8.0 trillion, planned spending now exceeds output, production must increase. This increase in production increases income, which in turn increases planned spending, and so it goes through a series of spending rounds.

The initial increase of $0.1 trillion in government purchases eventually increases the quantity of real GDP demanded at the given price level from $8.0 trillion to $8.5 trillion, shown as point *b* in Exhibit 1. Because output demanded increases by $0.5 trillion as a result of an increase of $0.1 trillion in government purchases, the government-purchases multiplier in our example is equal to 5. *As long as consumption is the only source of spending that varies with income, the multiplier for a change in government purchases, other things constant, equals*

EXHIBIT 1

Effect of a $0.1 Trillion Increase in Government Purchases on Aggregate Expenditure and Real GDP Demanded

As a result of a $0.1 trillion increase in government purchases, the aggregate expenditure shifts up by $0.1 trillion, increasing the level of real GDP demanded by $0.5 trillion.

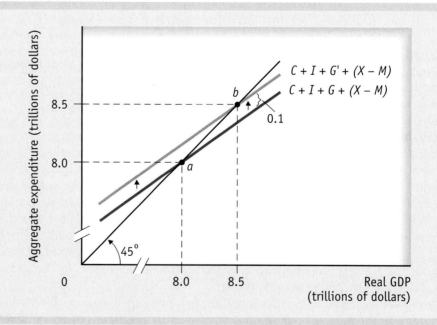

$1/(1 - \text{MPC})$, or $1/(1 - 0.8)$ in our example. Thus we can say that for a given price level, and assuming that only consumption varies with income,

$$\Delta \text{ real GDP} = \Delta G \times \frac{1}{1 - \text{MPC}}$$

where Δ means "change in". This same multiplier was discussed in Chapter 10, where we focused on shifts in consumption, investment, and net exports.

Changes in Net Taxes

A change in net taxes also affects the quantity of real GDP demanded, but the effect is less direct. A *decrease* in net taxes, other things constant, *increases* disposable income at each level of real GDP, so consumption increases. In Exhibit 2 we begin again at equilibrium point *a,* with real GDP equal to $8.0 trillion. To stimulate aggregate demand, suppose government cuts net taxes by $0.1 trillion, or by $100 billion, other things constant. We continue to assume that net taxes are autonomous—that is, that they do not vary with income. A $100 billion decrease in net taxes could result from a decrease in taxes, an increase in transfer payments, or some combination of the two. The $100 billion decrease in net taxes increases disposable income by $100 billion at each level of real GDP. Because households now have more disposable income, they spend more and save more at each level of real GDP.

But because households save some of the tax cut, consumption increases by less than the full tax cut. Specifically, *consumption spending at each level of real GDP*

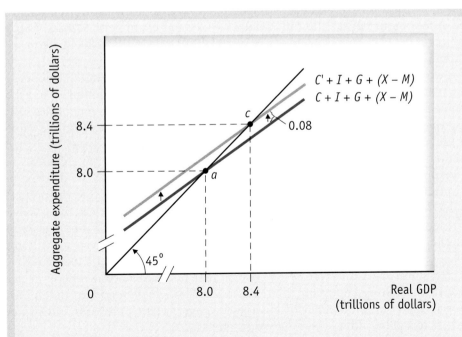

EXHIBIT 2

Effect of a $0.1 Trillion, or $100 Billion, Decrease in Autonomous Net Taxes on Aggregate Expenditure and Real GDP Demanded

As a result of a decrease in autonomous net taxes of $0.1 trillion, or $100 billion, consumers, who are assumed to have a marginal propensity to consume of 0.8, spend $80 billion and save $20 billion. The consumption function shifts up by $80 billion, or $0.08 trillion, as does the aggregate expenditure line. An $80 billion increase in the aggregate expenditure line eventually increases the level of real GDP demanded by $0.4 trillion. Keep in mind that the price level is assumed to be constant.

rises by the decrease in net taxes multiplied by the marginal propensity to consume. In our example, desired consumption spending at each level of real GDP increases by $100 billion times 0.8, or $80 billion. Decreasing net taxes by $100 billion causes the aggregate expenditure line to shift up by $80 billion at all levels of income, as shown in Exhibit 2. This initial increase in spending triggers subsequent rounds of spending, following a now-familiar pattern in the income-consumption cycle based on the marginal propensities to consume and to save. For example, the $80 billion increase in consumption increases output and income by $80 billion, which leads to $64 billion in consumption and $16 billion in saving, and so on through successive rounds. As a result, real GDP demanded eventually increases from $8.0 trillion to $8.4 trillion per year, or by $400 billion.

The effect of a change in net taxes on the quantity of real GDP demanded equals the resulting shift in the consumption function times the simple spending multiplier. Thus we can say that the effect of a change in net taxes is

$$\Delta \text{ real GDP} = (-\text{MPC} \times \Delta NT) \times \frac{1}{1 - \text{MPC}}$$

Here, the simple spending multiplier is applied to the shift in consumption that results from the change in net taxes. This equation can be rearranged as

$$\Delta \text{ real GDP} = \Delta NT \times \frac{-\text{MPC}}{1 - \text{MPC}}$$

Simple tax multiplier The ratio of a change in equilibrium real GDP demanded to the initial change in autonomous net taxes that brought it about; the numerical value of the simple tax multiplier is –MPC/(1 – MPC)

where $-\text{MPC}/(1 - \text{MPC})$ is the **simple tax multiplier,** which can be applied directly to the change in net taxes to yield the change in the quantity of real GDP demanded at a given price level (this tax multiplier is called *simple* because, by assumption, net taxes do not vary with income). For example, with an MPC of 0.8, the autonomous net tax multiplier equals −4. In our example, a *decrease* of $0.1 trillion in net taxes results in an *increase* in real GDP demanded of $0.4 trillion, assuming a given price level. As another example, an *increase* in net taxes of $0.2 trillion would, other things constant, *decrease* real GDP demanded by $0.8 trillion.

Note two differences between the government purchase multiplier and the simple tax multiplier. First, increases in government purchases and in net taxes have opposite effects on the level of real GDP demanded. Second, the absolute value of the multiplier for a given change in government purchases is larger by 1 than the multiplier for an identical change in net taxes. This holds because changes in government purchases affect aggregate spending directly—each $100 increase in government purchases increases spending in the first round by $100. In contrast, each $100 change in net taxes affects consumption indirectly by way of a change in disposable income. Thus, each $100 decrease in taxes or each $100 increase in transfer payments increases disposable income by $100, which, given an MPC of 0.8, increases consumption in the first round by $80; people save the other $20.

To summarize, an increase in government purchases or a decrease in net taxes, other things constant, increases real GDP demanded. Although not shown, the combined effect of changes in government purchases and in net taxes is found by adding their individual effects.

Thus far in this chapter, we have focused on the amount of real GDP demanded at a given price level. We are now in a position to bring aggregate supply into the picture.

INCLUDING AGGREGATE SUPPLY

In Chapter 11 we introduced the possibility that natural market forces may take a long time to close a contractionary gap. Let's consider the possible remedial effect of discretionary fiscal policy in such a situation.

Discretionary Fiscal Policy in Response to a Contractionary Gap

Let's begin with a short-run aggregate supply curve, as indicated by $SRAS_{130}$ in Exhibit 3. This supply curve implies that if the price level turns out to be 130, the economy will produce its potential level of output of $8.0 trillion. Suppose instead that the aggregate demand curve, AD, intersects aggregate supply at point e, yielding the short-run output of $7.5 trillion and price level of 125. Since output falls well short of the economy's potential, this opens a contractionary gap of $0.5 trillion, as Exhibit 3 shows, which increases unemployment to above the natural rate.

If markets adjust naturally to the resulting increase in unemployed resources, the nominal prices of resources would drop enough in the long run that the short-run aggregate supply curve would shift out to achieve an equilibrium at

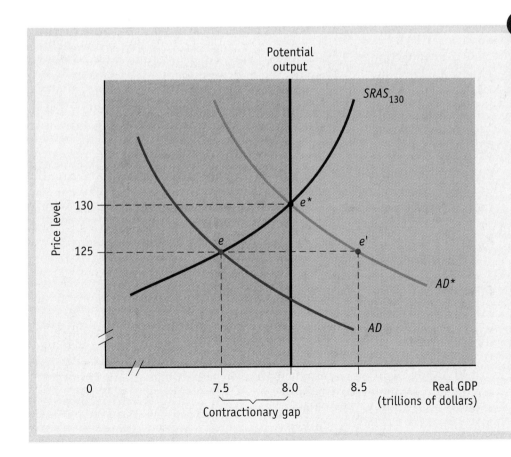

EXHIBIT 3

Discretionary Fiscal Policy to Close a Contractionary Gap

The aggregate demand curve, *AD*, and the short-run aggregate supply curve, $SRAS_{130}$, intersect at point *e*. Because the price level of 125 is below the expected price level of 130, the level of output falls short of the economy's potential. The resulting contractionary gap is $0.5 trillion. This gap could be closed by discretionary fiscal policy that increases aggregate demand by just the right amount. An increase in government purchases, a decrease in net taxes, or some combination of the two could shift aggregate demand to *AD'*, moving the economy to its potential level of output at *e**.

the economy's potential output. History suggests, however, that wages and other resource prices may be slow to adjust to a contractionary gap.

Suppose policy makers believe that the move back to potential output will take too long. If they introduce just the right fiscal stimulus through increased government purchases, reduced net taxes, or some combination of the two, they could increase aggregate demand enough to return the economy to its potential level of output. Suppose a $0.2 trillion increase in government purchases provides just enough fiscal stimulus to shift the aggregate demand curve to the right, as shown in Exhibit 3 by the shift from *AD* to *AD**. If the price level remains at 125, this additional spending will increase the quantity demanded from $7.5 to $8.5 trillion. This increase of $1.0 trillion reflects the simple multiplier effect, given a constant price level.

At the original price level of 125, however, there is an excess quantity demanded, which causes the price level to rise. As the price level rises, the quantity of real GDP supplied increases but the quantity of real GDP demanded decreases. The price level will rise until the quantity demanded equals the quantity supplied. In Exhibit 3, the new aggregate demand curve intersects the aggregate supply curve at *e**, where the price level is 130, the one originally expected, and output equals potential GDP of $8.0 trillion.

Since 130 was the price level on which producers originally based their production plans, the intersection at point *e** is not only a short-run equilibrium but also a long-run equilibrium. If fiscal policy makers are accurate enough (or lucky enough), they can provide the appropriate fiscal stimulus to close the contractionary gap and foster a long-run equilibrium at the economy's potential GDP. Note, however, that the increase in output is accompanied by a rise in the price level. What's more, if the federal budget was in balance before the fiscal stimulus, the increase in government spending creates a budget deficit. In fact, until recently, the federal government had been running substantial deficits each year since the early 1980s.

What if policy makers overshoot the mark, and aggregate demand turns out to be greater than needed to achieve potential GDP? In the short run, the economy will produce beyond its potential level of output. In the long run, firms and resource owners will adjust to the unexpectedly high price level. The short-run supply curve will shift back until it intersects the aggregate demand curve at potential output, increasing the price level further but reducing the level of output back to $8.0 trillion.

Discretionary Fiscal Policy in Response to an Expansionary Gap

Suppose the short-run equilibrium price level exceeds the level on which long-term contracts are based, so output exceeds potential GDP. In Exhibit 4, the short-run aggregate supply curve is again based on an expected price level of 130, but the aggregate demand curve, *AD'*, yields a higher actual price level. So the short-run level of equilibrium output is initially $8.5 trillion, an amount exceeding the economy's potential output of $8.0 trillion. The economy therefore faces an expansionary gap of $0.5 trillion. Ordinarily, this gap would be closed by an inward shift in the short-run aggregate supply curve, which would return the economy to the potential level of output but at a higher price level.

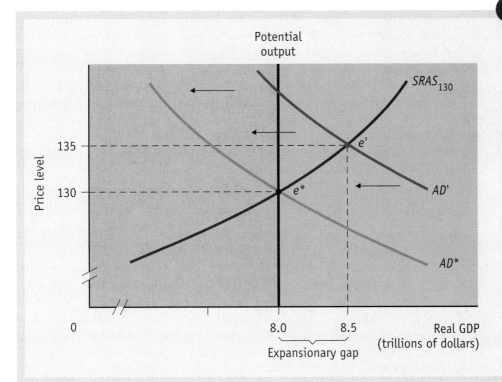

EXHIBIT 4

Discretionary Fiscal Policy to Close an Expansionary Gap

With the price level above the expected level of 130, there is an expansionary gap of $0.5 trillion. The gap could be eliminated by discretionary fiscal policy aimed at reducing aggregate demand by just the right amount. An increase in net taxes, a decrease in government purchases, or some combination of the two could shift the aggregate demand curve back to AD* and move the economy to potential output at point e*.

But the use of discretionary fiscal policy opens the door to another possibility. By reducing government purchases, increasing net taxes, or employing some combination of the two, the government can reduce aggregate demand, moving the economy to its potential level of output while avoiding an increase in the price level. If this policy is successful, the aggregate demand curve in Exhibit 4 will shift to the left from AD' to AD^*, and equilibrium will move from point e' to point e^*. Again, with just the right reduction in aggregate demand, output will fall to $8.0 trillion, the potential GDP. Closing an expansionary gap through fiscal policy rather than through natural market forces results in a lower price level, not a higher one. Increasing net taxes or reducing government purchases would also reduce a government deficit or increase a surplus.

Such precisely calculated fiscal policies as described here are hard to achieve, for their proper execution assumes that (1) the relevant spending multipliers can be predicted accurately, (2) aggregate demand can be shifted by the appropriate amount, (3) the potential level of output is accurately gauged, (4) various government entities can somehow coordinate their fiscal efforts, and (5) the shape of the short-run aggregate supply curve is known and will remain unaffected by the fiscal policy .

The Multiplier and the Time Horizon

In the short run, the aggregate supply curve slopes upward, so a shift in aggregate demand changes both the price level and the level of output. When aggregate supply gets in the act, the simple multiplier overstates the amount by which output changes. The exact change in equilibrium output in the short run depends on the steepness of the aggregate supply curve, which in turn depends on how sharply production costs increase as output expands. *The steeper the short-run aggregate supply curve, the less impact a given shift in the aggregate demand curve has on output and the more impact it has on the price level, so the smaller the spending multiplier.*

If the economy is already producing its potential output, then, in the long run, any change in fiscal policy aimed at stimulating demand will increase the price level but will not affect the output level. Thus, *if the economy is already producing its potential output, the spending multiplier is zero in the long run.*

You now have some idea of how fiscal policy can work in theory. Let's look at how it has been applied over the years.

THE EVOLUTION OF FISCAL POLICY

Classical economists A group of 18th- and 19th-century economists who believed that recessions were short-run phenomena that corrected themselves through natural market forces; thus they believed the economy was self-correcting

Before the 1930s, discretionary fiscal policy was seldom used explicitly to influence the performance of the macroeconomy. Prior to the Great Depression, public policy was shaped by the views of **classical economists**, who advocated *laissez-faire*, the belief that free markets were the best way to achieve national economic prosperity. Classical economists did not deny the existence of depressions and high unemployment, but they argued that the sources of such crises lay outside the market system, in the effects of wars, tax increases, poor growing seasons, and changing tastes. Such external shocks could reduce output and employment, but classical economists considered these to be short-run phenomena that would be corrected by natural market forces, such as changes in prices, wages, and interest rates.

Simply put, classical economists argued that if the economy's price level was too high to sell all that was produced, prices would fall until the quantity supplied equaled the quantity demanded; if wages were too high to employ all who wanted to work, wages would fall until the quantity of labor supplied equaled the quantity demanded; and if interest rates were too high to channel the amount saved into the amount invested, interest rates would fall until the amount saved equaled the amount invested.

So the classical approach implied that natural market forces, by way of flexible prices, wages, and interest rates, would move the economy toward its potential GDP. There appeared to be no need for government intervention in the economy. Before the onset of the Great Depression, most economists believed that an active fiscal policy would do more harm than good.

The Great Depression and World War II

Although classical economists acknowledged that capitalistic, market-oriented economies could experience temporary unemployment, the prolonged depression of the 1930s strained belief in the economy's ability to correct itself. As we discussed in Chapter 5, the Great Depression was marked by severe unemployment and much unused plant capacity. With abundant yet unemployed resources, output and income fell far short of the economy's potential.

The stark contrast between the natural market adjustments predicted by classical theory and the years of high unemployment during the Great Depression represented a collision of theory and fact. In 1936, John Maynard Keynes, of Cambridge University in England, published *The General Theory*, a book that challenged the classical view of the economy and touched off what has come to be called the Keynesian revolution. *Keynesian theory and policy were developed to address the problem of unemployment arising from the Great Depression.* Keynes's main quarrel with the classical economists was that prices and wages did not appear flexible enough to ensure the full employment of resources. According to Keynes, prices and wages were relatively inflexible—they were "sticky"—so natural market forces would not return the economy to full employment in a timely fashion. Keynes also believed business expectations might at times become so grim that even very low interest rates would not induce firms to invest all that consumers might save.

It is said that geologists learn more about the nature of the Earth's crust from one major upheaval, such as a huge earthquake or major volcanic eruption, than from a dozen more common events. Likewise, economists learned more about the economy from the Great Depression than from many more modest economic fluctuations. Even though this depression began seven decades ago, economists continue to sift through the data from that economic calamity, looking for hints about how the economy really works.

Three developments in the years following the onset of the Great Depression bolstered the use of discretionary fiscal policy in the United States. The first was the influence of Keynes's *General Theory,* in which he argued that natural forces would not necessarily close a contractionary gap. Keynes thought the economy could get stuck at a level of output that was well below its potential, requiring the government to increase aggregate demand so as to stimulate output and employment. The second development was the impact of World War II on output and employment. The demands of war greatly increased production and in the process eliminated cyclical unemployment during the war years, pulling the U.S. economy out of its depression. The third development, largely a consequence of the first two, was the passage of the Employment Act of 1946, which gave the federal government responsibility for promoting full employment and price stability.

Prior to the Great Depression, the dominant fiscal policy was to pursue a balanced budget. Indeed, to head off a modest federal deficit in 1932, a tax increase was approved, an increase that deepened the depression. In the wake of Keynes's *General Theory* and World War II, however, economists and policy makers grew more receptive to the idea that fiscal policy could be used to influence aggregate demand and thereby improve economic stability. No longer was the objective of fiscal policy to balance the budget but to promote full employment with price stability.

Automatic Stabilizers

So far this chapter has focused mostly on discretionary fiscal policy: conscious decisions to change taxes and government spending. Now let's get a clearer picture of automatic stabilizers. *Automatic stabilizers smooth fluctuations in disposable income over the business cycle, thereby boosting aggregate demand during periods of recession and dampening aggregate demand during periods of expansion.*

Let's look at the federal income tax. For simplicity, we earlier assumed net taxes to be independent of the level of income. In fact, the federal income tax system is progressive, meaning that the fraction of income paid in taxes increases as income increases. During an expansion, a growing fraction of income is claimed by taxes, slowing the growth in disposable income and, hence, the growth in consumption. Therefore, the progressive income tax relieves some of the inflationary pressure that might otherwise arise when output increases above its potential during an economic expansion. Conversely, when the economy is in recession, real GDP declines but taxes decline faster, so disposable income does not fall as much as real GDP. Thus the progressive income tax cushions declines in disposable income, in consumption, and in aggregate demand over the business cycle.

Another automatic stabilizer is unemployment insurance. During an economic expansion, the unemployment insurance system automatically increases the flow of unemployment insurance premiums from the income stream into the unemployment insurance fund, thereby moderating aggregate demand. During a recession, unemployment increases and the system reverses itself: Unemployment payments automatically flow from the insurance fund to those who become unemployed, thereby increasing their disposable income and propping up consumption and aggregate demand. Likewise, welfare spending automatically increases as more people become eligible during hard times. *As a result of these automatic stabilizers (1) real GDP fluctuates less than it otherwise would and (2) disposable income varies proportionately less than does real GDP.* And because disposable income varies less than real GDP, consumption also fluctuates less than does real GDP (as we saw in Exhibit 10 of Chapter 9). Because of the greater influence of automatic stabilizers, the economy is more stable today than it was during the Great Depression and before.

Unemployment insurance, welfare benefits, and the progressive income tax were initially designed not so much as automatic stabilizers but as income redistribution programs. Their beneficial roles as automatic stabilizers are secondary effects of the legislation. Automatic stabilizers do not eliminate economic fluctuations, but they do reduce their magnitude. The stronger and more effective the automatic stabilizers are, the less need there is for discretionary fiscal policy.

From the Golden Age to Stagflation

The 1960s were the Golden Age of fiscal policy. John F. Kennedy was the first U.S. president to put into practice the belief that a federal budget deficit could stimulate an economy experiencing a contractionary gap. He expanded the goals of fiscal policy from simply moderating business fluctuations to promoting long-term economic growth, and he set numerical targets of no more than 4 percent unemployment and no less than a 4.5 percent annual growth rate of output. Fiscal policy was also used on occasion to provide an extra kick to an expansion already under way, as in 1964, when Kennedy's successor, President Johnson, cut income tax rates to keep an expansion alive. *This tax cut, introduced to stimulate business investment, consumption, and employment, was perhaps the shining example of the successful use of fiscal policy during the 1960s.* The tax cut seemed to work wonders, increasing disposable income and consumption. The unemployment rate dropped below 5 percent for the first time in seven years, the inflation rate was under 2 percent, and the federal budget deficit in 1964 equaled only about 1 percent of GDP (compared to an average of 4 percent between 1982 and 1996).

Discretionary fiscal policy is a type of demand-management policy because the idea is to increase or decrease aggregate demand to smooth economic fluctuations. Demand-management policies were applied during much of the 1960s. But the 1970s were different. During the 1970s, the problem was stagflation—the double trouble of higher inflation and higher unemployment resulting from a decrease in aggregate supply. Aggregate supply dropped because of crop failures around the world, sharply higher oil prices, and other supply shocks. Demand-management policies were ill-suited to solving the problem of stagflation because an increase in aggregate demand would worsen inflation, whereas a decrease in aggregate demand would worsen unemployment.

Other concerns also caused economists and policy makers to question the effectiveness of discretionary fiscal policy: the difficulty of estimating the natural rate of unemployment, the time lags involved in implementing fiscal policy, the distinction between current and permanent income, and possible feedback effects of fiscal policy on aggregate supply. We will consider each of these concerns in turn.

Fiscal Policy and the Natural Rate of Unemployment

As we have seen, the unemployment rate that occurs when the economy is producing its potential GDP is called the *natural rate of unemployment.* For discretionary policy purposes, public officials must correctly estimate this natural rate. Suppose that the economy is producing its potential output of $8.0 trillion, as in Exhibit 5, and that the natural rate of unemployment is 5.0 percent. Also suppose that government officials believe the natural rate is 4.0 percent and they attempt to increase output and reduce unemployment through discretionary fiscal policy. As a result of the policy, the aggregate demand curve shifts to the

EXHIBIT 5

When Discretionary Fiscal Policy Overshoots

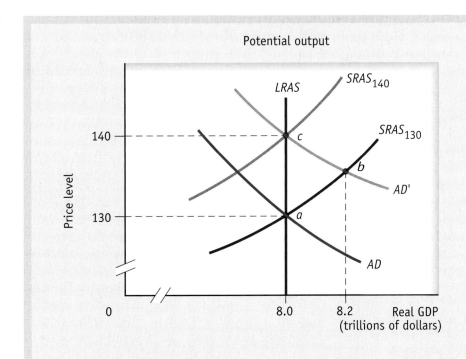

If public officials underestimate the natural rate of unemployment, they may attempt to stimulate aggregate demand even if the economy is producing its potential output, as at point *a.* In the short run, this expansionary policy yields a short-run equilibrium at point *b,* where the price level and output are higher and unemployment is lower, so the policy appears to succeed. But the resulting expansionary gap, will, in the long run, reduce the short-run aggregate supply curve from $SRAS_{130}$ to $SRAS_{140}$, eventually reducing output to its potential level of $8.0 trillion while increasing the price level to 140. Thus, attempts to increase production beyond potential GDP lead only to inflation in the long run.

right, from *AD* to *AD'*. In the short run this stimulation of aggregate demand expands output to $8.2 billion and reduces unemployment to 4.0 percent, so the policy appears to succeed. But stimulating aggregate demand opens up an expansionary gap, which in the long run pushes up the nominal price of resources, resulting in a leftward shift in the short-run aggregate supply curve from $SRAS_{130}$ to $SRAS_{140}$. This reduction in aggregate supply causes the price level to increase and the output level to fall back to the economy's potential of $8.0 trillion. Thus increases in output may temporarily persuade policy makers that their plan was a good one, but attempts to increase production beyond potential GDP in the long run lead only to inflation.

Lags in Fiscal Policy

The time required to approve and implement fiscal legislation may hamper its effectiveness and weaken discretionary fiscal policy as a tool of macroeconomic stabilization. Even if a fiscal prescription is appropriate for the economy at the time it is proposed, the months and sometimes years required to approve legislation and to implement the change mean the medicine could do more harm than good. The policy might kick in after the economy has already turned itself around. Since a recession is not usually identified as such until at least six months after it begins, and since the eight recessions since 1949 averaged only 11 months each, this leaves a narrow window in which to execute discretionary fiscal policy. (More will be said about timing problems in Chapter 16.)

Discretionary Policy and Permanent Income

It was once thought that discretionary fiscal policy could be turned on and off like a faucet, stimulating the economy at the right time and by just the right amount. Given the marginal propensity to consume, a relationship that is among the most stable in macroeconomics, tax changes could increase or decrease disposable income to bring about the desired change in consumption. A more recent view is that people base their consumption decisions not merely on changes in their current income but also on changes in their permanent income.

Permanent income Income that individuals expect to receive on average over the long term

   Permanent income is the income a person expects to receive on average over the long term. The short-term manipulation of tax rates to influence consumption will not have the desired effects as long as people view the tax changes as only temporary. In 1967, for example, at a time when the U.S. economy was producing its potential level of output, the escalating war in Vietnam increased military spending, pushing real GDP beyond its potential. The combination of a booming domestic economy and increased spending on a widening war produced an expansionary gap by 1968. That year, Congress approved a temporary tax *surcharge,* which raised income tax rates for 18 months. The idea behind this discretionary fiscal policy was to reduce disposable income, thereby reducing consumption and aggregate demand as a way of relieving inflationary pressure in the economy. But the reduction in aggregate demand turned out to be disappointingly small, and inflation was hardly affected. Although several factors help explain why higher taxes failed to reduce consumption, most economists agree that the *temporary* nature of the tax increase meant that consumers faced only a small decrease in their permanent income. Since permanent income changed little, consumption spending changed little. Consumers simply saved less. As another example, in late 1997 Japanese officials announced an income tax cut of about $15 billion, intended to stimulate Japan's flat economy. Economists were skeptical that the plan would work, largely because most people expected the cut to be repealed after a year.[1] In short, *to the extent that consumers base spending decisions on their permanent income, attempts to fine-tune the economy with tax-rate adjustments thought to be temporary will be less effective.*

Feedback Effects of Fiscal Policy on Aggregate Supply

So far we have limited our discussion of fiscal policy to its effect on aggregate demand. Fiscal policy may also affect aggregate supply, although often the effect is unintentional. For example, suppose the government increases unemployment benefits and finances these transfer payments with higher taxes on workers. If the marginal propensity to consume is the same for both groups, the reduction in spending by those whose taxes increase should just offset the increase in spending by transfer recipients. According to a theory of fiscal policy focusing on aggregate demand, there should be no change in aggregate demand and hence no change in equilibrium real GDP.

But consider the possible effects of these changes on labor supply. The unemployed, who benefit from increased transfers, now have less incentive to find work, so they may search at a more leisurely pace. Conversely, workers who find their after-tax wage reduced by the higher tax rates may be less willing to work extra hours or to work a second job since the higher marginal tax rates they face cut their opportunity cost of leisure. In short, the supply of labor could decrease as a result of offsetting changes in taxes and transfers. A decrease in the supply of labor would decrease aggregate supply, reducing the economy's potential GDP.

Both automatic stabilizers, such as unemployment insurance and the progressive income tax, and discretionary fiscal policy, such as changes in tax rates, may affect individual incentives to work, spend, save, and invest, although these effects are usually unintended. We should keep these secondary effects in mind when we evaluate fiscal policies. It was concern about the effects of taxes on the supply of labor that served as a basis for tax cuts introduced in 1981, as we will see next.

U.S. Budget Deficits of the 1980s and 1990s

In 1981, President Reagan and Congress agreed on a 23 percent reduction in average income tax rates and a major buildup in defense programs, with no substantial offsetting reductions in domestic programs. This tax cut reflected a supply-side philosophy that reductions in tax rates would make people more willing to work because they could keep more of what they earned. Lower taxes would increase the supply of labor and other resources in the economy, thereby increasing aggregate supply and the economy's potential GDP. In its strongest form, the supply-side theory held that enough additional real GDP would be generated by the tax cuts that total tax revenue would actually increase—a smaller share of a bigger pie would exceed a larger share of a smaller pie. What happened as a result of the tax cut? Let's examine events during the 1980s in the following case study.

---

1 See David Hamilton, "Japan's Prime Minister Slashes Taxes in Surprise Move to Boost Nikkei," *Wall Street Journal* (17 December 1997).

CaseStudy

Public Policy

The on-line magazine *Intellectual Capital* features a summary and two differing perspectives about supply-side economics in its October 10, 1996 issue at http://www.intellectualcapital.com/issues/96/1010/index.html. Supply-side economics emerged as an issue in the 1996 presidential campaign once Senator Dole chose ardent supply-side advocate Jack Kemp to be his running mate. First read the overview "Issue of the Week" article by Bob Kolasky for context. Then consider the different spins by Robert Shapiro of the Progressive Policy Institute and Stephen Moore of the Cato Institute. What does each side see as the factors that limit economic growth? What changes in public policies does each side advocate for promoting economic growth?

The Supply-Side Experiment

Taking 1981 to 1988 as the time frame for the examination, we can make some tentative observations about the effects of the federal income tax cut of 1981, which was phased in over three years. After the tax cut was approved but before it took effect, a recession hit the economy and the unemployment rate climbed to nearly 10 percent in 1982.

Although it is difficult to untangle the growth generated by the tax cuts from the cyclical upswing following the recession of 1981–1982, we can say that between 1981 and 1988 employment climbed by 15 million and unemployment fell by 2 million. Output per capita increased by about 2.0 percent per year between 1981 and 1988. This rate was higher than the 1.1 percent average annual increase between 1973 and 1981 but lower than the 2.2 percent annual growth rate between 1948 and 1973.

Does the growth in employment and in real GDP mean the supply-side experiment was a success? Part of the growth in employment and output could be explained by the economic stimulus provided by the huge federal deficits during the period. Although policy makers did not make a conscious decision to do so, their tax cuts, in effect, resulted in an expansionary fiscal policy. *The stimulus from the tax cut helped sustain a continued expansion during the 1980s—the longest peacetime expansion to that point in the nation's history.*

Despite the growth in employment, government revenues did not expand enough to offset the combination of tax cuts and increased government spending. Between 1981 and 1988, federal outlays grew at an average rate of 6.8 percent per year, and federal revenue grew at an average rate of 6.3 percent per year. So the tax cut failed to generate the revenue required to fund growing government spending. Prior to 1981, deficits had been relatively small compared to, say, GDP—typically less than 1 percent of GDP. But deficits grew to about $200 billion a year by the middle of the 1980s; relative to GDP, they averaged about 5 percent. These deficits were the largest the nation had ever experienced during peacetime. The recession of the early 1990s pushed the federal deficit up to 6 percent of GDP by 1992. *The national debt, which is the accumulation of annual deficits, more than quadrupled between 1981 and 1996.*

The extensive government borrowing during the 1980s pushed up U.S. interest rates, which attracted investment funds from abroad and increased the value of the dollar on foreign exchange markets. The ready supply of foreign capital meant that investment did not decline during the 1980s. High real U.S. interest rates, a strong dollar during the first half of the decade, and a stable political climate combined to make the United States a "safe haven" where foreigners could put their savings.

Sources: *Economic Report of the President*, February 1999; Herbert Stein, *The Fiscal Revolution in America*, 2nd ed. (Washington, D.C.: The AIE Press, 1996).

During the years of large federal deficits, the sum of U.S. consumption, investment, and government purchases exceeded U.S. income and output. How could this occur? Domestic spending could exceed domestic output because U.S. households, firms, and governments borrowed from abroad to help buy foreign goods. Since early 1976, U.S. imports have exceeded exports, and the resulting trade deficit has been financed in part by borrowing from abroad.

Given the effects of fiscal policy, particularly in the short run, we should not be surprised that elected officials might use discretionary fiscal policy to enhance their reelection prospects. Let's look at how political considerations may shape fiscal policies.

Discretionary Policy and Presidential Elections

After the recession of 1990–1991, the economy was slow to recover. At the time of the 1992 presidential election, the unemployment rate still languished at 7.5 percent, up two percentage points from where it stood in 1988, when President Bush was elected. The higher unemployment rate was too much of a hurdle to overcome and Bush lost to Clinton.

The link between economic performance and reelection success goes back a long way. Ray Fair of Yale University examined presidential elections dating back to 1916 and found that the state of the economy had a clear impact on the elections' outcomes. Specifically, he found that a declining unemployment rate and strong growth of real GDP per person during an election year increased the chances of election for the candidate of the incumbent party.

Another Yale economist, William Nordhaus, developed a theory of **political business cycles,** arguing that incumbent presidents use expansionary policies to stimulate the economy, often only temporarily, during an election year. They try to increase their chances of reelection by pursuing fiscal policies that reduce unemployment and increase output. For example, observers claim that President Nixon used expansionary policies to increase his chances for reelection in 1972.

The evidence to support the theory of political business cycles is not totally convincing. One problem is that the theory limits presidential motivation to reelection, when in fact presidents may have other policy objectives. For example, President Bush passed up an opportunity to sign a permanent tax cut for the middle class because that measure also called for tax increases on a much smaller group—upper-income taxpayers.

An alternative to the theory of political business cycles is that Democrats care relatively more about unemployment and relatively less about inflation than do Republicans. This view is supported by evidence indicating that during a Democratic administration, unemployment is more likely to fall and inflation is more likely to rise than during a Republican administration. Republican presidents tend to pursue contractionary policies soon after taking office and are more willing to endure a recession in order to reduce inflation. (The country suffered a recession in the second year of each of the last four Republican administrations.) Democratic presidents tend to pursue expansionary policies to reduce unemployment and are willing to put up with higher inflation to do so.

Sources: *Economic Report of the President,* February 1999; Ray Fair, "The Effects of Economic Events on Votes for President," *Review of Economics and Statistics* (May 1978): 159–172; and William Nordhaus, "Alternative Approaches to the Political Business Cycle," *Brookings Papers on Economic Activity* No. 2 (1989): 1–49.

*Case*Study

Public Policy

Beginning in 1998, President Clinton and the Republican Congress managed to move the federal budget from deficit to "surpluses as far as the forecasters can see." Could you have balanced the budget? Visit the Web site for the National Budget Simulation at http://garnet.berkeley. edu:3333/budget/budget.html and try your hand at the short game version. Descriptions of each category of spending can be found by clicking on the words to the right. What is the difference between spending and tax expenditure? Which types of spending are, in practical political terms, the least discretionary? Try to change interest payments. Why does the simulation give you only one option for this?

Political business cycles
Economic fluctuations that result when discretionary policy is manipulated for political gain

The large federal budget deficits of the 1980s and first half of the 1990s reduced the use of discretionary fiscal policy as a tool for economic stabilization. Because deficits were already large during economic expansions, it was hard to justify increasing deficits still more during a recession. For example, President Clinton proposed a modest stimulus package in early 1993 to boost the recovery that was under way. His opponents blocked the measure, arguing that it would increase the deficit.

Balancing the Federal Budget

Clinton did not get his way with the stimulus package, but he did manage to increase taxes substantially on high-income households in 1993. The Republican Congress elected in 1994 introduced more fiscal discipline on federal spending as part of a plan to balance the budget by the year 2002. Meanwhile the economy experienced a vigorous recovery fueled by growing consumer spending and rising business optimism based on the strongest stock market in history. The confluence of these events—tax increases on the rich, federal spending constraints, and a strengthening economy—changed the dynamic of the federal budget. Tax revenues gushed into Washington, growing an average of 8.0 percent per year between 1993 and 1998; federal spending remained in check, growing only 3.8 percent per year. By 1998 that one-two punch knocked out the federal deficit, a deficit that only six years earlier had topped $290 billion.

Toward the end of the 1990s, the U.S. economy performed extremely well. Whereas inflation and unemployment increased during the stagflation years of the 1970s, they both decreased during 1996, 1997, and 1998. During those three years, the U.S. inflation rate as measured by the CPI declined from 3.0 percent to 2.3 percent then to 1.6 percent; the unemployment rate dropped from 5.4 percent to 4.9 percent then to 4.5 percent. The inflation rate in 1998 was the lowest of any year since 1965, and the unemployment rate in 1998 was the lowest of any year since 1969. The declining unemployment rate boosted output; real GDP increased by 3.4 percent in 1996, and 3.9 percent in 1997 and in 1998. With the economy performing so well, there was no need to even consider using discretionary fiscal policy.

CONCLUSION

In this chapter we reviewed several considerations that reduce the size of the spending multiplier. In the short run, the aggregate supply curve slopes upward, so the impact on equilibrium output of any change in aggregate demand is blunted by a change in the price level. In the long run, the aggregate supply curve is vertical, so if the economy is already producing at its potential, the spending multiplier is zero. To the extent consumers respond primarily to changes in their permanent income, temporary changes in net taxes have less of an impact on consumption, so the net-tax multiplier will be smaller.

Throughout this chapter we assumed constant net taxes and constant net exports. In the real world, income taxes increase with income and net exports decrease with income. In the appendix to this chapter, we develop the spending multiplier that introduces these more realistic assumptions. The resulting spending multipliers and tax multipliers are smaller than those developed to this point.

Because of huge federal deficits between 1982 and 1996, discretionary fiscal policy had fallen out of favor. During this time, discretionary monetary policy took center stage as a tool of economic stabilization. Monetary policy is the regulation of the money supply by the Federal Reserve System. In the next three chapters we will introduce money and financial institutions, examine monetary policy, and discuss the impact of monetary and fiscal policy on economic stability and growth. After we introduce money, we will consider yet another reason why the simple spending multiplier is overstated.

SUMMARY

1. The tools of fiscal policy are automatic stabilizers and discretionary fiscal measures. Automatic stabilizers, such as the federal income tax, once implemented, operate year after year without congressional action. Discretionary fiscal measures require ongoing decisions about government spending and taxation.

2. The effect of a change in government purchases on aggregate demand is the same as that of a change in any other type of spending. The simple multiplier for government purchases equals $1/(1 - MPC)$.

3. A change in net taxes (taxes minus transfer payments) affects consumption by changing disposable income. A given change in net taxes does not affect spending as much as would an identical change in government purchases. The multiplier for a change in autonomous net taxes equals $-MPC/(1 - MPC)$.

4. An expansionary fiscal policy can close a contractionary gap by increasing government purchases or by reducing net taxes. Because the short-run aggregate supply curve slopes upward, an increase in aggregate demand will raise both output and the price level in the short run. Fiscal policy aimed at reducing aggregate demand in order to close an expansionary gap will reduce both output and the price level.

5. Fiscal policy focuses primarily on the demand side, not the supply side. The problems of the 1970s, however, resulted more from a decline in aggregate supply than from a decline in aggregate demand.

6. The tax cuts of the early 1980s were introduced as a way of increasing aggregate supply. But government spending grew faster than tax revenue, resulting in large budget deficits that stimulated aggregate demand, leading to the longest peacetime expansion up to that point in the nation's history. These huge deficits discouraged additional discretionary fiscal policy as a way of stimulating aggregate demand further, but recent success in erasing the deficit could spawn renewed interest in discretionary fiscal policy.

QUESTIONS FOR REVIEW

1. *(Fiscal Policy)* Define fiscal policy. Determine whether each of the following, other factors held constant, would lead to an increase, a decrease, or no change in the level of real GDP demanded:
   a. A decrease in government purchases
   b. An increase in net taxes
   c. A reduction in transfer payments
   d. A decrease in the marginal propensity to consume

2. *(The Multiplier and the Time Horizon)* Explain how the steepness of the short-run aggregate supply curve affects the government's ability to use fiscal policy to change real GDP.

3. *(Evolution of Fiscal Policy)* What did classical economists assume about the flexibility of prices, wages, and interest rates? What did this assumption imply about the self-correcting tendencies in an economy in recession? What disagreements did Keynes have with classical economists?

4. *(Automatic Stabilizers)* Often during recessions there is an increase in the number of young people who volunteer for military service. Could this rise be considered a type of automatic stabilizer? Why or why not?

5. *(Permanent Income)* "If the federal government wants to stimulate consumption by means of a tax cut, it should employ a permanent tax cut. If the government wants to stimulate saving in the short run, it should employ a temporary tax cut." Evaluate this statement.

6. *(Fiscal Policy)* Explain why effective discretionary fiscal policy requires information about each of the following:
   a. The slope of the short-run aggregate supply curve
   b. The natural rate of unemployment
   c. The size of the multiplier
   d. The speed with which self-correcting forces operate

7. *(Automatic Stabilizers)* Distinguish between discretionary fiscal policy and automatic stabilizers. Provide some

examples of automatic stabilizers. What is the impact of automatic stabilizers on disposable income as the economy moves through the business cycle?

8. *(Fiscal Policy Effectiveness)* Determine whether each of the following would make fiscal policy more effective or less effective:
   a. A decrease in the marginal propensity to consume
   b. Shorter lags in the effect of fiscal policy
   c. Consumers suddenly becoming more concerned about permanent income than about current income
   d. More accurate measurement of the natural rate of unemployment

9. *(CaseStudy: The Supply-Side Experiment)* Explain why it is difficult to determine whether or not the supply-side experiment was a success.

10. *(CaseStudy: Discretionary Policy and Presidential Elections)* Suppose that fiscal policy changes output faster than it changes the price level. How might such timing play a role in the theory of political business cycles?

11. *(Balancing the Federal Budget)* Now that the huge federal budget deficits of the 1980s and first half of the 1990s have been erased, why would policy makers be more inclined to use discretionary fiscal policy?

PROBLEMS AND EXERCISES

12. *(Changes in Government Purchases)* Assume that government purchases decrease by $10 billion, other factors held constant. Calculate the change in the level of real GDP demanded for each of the following values of the MPC. Then calculate the change if the government, instead of reducing its purchases, increased autonomous net taxes by $10 billion.
   a. 0.9   b. 0.8   c. 0.75   d. 0.6

13. *(Fiscal Multipliers)* Explain the difference between the government purchases multiplier and the net tax multiplier. If the MPC falls, what happens to the tax multiplier?

14. *(Changes in Net Taxes)* Using the income-expenditure model, graphically illustrate the impact of a $15 billion drop in government transfer payments on aggregate expenditure if the MPC equals 0.75. Explain why it has this impact. What is the impact on the level of real GDP demanded?

15. *(Fiscal Policy with an Expansionary Gap)* Using the aggregate demand–aggregate supply model, illustrate an economy with an expansionary gap. If the government is to close the gap by changing government purchases, should it increase or decrease those purchases? In the long run, what happens to the level of real GDP as a result of government intervention? What happens to the price level? Illustrate this on an AD–AS diagram, assuming that the government changes its purchases by exactly the amount necessary to close the gap.

16. *(Fiscal Policy)* This chapter shows that increased government purchases, with taxes held constant, can eliminate a contractionary gap. How could a tax cut achieve the same result? Would the tax cut have to be larger than the increase in government purchases? Why or why not?

17. *(Multipliers)* Suppose that investment, in addition to having an autonomous component, also has a component that varies directly with the level of real GDP. How would this affect the size of the government purchase and net tax multipliers?

EXPERIENTIAL EXERCISES

18. *(Fiscal Policy)* The University of Washington's Fiscal Policy Center at http://weber.u.washington.edu/~fpcweb/center/links.htm provides an extensive list of links about U.S. fiscal policy. Visit that site and use the links to determine what tax and spending proposals have been made in Congress during the past six months. Choose one of those proposals and use the AD–AS framework to explain its likely impact.

19. *(The Evolution of Fiscal Policy)* In the United States, fiscal policy is determined jointly by the president and Congress. The Congressional Budget Office at http://www.cbo.gov/index.html provides analysis to

Congress, and the Office of Management and Budget at http://www.whitehouse.gov/WH/EOP/OMB/html/ombhome.html does the same for the executive branch. Visit these Web sites to get a sense of the kinds of analysis these groups do and how they might be used in determining fiscal policy.

20. *(Wall Street Journal)* "Washington Wire" is a column that appears on the front page of the *Wall Street Journal* each Friday. Review the latest column to determine what fiscal policy proposals are under consideration. Do the proposals deal more with discretionary fiscal policy, or with automatic stabilizers? Are they designed to affect aggregate demand or aggregate supply?

Appendix

THE ALGEBRA OF DEMAND-SIDE EQUILIBRIUM

In this appendix, we continue to focus on aggregate demand, using algebra. In Appendix B to Chapter 10, we solved for real GDP demanded at a particular price level, then derived the simple spending multiplier for changes in spending, including government purchases. As derived in Appendix B to Chapter 10, the change in GDP demanded, here denoted as ΔY, resulting from a change in government purchases, ΔG, is

$$\Delta Y = \Delta G \times \frac{1}{1 - \text{MPC}}$$

The government spending multiplier is $1/(1 - \text{MPC})$. In this appendix, we first derive the multiplier for net taxes that do not vary with income. Then we incorporate variable net exports and proportional income taxes into the framework. *Note that multiplier effects assume a given price level, so we limit the analysis to shifts in the aggregate demand curve.*

NET-TAX MULTIPLIER

What is the effect on the quantity of GDP demanded of a $1 increase in net taxes that do not vary with income? We begin with Y, the equilibrium derived in Appendix B to Chapter 10:

$$Y = \frac{1}{1 - b} (a - bNT + I + G + X - M)$$

where b is the marginal propensity to consume and $a - bNT$ is that portion of consumption that is independent of the level of income (review Appendix B to Chapter 10 if you need a refresher).

Now let's increase net taxes by $1 to see what happens to the level of real GDP demanded. Increasing net taxes by $1 yields

$$Y' = \frac{a - b(NT + \$1) + I + G + X - M}{1 - b}$$

The difference between Y' and Y is

$$Y' - Y = \frac{\$1(-b)}{1 - b}$$

Since b is the marginal propensity to consume, this difference can be expressed as $1 times $-\text{MPC}/(1 - \text{MPC})$, which is the net-tax multiplier discussed in this chapter. With the MPC equal to 0.8, the net-tax multiplier equals $-0.8/0.2$, or -4, so the effect of increasing net taxes by $1 is to reduce GDP demanded by $4. For any change larger than $1, we simply scale up the results. For example, the effect of increasing net taxes by $1 billion is to reduce GDP demanded by $4 billion. A different marginal propensity to consume will yield a dif-

ferent multiplier. For example, if the MPC equals 0.75, the net-tax multiplier equals $-0.75/0.25$, or -3.

THE MULTIPLIER WHEN BOTH *G* AND *NT* CHANGE

Although in the chapter we did not discuss the combined effects of changes in both government purchases and net taxes, we can easily summarize these effects. Suppose that both increase by $1. We can bring together the two changes in the following equation:

$$Y^* = \frac{a - b(NT + \$1) + I + G + \$1 + X - M}{1 - b}$$

The difference between this equilibrium and Y (the income level before introducing any changes in G or NT) is

$$Y^* - Y = \frac{\$1(-b) + \$1}{1 - b}$$

which can be simplified to

$$Y^* - Y = \frac{\$1(1 - b)}{1 - b} = \$1$$

Equilibrium aggregate output demanded increases by $1 as a result of $1 increases in both government purchases and net taxes. This result is referred to as the *balanced budget multiplier*, which is equal to 1.

More generally, we can say that if ΔG represents the change in government purchases and ΔNT represents the change in net taxes, the resulting change in aggregate output demanded, ΔY, can be expressed as

$$\Delta Y = \frac{\Delta G - b\Delta NT}{1 - b}$$

The Multiplier with a Proportional Income Tax

A net tax of a fixed amount is relatively easy to manipulate, but it is not very realistic. Instead, suppose we introduce a **proportional income tax** rate equal to t, where t lies between zero and 1. Incidentally, the proportional income tax is also the so-called *flat tax* that has been discussed in Congress as an alternative to the existing progressive income tax. Tax collections under a proportional income tax equal real GDP, Y, times the tax rate, t. With tax collections of tY, disposable income equals

$$Y - tY = (1 - t)Y$$

We plug this value for disposable income into the consumption function to yield

$$C = a + b(1 - t)Y$$

To consumption, we add the other components of aggregate expenditure, I, G, and $X - M$, to get

$$Y = a + b(1 - t)Y + I + G + (X - M)$$

Moving the Y terms to the left-hand side of the equation yields

$$Y - b(1 - t)Y = a + I + G + (X - M)$$

or

$$Y[1 - b(1 - t)] = a + I + G + (X - M)$$

By isolating Y on the left-hand side of the equation, we get

$$Y = \frac{a + I + G + (X - M)}{1 - b(1 - t)}$$

The numerator on the right-hand side consists of the autonomous spending components. A $1 change in any of these components would change income by

$$\Delta Y = \frac{\$1}{1 - b(1 - t)}$$

Thus, the spending multiplier with a proportional income tax equals $1/[1 - b(1 - t)]$. Note that as the tax rate increases, the denominator increases, so the multiplier gets smaller. *The higher the proportional tax rate, other things constant, the smaller the multiplier.* Because a higher tax rate means a bigger reduction in disposable income, a higher tax rate reduces spending during each round of spending.

Including Variable Net Exports

The previous section assumed that net exports remained independent of the level of disposable income. If you have been reading the appendixes along with the chapters, you are already acquainted with how variable net exports fit into the picture. *The addition of variable net exports causes the aggregate expenditure line to flatten out, because net exports decrease as real income increases.* Real GDP demanded with variable net exports and a proportional income tax is

$$Y = a + b(1 - t)Y + I + G + X - m(1 - t)Y$$

where $m(1 - t)Y$ shows that imports are an increasing function of disposable income. The above equation reduces to

$$Y = \frac{a + I + G + X}{1 - b + m + t(b - m)}$$

The higher the proportional tax rate, t, or the higher the marginal propensity to import, m, the larger the denominator, so the smaller the spending multiplier. If the marginal propensity to consume is 0.8, the marginal propensity to import is 0.1, and the proportional income tax rate is 0.2, the spending multiplier would be about 2.3, or less than half our simple spending multiplier of 5.

Since we first introduced the simple spending multiplier, we have examined several factors that reduce that simple multiplier: (1) a marginal propensity to consume that responds primarily to permanent changes in income, not transitory changes, (2) a marginal propensity to import, and (3) a proportional income tax. The upward-sloping supply curve also reduces the effect of any given change in aggregate demand on equilibrium real GDP. After we introduce money in the next two chapters, we will consider additional factors that reduce the size of the spending multiplier.

APPENDIX QUESTIONS

1. *(The Algebra of Demand-Side Equilibrium)* Suppose that the autonomous levels of consumption, investment, government purchases, and net exports are $500 billion, $300 billion, $100 billion, and $100 billion, respectively. Suppose further that the MPC is 0.85, that the marginal propensity to import is 0.05, and that income is taxed at a proportional rate of 0.25.
   a. What is the level of real GDP demanded?
   b. What is the size of the government deficit (or surplus) at this output level?
   c. What is the size of net exports at the level of real GDP demanded?
   d. What is the level of saving at this output?

   e. What change in autonomous spending is required to change equilibrium real GDP demanded by $500 billion?

2. *(Spending Multiplier)* If the MPC is 0.8, the MPM is 0.1, and the proportional income tax rate is 0.2, what is the value of the spending multiplier? Determine whether each of the following would increase the value of the spending multiplier, decrease it, or leave it unchanged:
   a. An increase in the MPM
   b. An increase in the MPC
   c. An increase in the proportional tax rate
   d. An increase in autonomous net taxes

3. *(The Multiplier with a Proportional Income Tax)* Answer the following questions using the following data. Assume an MPC of 0.8.

Disposable Income	Consumption
$ 0	$ 500
500	900
1,000	1,300
1,500	1,700

a. Assuming that net taxes are equal to $200 regardless of the level of income, graph consumption against income (as opposed to disposable income).

b. How would an increase in net taxes to $300 affect the consumption function?

c. If the level of taxes were related to the level of income (i.e., income taxes were proportional to income), how would this affect the consumption function?

Money and the Financial System

Why are you willing to exchange a piece of paper bearing Alexander Hamilton's portrait and the number 10 in each corner for a pepperoni pizza with extra cheese? If Russia can't pay its bills, what's the problem with simply printing more rubles? Why are so few of the largest banks in the world American? How come someone was able to cash a check written on a pair of underpants? And why is there so much fascination with money, anyway? These and other questions are answered in this chapter, which introduces money and banking.

The word *money* comes from the name of the goddess in whose temple Roman money was coined. Money has come to symbolize all personal and business finance. You can read *Money* magazine and the "Money" section of *USA Today,* and you can watch TV shows such as *Moneyline, Moneyweek,* and

Your Money. You can articulate your preferences with money—after all, money talks. And when money talks, it has a lot to say, as in "put your money where your mouth is" and "show me the money." Money is the oil that lubricates the wheels of commerce. Just as oil makes for an easier fit among interacting gears, money reduces the friction—the transaction costs—of voluntary exchange. But too little oil can leave some parts creaking, and too much oil can gum up the works. Similarly, too little or too much money in circulation creates problems.

This chapter is obviously about money. We begin with the evolution of money, tracing its use from the most primitive economy to our own. Then we turn to monetary developments in the United States.

Topics discussed in this chapter include:

- Barter
- Functions of money
- Commodity and fiat moneys
- The Federal Reserve System
- Depository institutions
- Banking in the 1980s and 1990s

THE EVOLUTION OF MONEY

In the beginning there was no money. The earliest families were largely self-sufficient. Each family produced all it consumed and consumed all it produced, so there was little need for exchange. Without exchange, there was no need for money. When specialization first emerged, as some people went hunting and others took up farming, hunters and farmers had to trade. Thus the specialization of labor resulted in exchange, but the kinds of goods traded were limited enough that people could easily exchange their products directly for other products—a system called *barter.*

Barter and the Double Coincidence of Wants

Barter depends on a **double coincidence of wants,** which occurs only when a trader is willing to exchange his or her product for what another offers. If a hunter is willing to exchange hides for a farmer's corn, that's a coincidence. But if the farmer is also willing to exchange corn for the hunter's hides, that's a double coincidence—hence, the expression *double coincidence of wants.* As long as specialization was limited, say to two or three goods, mutually beneficial trades were relatively easy to discover—that is, trade wasn't much of a coincidence. As the economy developed, however, greater specialization in the division of labor increased the difficulty of finding the particular goods that each trader wanted to exchange. Rather than just two possible types of producers, there were, say, a hundred types of producers.

Double coincidence of wants A situation in which two traders are willing to exchange their products directly

In a barter system, traders must not only discover a double coincidence of wants, they must also agree on a rate of exchange—how many hides should be exchanged for a bushel of corn. If only two goods are produced, only one exchange rate has to be determined, but as the number of goods produced in the economy increases, the number of possible exchange rates grows quickly. Increased specialization raised the transaction costs of the barter system of exchange—exchange became more time-consuming and more cumbersome.

Sometimes differences between values of the units to be exchanged make barter difficult. For example, suppose the hunter wants to buy a home, which exchanges for 2,000 hides. The hunter would be hard-pressed to find a home seller in need of that many hides. These difficulties with barter led people, even in relatively simple economies, to use money.

Earliest Money and Its Functions

Nobody actually recorded the emergence of money. Thus we can only speculate about how it first came into use. Through experience accumulated from barter exchanges, traders may have found that they could easily find a buyer for certain goods. If a trader could not find a good that he or she desired personally, some good with a ready market could be accepted instead. So traders began to accept certain goods not for immediate consumption, but because these goods were readily accepted by others and therefore could be retraded later. For example, corn might become accepted because traders knew that it was always in demand. As one good became generally accepted in return for all other goods, that good began to function as **money.** *Any commodity that acquires a high degree of acceptability throughout an economy thereby becomes money.*

Money fulfills three important functions. Most importantly, it serves as a *medium of exchange.* Its function as a medium of exchange is what distinguishes money from other assets such as stocks, bonds, or real estate. Money also serves as a *unit of account* and a *store of value.* Let's consider each of these functions in turn.

Medium of Exchange. Separating the sale of one good from the purchase of another requires an item acceptable to all parties involved in the transactions. If a society, by luck or by design, can find one commodity that everyone will accept in exchange for whatever is sold, traders can save time, disappointment, and sheer aggravation. Suppose corn plays this role, a role that clearly goes beyond its usual function as food. We then call corn a medium of exchange because it is accepted in exchange by all buyers and sellers, whether or not they want corn to eat. A **medium of exchange** is anything that is generally accepted in payment for goods and services sold. The person who accepts corn in exchange for some product believes the corn can be used later to purchase whatever is desired.

In this example, corn both is a *commodity* and serves as *money,* so we call it a **commodity money.** The earliest money was commodity money. Consider some commodities used as money over the centuries. Cattle served as money, first for the Greeks and then for the Romans. In fact, the word *"pecuniary"* ("of or relating to money") derives from the Latin word *pecus,* meaning "cattle." Salt also served as money. Roman soldiers received part of their pay in salt; the salt portion was called the *salarium*—the origin of the word salary. The so-called precious metals—gold and silver—were long popular as commodity moneys. Other commodity moneys used at various times include tobacco and wampum (polished strings of shells) in colonial America, tea pressed into small cakes in Russia, and palm dates in North Africa. Whatever serves as a medium of exchange is called money—no matter what it is, no matter how it first came to serve as a medium of exchange, and no matter why it continues to serve this function.

Unit of Account. As one commodity, such as corn or tobacco, becomes widely accepted, the prices of all other goods come to be quoted in terms of that good. The chosen commodity becomes a common **unit of account,** a standard unit for quoting prices. If the price of shoes or pots is expressed in terms of bushels of corn, corn not only serves as a medium of exchange, it also becomes a com-

Money Anything that is generally accepted in exchange for goods and services

Medium of exchange Anything that facilitates trade by being generally accepted by all parties in payment for goods or services

Commodity money Anything that serves both as money and as a commodity

Unit of account A common unit for measuring the value of every good or service

mon denominator, a yardstick, for measuring the value of all goods and services. Rather than having to quote the rate of exchange for each good in terms of every other good, as is the case in a barter economy, people can measure the price of everything in terms of a common denominator, such as corn. For example, if a pair of shoes sells for two bushels of corn and a five-gallon pot sells for one bushel of corn, then one pair of shoes has the same value in exchange as two five-gallon pots.

Store of Value. Because people often do not want to make purchases at the time they sell something, the purchasing power acquired through a sale must somehow be preserved. Money serves as a **store of value** when it retains purchasing power over time. The better money is at preserving purchasing power, the better it serves as a store of value.

> **Store of value** Anything that retains its purchasing power over time

At this point it is useful to recall the distinction between a stock and a flow. Recall that a *stock* is an amount measured at a particular point in time, such as the amount of food in your refrigerator, the amount of money you have with you right now, or the amount of gasoline in your car's tank. In contrast, a *flow* is an amount per unit of time, such as the calories you consume per day, the income you earn per week, or the miles you drive per month. *Money* is a stock and *income* is a flow. Money is a medium of exchange and income is a reward for supplying services. Don't confuse money with income. The role of money as a stock is best reflected by money's role as a store of value.

Problems with Commodity Money

There are problems with most commodity moneys. *First,* if a commodity is perishable, such as corn or tobacco, it must be properly stored or its quality deteriorates; even then, it will not maintain its quality for long. *Second,* if a commodity is bulky, exchanges for major purchases are unwieldy. For example, if a new home cost 40,000 bushels of corn, many truckloads of corn would be needed to purchase one. *Third,* commodity money may not be easily divisible into smaller units. For example, when cattle served as money, any price that amounted to a fraction of a cow posed an exchange problem.

Fourth, if all of a particular commodity such as corn or tobacco is valued equally in exchange, regardless of quality, people will tend to keep the best and trade away the rest. As a result, the quality of the commodity in circulation will decline, reducing its acceptability. Sir Thomas Gresham noticed back in the 16th century that "bad money drives out good money," and this has come to be known as **Gresham's Law.** People tend to trade away inferior money and hoard the best; over time the supply of money shrinks and the quality that remains in circulation becomes less acceptable.

> **Gresham's Law** People tend to trade away inferior money and hoard the best

Fifth, commodity money usually ties up otherwise valuable resources as money, so commodity money has a relatively high opportunity cost, compared with, say, paper money. For example, gold that is used for money cannot at the same time be used to make jewelry, dental fillings, and so on.

A final problem of commodity money is that its value depends on its supply and demand, which may vary unpredictably. For example, if a bumper crop increased the supply of corn, corn as a medium of exchange would become less valuable, so more corn would be needed to exchange for any other good. This is what we call *inflation.* Likewise, any change in the demand for corn *as food,* such as occurred with the development of corn chips, would alter the amount available as a medium of exchange, and this, too, would affect the value of corn. Erratic fluctuations in the market for corn limit its usefulness as money, particularly as a unit of account and a store of value.

If people cannot rely on the value of corn over time, they will be reluctant to hold it or to enter contracts in terms of corn for future payment or receipt. More generally, *since the value of money depends on its supply being limited, anything that can be easily gathered or produced does not serve well as a commodity money.* For example, tree leaves or common rocks would not serve well as a commodity money. What all this boils down to is that *the best money is durable, portable, divisible, and of uniform quality, and has a low opportunity cost, and yet its supply can be carefully controlled.*

Coins

The division of commodity money into units was often quite natural, as in bushels of corn or heads of cattle. When rock salt was used as money, it was cut into uniform bricks. Since salt was usually of consistent quality, a trader had only to count the bricks to determine the amount of money. When silver and gold were used as commodity money, both their quantity and quality were open to question. Because precious metals could be *debased* by being alloyed with cheaper metals, the quantity and the quality of the metal had to be ascertained with each exchange.

This quality-control problem was addressed by coining the metal. *Coinage determined both the amount and quality of the metal.* The use of coins allowed payment by count rather than by weight. A table on which this money was counted came to be called the *counter,* a term still used today. Initially, coins were stamped on one side only, but undetectable amounts of the metal could be shaved from the smooth side of the coin. To prevent such shaving, coins were stamped on both sides. But another problem arose: small amounts of the metal could be clipped from the edges. To prevent clipping, coins were bordered with a well-defined rim and were milled around the edges. If you have a dime or a quarter, notice the tiny serrations on the edge and the words along the border. These features, throwbacks from the time when these coins were silver rather than cheaper metals, reduced one's chances of "getting clipped."

The power to coin was vested in the *seignior,* or feudal lord. The power to coin money was considered an act of sovereignty, and counterfeiting was an act of treason. If the face value of the coin exceeded the cost of coinage, the minting of coins became a source of revenue to the seignior. **Seigniorage** (pronounced *seen´-your-edge*) refers to the revenue earned from coinage by the seignior. **Token money** is money whose face value exceeds the value of the material from which it is made. Coins (and paper money) now in circulation in the United States are token money. For example, the 25-cent coin costs the U.S. Mint only about 3 cents to make. The Mint nets about $500 million per year from coin production.

Money and Banking

The word *bank* comes from the Italian word *banca,* meaning "bench," since Italian money changers originally conducted their business on benches. Banking spread from Italy to England, where London goldsmiths offered the community

Seigniorage The difference between the face value of money and the cost of supplying it; the "profit" from issuing money

Token money The name given to money whose face value exceeds the cost of producing it

"safekeeping" for money and other valuables. The goldsmiths had to give depositors their money back on request, but since withdrawals by some individuals tended to be offset by deposits by others, the amount of idle cash, or gold, in the vault usually remained relatively constant over time. Goldsmiths found that they could earn interest by making loans from this pool of idle cash.

Keeping money on deposit with a goldsmith was safer than leaving it where it could be easily stolen, but visiting the goldsmith each time money was needed was a nuisance. For example, a farmer might visit the goldsmith to withdraw enough money to buy a horse. The farmer would then pay the horse trader, who would promptly deposit the receipts with the goldsmith. Thus, money took a round trip from goldsmith to farmer to horse trader and back to goldsmith. Depositors grew tired of going to the goldsmith every time they needed to make a purchase, so goldsmiths instituted a practice whereby a purchaser, such as the farmer, could write the goldsmith instructions to pay someone else, such as the horse trader, a given amount from the purchaser's account. The payment amounted to having the goldsmith move gold from one stack (the farmer's) to another (the horse trader's). *These written instructions to the goldsmith were the first checks.* Checks have since become official-looking instruction forms, but they need not be, as evidenced by the actions of a Montana man who paid a speeding fine with a check written on a clean but frayed pair of underpants. The Western Federal Savings and Loan of Missoula honored the check.[1]

By combining the ideas of cash loans and checks, the goldsmith soon discovered how to make loans by check. Rather than lend idle cash, the goldsmith could create a checking account for the borrower. *The goldsmith could extend a loan by creating an account against which the borrower could write checks. In this way goldsmiths, or banks, were able to create a medium of exchange, or to "create money."* This money, though based only on an entry in the goldsmith's ledger, was accepted because of the public's confidence that these claims would be honored.

The total claims against the goldsmith consisted of claims by people who had deposited their money with the goldsmith plus claims created when the goldsmith extended loans. Because these claims exceeded the value of gold on reserve, this was the beginning of a **fractional reserve banking system,** a system in which the goldsmith's reserves amounted to only a fraction of claims against the goldsmith, or total deposits. The *reserve ratio* measures reserves as a proportion of total claims against the goldsmith, or total deposits. For example, if the goldsmith had gold reserves valued at $5,000 but deposits totaling $10,000, the reserve ratio would be 50 percent.

Paper Money

Another way a bank could create money was to issue bank notes. **Bank notes** were pieces of paper promising the bearer specific amounts of gold or silver when the notes were presented to the issuing bank for redemption. In London, goldsmith bankers introduced bank notes about the same time they introduced checks. *Whereas checks could be redeemed only if endorsed by the payee, notes could be redeemed by anyone who presented them.* Paper money was often "as good as gold,"

1 As reported in "Legal Briefs," *Newsweek* (3 Feburary 1992): 7.

Fractional reserve banking system A banking system in which only a portion of deposits is backed by reserves

Bank notes Papers promising a specific amount of gold or silver to bearers who presented them to issuing banks for redemption; an early type of money since the bearer could redeem it for gold. In fact, paper money was more convenient than gold because it took up less space and was easier to carry.

The amount of paper money issued by a bank depended on that bank's estimate of the proportion of notes that would be redeemed. The greater the redemption rate, the fewer notes could be issued based on a given amount of reserves. Initially, these promises to pay were issued by private individuals or banks, but over time governments took a larger role in printing and circulating notes.

Once paper money became widely accepted, it was perhaps inevitable that governments would begin issuing **fiat money,** which consists of paper money that derives its status as money from the power of the state, or by *fiat*. Fiat (pronounced *fee'at*) money is money because the government says it is money. The word is from the Latin, meaning "let it be done." Fiat money is not redeemable for anything other than more fiat money; it is not backed by a promise to pay something of intrinsic value. You can think of fiat money as mere paper money. It is acceptable not because it is intrinsically useful or valuable—as corn or gold is—but because the government requires that it be accepted as payment. Fiat money is declared to be **legal tender** by the government, meaning that creditors must accept it as payment for debts. *Gradually, people came to accept fiat money because they believed that others would accept it as well.* The currency issued in the United States today, and indeed paper money throughout most of the world, is fiat money.

In a way, a well-regulated system of fiat money is more efficient for an economy than commodity money. Fiat money uses only paper (the cost of labor and material per bill is about five cents), whereas commodity money requires that valuable commodities be used directly or held in reserve to support the system. As we shall see in the next chapter, paper money makes up only a small fraction of the total money supply. Most modern money consists of checking accounts, which amount to little more than electronic entries in the computers of the nation's banking system.

The Value of Money

Money has grown increasingly more abstract—from a physical commodity, to a piece of paper representing a claim on a physical commodity, to a piece of paper of no intrinsic value, to an electronic entry representing a claim on a piece of paper of no intrinsic value. So why does money have value? The commodity feature of early money bolstered confidence in its acceptability. Commodities such as corn and tobacco had value in use even if for some reason they became less acceptable in exchange. When paper money came into use, its acceptability was initially fostered by the promise to redeem it for gold, silver, or other items of value. But since most paper money throughout the world is now fiat money, there is no promise of redemption. So how come a piece of paper bearing the portrait of Alexander Hamilton and the number 10 in each corner can be exchanged for a large pepperoni pizza or anything else selling for $10? *People accept these pieces of paper because they believe others will do so.*

The value of money reflects in its *purchasing power:* the rate at which money exchanges for goods and services. The higher the price level, the

Fiat money Money not redeemable for any commodity; its status as money is conferred by the government

Legal tender Anything that creditors are required to accept as payment for debts

EXHIBIT 1

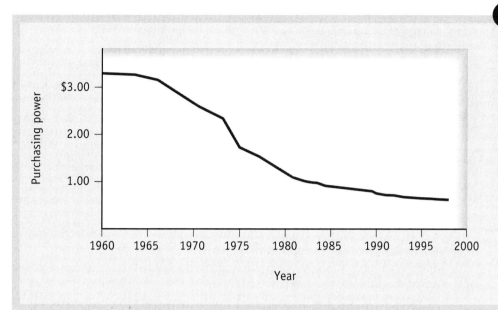

Purchasing Power of a Dollar Measured in 1982–1984 Constant Dollars

An increase in the price level reduces the amount of goods and services that can be purchased with a dollar. Since 1960, the price level has risen every year, so the purchasing power of the dollar has fallen continually.

Source: *Economic Report of the President*, February 1999.

fewer goods and services that can be purchased with each dollar, so the less each dollar is worth. The purchasing power of each dollar over time varies inversely with changes in the price level. As the price level increases, the purchasing power of money falls. To measure the purchasing power of the dollar in a particular year, first compute the price index for that year, then divide 100 by that price index. For example, relative to the base period of 1982–1984, the consumer price index for January 1999 was 164.3. The purchasing power of a dollar was therefore 100/164.3, or about $0.61, measured in 1982–1984 dollars. Exhibit 1 chronicles the steady decline since 1960 in the value of the dollar.

When Money Performs Poorly

One way to understand the functions of money is to look at situations in which money did not perform these functions well. In Chapter 7, we examined hyperinflation in Brazil. With prices growing by the hour, money no longer represented a stable store of value, so people couldn't wait to exchange rapidly inflating money for goods or for a "harder" currency—that is, one whose value was relatively stable. And with the price level rising rapidly, some merchants were quicker to raise their prices than others, so relative prices became distorted. Thus, money became less useful as a unit of account, or as a way of comparing the price of one good to that of another.

At some point, the inflation rate may become so high that people will no longer accept the nation's money and instead will resort to barter. Likewise, if the supply of money dries up because of hoarding or if the price system is not allowed to function properly, barter may be the only remaining alternative. The following case study discusses instances when money performed poorly.

CaseStudy

Other Times, Other Places

Are U.S. dollars still flowing into Russia? Find out from the Bank of Russia's statistics page at http://www.cbr.ru/ eng/system/statistics.html. Look under "Foreign Currency Brought into and Taken out of the Russian Federation by Authorised Banks" to see how the flow of dollars has changed over time. For an Internet guide to Russian banks and finance, visit *Russia on the Net* at http://www.ru/.

When the Monetary Systems Break Down

After Germany lost World War II, money in that country became almost useless because, despite tremendous inflationary pressure in the economy, those who won the war imposed strict price controls. Since prices were set well below what people thought they should be, sellers stopped accepting money, and this forced people to barter. Experts estimate that because of the lack of a viable medium of exchange, the German economy produced only half the output that it would have produced with a smoothly functioning monetary system. The "economic miracle" that occurred in Germany immediately after 1948 can be credited in large part to that country's adoption of a reliable monetary system.

Money became extremely scarce during the 19th century in Brazil because of a copper shortage. Money-financed transactions were difficult because copper coins could no longer be minted, and people hoarded rather than traded the limited supply of coins. In response to this crisis, some merchants and tavern-keepers printed vouchers redeemable for goods and services. These vouchers circulated as money until copper coins reappeared. Similarly, people dealt with the shortage of money in the early American colonies by keeping careful records, showing who owed what to whom.

For a more recent example, consider Panama, a Central American country that relies on the U.S. dollar as a medium of exchange. In 1988, the United States, in response to charges that the leader of Panama was involved in drug dealing, froze Panamanian assets in the United States. This touched off a panic in Panama as bank depositors tried to withdraw their funds; banks were forced to close for nine weeks. Dollars were hoarded, so people resorted to barter. Because barter is much less efficient than a smoothly functioning monetary system, Panama's GDP reportedly fell by 30 percent in 1988.

In Russia, the hyperinflation of the ruble following the breakup of the Soviet Union increased Russian demand for so-called hard currencies, especially the dollar. A Russian central banker estimated that in 1995 the value of Russians' dollar holdings exceeded the value of their ruble holdings. In keeping with Gresham's Law, Russians preferred to trade their rubles and hoard their dollars.

Sources: Peter White, "The Power of Money," *National Geographic* (January 1993): 80–107; Frederic Dannen and Ira Silverman, "The Supernote," *New Yorker* (23 October 1995): 50–55; and "Russia Official Nods to Money Boost," *New York Times* (30 September 1998).

Thus, when the supply of money shrinks as a result of hoarding or when the official money fails to serve as a medium of exchange, some other mechanism often emerges to facilitate exchange. But because more resources must be diverted from production to exchange, this second-best alternative is seldom as efficient as a smoothly functioning monetary system. A poorly functioning monetary system results in higher transaction costs. *It has been said that no machine increases the economy's productivity as much as properly functioning money.* Indeed, it seems hard to overstate the value of a reliable monetary system.

Let's turn now to a discussion of the U.S. monetary system, beginning with the development of money and banking in the United States.

FINANCIAL INSTITUTIONS IN THE UNITED STATES

You have already learned about the origin of modern banks: Goldsmiths lent money from deposits they held for safekeeping. So you already have some idea of how banks operate. Recall from the circular flow model discussed earlier that household saving flows into financial markets, where it is lent to investors. Financial institutions accumulate funds from savers and lend these funds to borrowers, thereby serving as intermediaries between savers and borrowers. Financial institutions, or **financial intermediaries,** earn a profit by "buying low and selling high"—that is, by paying a lower interest rate to savers than they charge borrowers.

Financial intermediaries Institutions that serve as go-betweens, accepting funds from savers and lending them to borrowers

Commercial Banks and Thrifts

A wide variety of financial intermediaries respond to the economy's demand for financial services. **Depository institutions,** such as commercial banks, savings and loan associations, mutual savings banks, and credit unions, obtain funds primarily by accepting *deposits* from the public—hence their name. Our emphasis will be on depository institutions because they play a key role in providing the nation's money supply. Depository institutions can be classified broadly into two types: commercial banks and thrift institutions.

Depository institutions Commercial banks and thrift institutions that accept deposits from the public

Commercial banks are the oldest, largest, and most diversified of depository institutions. They are called **commercial banks** because historically they made loans primarily to *commercial* ventures, or businesses, rather than to households. Commercial banks hold two-thirds of all deposits held by depository institutions. Until recently, commercial banks were the only depository institutions that offered demand deposits, or checking accounts. **Demand deposits** are so named because a depositor with such an account can write a check *demanding* those deposits at any time.

Commercial banks Depository institutions that make short-term loans primarily to businesses

Thrift institutions, or **thrifts,** include savings and loan associations, mutual savings banks, and credit unions. Historically, savings and loan associations and mutual savings banks specialized in making mortgage loans, which are loans to finance real estate purchases. Credit unions extend loans only to their "members" to finance homes or other major consumer purchases, such as new cars.

Demand deposits Accounts at financial institutions that pay no interest and on which depositors can write checks to obtain their deposits at any time

Thrift institutions, or **thrifts** Savings and loan institutions, mutual savings banks, and credit unions; depository institutions that make long-term loans primarily to households

Development of the Dual Banking System

Before 1863, commercial banks in the United States were chartered by the states in which they operated, so they were called *state banks.* These banks, like the English goldsmiths, issued bank notes. More than 10,000 different kinds of notes circulated and nearly all were redeemable for gold. The National Banking Act of 1863 and its later amendments created a new system of federally chartered banks called *national banks.* These national banks were authorized to issue notes and were regulated by the Office of the Comptroller of the Currency, part of the U.S. Treasury. At this time, a tax was introduced on the notes issued by state-chartered banks, the idea being to tax state bank notes out of existence. But state banks survived by substituting checks for notes. Borrowers were issued checking accounts rather than bank notes. State banks held on, and to this day the United States has a *dual banking system* consisting of both state banks and national banks.

Birth of the Federal Reserve System

During the 19th century, the economy experienced a number of panic "runs" on banks by depositors seeking to withdraw their funds. A panic was usually set off by the failure of some prominent financial institution. Following such a failure, other banks were besieged by fearful customers. Borrowers wanted additional loans and extensions of credit, and depositors wanted their money back. Similar bank panics have occurred recently in Russia and parts of Asia. The failure of the Knickerbocker Trust Company in New York triggered the Panic of 1907. This financial calamity underscored the lack of banking stability and so aroused the public that in 1908 Congress established the National Monetary Commission to study the banking system and make recommendations. That group's deliberations led to the Federal Reserve Act, passed in 1913 and implemented in 1914, which established the **Federal Reserve System** as the central bank and monetary authority of the United States.

Nearly all industrialized countries had formed central banks by 1900—the Bundesbank in Germany, the Bank of Japan, the Bank of England. The American public's suspicion of such monopoly power led to the establishment of not one central bank but 12 separate banks in 12 Federal Reserve districts around the country. The new banks were named after the cities in which they were located—the Federal Reserve Bank of Boston, New York, Chicago, San Francisco, and so on. *Throughout most of its history, the United States had what is called a decentralized banking system. The Federal Reserve Act moved the country toward a system that was partly centralized and partly decentralized.* All national banks became members of the Federal Reserve System and were thus subject to new regulations issued by *the Fed*, as it came to be known. For state banks, membership was voluntary; most state banks did not join because their owners did not want to comply with the new regulations.

Powers of the Federal Reserve System

According to the 1913 Act, the Federal Reserve Board was "to exercise general supervision" over the Federal Reserve System to ensure sufficient money and credit in the banking system to support a growing economy. The power to issue bank notes was taken away from national banks and turned over to the Federal Reserve banks. (Take out a dollar bill and notice what it says across the top: FEDERAL RESERVE NOTE. The seal to the left of George Washington's portrait identifies which Reserve bank issued the note.) The Federal Reserve was also given other powers: *to buy and sell government securities, to extend loans to member banks, to clear checks, and to require that member banks hold reserves equal at least to a specified fraction of their deposits.*

Federal Reserve banks typically do not deal with the public directly. Each may be thought of as a bankers' bank. Reserve banks hold deposits of member banks, just as depository institutions hold deposits of the public. Reserve banks extend loans to member banks just as depository institutions extend loans to the public.

Federal Reserve banks are so named because they hold member bank *reserves* on deposit. **Reserves** are funds that banks have on hand or on deposit with the Fed to promote banking safety, to facilitate interbank transfers of

Federal Reserve System
The central bank and monetary authority of the United States; also known as "the Fed"

Reserves Funds that banks use to satisfy the cash demands of their customers and the reserve requirements of the Fed; reserves consist of deposits at the Fed plus currency physically held by banks

funds, to satisfy the cash demands of their customers, and to comply with Federal Reserve regulations. These reserves allow Reserve banks to clear checks written by a depositor at one commercial bank and deposited in another commercial bank. This check clearance process is, on a larger scale, much like the goldsmith's moving of gold reserves from the farmer's account to the horse trader's account. Reserve banks also make loans to banks. The interest rate charged to banks for these so-called *discount loans* is called the *discount rate.* By making discount loans to banks, the Fed can increase reserves in the banking system.

Member banks are required to own stock in the Federal Reserve bank in their district, and this stock ownership entitles them to a specified dividend. Any additional profit earned by the Reserve banks is turned over to the U.S. Treasury.

Banking During the Great Depression

From 1913 to 1929, both the Federal Reserve System and the national economy performed relatively well. Then the stock market crash of 1929 was followed by the Great Depression, bringing a new set of problems for the Federal Reserve System. Frightened depositors wanted their money back, precipitating bank runs. But the Fed failed to respond to the crisis; it failed to act as a lender of last resort—that is, it did not lend banks the money they needed to satisfy deposit withdrawals in cases of runs on otherwise sound banks. Between 1930 and 1933, about 9,000 banks failed in the United States—roughly half the banks in the nation.

The Federal Reserve System had been established precisely to prevent such panics and to add stability to the banking system. What went wrong? In a word, everything. Between 1930 and 1933, the support offered by the Federal Reserve System seemed to crumble in stages. As businesses failed, they were unable to repay their loans. These defaults on loans led to the initial bank failures. As the crisis deepened, the public grew more concerned about the safety of bank deposits, so cash withdrawals increased. To satisfy the increased demand for currency, banks were forced to sell their holdings of stocks and bonds. But with many banks trying to sell and with few buyers, securities markets collapsed, sharply reducing the market value of these bank assets. Many banks did not have the resources to survive.

Because the Fed failed to understand the extent of the problem and its role as the lender of last resort, it failed to extend loans on a large scale to banks experiencing short-run shortages of cash (in contrast, the Fed was a ready source of loans a half century later during the stock market crash of 1987). The Fed failed to act because it did not understand either the gravity of the situation or its own power to assist troubled banks. The Fed viewed bank failure as a regrettable but inevitable consequence of poor management or prior speculative excesses, or simply as the effect of a collapsing economy. The Fed did not seem to understand that the banking system's instability was contributing to the deterioration of the economy. For example, the stock market collapsed between 1929 and 1933 in part because many banks were trying to sell their securities at the same time. And the collapse came just when banks were badly in need of cash. Fed officials appeared concerned primarily with the solvency of the Federal Reserve banks. They did not realize that because Federal Reserve banks had unlimited money-creating power, they could not fail.

Roosevelt's Reforms

In his first inaugural address, President Franklin D. Roosevelt said, "The only thing we have to fear is fear itself," a view that was especially applicable to a fractional reserve banking system. Most banks were sound as long as people had confidence in the safety of their deposits. *But if many people became frightened and tried to withdraw their money, they could not do so because each bank held reserves amounting to only a fraction of its deposits.*

Upon taking office in early 1933, President Roosevelt attempted to soothe prevailing fears by declaring a "banking holiday," which closed all banks for a week. A national suspension of banking business for a week was unprecedented, yet it was welcomed as a sign that something would be done. Roosevelt also proposed the Banking Acts of 1933 and 1935 and other measures aimed at shoring up the banking system and centralizing the power of the Federal Reserve in Washington. Let's consider the most important features of this legislation.

Board of Governors. The Federal Reserve Board was renamed the Board of Governors and became responsible for setting and implementing the nation's monetary policy. *Monetary policy* is the regulation of the economy's money supply to promote macroeconomic objectives. All 12 Reserve banks came under the authority of the Board of Governors, which consists of seven members appointed by the president and confirmed by the Senate. Each governor serves a 14-year term, with terms staggered so that one governor is appointed every two years. The president also appoints one of the governors to chair the board for a 4-year term. A president bent on changing the direction of monetary policy could be sure of changing only two members in a single presidential term. Board membership is relatively stable, and in one 4-year term a president has only limited control over the board's monetary policy. *The idea was to insulate monetary authorities from short-term political pressure by elected officials.*

Federal Open Market Committee. Originally, the power of the Federal Reserve was vested in each of the 12 Reserve banks. The Banking Acts established the *Federal Open Market Committee (FOMC)* to consolidate decisions about the most important tool of monetary policy—**open-market operations,** which are purchases and sales of U.S. government securities by the Fed (open-market operations and other tools of monetary policy will be examined in the next chapter). The FOMC consists of the seven board governors plus five of the 12 presidents from the Reserve banks; the group is headed by the chair of the Board of Governors. Open-market operations are carried out by the New York Federal Reserve bank, and the president of the New York Fed is always on the FOMC. The organizational structure of the Federal Reserve System as it now stands is presented in Exhibit 2. That exhibit shows that the presidential appointment of Board members is subject to Senate confirmation. The FOMC and the Federal Advisory Committee (which consists of a commercial banker from each of the 12 Reserve districts) advise the Board.

Regulating the Money Supply. As we saw earlier, because reserves amount to only a fraction of deposits, we have a *fractional reserve* banking system. Specific reserve requirements had been established by the Federal Reserve Act of 1914. Member banks were required to hold reserves equal to a certain percentage of their deposits, say from 3 percent to 12 percent depending on the type of deposit and the type of bank. The Banking Acts of 1933 and 1935 authorized the

Open-market operations Purchases and sales of government securities by the Federal Reserve in an effort to influence the money supply

EXHIBIT 2

Organization Chart for the Federal Reserve System

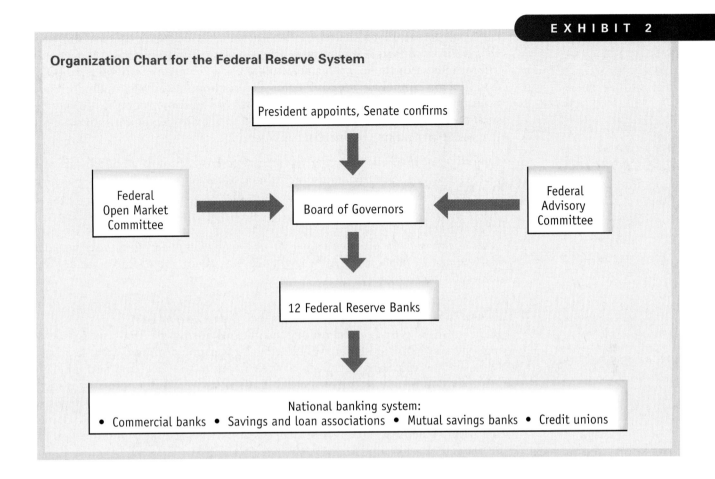

Board of Governors to vary reserve requirements within a range, thereby giving the Fed an additional tool of monetary policy.

Thus, as of 1935, the Federal Reserve System had a variety of tools to regulate the money supply, including *(1) conducting open-market operations—buying and selling U.S. government securities; (2) setting the discount rate—the interest rate charged by Reserve banks for loans to member banks; and (3) setting legal reserve requirements for member banks.* We will explore these tools in greater detail in the next chapter.

Deposit Insurance. One cause of bank failures during the depression was the lack of confidence in the safety of bank deposits. The Federal Deposit Insurance Corporation (FDIC) was established in 1933 to insure the first $2,500 of each deposit account. Today the insurance ceiling is $100,000 per account. Members of the Federal Reserve System are required to purchase FDIC insurance; the program is voluntary for other banks. About 97 percent of commercial banks and about 90 percent of savings and loan associations are insured by the FDIC. The rest are insured by private companies or state reserve funds. *Deposit insurance, by calming fears about the safety of deposits, worked wonders to reduce bank runs.*

Restricting Bank Investment Practices. As part of the Banking Act of 1933, commercial banks were forbidden to buy or sell corporate stocks and bonds. The belief was that when commercial banks hold assets that fluctuate widely in value, the stability of the banking system is endangered. *The act limited bank assets primarily to loans and to government securities—bonds issued by federal, state, and local governments.* A *bond* is an IOU promising the lender an annual interest payment and full repayment of the loan on a certain date, so a government bond is an IOU from the government. Also, bank failures were thought to have resulted in part from interest-rate competition among banks for customer deposits. To reduce such competition, the Fed was empowered to set the maximum interest rates that could be paid on commercial bank deposits.

Objectives of the Fed. Over the years, the Fed has accumulated additional objectives. Six goals are frequently mentioned as objectives of the Fed's policies: (1) a high level of employment in the economy, (2) economic growth, (3) price stability, (4) stability in interest rates, (5) stability in financial markets, such as the stock market, and (6) stability in foreign-exchange markets. *We can boil these goals down to high employment, economic growth, and stability in prices, interest rates, financial markets, and exchange rates.* As we will see, not all of these objectives can be achieved simultaneously.

From the Great Depression to Deregulation

Restrictions imposed on depository institutions during the 1930s made banking a heavily regulated industry. The federal government insured most deposits. Depository institutions lost much of their freedom to wheel and deal. The assets they could acquire were carefully limited, as were the interest rates they could offer depositors. Households typically left their money in savings deposits earning 4 percent interest or less; checking deposits earned no interest. Banks and thrifts quietly accepted these deposits and made loans, earning their profit on the interest differential.

Federal Reserve ceilings on interest rates reduced interest-rate competition for deposits *among* depository institutions. As long as the interest-rate ceilings were at or above prevailing market rates of interest, the banking system as a whole did not have to worry about outside competition for customer deposits. When market interest rates rose above the ceiling that banks and thrifts could offer, however, many savers withdrew their deposits and put them into higher-yielding alternatives.

The surge of inflation during the 1970s increased interest rates in the economy, and banking has not been the same since. In 1972, Merrill Lynch, a major brokerage house, introduced an account combining a **money market mutual fund** with check-writing privileges. Money market mutual fund shares are claims on a portfolio, or collection, of short-term interest-earning assets. By pooling the funds of many shareholders, the managers of a mutual fund can acquire a diversified portfolio of assets offering shareholders higher rates of interest than those available at most depository institutions. Money market mutual funds proved to be stiff competition for bank deposits, especially demand deposits, which paid no interest.

Depository institutions use savers' deposits to make loans; when savers withdrew their deposits, banks and thrifts had to replace the funds needed to support their loans by borrowing at prevailing interest rates, which were typically higher than the rates they earned on their existing loans. Because their loans were typically for short periods, commercial banks got in less trouble than thrifts when interest rates rose. But thrifts had made loans for long-term mortgages, loans that

Money market mutual fund　A collection of short-term interest-earning assets purchased with funds collected from many shareholders

would not be fully repaid for decades. *Because thrifts had to pay more interest to borrow funds than they were earning on these mortgages, they were in big trouble and many failed.*

Bank Deregulation

In response to the loss of deposits and other problems of depository institutions, Congress tried to ease regulations, thereby giving banks and thrifts greater discretion in their operations. For example, the interest-rate ceilings for deposits were eliminated, and all depository institutions were authorized to offer checking accounts. Thrifts were given wider latitude in making loans and in the kinds of assets they could acquire. Additionally, all depository institutions were allowed to offer money market deposit accounts, whose value jumped from only $8 billion in 1978 to $200 billion in 1982.

Some states, such as California and Texas, largely deregulated state-chartered savings and loan associations. The combination of deposit insurance, unregulated interest rates, and wider latitude in the kinds of assets that could be purchased gave savings and loan associations a green light to compete for large deposits in national markets and to acquire assets as they pleased. Once-staid financial institutions moved into the fast lane.

Thus thrifts could wheel and deal, but with the benefit of deposit insurance. The combination of deregulation and deposit insurance encouraged some thrifts already in financial trouble to take big risks—to "bet the bank"—because their depositors would be protected by deposit insurance. This created a so-called *moral hazard,* which in this case is the tendency of bankers to take unwarranted risks when they believe the government is providing a safety net. Banks that were already virtually bankrupt—so-called "zombie" banks—were able to attract additional deposits because of deposit insurance. Zombie banks, by offering higher interest rates, also attracted deposits away from healthy banks.

Meanwhile, since deposits were insured, most depositors paid little attention to their bank's health. *Thus deposit insurance, originally introduced during the Great Depression to prevent bank panics, caused depositors to become complacent about the safety of their deposits. Worse still, it caused those who ran the banks and thrifts to take unwarranted risks because they were gambling with other people's money.*

Bailing Out the Thrifts

Losses in the savings and loan industry topped $10 billion in 1987 and $20 billion in 1988. The result was a disaster, and depository institutions, particularly thrifts, failed at record rates. Thrift failures began growing in the mid-1980s, peaking at 327 in 1989. The insolvency and collapse of a growing number of thrifts prompted Congress, in August 1989, to approve the largest financial bailout of any industry in history—a measure that would eventually cost about $250 billion. Taxpayers paid nearly two-thirds of the total, and the thrift industry paid the remaining third through higher deposit insurance premiums. The money was spent to shut down failing thrifts and pay off insured depositors.

Part of the cleanup involved selling more than $450 billion of office buildings, shopping malls, apartment buildings, land, and other assets formerly taken over by insolvent thrifts because of bad loans. A glut of such properties dragged down market values and reduced the federal government's ability to recoup its losses from deposit insurance. Still, the mess was cleaned up in the early 1990s and the number of failures dropped sharply. Exhibit 3 shows failures by year.

EXHIBIT 3

Annual Failures of U. S. Thrift Institutions

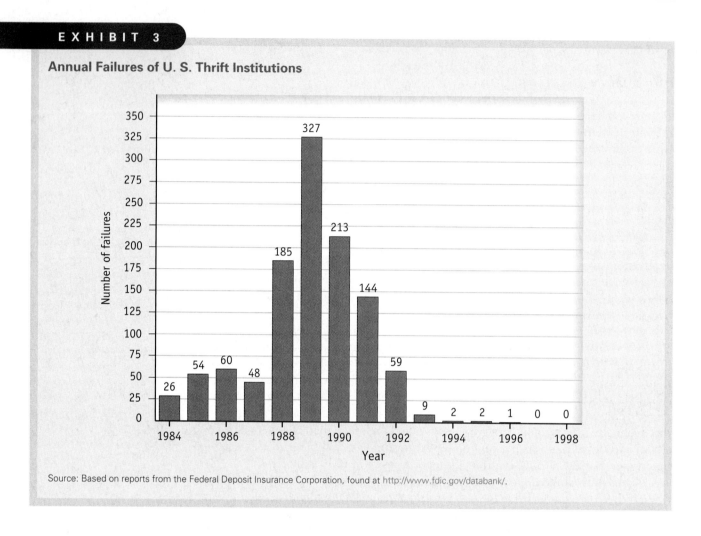

Source: Based on reports from the Federal Deposit Insurance Corporation, found at http://www.fdic.gov/databank/.

From their peak of 327 in 1989, the number of thrift failures dropped to zero in 1997 and 1998. Because of failures and mergers, the number of thrift institutions dropped from about 3,700 in 1986 to under 1,900 in 1998.

Commercial Banks Were Also Failing

The U.S. banking system experienced more change and upheaval during the 1980s and early 1990s than at any other time since the Great Depression. As they had in the case of thrifts, risky decisions based on deposit insurance coupled with the slump in property values also hastened the demise of many commercial banks. Hundreds of troubled banks, such as Continental Illinois, First Republic Bank of Dallas, and the Bank of New England, were taken over by the FDIC or forced to merge with healthier competitors. Banks in Texas and Oklahoma failed when loans to oil drillers and farmers went sour. Banks in the Northeast failed because falling real estate values caused borrowers to default. Exhibit 4 shows the number of bank failures per year since 1935. The rising tide of failures during the 1980s is clear.

The United States was not alone in experiencing banking problems in the 1980s and 1990s. A wave of banking trouble swept around the world. Countries

EXHIBIT 4

Commercial Bank Failures per Year Since 1934

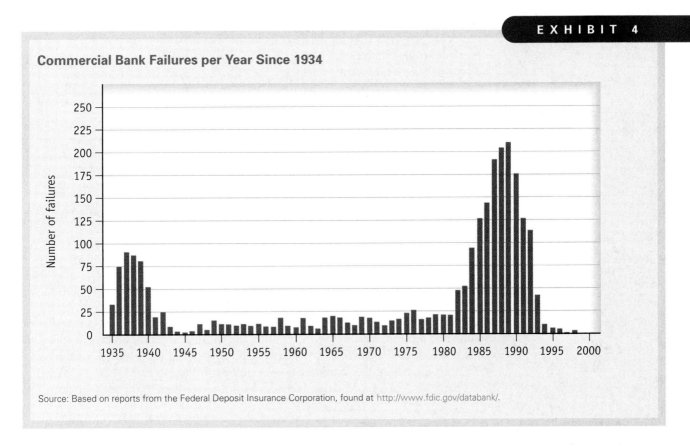

Source: Based on reports from the Federal Deposit Insurance Corporation, found at http://www.fdic.gov/databank/.

where huge bank losses occurred include Argentina, Chile, Venezuela, Mexico, Brazil, Finland, Uruguay, Sweden, Colombia, Norway, Russia, and countries in Eastern Europe.

The Structure of U.S. Banking

The United States now has about 9,000 commercial banks—more than any other country, but down from 14,500 in 1984. Other industrial countries have fewer than 1,000 commercial banks, and Japan has fewer than 100. The 10 largest U.S. commercial banks hold less than half the U.S. banking industry assets. In contrast, as few as a half dozen banks hold over half the assets in other developed countries, such as Australia, Canada, Japan, and the United Kingdom. *So the United States has more banks than other countries, and U.S. bank assets are distributed more evenly across banks.*

The large number of banks in this country reflects past government restrictions on *branches,* which are additional offices that carry out banking operations. The combination of intrastate and interstate restrictions on branching spawned the many commercial banks that exist today, most of which are relatively small. *Restrictions on interstate banking create inefficiencies, since banks cannot achieve optimal size and cannot as easily diversify their portfolio of loans among different regions.*

In recent years, two developments have allowed banks to get around branching restrictions: bank holding companies and mergers. A **bank holding company** is a corporation that may own several different banks. Many states now permit holding companies to cross state lines, thereby skirting federal

Bank holding company A corporation that owns banks

prohibitions against interstate banking. Moreover, a holding company can provide other services that banks are not authorized to offer, such as financial advising, leasing, insurance, issuing credit cards, and selling securities. Holding companies have blossomed in recent years, and the nation's major banks are all owned by holding companies. More than three-quarters of the nation's checking deposits are in banks owned by holding companies.

Another important development that has allowed banks to expand their geographical reach is mergers, which have spread the presence of some banks across the country. Banks are merging because they want more customers and expect the higher volume of transactions to reduce operating costs per customer. Nationwide banking is also seen as a way of avoiding the concentration of bad loans that sometimes occur in one geographical area. The merger movement was fueled by a rising stock market during the 1990s and by federal legislation passed in 1994 that facilitates consolidation of merged banks.

NationsBank and BankAmerica merged in 1998 to create Bank of America, the nation's largest bank and the first one to stretch coast to coast. The new bank in 1998 held $1 of every $12 Americans put in banks; its 4,800 branch offices and 14,000 ATMs spanned 27 states and 38 countries.

U.S. bank profits increased to record levels by the mid-1990s, so the industry has turned around. As shown in Exhibit 4, the number of bank failures dropped to only three in 1998, down from well over 200 in 1988. But a national banking system is no guarantee that banks will not fail. The following case study discusses recent banking problems in Japan, a country with fewer than 100 commercial banks.

Banking Troubles in Japan

CaseStudy

Other Times, Other Places

During the Japanese banking crisis, Fuji Bank survived by restructuring while the Nippon Credit Bank was taken over by the government. How are they doing now? Go to their English language home pages at http://www.fujibank.co.jp/eng/fb/home.html for Fuji Bank and http://www.ncb.co.jp/lr/English/1998/index.html for the Nippon Credit Bank. Review some of their recent news releases. What plans does the Japanese government have for the Nippon Credit Bank? Does the government intend to privatize the bank or has it already done so?

Prior to the 1980s, financial markets in Japan were heavily regulated, with severe restrictions on interest rates that banks could offer. As a result of financial deregulation, banks became more aggressive in attracting deposits and more willing to make riskier loans, particularly in the real estate sector. For example, the Kizu Credit Cooperative, by offering high interest rates on deposits, increased deposits from $2 billion in 1988 to $12 billion by 1995. Kizu lent these deposits to finance real estate loans.

When Japanese property values collapsed in the 1990s, banks were in trouble. As the bad loans piled up, Japan experienced its first bank failures since World War II. Banks that grew the fastest during the go-go era, such as Kizu, became some of the first casualties. According to the Japanese finance minister, bank losses in the country totaled $350 billion by 1997.

Although many Japanese banks failed, regulatory officials appeared reluctant to close down banks that were financially insolvent. Regulators seemed to be following a "too-big-to-fail" philosophy by promising that none of the nation's 21 largest banks would be allowed to fail. But that approach was violated in late 1997 when Hokkaido Takushuku Bank, Japan's tenth largest, failed. After the failure, the Japanese government immediately extended emergency central bank loans and arranged for another bank to take over the failed bank's deposits and outstanding loans. All deposits were protected, but the bank's shareholders lost their investment. Following that bank's collapse, some other Japanese banks found it difficult to borrow.

Even after such bank failures, much of the Japanese banking system consists of zombies, living-dead banks kept alive only by transfusions from the Bank of Japan, the central bank. As the economy worsened in 1998, with GDP contracting by 3.3 percent, the stock of bad loans soared to an estimated 30 percent of GDP. This makes Japan's banking problem about five times bigger, in relative terms, than America's savings-and-loan problem.

One problem with the banking crisis in Japan is that nobody knows how bad off banks really are because reporting requirements there are much looser than in the United States. This so-called *lack of transparency* in accounting magnifies the impact of the information that does become public. For example, in September 1998, Fuji Bank reported that its problem loans were 50 percent larger than it had previously disclosed. Fuji also said that the reserves it set aside to cover these loans were far below what most observers believed would be sufficient. The effect of these announcements was a huge drop in Fuji's share price, along with share prices of other banks. To resolve its banking crisis, the Japanese government in 1998 began using public funds to bail out troubled banks. By early 1999, about $75 billion had been earmarked to shore up 15 major banks. But with Japan stuck in its worst recession in decades, banking troubles were expected to continue.

Sources: David Sanger, "Japanese Tell U.S. That Their Banks Are in Big Trouble," *New York Times* (5 October 1998); Bill Spindle, Norihiko Shirouzu, and Jason Sapsford, "Bleak Economy Emerges from Japanese Survey," *Wall Street Journal* (1 October 1998); "Time to Wake Up," *Economist* (26 September 1998), pp. 21–23; and Houtan Bassiri, "Japan Banks Step Toward Recovery with More Public Funds," *Dow-Jones Newswire* (14 February 1999).

CONCLUSION

Money has grown increasingly more abstract over time, moving from commodity money to paper money that represented a claim on some commodity such as gold, to paper money with no intrinsic value. As you will see, paper money constitutes only a fraction of the money supply. Most modern money consists of electronic entries in the banking system's computers. So money has changed from a physical commodity to an electronic entry. Money today not so much changes hands as changes computer accounts.

Money and banking have been intertwined ever since the early goldsmiths offered to hold customers' valuables for safekeeping. Banking has since evolved from one of the most staid industries to one of the most competitive. Deregulation and branching innovations have increased competition and have expanded the types of bank deposits. Reforms have given the Fed more uniform control over all depository institutions and have given the institutions greater access to the services provided by the Fed. Thus all depository institutions can compete on more equal footing.

Deregulation provides greater freedom not only to prosper but also to fail. Failures of depository institutions create a special problem, however, because these institutions provide the financial underpinning of the nation's money supply, as you will see in the next chapter. There we will examine more closely how banks operate and supply the nation's money.

SUMMARY

1. Barter was the first form of exchange. As specialization grew, it became more difficult to discover the double coincidence of wants required for barter. The time and inconvenience associated with barter led even simple economies to introduce money.

2. Anything that acquires a high degree of acceptability throughout an economy as a medium of exchange thereby becomes money. The first moneys were commodities, such as salt or gold. Eventually what changed hands was a piece of paper that could be redeemed for something of value, such as gold. As paper money became widely accepted, governments introduced fiat money, which is paper money that cannot be redeemed for anything other than more paper money. Fiat money is given its status as money by law, or by fiat. Most currencies throughout the world today are fiat money. People accept fiat money because they believe others will do so as well.

3. The value of money depends on how much it will buy. If money fails to serve as a medium of exchange, traders will resort to some second-best means of exchange, such as barter, a careful system of record-keeping, or some informal commodity money. If a monetary system breaks down, more time must be devoted to exchange, leaving less time for production, so the economy's efficiency suffers.

4. The Federal Reserve System was established in 1914 to stabilize the banking system. After many banks failed during the Great Depression, the Fed's powers were increased and centralized. Its control over all depository institutions was extended by legislation passed during the 1980s. The primary powers of the Fed are to (1) conduct open-market operations (buying and selling U.S. government securities to control the money supply), (2) set the discount rate (the rate at which depository institutions can borrow from the Fed), and (3) establish and enforce reserve requirements for depository institutions.

5. Regulations introduced during the Great Depression turned banking into a closely regulated and largely predictable industry. But high interest rates during the 1970s disturbed the quiet life of depository institutions. Reforms in the 1980s were designed to give depository institutions greater flexibility in competing with other kinds of financial intermediaries. Many thrifts used this flexibility to gamble on investments, but these gambles often failed, causing hundreds of thrifts to go bankrupt. In 1989, Congress approved a measure to close failing thrifts, pay off insured deposits, and regulate more closely the operations of remaining thrifts. Commercial banks also experienced record numbers of failures during the 1980s, but their problems were not as serious as those affecting the thrifts. By the mid-1990s, commercial banks and thrifts were thriving once again in the United States, although they remained troubled in Japan. Mergers of banks are creating a national banking system.

QUESTIONS FOR REVIEW

1. *(Barter)* Define a double coincidence of wants and explain its role in a barter system.

2. *(Money Versus Barter)* "Without money, everything would be more expensive." Explain this statement. Then take a look at a Web page devoted to barter at http://www.ex.ac.uk/~RDavies/arian/barter.html. What are some current developments in barter exchange?

3. *(Functions of Money)* What are the three important functions of money? Define each of them.

4. *(Functions of Money)* "If an economy had only two goods (both *nondurable*), there would be no need for money because exchange would always be between those two goods." What important function of money does this statement disregard?

5. *(Characteristics of Money)* Why is universal acceptability such an important characteristic of money? What other characteristics can you think of that might be important to market participants?

6. *(Commodity Money)* Why do you think rice was chosen to serve as money in medieval Japan? What would happen to the price level if there was a particularly good rice harvest one year?

7. *(Commodity Money)* Early in U.S. history, tobacco was used as money. If you were a tobacco farmer and had two loads of tobacco that were of different qualities, which would you use for money and which for smoking? Under what conditions would you use both types of tobacco for money?

8. *(Origins of Banking)* Discuss the various ways in which London goldsmiths functioned as early banks.

9. *(Types of Money)* Complete each of the following sentences:
   a. If the face value of a coin exceeds the cost of coinage, the resulting revenues to the issuer of the coin are known as _____.
   b. A product that serves both as money and as a commodity is _____.
   c. Coins and paper money circulating in the United States have face values that exceed the value of the material from which they are made. Therefore, they are forms of _____.
   d. If the government declares that creditors must accept a form of money as payment for debts, the money becomes _____.
   e. A common unit for measuring the value of every good or service in the economy is known as a(n) _____.

10. *(Fiat Money)* Most economists believe that the better fiat money serves as a store of value, the more acceptable it is. What does this statement mean? How could people lose faith in money?

11. *(The Value of Money)* When the value of money was based on its gold content, new discoveries of gold were frequently followed by periods of inflation. Explain.

12. *(Case**Study**: When the Monetary Systems Break Down)* In countries where the monetary system has broken down, what are some alternatives to which people have resorted to carry out transactions?

13. *(Depository Institutions)* What is a depository institution and what types of depository institutions are found in the United States? How do they act as intermediaries between savers and borrowers? Why do they play this role?

14. *(Federal Reserve System)* What are the main powers and responsibilities of the Federal Reserve System?

15. *(Bank Deregulation)* Some economists argue that deregulated deposit rates combined with deposit insurance led to the insolvency of many depository institutions. On what basis do they make such an argument?

16. *(The Structure of U.S. Banking)* Discuss the impact of bank mergers on the structure of American banking. Why do banks wish to merge?

17. *(Case**Study**: Banking Troubles in Japan)* Discuss problems with the banking system in Japan. In what ways are they similar to U.S. banking problems in the late 1980s and early 1990s? What is the current status of bank restructuring in Japan?

EXPERIENTIAL EXERCISES

18. *(When Money Performs Poorly)* Visit Glyn Davies' History of Money site at http://mirrors.org.sg/money/llyfr.html. Click on "A Comparative Chronology of Money" and check the years since 1939. How many hyperinflations are mentioned for those years? What does that tell you about the relationship between monetary systems and economic well-being?

19. *(Bank Deregulation)* The Federal Reserve Bank of Philadelphia's *Business Review* often runs informative articles that are accessible to introductory economics students. Read the article by Ted Temzelides entitled "Are Bank Runs Contagious?" in the November/December 1997 issue at http://www.phil.frb.org/econ/br/brnd97in.html. What is his conclusion and how does it relate to the discussion of banking regulation in this chapter?

20. The *Wall Street Journal* prints several features that track key interest rates. The daily Money Rates box lists the current prime lending rate, along with a variety of short-term rates. The weekly Key Interest Rates table reports on Treasury securities. And a weekly Consumer Savings Rates List shows the rates paid by 100 large banks. Take a look at these sources—you can find them on the Money and Credit Markets pages—and determine the extent to which all these interest rates move together.

14

Banking and the Money Supply

What role do banks play in creating money? Why are banks more likely to be

called First Trust, Security National, or Federal Savings rather than Benny's

Bank, Easy Money Bank and Trust, or Loans 'R' Us? Why are we so interested

in banks, anyway? After all, isn't banking a business like any other—dry clean-

ing, auto manufacturing, or home remodeling? Why not devote this chapter to

the home-remodeling business? Answers to these and related questions are ad-

dressed in this chapter, which examines banking and the money supply.

In this chapter, we take a closer look at the role banks play in the economy.

Banks are special in macroeconomics because, like the London goldsmith, they

can convert a borrower's IOU into money, and an adequate supply of money is

a key ingredient in a healthy economy. Since regulatory reforms have eliminated many of the distinctions between commercial banks and thrift institutions, and since thrifts represent a dwindling share of depository institutions, from here on, all depository institutions will usually be referred to more simply as *banks*.

We first consider the role of banks in the economy and the types of deposits they hold. We then examine how banks work and see how the money supply expands through the creation of deposits. We also consider the operation of the Federal Reserve System in more detail. As we will see, the Federal Reserve, or the Fed, attempts to control money supply indirectly by controlling bank reserves. Topics discussed in this chapter include:

- Checkable deposits
- Monetary aggregates
- Balance sheets
- Money creation process
- Money multipliers
- Tools of the Fed

BANKS, THEIR DEPOSITS, AND THE MONEY SUPPLY

Banks attract funds from savers and lend these funds to borrowers. Savers need a safe place for their money and borrowers need credit; banks try to earn a profit by serving both groups. To inspire depositor confidence, banks present an image of sober dignity—an image meant to foster trust and assurance. For example, they are more apt to be called First Trust, Security National, or Federal Savings rather than Benny's Bank, Easy Money Bank and Trust, or Loans 'R' Us. In contrast, *finance companies* are financial intermediaries that do not get their funds from depositors, so they can choose names aimed more at borrowers—names such as Household Finance and The Money Store.

Banks Are Financial Intermediaries

By bringing together the two sides of the market, banks serve as financial intermediaries, or as go-betweens. They gather various amounts from savers and repackage these funds into the amounts demanded by borrowers. Usually savers want to save relatively small amounts, while borrowers want to borrow relatively large amounts, so banks repackage the various small savings into larger amounts for borrowers. Some savers need their money back next week, some next year, some only after retirement. Likewise, different borrowers want to borrow for different lengths of time. Banks, as intermediaries, offer desirable durations to both savers and borrowers.

Coping with Asymmetric Information. Banks, as lenders, try to identify borrowers who are willing to pay interest and are able to repay the loans. But borrowers have more reliable information about their own credit history and financial plans than do lenders. Thus in the market for loans there is **asymmetric information:** a disparity in the information known by each party to the transaction. This asymmetry would not create a problem if borrowers could be trusted to report relevant details to lenders. Some borrowers, however, have an incentive to suppress critical information, such as other debts, a troubled financial history, or plans to invest the borrowed funds in a risky venture. Because they have experience and expertise in evaluating the creditworthiness of loan applicants, banks have a greater ability to cope with asymmetric information than an individual saver would. Moreover, because banks have experience in

Asymmetric information
Unequal information known by each party to a transaction; borrowers usually have more information about their creditworthiness than do lenders

depositor requests for funds, so banks often hold excess reserves or hold some assets that can be easily converted to cash to satisfy any unexpected demand for funds. Banks may also want to have excess reserves on hand in case a valued customer needs an immediate loan.

Liquidity A measure of the ease with which an asset can be converted into money without significant loss in its value

The bank manager must therefore structure the portfolio of assets with an eye toward liquidity but must not forget that the bank's survival also depends on profitability. **Liquidity** is the ease with which an asset can be converted into cash without a significant loss of value. *The objectives of liquidity and profitability are at odds.* For example, the bank will generally find that the assets offering a higher interest rate are less liquid than other assets offering a lower interest rate. The most liquid asset is bank reserves, either in the bank's vault as cash or on account with the Fed, but reserves earn no interest.

At one extreme, suppose a bank is completely liquid, holding all its assets as cash reserves. Such a bank would clearly have no difficulty meeting depositors' demands for funds. The bank is playing it safe—too safe. Since it holds no interest-earning assets, it will earn no income and will fail. At the other extreme, suppose a bank uses all its excess reserves to acquire high-yielding but illiquid assets, such as long-term loans. Such a bank will run into problems whenever withdrawals exceed new deposits. The bank portfolio manager's task is to strike just the right balance between liquidity, or safety, and profitability.

Federal funds market A market for overnight lending and borrowing of reserves among banks; the market for reserves on account with the Fed

Since reserves earn no interest, banks usually try to keep their excess reserves to a minimum. Banks continuously "sweep" their accounts to find excess reserves that can be put to some interest-bearing use. They do not let excess reserves remain idle even overnight. The **federal funds market** provides for day-to-day lending and borrowing among banks of excess reserves on account at the Fed; these funds usually do not leave the Fed—they shift among accounts. For example, suppose that at the end of the business day Home Bank has excess reserves of $50,000 on account at the Fed and wants to loan that amount to another bank that finished the day with a reserve deficiency of $50,000. These two banks are brought together by a broker who specializes in the market for federal funds—that is, the market for excess reserves at the Fed. The interest rate paid on this loan is called the **federal funds rate,** and it is this rate the Fed targets as a tool of monetary policy, but more on that later.

Federal funds rate The interest rate prevailing in the federal funds market; the interest rate banks charge one another for overnight borrowing

Let's now discuss how Home Bank and the banking system as a whole can create money.

HOW BANKS CREATE MONEY

This chapter is really about how fiat money is created. We are now in a position to examine how an individual bank and the banking system as a whole can create money. Our discussion will focus on the behavior of commercial banks because these are the largest and most important depository institutions, although thrifts can carry out similar activities.

Creating Money Through Excess Reserves

As we shall see, excess reserves are the raw material the banking system employs to support the creation of money. The Fed can influence the amount of excess reserves by (1) buying or selling U.S. government bonds, (2) extending discount loans to banks, and (3) changing the required reserve ratio. By far the most important of these is buying or selling U.S. government bonds, bonds originally issued by the U.S. Treasury.

Assume there are no excess reserves in the banking system initially and that the reserve requirement on checkable deposits is 10 percent. To get our analysis rolling, suppose the Federal Reserve buys a $1,000 U.S. government bond from Home Bank. To pay for the bond, the Fed simply increases Home Bank's reserve account with the Fed by $1,000. Where does the Fed get these reserves? It makes them up—creates them out of electronic ether, out of thin air!

In the transaction, Home Bank has exchanged one asset, a U.S. bond, for another asset, reserves on deposit with the Fed. So far the money supply has not changed, because neither U.S. bonds nor Home Bank's reserves are part of the money supply. But the increase in excess reserves fuels an increase in the money supply.

The story, in brief, is this. A bank's lending is limited to the amount of its excess reserves. Suppose Home Bank makes a loan by increasing the borrower's checkable deposits by $1,000. Since checkable deposits are money, the bank, by making the loan, has created money in the amount of $1,000. These borrowed funds eventually get spent and end up as $1,000 in someone else's checkable deposits, perhaps in another bank, so the money supply remains $1,000 higher. That bank, after setting aside required reserves of, say, $100, can lend out its excess reserves of $900 by increasing a new borrower's checkable deposits, thereby adding $900 more to the money supply, or M1. The money supply continues to expand in this fashion until no excess reserves are left in the banking system. Let's look at the deposit creation process in greater detail in the following series of rounds.

Round One. We begin with the Fed buying a $1,000 U.S. bond from Home Bank. After selling that bond, Home Bank has $1,000 in excess reserves. Rather than sit on these reserves and earn no interest, Home Bank can make loans for the full amount of excess reserves. Suppose Home Bank is your regular bank and you apply for a $1,000 student loan. Home Bank approves your loan and consequently increases your checking account by $1,000. *Home Bank has converted your promise to repay the loan, your IOU, into a $1,000 checkable deposit. Because checkable deposits are part of M1, this action increases the money supply by $1,000.* In the process, Home Bank's excess reserves have become required reserves. As shown in Exhibit 4, Home Bank's assets increase by $1,000, as do its liabilities. On the asset side, loans increase by $1,000 because your IOU becomes an asset to the bank. On the liability side, checkable deposits increase by $1,000 because Home Bank has increased your account by that amount. Home Bank has created money based on your promise to repay the loan.

EXHIBIT 4

Changes in Home Bank's Balance Sheet After Home Bank Lends You $1,000

Home Bank's Balance Sheet

Assets		Liabilities and Net Worth	
Loans	+ 1,000	Checkable deposits	+ 1,000

Round Two. When you write a $1,000 check for tuition, your college promptly deposits the check in its checking account at College Bank. College Bank then increases the college's account by $1,000 and presents your check to the Fed. The Fed reduces Home Bank's reserve account by $1,000 and increases College Bank's reserve account by the same amount. The Fed then sends the check to Home Bank, which reduces your checkable deposits by $1,000. The Fed has "cleared" your check by settling the claim that College Bank had on Home Bank. So far, the $1,000 in checkable deposits, the newly created money, has simply shifted from Home Bank to College Bank.

But College Bank now has $1,000 more in reserves on deposit with the Fed. After setting aside $100, or 10 percent of your college's increase in deposits, as required reserves, College Bank has $900 in excess reserves. College Bank can thus make a loan or purchase some other interest-bearing asset. Suppose the bank lends $900 to an enterprising business student who plans to open an all-night bait-and-bagel shop to lure early morning anglers on their way to a nearby fishing spot. College Bank extends the loan by providing this student with a checking account balance of $900. As shown in Exhibit 5, College Bank's assets increase by the $900 loan, and its liabilities increase by the $900 added to the student's checkable deposits. *College Bank has converted the student's promise to repay the loan into a checkable deposit, which is money.*

Suppose the student writes a $900 check for equipment purchased at a hardware store, which deposits the check into an account at Merchants Trust. Merchants Trust increases the hardware store's checkable deposits by $900 and sends the check to the Fed, which increases Merchants Trust's reserves by $900 and decreases College Bank's reserves by the same amount. The Fed then sends the check to College Bank, which reduces the student's checkable deposit account by $900. So deposits at the Fed and checkable deposits decrease by $900 at College Bank and increase by that amount at Merchants Trust.

At this point, checkable deposits in the banking system total $1,900 more than before we started: Your college still has $1,000 more in checkable deposits at College Bank because you paid tuition, and the hardware store has $900 more in its account at Merchants Trust because of the enterprising student's equipment purchase.

Round Three and Beyond. Merchants Trust sets aside $90 of the $900 deposited as required reserves, leaving $810 in excess reserves. Suppose it loans $810 to an English major who is starting a new venture called "Note This," a note-taking service for students in large classes. Exhibit 6 shows that Merchants Trust's assets are up by $810 in loans, and its liabilities are up by the same amount in checkable deposits.

EXHIBIT 5

Changes in College Bank's Balance Sheet After the Bank Makes a $900 Loan

Assets		Liabilities and Net Worth	
Loans	+ 900	Checkable deposits	+ 900

Assets		Liabilities and Net Worth	
Loans	+ 810	Checkable deposits	+ 810

Wha
buys it fr
Fed has i
notes, wh
lic, for a
dealer pu
ends up i
pansion p

Excess
and M
The ban
money su
$1,000 ir
checkabl
cess reserv
the sourc
$10,000 i

The r
in the ba
simple n
or 1/r, wh
cent, or C
multiple e

ch

The s
that borr
cash. The
must be h
quiremen
aside twic
case woul
deposits re
fore be $1
by only ha
serves fuel
from the ba

On th
would set
for loans.
$1,000 in
could inci
Thus the
ity to crea

In sum
into the b
greater tha
and the se

The loan of $810 is spent at the college bookstore on notebooks and computer software. The bookstore then deposits the check in its account at Fidelity Bank. Fidelity Bank credits the bookstore's checkable deposits with $810 and sends the check to the Fed for clearance. The Fed reduces Merchants Trust's reserves by $810 and increases Fidelity Bank's by the same amount. The Fed then sends the check to Merchants Trust, which reduces the English major's checkable deposits by $810. So deposits at the Fed and checkable deposits are down by $810 at Merchants Trust and up by the same amount at Fidelity Bank.

At this point checkable deposits in the banking system, and the money supply in the economy, are up by $2,710: your college's $1,000 checkable deposit at College Bank, plus the hardware store's $900 checkable deposit at Merchants Trust, plus the bookstore's $810 checkable deposit at Fidelity Bank. We could continue the deposit expansion process with Fidelity Bank, which sets aside $81 in required reserves and uses the $729 in excess reserves as a basis for additional loans, but by now you get the idea.

Notice the pattern of deposits and loans emerging from the analysis. Each time a bank receives a new deposit, 10 percent is set aside to satisfy the reserve requirement. The rest becomes excess reserves, which can be left idle or can serve as a basis for making loans or purchasing government bonds. In our example, excess reserves support loans that were then spent by the borrowers. This spending became another bank's checkable deposits, thereby generating excess reserves to support still more loans. Thus the excess reserves created initially by the Federal Reserve's purchase of U.S. bonds were passed from one bank to the next in the chain. Each bank set aside 10 percent of new deposits as required reserves, then used the remaining 90 percent to support additional lending.

An individual bank can lend no more than its excess reserves. When the borrower spends the amount loaned, reserves at one bank usually fall, but total reserves in the banking system do not. A check drawn against one account will typically be deposited in another account—if not in the same bank, then in another. Thus when a bank makes a loan and creates checkable deposits, the excess reserves on which that loan was based usually find their way back into the banking system. The recipient bank uses most of the new deposit to extend more loans and create more checkable deposits. The potential expansion of checkable deposits in the banking system therefore equals some multiple of the initial increase in excess reserves. Note that our example assumes that banks do not allow excess reserves to sit idle and that the public does not choose to hold some of the newly created money as cash. If excess reserves remained just that, they obviously would not fuel an expansion of the money supply. And if people choose to hold some of the newly created money as cash rather than in checking accounts, then the borrowed funds would not provide additional reserves in the banking system.

lower discount rate reduces the cost of borrowing, encouraging banks to borrow reserves from the Fed. More bank reserves usually result in more bank lending and an increased money supply. On the other hand, a higher discount rate increases the cost of borrowing reserves from the Fed, resulting in less bank lending and a reduced money supply. The Fed's Board of Governors (not the FOMC) sets the discount rate by majority vote.

The Fed uses the discount rate more as a signal to financial markets about its monetary policy than as a tool for increasing or decreasing the money supply. The discount rate might also be thought of as an emergency tool for injecting liquidity into the banking system in the event of some financial crisis, such as a stock market crash.

The discount rate is a relatively imperfect tool for monetary policy because there is no guarantee that banks will necessarily borrow more even if the discount rate is reduced. If business prospects look poor and if banks view lending as risky, then even a lower discount rate may not entice banks to borrow from the Fed. Still, changes in the discount rate signal the Fed's intentions about monetary policy.

Reserve Requirements

The Fed also influences the money supply through reserve requirements, which are regulations regarding the minimum amount of reserves that banks must hold against deposits. Reserve requirements influence how much money the banking system can create with each dollar of reserves. If the Fed increases the reserve requirement, then banks must hold more reserves, reducing the amount of each dollar on deposit that can be lent out, which has the effect of reducing the money supply. On the other hand, a decrease in the reserve requirement increases the fraction of each dollar on deposit that can be lent out, which has the effect of increasing the money supply. Reserve requirements can be changed by a simple majority vote by the Board of Governors. But since changes in the reserve requirement are disruptive to the banking system, the Fed seldom employs them as a tool of monetary policy.

The Fed Is a Money Machine

Over three-fourths of the Federal Reserve's assets are U.S. government bonds. These bonds, the result of open-market operations, are IOUs from the federal government and assets of the Fed. *Over three-fourths of the Fed's liabilities are Federal Reserve notes in circulation.* These notes—U. S. currency—are IOUs from the Fed and are therefore liabilities of Fed. The Fed's primary asset—U.S. government bonds—earns interest, whereas the Fed's primary liability—Federal Reserve notes—requires no interest payments by the Fed. *The Fed is therefore both literally and figuratively a money machine. It is literally a money machine because it supplies the economy with Federal Reserve notes, and it is figuratively a money machine because its main asset earns interest but its main liability requires no interest payments.* The Fed also earns revenue from various services it provides. After financing its operating costs, the Fed turns over any remaining income to the U.S. Treasury to help fund the federal government.

We will learn more about the Fed's monetary policy in the next chapter. For a change of pace, let's close with a case study that looks at new developments in banking sparked by the revolution in personal computers and the Internet.

Banking on the Net

The Security First Network Bank (SFNB) never closes. It's open 24 hours a day, 365 days a year. Bank customers can pay bills, check account balances, and buy financial services from anywhere in the world—anywhere they have access to a personal computer and the Internet. SFNB was the nation's first "virtual" bank, authorized by regulators to offer full banking services on the Internet. Accounts are insured by the Federal Deposit Insurance Corporation. And the bank can accept deposits from customers in all 50 states. Deposits are accepted through the mail, direct deposit (such as with payroll checks), and electronic transfers. Depositors can also use ATM cards to carry out transactions or get cash at thousands of locations.

Incidentally, Internet banking is not quite the same thing as home banking. Internet banking requires no special software beyond your browser, nor is any banking data stored on your hard drive. The Internet customer need only log on to benefit from all the features of a bank. In contrast, home banking may require special software, and customers may be able to access their accounts only through computers on which the application is installed.

With hundreds of banks now accessible via the Internet, customers are increasingly shopping nationwide, even worldwide, for the best rates for deposits, credit cards, or loans. So a customer in St. Louis can get a housing mortgage in Atlanta, a car loan in Phoenix, a credit card in Boston, and a checking account in Chicago. And most banks offer an on-screen calculator so potential customers can figure out what size loan they can afford.

The Internet could become the biggest market in history, and banks want to become part of the picture. Over the long run, the Internet offers convenience for customers and potential cost savings for banks. Like telephone banking, which now accounts for one-fourth of all bank transactions, the Internet reduces the need for branches and branch personnel. Citibank, for example, encourages on-line use by eliminating fees for those who bank via computer. By 2005, three-quarters of U.S. households are expected to be doing some form of on-line banking.

Sources: Saul Hansell, "Online Banking Doesn't Always Cover the Basics," *New York Times* (10 November 1997); Peter Truell, "Industry Trend Seen as Citicorp, Travelers Plan Major Layoffs," *New York Times* (18 September 1998). SFNB's Internet address is http://www.sfnb.com. For access to hundreds of banking sites on the Internet see "Banks," USA Online at http://www.usaol.com/YP/banks/banks.html.

CaseStudy

The Information Economy

Two Web sites provide evaluations of the quality of Internet banking. The *Wall Street Journal*'s on-line money magazine, *Smart Money*, presents the results of its latest survey of the Internet services of the 15 largest U.S. banks at http://www.smartmoney.com/ ac/bestbuys/banking/index. cfm?story=ebank. On what basis do they decide which is the best? Gomez Advisors lists their top 20 at http://www.gomez.com/ Finance/Banks/Scorecard/ index.cfm?cat=1. Go to the methodology section to learn how they score the services of the banks. More detailed information about each bank can be found by clicking on the bank's name.

CONCLUSION

Banks play a unique role in the economy because they can transform someone's IOU into a checkable deposit, and a checkable deposit is money. The banking system's ability to expand the money supply depends on the amount of excess reserves in that system. Through open-market operations, changes in the discount rate, or changes in reserve requirements, the Fed can vary the amount of excess reserves in the banking system. In our example, it was the purchase of a $1,000 U.S. bond that started the ball rolling. The Fed can also increase reserves by lowering the discount rate enough to stimulate bank borrowing from the Fed (although the Fed uses changes in the discount rate more to signal its policy goals than to alter the money supply). And, by reducing the required reserve ratio, the Fed not only instantly creates excess reserves in the banking system but also increases the money multiplier. In practice, the Fed rarely changes the reserve requirement because of the disruptive effect of such a change on the banking system. *To control the money supply, the Fed relies primarily on open-market operations.*

Open-market operations can have a direct affect on the money supply, as when the Fed buys bonds from the public for cash. But the Fed's primary effect on the money supply is indirect, as when the Fed's bond purchase increases bank reserves, which then serve as fuel for the money multiplier. In the next chapter, we will consider the effects of the money supply on the economy.

SUMMARY

1. Banks are unlike other businesses because they can turn a borrower's IOU into money—they can create money. Banks match the different desires of savers and borrowers. Banks also evaluate loan applications and diversify portfolios of assets to reduce the risk to any one saver.

2. The money supply is narrowly defined as M1, which consists of currency held by the nonbanking public plus checkable deposits and travelers checks. Broader monetary aggregates include other kinds of deposits. M2 includes M1 plus savings deposits, small-denomination time deposits, and money market mutual funds. M3 includes M2 plus large-denomination time deposits.

3. In acquiring portfolios of assets, banks attempt to maximize profits while maintaining enough liquidity to satisfy depositors' demands for funds.

4. Any single bank can expand the money supply by the amount of its excess reserves. For the banking system as a whole, the maximum expansion of the money supply equals a multiple of excess reserves. The simple money multiplier equals the reciprocal of the reserve ratio. The money multiplier is reduced to the extent that borrowers sit on their proceeds, the public withdraws cash from the banking system, and banks allow excess reserves to remain just that.

5. The key to changes in the money supply is the Fed's impact on excess reserves in the banking system. To increase excess reserves and, hence, to increase the money supply, the Fed can buy U.S. government bonds, reduce the discount rate, or lower the reserve requirement. To reduce excess reserves and, hence, to reduce the money supply, the Fed can sell U.S. government bonds, increase the discount rate, or increase the reserve requirement. By far the most important monetary tool for the Fed is open-market operations—buying or selling U.S. bonds.

QUESTIONS FOR REVIEW

1. *(Banks as Financial Intermediaries)* In acting as financial intermediaries, what needs and desires of savers and borrowers must banks consider?

2. *(CaseStudy: Tracking the Supernote)* Why did the U.S. government consider it important to redesign the $100 bill in order to combat the effects of the "supernote"?

3. *(Monetary Aggregates)* Determine whether each of the following is included in any of the M1, M2, or M3 measures of the money supply:
   a. Currency held by the nonbanking public
   b. Available credit on credit cards held by the nonbanking public
   c. Savings deposits

d. Large-denomination time deposits
e. Money market mutual fund accounts

4. *(Monetary Aggregates)* Suppose that $1,000 is moved from a savings account at a commercial bank to a checking account at the same bank. Which of the following statements are true and which are false?
   a. The amount of currency in circulation will fall.
   b. M1 will increase.
   c. M2 will increase.

5. *(Bank Deposits)* Explain the differences among checkable deposits, demand deposits, savings deposits, and time deposits. Explain whether each of these deposits represents a bank asset or a bank liability.

6. *(Reserve Accounts)* Explain why a reduction in the required reserve ratio cannot, at least initially, increase total reserves in the banking system. Is the same true of lowering the discount rate? What would happen if the Fed bought U.S. bonds from, or sold them to, the banking system?

7. *(Liquidity Versus Profitability)* Why must a bank manager strike a balance between liquidity and profitability on the bank's balance sheet?

8. *(Creating Money)* Often it is claimed that banks create money by making loans. How can commercial banks create money? Is the government the only institution that can legally create money?

9. *(Fed Tools of Monetary Control)* What three tools can the Fed can use to change the money supply? Which tool is used most frequently? What are two limitations on the money expansion process?

10. *(Discount Rate)* What is the difference between the federal funds rate and the discount rate? What is the ultimate impact on the money supply of an increase in the discount rate?

11. *(Federal Funds Market)* What is the federal funds market? How does it help banks strike a balance between liquidity and profitability?

12. *(The Fed Is a Money Machine)* Why is the Fed both literally and figuratively a money machine?

13. *(Case**Study:** Banking on the Net)* What impact is increased Internet banking likely to have on money's function as a medium of exchange?

PROBLEMS AND EXERCISES

14. *(Monetary Aggregates)* Calculate M1, M2, and M3 using the following information:

Large-denomination time deposits	$304 billion
Currency and coin held by non-banking public	$438 billion
Checkable deposits	$509 billion
Small-denomination time deposits	$198 billion
Travelers checks	$18 billion
Savings deposits	$326 billion
Money market mutual fund accounts	$637 billion

15. *(Money Creation)* Show how each of the following *initially* affects bank assets, liabilities, and reserves. Do *not* include the results of bank behavior resulting from the Fed's action. Assume a required reserve ratio of 0.05.
   a. The Fed purchases $10 million worth of U.S. government bonds from a bank.
   b. The Fed loans $5 million to a bank.
   c. The Fed raises the required reserve ratio to 0.10.

16. *(Money Creation)* Show how each of the following would initially affect a bank's assets and liabilities.

   a. Someone makes a $10,000 deposit.
   b. A bank makes a loan of $1,000 by establishing a checking account for $1,000.
   c. The loan described in part (b) is spent.
   d. A bank must write off a loan because the borrower defaults.

17. *(Reserve Accounts)* Suppose that a bank's customer deposits $4,000 in her checking account. The required reserve ratio is 0.25. What are the required reserves on this new deposit? What is the largest loan that the bank can make on the basis of the new deposit? If the bank chooses to hold reserves of $3,000 on the new deposit, what are the excess reserves on the deposit?

18. *(Money Multiplier)* Suppose that the Federal Reserve lowers the required reserve ratio from 0.10 to 0.05. How does this affect the simple money multiplier, assuming that excess reserves are held to zero and there are no currency leakages? What are the money multipliers for required reserve ratios of 0.15 and 0.20?

19. *(Money Creation)* Suppose Bank A, which faces a reserve requirement of 10 percent, receives a $1,000 deposit from a customer.

a. Assuming that it wishes to hold no excess reserves, determine how much the bank should lend. Show your answer on Bank A's balance sheet.

b. Assuming that the loan shown in Bank A's balance sheet is redeposited in Bank B, show the changes in Bank B's balance sheet if it lends out the maximum possible.

c. Repeat this process for three additional banks: C, D, and E.

d. Using the simple money multiplier, calculate the total change in the money supply resulting from the $1,000 initial deposit.

e. Assume Banks A, B, C, D, and E each wish to hold 5 percent excess reserves. How would holding this level of excess reserves affect the total change in the money supply?

20. *(Monetary Control)* Suppose the money supply is currently $500 billion and the Fed wishes to increase it by $100 billion.

a. Given a required reserve ratio of 0.25, what should it do?

b. If it decided to change the money supply by changing the required reserve ratio, what change should it make?

EXPERIENTIAL EXERCISES

21. *(Fed Tools of Monetary Control)* Review the Fed's on-line brochure on the Federal Open Market Committee at http://www.bog.frb.fed.us/pubs/frseries/frseri2.htm, especially the sections entitled "The Decision-making Process" and "Reports." What information does the FOMC consider as it plans open-market operations? Look at the minutes of the most recent meeting to determine what kinds of open-market operations are going on now.

22. *(CaseStudy: Banking on the Net)* The *Journal of Internet Banking and Commerce* at http://www.arraydev.com/commerce/jibc/current.htm is a Web-based magazine devoted to Internet banking and related issues.

Take a look at the current edition and see if you can determine what effect electronic banking is having on the Fed's ability to control the U.S. money supply. Also see what you can learn about the status of Internet banking outside the United States.

23. *(Wall Street Journal)* If you have access to the Interactive Edition of the *Wall Street Journal,* you can use the Briefing Books feature to obtain data on over 10,000 public companies. Use this feature to locate the Briefing Book on a large commercial bank in your area. Look at some of its press releases to determine how this bank has been influenced by Federal Reserve regulations and monetary policy operations.

Monetary Theory And Policy

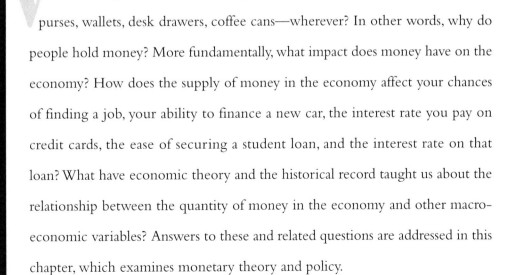

W hy do people maintain checking accounts and have cash in their pockets, purses, wallets, desk drawers, coffee cans—wherever? In other words, why do people hold money? More fundamentally, what impact does money have on the economy? How does the supply of money in the economy affect your chances of finding a job, your ability to finance a new car, the interest rate you pay on credit cards, the ease of securing a student loan, and the interest rate on that loan? What have economic theory and the historical record taught us about the relationship between the quantity of money in the economy and other macro-economic variables? Answers to these and related questions are addressed in this chapter, which examines monetary theory and policy.

Visit the McEachern
Interactive Study Center
for this chapter at
http://mcisc.swcollege.com

The supply of money in the economy affects you in a variety of ways, but to understand those effects we must dig a little deeper. Thus far we have focused on how the banking system creates money. But a more fundamental question is how the money supply affects the economy. The Fed's role in supplying money to the economy is called *monetary policy*. The study of the effect of money on the economy is called *monetary theory*. A central concern of monetary theory is the effect of the money supply on the economy's price level and on the level of output.

Until now, we have not emphasized differences among competing theories of how the economy works. Traditionally, economists have maintained that there are two channels through which a change in the money supply may affect aggregate demand: an indirect channel, working through changes in the interest rate, and a direct channel, where changes in the supply of money directly affect how much people want to spend. There was a time when the major debate among macroeconomists involved the relative importance of each channel. One group of economists believed the indirect channel was more important and the other believed the direct channel was more important. Most economists now find some validity with each channel.

In this chapter, we consider the theory behind each channel. Note that although these two theories are different, they are not mutually exclusive. Each traces a different path between changes in the money supply and changes in aggregate demand, and both paths could operate at the same time. Topics discussed in this chapter include:

- Demand and supply of money
- Indirect and direct channels to aggregate demand
- Equation of exchange
- Velocity of money
- Monetary targets

MONEY AND THE ECONOMY: THE INDIRECT CHANNEL

Let's begin by reviewing the important distinction between the *stock of money* and *the flow of income*. How much money do you have with you right now? That amount is a *stock*. Income, in contrast, is a *flow*, indicating how much money you earn per period of time. Income has no meaning unless the time period is specified. You would not know whether to be impressed that a friend earned $100 unless you knew whether this was earnings per week, per day, or per hour.

Demand for money The relationship between how much money people want to hold and the interest rate

The **demand for money** is a relationship between how much money people want to hold and the interest rate. Keep in mind that the quantity of money held is a stock measure. It may seem odd at first to be talking about the demand for money. You might think people would demand all the money they could get their hands on. But remember that money, the stock, is not the same as income, the flow. People express their demand for income by selling their labor and other resources. People express their demand for money by holding some of their wealth as money rather than holding other assets that would earn more interest.

But we are getting ahead of ourselves. The question we want to ask initially is why people demand money. Why do people maintain checking accounts and have cash in their pockets, purses, wallets, desk drawers, coffee cans—wherever? The most obvious reason people demand money is that it is a convenient medium of exchange. *People demand money to carry out market transactions.*

The Demand for Money

Because barter represents an insignificant portion of exchange in the modern industrial economy, households, firms, governments, and foreigners need money to conduct their daily transactions. Consumers need money to buy products, and firms need money to buy resources. *Money allows people to carry out their economic transactions more easily.* When credit cards are involved, the payment of money is delayed briefly, but all accounts must eventually be settled with money.

The greater the value of transactions to be financed in a given period, the greater the demand for money. So the more active the economy is—that is, the greater the volume of exchange as reflected by the level of real output—the greater the demand for money. Also, the higher the price level, the greater the demand for money. The more things cost on average, the more money is required to purchase them.

Your demand for money supports expenditures you expect in the course of your normal economic affairs plus various unexpected expenditures. If you plan to buy lunch tomorrow, you will carry enough money to pay for it. But you also may want to be able to pay for other possible contingencies. For example, you could have car trouble or you could come across an unexpected sale on a favorite item. You may have a little extra money with you right now for who knows what. Even *you* don't know.

The demand for money is rooted in money's role as a medium of exchange. But as we have seen, money is more than a medium of exchange; it is also a store of value. Because a household's income and expenditures are not perfectly matched each period, purchasing power is often saved to finance future expenditures. People save for a new home, for college, for retirement. The view of money that emphasizes the indirect channel focuses on two ways in which people can store their purchasing power: (1) in the form of money and (2) in the form of other financial assets, such as corporate and government securities. When people purchase bonds and other financial assets, they are lending their money and are paid interest for doing so.

The demand for any asset is based on the flow of services it provides. The big advantage of money as a store of value is its liquidity: Money can immediately be exchanged for whatever is for sale. In contrast, other financial assets, such as corporate or government bonds, must first be *liquidated*, or exchanged for money, which can then be used to buy goods and services. Money, however, has one major disadvantage when compared to other types of financial assets. Money in the form of currency and travelers checks earns no interest, and the interest rate earned on checkable deposits is typically below that earned on other financial assets. So those who hold their wealth in the form of money forgo some interest that they could earn by holding some other financial asset. For example, suppose a corporation could earn 3 percent more by holding financial assets other than money. The opportunity cost of holding $10 million as money rather than as some other financial asset would amount to $300,000 per year. *The interest forgone is the opportunity cost of holding money.*

Money Demand and Interest Rates

When the market interest rate is low, other things constant, the cost of holding money—the cost of maintaining liquidity—is low, so people hold a larger fraction of their wealth in the form of money. When the market interest rate is

E X H I B I T   1

Demand for Money

The demand for money curve, D_m, slopes downward. As the interest rate falls, so does the opportunity cost of holding money; the quantity of money demanded increases.

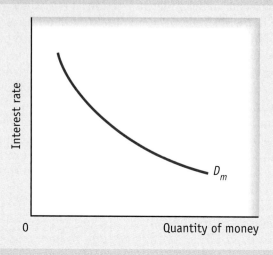

high, the cost of holding money is high, so people hold less of their wealth in money and more of their wealth in other financial assets that pay more interest. Thus, *other things constant, the quantity of money demanded varies inversely with the market interest rate.*

The money demand curve, D_m, in Exhibit 1 shows the quantity of money people in the economy demand at alternative interest rates, other things constant. Both the quantity of money and the interest rate are in nominal terms. *The money demand curve slopes downward because the lower the interest rate, the lower the opportunity cost of holding money.* Movements along the curve reflect the effects of changes in the interest rate on the quantity of money demanded, other things constant. The quantity of money demanded is inversely related to the price of holding money, which is the interest rate. *Held constant along the curve are the price level and real GDP. If either increases, the demand for money increases, as reflected by a shift to the right in the entire money demand curve.*

Supply of Money and the Equilibrium Interest Rate

The supply of money—the stock of money available in the economy at a particular time—is determined primarily by the Fed through its control over currency and over excess reserves in the banking system. The supply of money, S_m, is depicted as a vertical line, as in Exhibit 2. *A vertical supply curve implies that the quantity of money supplied is independent of the interest rate.*

The intersection of the supply of money, S_m, and the demand for money, D_m, determines the equilibrium interest rate, i—the interest rate that equates the quantity of money supplied in the economy with the quantity of money demanded. At interest rates above the equilibrium level, the opportunity cost of holding money is higher, so the quantity of money people want to hold is less than the quantity supplied. At interest rates below the equilibrium level, the opportunity cost of holding money is lower, so the quantity of money people want to hold is greater than the quantity supplied.

EXHIBIT 2

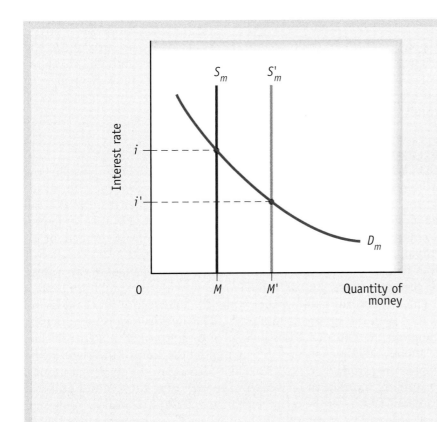

Effect of an Increase in the Money Supply

Since the supply of money is determined by the Federal Reserve, it can be represented by a vertical line. The intersection of the supply of money, S_m, and the demand for money, D_m, determines the equilibrium interest rate, i. Following an increase in the money supply to S'_m, the quantity of money supplied exceeds the quantity demanded at the original interest rate, i. People who are holding more money than they would like attempt to exchange money for bonds or other financial assets. In doing so, they drive the interest rate down to i', where quantity demanded equals the new quantity supplied.

If the Fed increases the money supply, the money supply curve shifts to the right, as shown by the movement from S_m to S'_m in Exhibit 2. The quantity supplied now exceeds the quantity demanded at the original interest rate, i. Because of the increased supply of money, there is now more money in the hands of the public, so people are *able* to hold a greater quantity of money. But at interest rate i they are *unwilling* to hold that much. Since people are now holding more of their wealth as money than they would like, they exchange some money for other financial assets, such as bonds.

As people try to exchange money for bonds, the market rate of interest falls. As the demand for bonds increases, bond issuers can pay less interest yet still attract enough buyers. The interest rate falls until the quantity demanded just equals the quantity supplied. With the decline in the interest rate to i' in Exhibit 2, the opportunity cost of holding money falls enough so the public is willing to hold the now-larger stock of money. *For a given demand for money curve, increases in the supply of money drive down the market interest rate, and decreases in the supply of money drive up the market interest rate.*

Now that you have some idea how money demand and supply determine the market interest rate, you are ready to see how money fits into the model of the macroeconomy developed thus far. Specifically, let's see how changes in the supply of money affect aggregate demand and equilibrium output.

NetBookmark

Bloomberg.com's financial news network provides quick links to the latest key interest rates and currency exchange rates at its markets Web site at http://www.bloomberg.com/markets/index.html. Bloomberg also offers numerous other resources over the Web, including BloombergTV financial news.

MONEY AND AGGREGATE DEMAND

Monetary policy influences the market interest rate, which, in turn, affects the level of planned investment, a component of aggregate demand. This is the indirect channel of money, where money affects the economy through changes in the interest rate. Let's work through the chain of causation in a specific economic setting.

Interest Rates and Planned Investment

Suppose the Federal Reserve believes that the economy is operating well below its potential level of output and decides to increase the money supply to stimulate output and employment. Recall from the previous chapter that the Fed can expand the money supply by (1) purchasing U.S. government bonds, (2) lowering the discount rate, the rate at which banks can borrow from the Fed, or (3) lowering the reserve requirement.

The four panels of Exhibit 3 trace the links between changes in the money supply and changes in aggregate demand. We begin with the equilibrium interest rate i, which is determined in panel (a) by the intersection of the demand for money, D_m, with the supply of money, S_m. This intersection is identified by point a. Suppose the Fed purchases U.S. government bonds and thereby increases the money supply, as shown in panel (a) by the shift to the right in the money supply curve from S_m to S'_m. After the increase in the supply of money, people are holding more of their wealth in money than they would prefer at the initial interest rate i, so they try to exchange one form of wealth, money, for other financial assets. This greater willingness to lend has no direct effect on aggregate demand, but it does reduce the market interest rate.

A decline in the interest rate to i', other things constant, reduces the opportunity cost of financing new plants and equipment, thereby making new business investment more profitable. Likewise, a lower interest rate reduces the cost of mortgages on new housing, so housing investment increases. Thus the decline in the rate of interest increases the quantity of investment demanded. Panel (b) shows the demand for investment, D_I, first introduced in Chapter 9. When the interest rate falls from i to i', investment spending increases from I to I'.

The aggregate expenditure line in panel (c) shifts upward by the increase in planned investment, from AE to AE'. The spending multiplier magnifies this increase in investment, leading to a greater increase in the quantity of real GDP demanded at each price level. The quantity demanded increases from Y to Y', as reflected in panel (c) by the intersection of the new aggregate expenditure function with the 45-degree line. This same increase is also reflected in panel (d), given price level P, by the horizontal shift in the aggregate demand curve from AD to AD'.

The sequence of events can be summarized as follows:

$$M\uparrow \rightarrow i\downarrow \rightarrow I\uparrow \rightarrow AE\uparrow \rightarrow AD\uparrow$$

An increase in the money supply, M, reduces the interest rate, i. The lower interest rate stimulates investment spending, I, which shifts up the aggregate expenditure line. This increase in the quantity of real GDP demanded at a particular price level is reflected by a shift to the right in the aggregate demand curve,

EXHIBIT 3

**Effects of an Increase in the Money Supply on
Interest Rates, Investment, Aggregate Expenditure, and Aggregate Demand**

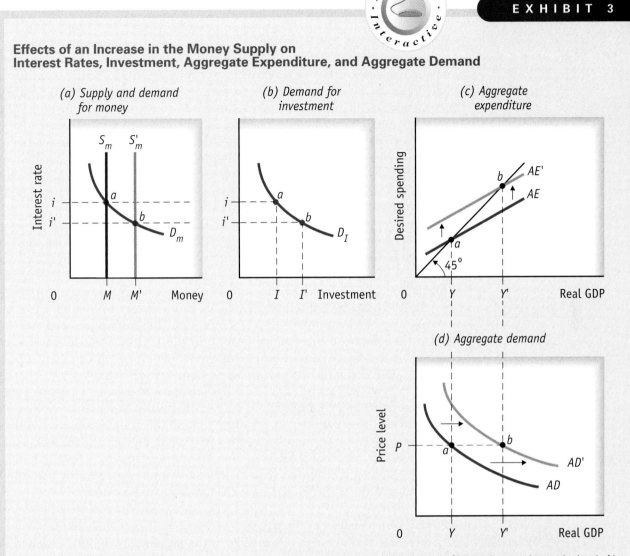

In panel (a), an increase in the money supply drives the interest rate down to *i*'. With the cost of borrowing now lower, the level of investment spending increases from *I* to *I*', as shown in panel (b). More investment spending drives aggregate expenditure up from *AE* to *AE*', as shown in panel (c). The increased expenditure sets off the multiplier process, so the quantity of aggregate output demanded increases from *Y* to *Y*'. The increase is shown by the shift to the right in the aggregate demand curve in panel (d).

from *AD* to *AD*'.[1] The entire sequence is also traced out in each panel by the movement from points *a* to *b*.

---

1 The graphs are actually more complicated than those presented here. Since the demand for money depends on the level of real GDP, an increase in real GDP would shift the money demand curve to the right in panel (a). For simplicity, we have not shown a shift in the money demand curve. If we had shifted the money demand curve, the equilibrium interest rate would still have fallen, but not by as much, so investment and aggregate demand would not have increased by as much.

Let's now consider the effect of a Fed-orchestrated reduction in interest rates. In Exhibit 3 such a policy can be traced by moving from point *b* to point *a* in each panel, but we will dispense with a blow-by-blow discussion of the graphs. Suppose the Federal Reserve decides to reduce the money supply to cool down an overheated economy. A decrease in the money supply would create an excess demand for money at the initial interest rate, so people will attempt to exchange other financial assets for money. These efforts to get more money raise the market interest rate, or the opportunity cost of holding money. The interest rate increases until the quantity of money demanded declines just enough to equal the now-lower quantity of money supplied.

At the higher interest rate, businesses find it more costly to finance plants and equipment, and households find it more costly to finance new homes. Hence a higher rate of interest reduces investment. The resulting decline in investment is magnified by the spending multiplier, leading to a greater decline in aggregate demand.

As long as the interest rate is sensitive to changes in the money supply, and as long as the quantity of investment is sensitive to changes in the interest rate, changes in the supply of money affect planned investment. The extent to which a given change in planned investment affects aggregate demand depends on the size of the spending multiplier.

Let's examine a recent example of a Fed-orchestrated reduction in interest rates. At 2:15 P.M. on September 29, 1998, immediately following a regular meeting of the Federal Open Market Committee, the Fed announced that "to cushion the effects on prospective growth in the United States of increasing weakness in foreign economies," it planned to increase the money supply enough to push down the federal funds rate from a target of 5.5 percent to a target of 5.25 percent. This was the Fed's first interest rate cut since January 1996. As you know, the federal funds rate is the one that banks charge one another for overnight loans. The next day, major banks around the country announced they would lower their prime interest rate, the interest rate they charge their best customers, by 0.25 percentage points. Thus, by announcing a cut in the federal funds rate, the Fed was able to reduce the prime interest rate in the economy. We will learn more about interest rate changes later in the chapter.

Adding Aggregate Supply

Even after tracing the effect of a change in the money supply on aggregate demand, we still have only half the story. To determine the effects of monetary policy on the equilibrium level of real GDP in the economy, we need the supply side. An aggregate supply curve can help show how a given shift in the aggregate demand curve affects real GDP and the price level. In the short run, the aggregate supply curve slopes upward, so the quantity supplied will expand only if the price level increases. *For a given shift in the aggregate demand curve, the steeper the short-run aggregate supply curve, the smaller the increase in real GDP and the larger the increase in the price level.*

Assume the economy is producing at point *a* in Exhibit 4, where the aggregate demand curve, *AD*, intersects the short-run aggregate supply curve, AS_{130}, yielding a short-run equilibrium output of $7.8 trillion and a price level of 125. As you can see, the actual price level of 125 is below the expected price level of 130, so the short-run equilibrium output of $7.8 trillion is below the economy's potential of $8.0 trillion, yielding a contractionary gap of $0.2 trillion.

EXHIBIT 4

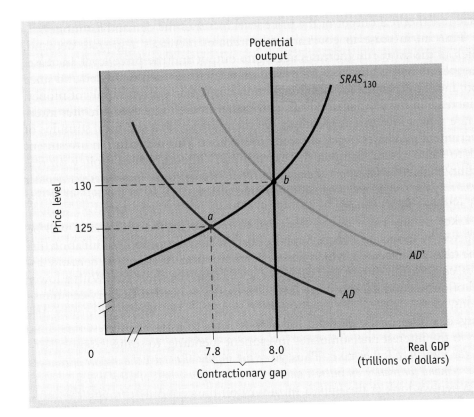

Expansionary Monetary Policy to Correct a Contractionary Gap

At point *a*, the economy is producing below potential. There is a contractionary gap equal to $0.2 trillion. If the Federal Reserve increases the money supply, the aggregate demand curve shifts to *AD'*. Equilibrium will be reestablished at point *b*, with price level 130 and output at the potential level of $8.0 trillion.

The Fed can wait to see whether natural market forces close the gap as the short-run aggregate supply curve shifts to the right, or it can intervene and attempt to close the gap with an expansionary monetary policy. For example, in 1992 and 1993 the Fed aggressively increased the money supply in order to lower interest rates and stimulate aggregate demand. If the Fed increases the money supply by exactly the appropriate amount, this increases the aggregate demand curve enough to achieve a new equilibrium at point *b*, where the economy is producing its potential output. Given all the connections in the chain of causality between changes in the money supply and changes in equilibrium output, however, it would actually be quite remarkable for the Fed to execute monetary policy so precisely—but more on that later.

To review: *The indirect effect of an increase in the money supply is to reduce the market interest rate, resulting in an increase in planned investment and a consequent increase in aggregate demand. As long as the short-run aggregate supply curve slopes upward, the short-run effect of an increase in the money supply is an increase in both real output and the price level.*

Fiscal Policy with Money

Now that we have considered the indirect effect that money has on aggregate demand and equilibrium output, we can take another look at fiscal policy. Suppose there is an increase in government purchases, other things constant. In Chapter 12, we found that an increase in government purchases increases aggregate demand and, in the short run, leads to both a greater output and a higher price

EXPERIENTIAL EXERCISES

23. *(Money Supply Versus Interest Rate Targets)* A favorite activity of many macroeconomists is Fed-watching. Go to the Federal Reserve Board's Web site and look for the most recent Congressional testimony of the Board Chairperson at http://www.bog.frb.fed.us/boarddocs/testimony/. Is the Fed targeting interest rates, the money supply, or something else?

24. *(Targets After 1982)* The Federal Reserve Bank of Cleveland's monthly publication *Economic Trends* at http://www.clev.frb.org/research/ is available on-line. Choose a recent issue and click on "Monetary Pol-

icy." What are some current developments in monetary policy? See if you can illustrate them using the *AD–AS* model.

25. *(Wall Street Journal)* The Federal Reserve Report appears in each Friday's *Wall Street Journal*. You can find it in the Money and Investing section. In addition to the weekly report, a monthly chart shows the recent performance of money supply indicators, compared with Fed targets. Does it look as if the Fed has been hitting its targets over the last year?

The Policy Debate:
Active or Passive?

Visit the McEachern
Interactive Study Center
for this chapter at
http://mcisc.swcollege.com

D oes the private sector work fairly well on its own or does it require active government intervention? If people expect government intervention to prod the economy along, does this expectation affect people's behavior? Does government intervention do more harm than good? What is the relationship between unemployment and inflation in the short run and in the long run? Answers to these and other questions are provided in this chapter, which examines the policy debate regarding the appropriate role for government in economic stabilization.

You have now studied both fiscal and monetary policy and are in a position to take a broader view of the impact of public policy on the U.S. economy. This chapter distinguishes between two approaches: the *active approach* and the *passive approach*. The active approach views the private sector as relatively unstable and unable to recover from shocks when they occur. According to advocates of an active approach, economic fluctuations arise primarily from the private sector, particularly investment, and natural market forces may not be much help when the economy gets off track. To move the economy to its potential output, the active approach calls for the use of discretionary policy.

The passive approach, on the other hand, considers the private sector to be relatively stable and able to recover from shocks when they occur. According to advocates of a passive approach, when the economy gets off track, natural market forces nudge it back on course. Not only is active government intervention unnecessary, but such activism, according to advocates of the passive approach, often does more harm than good.

In this chapter, we will consider the pros and cons of *active* intervention in the economy versus *passive* reliance on natural market forces. We will also examine the role that expectations play in determining the effectiveness of stabilization policy. You will learn why unanticipated stabilization policies have more impact on employment and output than do anticipated ones. Finally, the chapter explores the trade-off between unemployment and inflation. As you read, keep in mind that issues of macroeconomic policy remain the most widely debated of economic questions. Topics discussed in this chapter include:

- Active versus passive policies
- Self-correcting mechanisms
- Rational expectations
- Policy rules and policy credibility

- The time-inconsistency problem
- Short-run and long-run Phillips curves
- Natural rate hypothesis

ACTIVE POLICY VERSUS PASSIVE POLICY

According to the *active approach,* discretionary fiscal or monetary policy can reduce the costs imposed by an unstable private sector. According to the *passive approach,* discretionary policy contributes to the instability of the economy and is therefore part of the problem, not part of the solution. The two approaches differ in their assumptions about how well natural market forces operate.

Closing a Contractionary Gap

Perhaps the best way to describe each approach is by examining a particular macroeconomic problem. Suppose the economy is in short-run equilibrium at point *a* in panel (a) of Exhibit 1, with a real GDP of $7.8 trillion, which is below the economy's potential output of $8.0 trillion. The contractionary gap of $0.2 trillion drives unemployment above the natural rate (the rate of unemployment when the economy is producing its potential output). This gap could have resulted from lower than expected aggregate demand or some adverse supply shock that temporarily decreased short-run aggregate supply. What should public officials do when confronted with this gap?

Those who subscribe to the passive approach, like their classical predecessors, have more faith in the *self-correcting mechanisms* of the economy than do those who favor the active approach. In what sense is the economy self-correcting? According to the passive approach, wages and prices are flexible enough to adjust within a reasonable period to labor shortages or surpluses. The high unemployment in panel (a) will cause wages to fall, which will reduce production

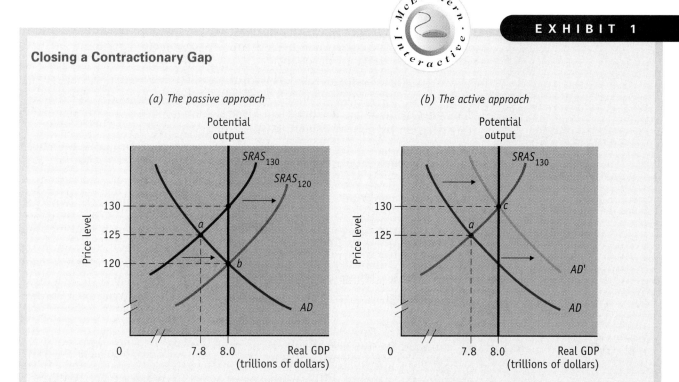

EXHIBIT 1

Closing a Contractionary Gap

(a) The passive approach

(b) The active approach

At point *a* in both panels, the economy is in short-run equilibrium, with unemployment above the natural rate. According to the passive approach, that high unemployment will eventually cause wages to fall, reducing firms' cost of doing business. The decline in costs will cause the short-run aggregate supply curve to shift out to $SRAS_{120}$, moving the economy to its potential level of output at point *b* in panel (a). In panel (b), the government employs an active approach to shift the aggregate demand curve from *AD* to *AD'*. If the policy works, the economy moves to its potential level of output at point *c*.

costs, which will shift the short–run aggregate supply curve rightward. (Money wages need not actually fall; money wage increases may simply lag behind increases in the price level, so that real wages fall.) According to the passive approach, the short–run aggregate supply curve will, within a reasonable period, shift from $SRAS_{130}$ to $SRAS_{120}$, moving the economy to its potential level of output at point *b. According to the passive approach, the economy is inherently stable, gravitating in a reasonable amount of time toward potential GDP. Consequently, advocates of passive policy see little reason for active government intervention.* The passive approach is to let natural market forces close the contractionary gap. So the prescription of passive policy is to do nothing special.

Advocates of an active approach, on the other hand, believe that prices and wages are not very flexible, particularly in the downward direction. They think that when adverse supply shocks or sagging demand result in unemployment that exceeds the natural rate, the economy does not quickly adjust to eliminate this unemployment. Advocates of the active approach argue that even when there is much unemployment in the economy, the renegotiation of long–term wage contracts in line with a lower expected price level may take a long time.

If so, the wage reductions required to shift the short-run aggregate supply curve outward may also take a long time, even years. The longer it takes natural market forces to lower unemployment to the natural rate, the greater the output forgone during the adjustment period and the greater the economic and psychological costs to those unemployed during that period. Because advocates of an active policy associate a high cost with the passive approach, they believe that the economy needs an active stabilization policy to alter aggregate demand and achieve the natural rate of output and price stability.

A decision by public officials to intervene in the economy to speed the return to potential output—that is, a decision to use discretionary policy—reflects an active approach. In panel (b) of Exhibit 1, we begin at the same point *a* as in panel (a). At point *a,* short-run equilibrium output is below potential output, so the economy is experiencing a contractionary gap. Through monetary policy, fiscal policy, or some mix of the two, active policy attempts to increase aggregate demand from *AD* to *AD'*, moving equilibrium from point *a* to point *c* and closing the contractionary gap. One cost of such a policy is an increase in the price level, or inflation. To the extent that the stimulus to aggregate demand worsens the federal budget deficit, another cost of active policy is an increase in the national debt, a cost that will be examined more closely in the next chapter.

Closing an Expansionary Gap

Let's consider the situation in which the short-run equilibrium output exceeds the economy's potential. Suppose that the actual price level of 135 exceeds the expected price level of 130, causing an expansionary gap of $0.2 trillion, as shown in Exhibit 2. The passive approach argues that natural market forces will prompt firms and workers to negotiate higher wages. These higher nominal wages will increase production costs, shifting the short-run supply curve up and to the left, from $SRAS_{130}$ to $SRAS_{140}$, as shown in panel (a). This leads to a higher price level and lowers output to the economy's potential. So the natural adjustment process will result in a higher price level, or inflation.

An active approach sees discretionary policy as a way of returning the economy to its potential output without an increase in the price level, or inflation. Advocates of active policy believe that if aggregate demand can be reduced from *AD"* to *AD'*, as shown in panel (b) of Exhibit 2, then the equilibrium point will move down along the initial aggregate supply curve from *d* to *c. Whereas the passive approach relies on natural market forces to close an expansionary gap through a decrease in the short-run aggregate supply curve, the active approach relies on just the right discretionary policy to close the gap through a decrease in aggregate demand.* The passive approach results in a higher price level, but the active approach results in a lower price level. Thus the correct discretionary policy can relieve the inflationary pressure associated with an expansionary gap. Whenever the Fed attempts to cool an overheated economy, as it did in 1994, it employs an active monetary policy to close an expansionary gap. In 1994, the economy was flying high, with output exceeding potential, and the Fed was trying to orchestrate a so-called soft landing.

Problems with Active Policy

The timely adoption and implementation of an appropriate active policy is not easy. One problem is identifying the economy's potential output level and the unemployment at that level. Suppose the natural rate of unemployment is 5

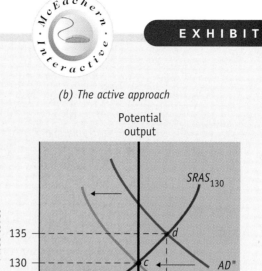

EXHIBIT 2

Policy Responses to an Expansionary Gap

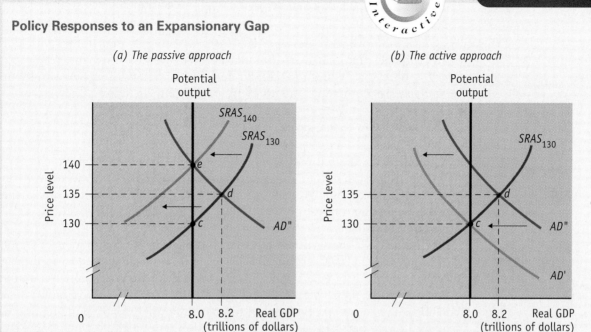

(a) The passive approach

(b) The active approach

At point *d* in both panels, the economy is in short-run equilibrium, producing $8.2 trillion. Unemployment is below the natural rate. In the passive approach reflected in panel (a), the government makes no change in policy, so natural market forces will eventually bring about a higher negotiated wage, shifting the short-run supply curve up to $SRAS_{140}$. The new equilibrium at point *e* will result in a higher price level and a lower level of output and employment. An active policy might be able to reduce aggregate demand, shifting the equilibrium from point *d* to point *c* in panel (b), thus closing the expansionary gap without increasing the price level.

percent, but policy makers believe it is 4 percent. As they pursue their elusive objective of 4 percent, they will find that output is constantly pushed beyond its potential, creating higher prices in the long run but no permanent reduction in unemployment. Recall that in the short run, if output is pushed beyond the economy's potential, an expansionary gap opens up, which will cause an upward shift in the short-run aggregate supply curve until the economy returns to its potential level of output at a higher price level.

Even if policy makers can accurately estimate the economy's potential level of output, formulating an effective policy requires detailed knowledge of current and future economic conditions. To pursue an effective active policy, policy makers must *first* be able to forecast what aggregate demand and aggregate supply would be without government intervention. Simply put, they must be able to predict what would happen with a passive policy. *Second,* policy makers must have the tools necessary to achieve the desired result relatively quickly. *Third,* policy makers must be able to forecast the effects of an active policy on the economy's key performance measures. *Fourth,* policy makers must work together. Congress and the president pursue fiscal policy while the Fed directs monetary policy; these groups often fail to coordinate their efforts. To the extent that an active policy requires coordination, the policy may not work as desired. In early 1995, for example, Congress was considering an expansionary tax cut at the same time the Fed was pursuing a contractionary monetary policy. *Fifth,* policy makers must be able to implement the appropriate policy, even if that policy involves short-term political costs. For example, during inflationary times the optimal policy may call for a tax increase or a tighter monetary policy, policies that may be unpopular because they increase unemployment. *Finally,* policy makers must be able to deal with a variety of lags. As we will see next, these lags compound the problems of pursuing an active policy.

The Problem of Lags

So far we have ignored the time required to implement policy. That is, we have assumed that the desired policy was selected and implemented instantaneously. We have also assumed that, once implemented, the policy will work as advertised—again, in no time. Actually, there may be long, sometimes unpredictable, lags at several stages in the process. These lags reduce the effectiveness and increase the uncertainty of active policies.

Recognition lag The time needed to identify a macroeconomic problem and assess its seriousness

First, there is a **recognition lag,** which is the time it takes to identify a problem and determine how serious it is. For example, time is required to accumulate evidence that the economy is indeed performing below its potential. Even if initial data spell trouble, these data are often subsequently revised. Therefore, policy makers must await additional evidence of trouble rather than risk responding to what may turn out to be a false alarm. Since a recession is not identified until more than six months after it begins and since the average recession lasts about a year, a typical recession will be more than half over before it is officially recognized as such.

Decision-making lag The time needed to decide what to do once a macroeconomic problem has been identified

Even after enough evidence has accumulated, policy makers usually take additional time deciding what to do, so there is a **decision-making lag.** In the case of discretionary fiscal policy, Congress and the president must develop and agree upon an appropriate course of action. Fiscal legislation usually takes months to approve; it could take more than a year. On the other hand, the Fed can decide on the appropriate monetary policy more quickly, so the decision-making lag is shorter for monetary policy.

Implementation lag The time needed to introduce a change in monetary or fiscal policy

Once a decision has been made, the new policy must be introduced, which often involves an **implementation lag.** Again, monetary policy has the advantage: After a policy has been adopted, the Fed can buy or sell U.S. bonds, change the discount rate, or alter reserve requirements relatively quickly. The implementation lag is longer for fiscal policy. For example, if tax rates change, new tax forms must be printed and distributed. If government spending changes, the appropriate government agencies must get involved. The implementation of fiscal policy can take more than a year. For example, in February 1983, the nation's unemployment rate reached 10.3 percent, with 11.5 million unemployed. The following month, Congress passed the Emergency Jobs Appropriation Act, providing $9 billion to create what supporters claimed would be hundreds of thousands of new jobs. Fifteen months later, only $3.1 billion had been spent and only 35,000 new jobs had been created, according to a U.S. General Accounting Office study. By that time, the economy had recovered on its own, reducing the unemployment rate to 7.1 percent and adding 6.2 million jobs! So this public spending program was implemented only after the recession had bottomed out. Likewise, in the spring of 1993, President Clinton proposed a $16 billion stimulus package to help boost what appeared to be a sluggish recovery. The measure was defeated because it would have added to a large federal deficit, yet the economy still gained 5.6 million jobs between January of 1993 and December of 1994.

Once a policy has been implemented, there is an **effectiveness lag** before the full impact of the policy registers on the economy. One problem with monetary policy is that the lag between a change in the money supply and its effect on aggregate demand and output is long and variable, ranging from several months up to three years. Fiscal policy, once enacted, usually requires 3 to 6 months to take effect and between 9 and 18 months to register its full effect.

These various lags make active policy difficult to execute. The more variable the lags, the harder it is to predict when a particular policy will take hold and what the state of the economy will be at that time. To advocates of passive policy, these lags are reason enough to avoid discretionary policy. *Advocates of a passive approach argue that an active stabilization policy imposes troubling fluctuations in the price level and real GDP because it often takes hold only after self-correcting market forces have already returned the economy to its potential output level.*

Talk in the media about "jump-starting" the economy reflects the active approach, which views the economy as a sputtering machine that can be fixed by an expert mechanic. The passive approach views the economy as more like a supertanker on automatic pilot. The policy question then becomes whether to trust that automatic pilot (the self-correcting tendencies of the economy) or to try to override the mechanism with active discretionary policies.[1]

Effectiveness lag The time necessary for changes in monetary or fiscal policy to have an effect on the economy

Review of Policy Perspectives

The active and passive approaches embody different views about the natural stability of the economy and the ability of Congress or the Fed to implement appropriate discretionary policies. Hence they disagree about the role of public policy in the economy. As we have seen, advocates of an active approach think that the natural adjustments of wages and prices can be excruciatingly slow, particularly when unemployment is high, as it was during the Great Depression. Prolonged high unemployment means that much output must be sacrificed, and the unemployed must suffer personal hardship during the slow adjustment period. If high unemployment lasts a long time, labor skills may grow rusty, and some long-term unemployed workers may drop out of the labor force. Therefore prolonged unemployment may cause the economy's potential GDP to fall, as the case study of hysteresis in Chapter 11 suggested.

Thus, active policy associates a high cost with the failure to pursue a discretionary policy. And, despite the lags involved, advocates of active policy prefer action—through fiscal policy, monetary policy, or some combination of the two—to inaction. Passive policy advocates, on the other hand, believe that uncertain lags and ignorance about how the economy works prevent policy makers from accurately determining and effectively implementing the appropriate active policy. Therefore the passive approach, rather than pursuing a misguided activist policy, relies more on the economy's natural ability to correct itself and on the government's automatic stabilizers.

Differences between active and passive approaches emerged during the presidential campaign of 1992, when the economy was slow to recover from a recession, as is discussed in the following case study.

---

1 This analogy was contributed by J. W. Mixon, Jr., to *The Teaching Economist,* Issue 4 (Spring 1992): 3, W. A. McEachern, ed.

CaseStudy
Public Policy

President Bush's last State of the Union address was on January 28, 1992—a time when the country had been experiencing a mild recession. The text of his speech is available from the Bush Presidential Library at http://www.csdl. tamu.edu/bushlib/papers/ 1992/92012801.html. Read it to determine whether he was in favor of an active or passive approach to dealing with the recession. President Clinton's State of the Union address can be found under "Read Speeches by the President" at the White House Web site, http://www.pub. whitehouse.gov/WH/ Publications/html/ Publications.html. Given current economic conditions, how activist does Clinton appear to be? Is he seeking additional government programs and targeted tax cuts? For what purposes?

Active Versus Passive Presidential Candidates

During the third quarter of 1990, after the longest peacetime expansion this century, the U.S. economy slipped into a recession, touched off by the uncertainty generated when Iraq invaded Kuwait. Because of the large federal deficit prevailing at the time, policy makers were reluctant to employ discretionary fiscal policy to stimulate the economy. That task was left to monetary policy. The Fed supplied enough additional reserves to the banking system to lower the federal funds rate. The Fed also cut the discount rate several times. These moves were aimed at stimulating spending. The recession lasted only nine months, but the recovery was sluggish.

That sluggish recovery was the economic setting for the presidential election of 1992 between Republican President George Bush and Democratic challenger Bill Clinton. Since monetary policy did not seem to be providing a sufficient kick, was an additional fiscal stimulus a viable option? With the federal budget deficit in 1992 already nearing $300 billion, a record level, would a higher deficit do more harm than good?

Bush's biggest liability during the campaign was the sluggish recovery and ballooning federal deficit; these were Clinton's biggest political assets. Clinton's economic positions were that (1) Bush had not done enough to revive the economy; (2) Bush and his predecessor, President Reagan, were responsible for the huge federal deficits; and (3) Bush could not be trusted because he broke his 1988 campaign pledge of no new taxes by signing a tax increase in 1990 to reduce the deficits. Clinton called for raising the marginal tax rate on the top 2 percent of taxpayers and cutting taxes for the middle class. He also promised to create jobs through government spending that would "invest in America."

Bush tried to point out that, technically, the recession was over and the economy was on the right track. He blamed a Democratic Congress for blocking his recovery proposals, and he renewed his pledge of no new taxes (saying he really meant it this time). In fact, Bush promised to cut taxes by 1 percent, arguing that this would reallocate spending from government back to households.

Although both candidates were short on specifics, Clinton saw a stronger role for government, and Bush saw a stronger role for the private sector. Clinton's approach was more *active,* and Bush's approach was more *passive.* In the end, the negative economic reports that dominated the news during the campaign made people willing to gamble on Clinton. Evidently, during hard times, an active policy has more voter appeal than a passive one. Ironically, the economy at the time was much stronger than was conveyed by the media and by challenger Clinton. The growth in real GDP in 1992 turned out to be 2.7 percent, which is quite respectable by current standards and better than the average real GDP growth of 2.6 percent achieved during Clinton's first term.

Sources: David Wessel, "Wanted: Fiscal Stimulus Without Higher Taxes," *Wall Street Journal* (5 October 1992); Herbert Stein, "The Inane Campaign Gives Me a Pain," *Wall Street Journal* (7 October 1992); and *Economic Report of the President*, February 1999.

ROLE OF EXPECTATIONS

The effectiveness of a particular government policy depends in part on what people expect. As we saw in Chapter 11, the short-run aggregate supply curve is drawn for a given expected price level reflected in long-term wage contracts. If workers and firms expect continuing inflation, their wage agreements will reflect these inflationary expectations. One approach in macroeconomics, called **rational expectations,** argues that people form expectations on the basis of all available information, including information about the probable future actions of policy makers. Thus aggregate supply depends on what sort of macroeconomic course policy makers are expected to pursue. For example, if people were to observe that policy makers try to stimulate aggregate demand every time real output falls below potential, people will come to anticipate the effects of this policy on the price level and output. Robert Lucas, of the University of Chicago, won the 1995 Nobel prize for his work in rational expectations.

Rational expectations A school of thought that claims people form expectations based on all available information, including the probable future actions of government policy makers

Monetary authorities are required to testify before Congress regularly, indicating the monetary policy they plan to pursue. The Fed also announces any changes in interest rate targets after each meeting, held every six weeks. We will consider the role of expectations in the context of monetary policy by examining the relationship between policy pronouncements and equilibrium output. We could employ a similar approach with fiscal policy, but active discretionary fiscal policy over the last two decades was hobbled by high federal deficits. To be sure, there were still tax increases, as in 1993, and tax cuts, as in 1997, and now that the federal deficit has been erased policy makers will turn once again to discretionary fiscal policy. Still, monetary policy has been at center stage for the last two decades.

Monetary Policy and Expectations

Suppose the economy is producing the potential rate of output. At the beginning of the year, firms and employees must negotiate wage agreements. While labor negotiations are under way, the Fed announces that throughout the year its monetary policy will aim at serving the money needs of an economy producing at the potential level. Thus the Fed plans to keep the price level constant. This seems to be the appropriate policy since unemployment is already at the natural rate. Until the year is under way and monetary policy is actually implemented, however, the public cannot be sure what the Fed will do. Firms and workers understand that the Fed's constant-price plan appears optimal under the circumstances, since an expansionary monetary policy would result simply in higher inflation in the long run.

As long as wage increases do not exceed the growth in labor productivity, the Fed's plan of a constant price level should work out. Alternatively, workers could try for higher wage growth, but that option would ultimately lead to inflation. Suppose workers and firms believe the Fed's pronouncements and agree on wage settlements based on expectations of a constant price level. If the Fed follows through, as promised, then the price level will turn out as expected. Output will remain at the economy's potential, and unemployment will remain at the natural rate. The situation is depicted in Exhibit 3, where the short-run aggregate supply curve, $SRAS_{130}$, is based on wage contracts reflecting an expected price level of 130. If the Fed follows the announced course, aggregate demand

EXHIBIT 3

Short-Run Effects of an Unexpected Expansionary Monetary Policy

At point *a*, firms and workers expect the price level to be 130; supply curve $SRAS_{130}$ reflects those expectations. If the Federal Reserve unexpectedly pursues an expansionary monetary policy, the aggregate demand curve will be *AD'* rather than *AD*. Output will temporarily rise above the potential rate (at point *b*), but in the long run it will fall back to the potential rate at point *c*. The short-run effect of monetary policy is a higher level of output, but the long-run effect is just an increase in the price level.

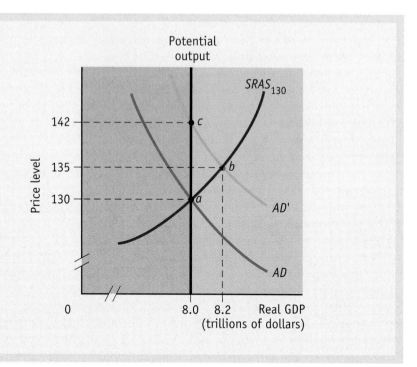

will be *AD* and equilibrium will be at point *a*, where the price level is as expected and the economy is producing $8.0 trillion, the potential level of output.

Suppose, however, that after workers and firms have agreed on nominal wages—that is, after the short-run aggregate supply curve has been determined—public officials become dissatisfied with the prevailing level of unemployment. Perhaps election-year concerns about unemployment or a false alarm about the onset of a recession prompts elected officials to persuade the Fed to stimulate aggregate demand.

An expansionary monetary policy increases aggregate demand from *AD*, the level anticipated by firms and employees, to *AD'*. This unexpected policy stimulates output and employment in the short run to equilibrium point *b*. Output increases to $8.2 trillion, and the price level increases to 135. This temporary boost in output and reduction in unemployment lasts perhaps long enough to help public officials get reelected.

So the price level is now higher than workers expected, which means that the wage they agreed to buys less in real terms. At their next opportunity, they will negotiate higher wages. These higher wage agreements will eventually cause the short-run aggregate supply curve in Exhibit 3 to shift up to the left, intersecting *AD'* at point *c*, the economy's potential output. (To keep the diagram less cluttered, the shifted short-run aggregate supply curve is not shown.) So output once again returns to the economy's potential GDP, but in the process the price level rises to 142.

Thus the unexpected expansionary monetary policy causes a short-run increase in output and employment. But in the long run the increase in the aggregate demand results only in a higher price level, and a higher inflation rate, than had been expected. After a short-run surge in output, the short-run aggregate supply curve shifts to the left, the price level climbs, and output returns once again to the economy's potential.

The **time-inconsistency problem** arises when policy makers have an incentive to announce one policy to influence expectations but then pursue a different policy once those expectations have been formed and acted on. As we shall see in the next section, one solution to the time-inconsistency problem is to take discretion away from the policy makers so that once a policy is announced, it cannot be changed.

Anticipating Monetary Policy

Workers may be fooled once by the Fed's actions, but they won't be fooled again. Suppose Fed policy makers become alarmed by the high inflation. The next time around, the Fed once again announces that it plans a monetary policy that will hold the price level constant at 142, a policy aimed at keeping real GDP at its potential. From their previous experience, however, workers and firms have learned that the Fed is willing to accept higher inflation in exchange for a temporary reduction in unemployment. Consequently, they take the Fed's announcement with a grain of salt. Workers, in particular, do not want to get caught again with their real wages down should the Fed implement a stimulative monetary policy, so a high wage-increase settlement is reached.

In effect, workers and firms are betting that monetary authorities will pursue an expansionary monetary policy regardless of their pronouncement to the contrary. The short-run aggregate supply curve reflecting these high wage-increase agreements is depicted by $SRAS_{152}$ in Exhibit 4, where 152 is the expected price level. Note that AD' is the aggregate demand that would result if the Fed's announced constant-price-level policy were pursued; that demand curve intersects the potential output line at point c, where the price level is 142. But AD'' is the aggregate demand that firms and workers expect based on an expansionary policy. They have agreed to wage settlements that will produce the economy's potential level of output if the Fed behaves as *expected*, not as *announced*. Thus, a price level of 152 is based on rational expectations. In effect, workers and firms expect the expansionary policy to shift aggregate demand from AD' to AD''.

Monetary authorities must now decide whether to stick with their announced plan of holding the price level constant or follow a more expansionary monetary policy. If they pursue the constant-price-level policy, aggregate demand will turn out to be AD' and short-run equilibrium will occur at point d. Short-run output will fall below the economy's potential, resulting in unemployment exceeding the natural rate. If monetary authorities want to keep the economy performing at its potential, they have only one alternative—to match expectations. Monetary authorities *must* pursue an expansionary monetary policy, a course of action that reinforces public skepticism of policy announcements. This expansionary policy will result in an aggregate demand of AD'', leading to an equilibrium at point e, where the price level is 152 and output equals the economy's potential.

Thus firms and workers enter their negotiations with the realization that the Fed has an incentive to pursue an expansionary monetary policy. Therefore workers and firms agree to high wage increases, and the Fed follows with an expansionary policy, one that results in more inflation. Once workers and firms

Short-Run Effects of the Fed Pursuing a More Expansionary Policy than Announced

The Fed announces a monetary policy that will keep the price level at 142. Firms and workers, however, do not believe the announcement; they think the monetary policy will be expansionary. The short-run aggregate supply curve, $SRAS_{152}$, reflects their forecasts of the price level. The Fed must then decide what to do. If it follows the noninflationary policy, aggregate demand will be AD', and output will fall below potential to point d. To keep the economy performing at its potential, the Fed must increease the money supply by as much as workers and firms expected.

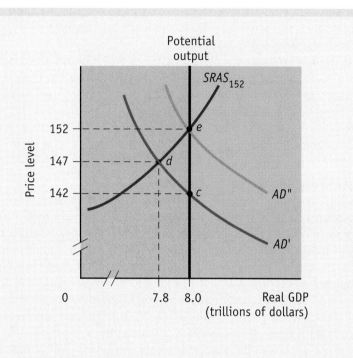

come to expect an expansionary monetary policy and the resulting inflation, such a policy does not spur even a temporary boost in output beyond the economy's potential. *Economists of the rational expectations school believe that if the economy is already producing its potential output, an expansionary monetary policy, if fully and correctly anticipated, will have no effect on output or employment. Only unanticipated or incorrectly anticipated changes in policy can temporarily influence output and employment.*

Policy Credibility

If the economy is already producing its potential output, an unexpected expansionary monetary policy would increase output and employment temporarily. The costs, however, include not only inflation in the long term but also a loss of credibility the next time around. Is there any way out of this? For the Fed to pursue a policy consistent with a constant price level, its announcements must somehow be *credible,* or believable. Firms and workers must believe that when the time comes to make a hard decision, the Fed will follow through as promised. Perhaps the Fed could offer some sort of insurance policy to make everyone believe that policy makers who deviate from the set course will pay dearly—for example, the chairman of the Fed could promise to resign if the Fed does not pursue the announced course. Ironically, policy makers are often more credible and therefore more effective if they have their discretion taken away. In this case, a hard-and-fast rule could be substituted for a policy maker's discretion. Policy rules will be considered in the next section.

Consider the problems facing central banks in countries that have experienced hyperinflation. For an anti-inflation policy to succeed at the least possible cost in forgone output, the public must believe the announcements of central bankers. How do they establish credibility? Some economists believe that the most efficient anti-inflation policy is **cold turkey,** which is to announce and execute tough measures to stop inflation, such as halting the growth in the money supply. For example, in 1985 the annual rate of inflation in Bolivia was running at 20,000 percent when the new government announced a stern policy. The restrictive measures worked and inflation was stopped within a month, with only a 5 percent loss on output. Around the world, credible anti-inflation policies have been successful.[2] Drastic measures may involve costs. For example, some economists argue that the Fed's dramatic efforts to curb high U.S. inflation during the early 1980s precipitated the worst recession since the Great Depression. Some say that the Fed's pronouncements were not credible and therefore resulted in a recession.

Much depends on the Fed's time horizon. If policy makers take the long view of their duties, they will be reluctant to risk their long-run policy effectiveness for a temporary reduction in unemployment. If Fed officials realize that their credibility is hard to develop but easy to undermine, they will be reluctant to pursue policies that will ultimately increase inflation.

Often Congress tries to pressure the Fed to stimulate the economy. By law the Fed must "promote effectively the goals of maximum employment, stable prices, and moderate long-term interest rates." The law leaves it up to the Fed to determine how best to pursue these goals. The Fed does not rely on congressional appropriations, so Congress cannot attempt to influence the Fed by withholding funds. In fact, the Fed makes a "profit" of nearly $20 billion a year, which it turns over to the U.S. Treasury. Thus, although the U.S. president appoints members of the Board of Governors, and these appointments must be approved by the Senate, the Fed operates fairly independently of the president and Congress. Consider central bank independence around the world in the following case study.

Cold turkey The announcement and execution of tough measures to reduce high inflation

Central Bank Independence and Price Stability

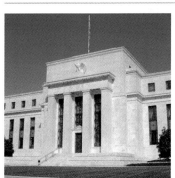

Some economists argue that the Fed would do better in the long run if it were committed to the single goal of price stability. Look, for example, at the Japanese experience. Since 1975, the Japanese central bank has had a strong commitment to low inflation, and inflation in Japan since 1975 has averaged only half the U.S. rate.

Some economists argue that to focus on price stability, a central bank should be insulated from political influence. When the Fed was established, several features insulated it from the ordinary political process—the 14-year terms with staggered appointments, for example. Also, the Fed is prohibited from purchasing securities directly from the

CaseStudy
Public Policy

Argentina limited its central bank's ability to issue new currency by creating a currency board, which required that each new peso be backed by one U.S. dollar held in reserve by the bank. "Are Currency Boards a Cure for All Monetary Problems?" is an article from the IMF publication, *Finance and Development*, which explores the use of independent currency boards to control the supply of money in advanced industrial countries. It can be found

---

2 For a discussion about how four hyperinflations in the 1920s ended, see Thomas Sargent, "The Ends of Four Big Inflations," *Inflation: Causes and Consequences,* Robert Hall, ed. (Chicago: University of Chicago Press, 1982): 41–98.

at http://imfnt1x.imf.org/
external/pubs/ft/fandd/1998/
12/enoch.htm. **What are the
benefits of imposing such
strict rules? How does a currency board derive its own
credibility?**

U.S. Treasury (the Fed purchases these securities in so-called secondary markets). What's more, since the Fed has its own source of income (interest on government securities and discount loans), it does not rely on Congress for a budget.

Does this independence affect performance? When central banks for 17 advanced industrial countries were ranked from least independent to most independent, inflation turned out to be the lowest in countries with the most independent central banks and highest in countries with the least independent central banks. For example, the most independent central banks were in Germany and Switzerland, and their inflation rates from 1973 to 1988 averaged about 3 percent per year. The least independent banks during that period were in Spain, New Zealand, Australia, and Italy, where inflation averaged 11.5 percent per year. The U.S. central bank is considered relatively independent; our inflation rate, which averaged 6.5 percent per year between 1973 and 1988, fell between the most independent and least independent groups.

The tendency around the world is toward greater central bank independence. Since 1988, for example, Australia and New Zealand have amended laws governing their central banks to make price stability the primary goal. Chile, Colombia, and Argentina, developing countries that recently experienced hyperinflation, have legislated more central bank independence. And the Maastricht agreement, which defined the framework for establishing a single European currency, the euro, identified price stability as the main objective of the new European central bank.

Sources: Alberto Alesina and Lawrence Summers, "Central Bank Independence and Macroeconomic Performance: Some Comparative Evidence," *Journal of Money, Credit and Banking*, 25 (May 1993): 151–162; Paul Lewis, "Bundesbank Puts Politicians on Notice," *New York Times* (23 October 1997); and Patricia Pollard, "Central Bank Independence and Economic Performance," *Federal Reserve Bank of St. Louis* (July/August 1993): 21–36.

POLICY RULES VERSUS DISCRETION

As noted earlier, the active approach views the economy as inherently unstable and in need of discretionary policy to eliminate excessive unemployment when it arises. The passive approach views the economy as so stable that discretionary policy is not only unnecessary but may actually cause destabilizing swings in aggregate demand that ultimately lead to more inflation. In place of discretionary policy, the passive approach often calls for predetermined rules to guide the actions of policy makers. In the context of fiscal policy, these rules take the form of automatic stabilizers, such as unemployment insurance, a progressive income tax, and transfer payments, all of which are aimed at offsetting the effects of business fluctuations. In this section, we examine the arguments for rules versus discretion in the context of monetary policy.

Rationale for Rules

The rationale for passive rules rather than the use of active discretion arises from different views of how the economy works. One view holds that *the economy is so complex and economic aggregates interact in such obscure ways and with such varied lags that policy makers cannot comprehend what is going on well enough to pursue an active monetary or fiscal policy.* Milton Friedman is perhaps the best-known advocate of this position. He argues that although there is a link between money growth and the growth in nominal GDP, the exact relationship is hard to pin down because of long lags in the response of economic activity to changes in money growth. If the central bank adopts a discretionary policy that is based on an incorrect estimate of the lag structure, the money supply may expand just when a tighter monetary policy would be more appropriate. To avoid the timing problem, Friedman recommends that the Fed follow a fixed-growth-rate monetary policy year after year, such as an annual growth rate of 3 percent in the money supply. Changes in the financial structure of the economy since the early 1980s have made reliance on the fixed-growth-rate rule problematic. But the argument is that the Fed should announce and then pursue some clear, identifiable policy rule.

A comparison of economic forecasters and weather forecasters may help shed light on the position of those who advocate the use of a passive rule. Suppose you are in charge of the heating and cooling system at a major shopping mall. You realize that weather forecasters have a poor record in your area, particularly in the early spring, when days can be either warm or cold. Each day you must guess what the temperature will be and, based on that guess, decide whether to fire up the heater, turn on the air conditioner, or leave them both off. Because the mall is so large, you must start up the system long before you know for sure what the weather will be. Once the system has been turned on, it cannot be turned off until much later in the day.

Suppose you guess the day will be cold, so you turn on the heat. If the day turns out to be cold, your policy is correct and the mall temperature will be just right. But if the day turns out to be warm, the heater will make the mall unbearable. You would have been better off with nothing. In contrast, if you turn on the air conditioner expecting a warm day but the day turns out to be cold, the mall will be freezing. The lesson is that if you are unable to predict the weather, you should use neither heat nor air conditioning. Similarly, if monetary officials cannot predict the course of the economy, they should not try to fine-tune monetary policy. Complicating the prediction problem is the fact that monetary officials are not sure about the lags involved with monetary policy. The situation is comparable to your not knowing for sure when you turn the switch to "on" how long the system will actually take to come on.

This analogy applies only if the cost of doing nothing—using neither heat nor air conditioning—is relatively low. In the early spring, you can assume that there is little risk of the weather being so cold that water pipes freeze or so hot that the walls sweat. A similar assumption in the passive view is that the economy is inherently stable and periods of prolonged unemployment are unlikely. In such an economy, the costs of *not* intervening are relatively low. In contrast, advocates of active policy believe that there can be wide and prolonged swings in the economy (analogous to wide and prolonged swings in temperature), so doing nothing involves significant risks.

Rules and Rational Expectations

Another group of economists also advocates passive rules, but not because they believe we know too little about how the economy works. Proponents of the rational expectations approach, introduced earlier in this chapter, claim that people on average have a pretty good idea about how the economy works and what to expect from government policy makers. Individuals and firms know enough

NetBookmark

The Region, a publication of the Minneapolis Federal Reserve Bank, has conducted interviews with Nobel prize winners and other noted economists. These are all now available on-line at http://minneapolisfed.org/ pubs/region/int.html. Be sure to check out the interviews with Milton Friedman, the most important contemporary monetarist, Robert Lucas, and James Buchanan.

about the monetary and fiscal policies pursued in the past to forecast, with reasonable accuracy, future policies and their effects on the economy. Some individuals will forecast too high and some too low, but on average forecasts will turn out to be about right. *To the extent that monetary policy is fully anticipated by workers and firms, it has no effect on the level of output; it affects only the price level.* Thus only unexpected changes in policy can bring about short-run changes in output.

Since, in the long run, changes in the money supply affect only the rate of inflation, not real output, followers of the rational expectations theory believe that the Fed should not try to pursue a discretionary monetary policy. Instead, the Fed should follow a predictable monetary rule. A monetary rule would reduce monetary surprises and keep output near the natural rate. *Whereas Friedman advocates a rule because of the Fed's ignorance about the lag structure of the economy, rational expectations theorists advocate a predictable rule to avoid monetary surprises, which result in unnecessary departures from the natural rate of output.*

Despite support by some economists for explicit rules rather than discretion, central bankers appear reluctant to follow hard-and-fast rules about the course of future policy. Discretion appears to rule the day. As Paul Volcker, the former Fed chairman, argued:

> *The appeal of a simple rule is obvious. It would simplify our job at the Federal Reserve, make monetary policy easy to understand, and facilitate monitoring of our performance. And if the rule worked, it would reduce uncertainty. . . . But unfortunately, I know of no rule that can be relied on with sufficient consistency in our complex and constantly evolving economy.*[3]

Thus far we have looked at active stabilization policy, which focuses on shifts in the aggregate demand curve, and passive stabilization policy, which relies more on natural shifts in the short-run aggregate-supply curve. In the final section we focus on an additional model, the Phillips curve, which sheds more light on the relationship between aggregate demand and aggregate supply.

THE PHILLIPS CURVE

At one time, policy makers thought they faced a fairly stable long-run tradeoff between inflation and unemployment. This view was suggested by the research of New Zealand economist A. W. Phillips, who in 1958 published an article that examined the historical relation between inflation and unemployment in the United Kingdom.[4] Based on about 100 years of evidence, his data traced out an inverse relationship between the unemployment rate and the rate of change in money wages (serving as a measure of inflation). This relationship implied that the opportunity cost of reducing unemployment was higher inflation, and the opportunity cost of reducing inflation was higher unemployment.

The possible options with respect to unemployment and inflation are illustrated by the hypothetical **Phillips curve** in Exhibit 5. The unemployment rate is measured along the horizontal axis and the inflation rate along the vertical axis. Let's begin at point *a,* which depicts one possible combination of unemployment and inflation. Fiscal or monetary policy could be used to stimulate output and

Phillips curve A curve showing possible combinations of the inflation rate and the unemployment rate

---

3 Statement of Paul Volcker, then chairman of the Board of Governors of the Federal Reserve System, before the Committee on Banking, Finance, and Urban Affairs, U.S. House of Representatives, August 1983.
4 A. W. Phillips, "Relation Between Unemployment and the Rate of Change in Money Wage Rates in the United Kingdom, 1861–1957," *Economica* 25 (November 1958): 283–299.

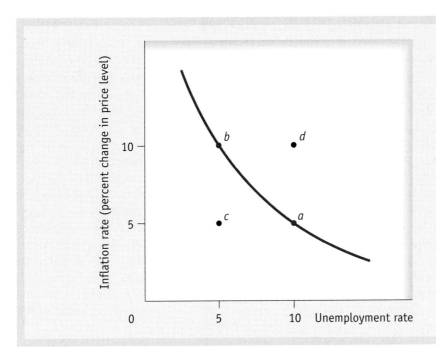

EXHIBIT 5

Hypothetical Phillips Curve

Points *a* and *b* lie on the Phillips curve and represent alternative combinations of the inflation rate and the un-employment rate that are attainable as long as the curve itself does not shift. Points *c* and *d* are off the curve; they are not attainable combinations.

thereby reduce unemployment, moving the economy from point *a* to point *b*. Notice, however, that the reduction in unemployment comes at the cost of higher inflation. A reduction in unemployment with no change in inflation would be represented by point *c*. But as you can see, this alternative is not an option available on the curve. Thus policy makers were thought to face a difficult trade-off: They could choose either lower inflation or lower unemployment, but not both.

Not everyone accepted the implications of the Phillips curve, but during the 1960s, policy makers increasingly came to believe that they faced a stable, long-run trade-off between unemployment and inflation. The Phillips curve was based on an era when inflation was low and the primary disturbances in the economy were shocks to aggregate demand. Changes in aggregate demand can be viewed as movements along a given short-run aggregate supply curve. If aggregate demand increased, the price level increased, but unemployment fell. If aggregate demand decreased, the price level decreased, but unemployment increased. Many economists therefore assumed that there was a trade-off between inflation and unemployment. Hence, with appropriate demand-management policies, government policy makers could choose any point along the Phillips curve.

The 1970s proved this view wrong for two reasons. First, some of the biggest disturbances were adverse *supply* shocks, such as those created by the oil embargoes and worldwide crop failures. These shocks shifted the aggregate supply curve to the left. A reduction in aggregate supply led to both higher inflation *and* higher unemployment. This stagflation was at odds with the Phillips curve. Second, economists learned that when short-run equilibrium output exceeds potential output, an expansionary gap opens. As this gap is closed by the upward movement of the short-run aggregate supply curve, the results are greater inflation *and* higher unemployment—again, results inconsistent with a given Phillips curve.

The combination of high inflation and high unemployment resulting from stagflation and expansionary gaps is represented by an outcome such as point *d* in Exhibit 5. By the end of the 1970s, increases in inflation and unemployment suggested either that the Phillips curve had shifted outward or that it no longer described economic reality. The situation called for a reexamination of the Phillips curve, a reexamination that led economists to distinguish between the short-run Phillips curve and the long-run Phillips curve.

The Short-Run Phillips Curve

To discuss the underpinnings of the Phillips curve, we must return to the short-run aggregate supply curve. Let's begin by assuming that the price level this year is reflected by a price index of, say, 100. Suppose that people expect prices to be about 3 percent higher next year. So the price level expected for next year is 103. Workers will therefore negotiate wage contracts based on an expected price level of 103, which is 3 percent higher than the current price level. As the short-run aggregate supply curve in panel (a) of Exhibit 6 indicates, if *AD* is the aggregate demand curve and the price level is 103, as expected, output will equal the economy's potential GDP, shown here to be $8.0 trillion. Recall that when the economy produces its potential GDP, unemployment is equal to the natural rate.

The short-run relationship between inflation and unemployment is presented in panel (b) of Exhibit 6 under the assumption that people expect the inflation rate to be 3 percent. The unemployment rate is measured along the horizontal axis and the inflation rate along the vertical axis. Panel (a) shows that when the inflation rate is 3 percent, the economy produces its potential GDP. When the economy produces its potential GDP, unemployment is at the natural rate, which we assume to be 5 percent in panel (b). The combination of 3 percent inflation and 5 percent unemployment is reflected by point *a* in panel (b), which corresponds to point *a* in panel (a).

What if aggregate demand turns out to be greater than expected, as indicated by *AD'* in panel (a)? In the short run, the greater demand results in equilibrium at point *b*, with a price level of 105 and an output level of $8.1 trillion. Since the price level is greater than the level reflected in wage contracts, the inflation rate is also greater than expected. Specifically, the inflation rate turns out to be 5 percent, not 3 percent. Output now exceeds potential, so the unemployment rate falls below the natural rate to 4 percent. This combination of a higher inflation rate and a lower level of unemployment is depicted by point *b* in panel (b), which corresponds to point *b* in panel (a).

What if aggregate demand turns out to be lower than expected, as indicated by *AD"* in panel (a)? In the short run, the lower demand results in equilibrium at point *c,* where the price level of 101 is lower than the expected level reflected in labor contracts, and output of $7.9 trillion is below potential GDP. With a lower-than-expected price level, the inflation rate is 1 percent rather than the expected 3 percent. With output below the economy's potential, the unemployment rate is 6 percent, which exceeds the natural rate. This combination of lower-than-expected inflation and higher-than-expected unemployment is reflected by point *c* on the curve in panel (b).

Note that the short-run aggregate supply curve in panel (a) can be used to establish the inverse relationship between the inflation rate and the level of

EXHIBIT 6

Relationship Between the Short-Run Aggregate Supply Curve and the Short-Run Phillips Curve

(a) Short-run aggregate supply curve

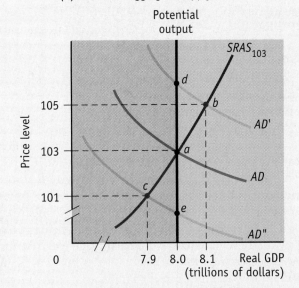

(b) Short-run and long-run Phillips curves

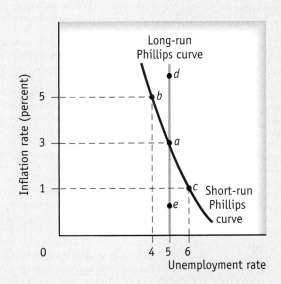

If people expect a price level of 103, which is 3 percent higher than the current level, and if AD is the aggregate demand curve, then the price level will actually be 103 and output will be at the potential rate. Point a in both panels represents this situation. Unemployment will be at the natural rate, 5 percent

If aggregate demand is higher than expected (AD' instead of AD), the economy will be at point b in both panels. If aggregate demand is less than expected (AD" rather than AD), short-run equilibrium will be at point c; the price level, 101, will be lower than expected, and output will be below the potential rate. The lower inflation rate and higher unemployment rate are shown as point c in panel (b). In panel (b), points a, b, and c trace the short-run Phillips curve.

In the long run, the actual price level equals the expected price level and output is at the potential level, $8.0 trillion, in panel (a), and unemployment is at the natural rate, 5 percent, in panel (b). Points a, d, and e represent that situation; they lie on the vertical long-run Phillips curve.

unemployment illustrated in panel (b). This latter curve is called a **short–run Phillips curve,** and it is generated by the intersection of alternative aggregate demand curves along a given short–run aggregate supply curve. *The short–run Phillips curve is based on labor contracts that reflect a given expected price level, which implies a given expected rate of inflation.* The short–run Phillips curve in panel (b) is based on an expected inflation rate of 3 percent. If inflation turns out as expected, unemployment equals the natural rate. If inflation is higher than expected, unemployment in the short run falls below the natural rate. If inflation is lower than expected, unemployment in the short run exceeds the natural rate.

Short-run Phillips curve A curve, based on an expected inflation rate, that reflects an inverse relationship between the inflation rate and the level of unemployment

The Long-Run Phillips Curve
If inflation is higher than was expected, output can exceed the economy's potential in the short run but not in the long run. Labor shortages and worker dissatisfaction with shrinking real wages will lead to higher wage agreements during the next round of negotiations. The short–run aggregate supply curve

will shift up to the left until it passes through point *d* in panel (a) of Exhibit 6, returning the economy to its potential level of output. Point *d* corresponds to a higher price level, and hence a higher rate of inflation. But notice that the higher inflation is no longer associated with reduced unemployment.

With the closing of the expansionary gap, the economy experiences both higher unemployment and higher inflation. At point *d* in panel (a) the economy is producing its potential GDP, which means that unemployment equals the natural rate. This combination of the natural rate of unemployment and higher inflation is depicted by point *d* in panel (b). The unexpectedly higher aggregate demand curve has no lasting effect on output or unemployment. Note that whereas points *a, b,* and *c* are on the same short-run Phillips curve, point *d* is not.

To trace the long-run effects of a lower-than-expected price level, let's return to point *c* in panel (a) of Exhibit 6. At this point, the actual price level is below the expected level, so output is below potential GDP. If firms and workers negotiate lower money wages (or if the growth in nominal wages trails inflation), the short-run aggregate supply curve will shift to the right until it passes through point *e*, where the economy returns once again to its potential level of output. Both inflation and unemployment will fall, as reflected by point *e* in panel (b).

Note that points *a, d,* and *e* in panel (a) depict long-run equilibrium points, in the sense that the expected price level equals the actual price level. At those same points in panel (b), the expected inflation rate equals the actual rate, so unemployment equals the natural rate. We can connect points *a, d,* and *e* in panel (b) to form what is called the **long-run Phillips curve.** *When employers and workers have the time and the ability to adjust fully to any unexpected change in aggregate demand, the long-run Phillips curve is a vertical line drawn at the economy's natural rate of unemployment,* as shown in panel (b). As long as prices and wages are flexible, the rate of unemployment, in the long run, is independent of the rate of inflation. *Thus, according to proponents of this type of analysis, in the long run, policy makers cannot choose between unemployment and inflation. They can choose only among alternative rates of inflation.*

Long-run Phillips curve A vertical line drawn at the economy's natural rate of unemployment that traces equilibrium points that can occur when employers and workers have the time to adjust fully to any unexpected change in aggregate demand

Natural rate hypothesis The natural rate of unemployment is largely independent of the stimulus provided by monetary or fiscal policy.

The Natural Rate Hypothesis

As defined in Chapter 11, the natural rate of unemployment is the rate that is consistent with the economy's potential level of output, which we have discussed extensively already. An important idea that emerged from this reexamination of the Phillips curve is the **natural rate hypothesis,** which states that in the long run the economy tends toward the natural rate of unemployment. This natural rate is largely independent of the level of the *aggregate demand* stimulus provided by monetary or fiscal policy. Policy makers may be able to push the economy beyond its natural, or potential, rate of production temporarily, but only if the public does not anticipate the resulting level of aggregate demand and the resulting price level. The natural rate hypothesis implies that *regardless of policy makers' concerns about unemployment, the policy that results in low inflation is generally going to be the optimal policy in the long run.*

Evidence of the Phillips Curve

What has been the actual relationship between unemployment and inflation in the United States? In Exhibit 7, each year since 1960 is represented by a point, with the unemployment rate measured along the horizontal axis and the infla-

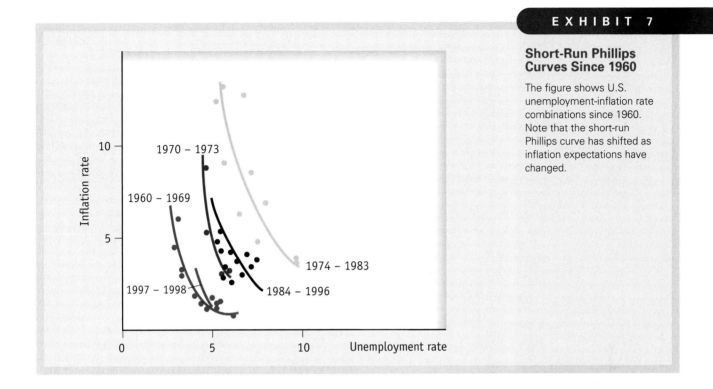

EXHIBIT 7

Short-Run Phillips Curves Since 1960

The figure shows U.S. unemployment-inflation rate combinations since 1960. Note that the short-run Phillips curve has shifted as inflation expectations have changed.

tion rate measured along the vertical axis. Superimposed on these points is a series of short-run Phillips curves showing patterns of unemployment and inflation during five distinct periods since 1960. Remember, each short-run Phillips curve is drawn for a given *expected rate of inflation*. A change in inflationary expectations results in a shift of the short-run Phillips curve.

The clearest trade-off between unemployment and inflation occurred between 1960 and 1969; the points for those years fit neatly along the curve. In the early part of the decade, inflation was low but unemployment was high; as the 1960s progressed, unemployment declined but actual inflation increased. The inflation rate during the decade averaged only 2.5 percent, and the unemployment rate averaged 4.8 percent.

The short-run Phillips curve shifted up to the right for the period from 1970 to 1973, when inflation and unemployment both climbed to an average of 5.2 percent. In 1974, sharp increases in oil prices and crop failures around the world reduced aggregate supply, which sparked another shift in the Phillips curve. Although points for the decade between 1974 and 1983 do not lie as neatly along the curve as points for earlier periods do, a trade-off between inflation and unemployment is still evident. During the 1974–1983 period, inflation rose on average to 8.2 percent and unemployment climbed on average to 7.5 percent.

After recessions in the early 1980s, the short-run Phillips curve seems to have shifted downward since 1983. Average inflation for 1984–1996 fell to 3.7 percent and average unemployment fell to 6.1 percent. Finally, data for 1997 and 1998 suggest that a new, lower short-run Phillips curve may be forming, with average inflation of only 1.6 percent and average unemployment of 4.7.

Thus the Phillips curve shifted outward between the 1960s and the early 1980s. Since then, the Fed has learned more about how to control inflation, thereby shifting the Phillips curve back to about where it was during the 1960s.

CONCLUSION

This chapter examined the implications of active and passive policy. The important question is whether the economy is (1) essentially stable and self-correcting when it gets off track or (2) essentially unstable and in need of active intervention. Advocates of active policy believe that the Fed or Congress should reduce economic fluctuations by stimulating aggregate demand when output falls below its potential level and by dampening aggregate demand when output exceeds its potential level. Advocates of active policy argue that government attempts to insulate the economy from the ups and downs of the business cycle may be far from perfect but are better than nothing. Some activists also believe that high unemployment may be self-reinforcing, because some unemployed workers lose valuable job skills and grow to accept unemployment as a way of life, as has happened in Europe.

Advocates of passive policy, on the other hand, believe that discretionary policy may contribute to the cyclical swings in the economy, leading to higher inflation in the long run with no permanent boost in either output or employment. This group favors passive rules for monetary policy and automatic stabilizers for fiscal policy.

The active-passive debate in this chapter has focused primarily on monetary policy because discretionary fiscal policy, until quite recently, had been hampered by large federal deficits that ballooned the national debt. In the next chapter, we will take a closer look at the federal budget, recent federal deficits, and federal debt.

SUMMARY

1. Advocates of active policy view the private sector—particularly fluctuations in investment—as the main source of economic instability in the economy. Activists argue that the return to potential output can be slow and painful, so the Fed or Congress should intervene with monetary or fiscal policy to stimulate aggregate demand when actual output falls below potential output.

2. Advocates of passive policy argue that the economy has a natural resiliency that will cause output to return to its potential level within a reasonable amount of time if upset by some shock. They point to the variable and uncertain lags associated with discretionary policy as reason enough to steer clear of active intervention.

3. The passive policy approach suggests that the government should follow clear and predictable policies and avoid trying to stimulate or dampen aggregate demand over the business cycle. Passive policies are reflected in automatic fiscal stabilizers and in explicit monetary rules, such as a fixed rate of growth in the money supply.

4. At one time, public officials thought they faced a stable trade-off between higher unemployment and higher inflation. Recent evidence suggests that if there is a trade-off, it exists only in the short run, not in the long run. Expansionary fiscal or monetary policies, if unexpected, can stimulate output and employment in the short run. But if the economy is already at or near its potential output, these expansionary policies will, in the long run, result only in higher inflation.

QUESTIONS FOR REVIEW

1. *(Active Versus Passive Policy)* Contrast the passive policy view of the behavior of wages and prices during a contractionary gap to the active policy view.

2. *(Active Policy)* Why do proponents of active policy recommend government intervention to close an expansionary gap?

3. *(Active Versus Passive Policy)* According to advocates of passive policy, what variable naturally adjusts in the labor market, shifting the short-run aggregate supply curve to restore unemployment to the natural rate? Why does the active policy approach assume that the short-run aggregate supply curve shifts upward more easily and quickly than it shifts downward?

4. *(Review of Policy Perspectives)* Why may an active policy approach be more politically popular than a passive approach, especially during a recession?

5. *(Macroeconomic Policy)* Some economists argue that only unanticipated increases in the money supply can affect real GDP. Explain why this may be the case.

6. *(Anticipating Monetary Policy)* In 1993 the Fed began announcing its interest rate targets immediately following each meeting of the Federal Open Market Committee. Prior to that, observers were left to draw inferences about Fed policy based on the results of that policy. What is the value of this new openness?

7. *(Policy Credibility)* What is policy credibility and how is it relevant to the problem of reducing the inflation rate? How is credibility related to the time-inconsistency problem?

8. *(CaseStudy: Central Bank Independence and Price Stability)* One source of independence for the Fed, as suggested in Chapter 13, is the length of term for members of the Board of Governors. In Chapter 15, we learned that the Fed is a "money machine." Does this suggest another source of Fed independence from Congress?

9. *(Rationale for Rules)* Some economists call for predetermined rules to guide the actions of government policy makers. What are the two rationales that have been given for such rules?

10. *(Rational Expectations and Policy)* Suppose that people in an election year believe that public policy makers are going to pursue expansionary policies to enhance their reelection prospects. How could such expectations put pressure on officials to pursue expansionary policies even if they hadn't been planning to?

11. *(Short-Run Phillips Curve)* Why does a movement leftward and upward along the short-run Phillips curve imply a declining real wage for workers? Would workers allow this decline to continue unabated? How would the short-run Phillips curve eventually adjust to changes in workers' perceptions about their real wages?

12. *(Potential GNP)* Why is it hard for policy makers to decide if the economy is operating at its potential output level? Why is this uncertainty a problem?

13. *(Phillips Curves)* Describe the different policy trade-offs implied by the short-run Phillips curve and the long-run Phillips curve. What forces shift the long-run Phillips curve?

PROBLEMS AND EXERCISES

14 *(Active Versus Passive Policy)* Discuss the role each of the following plays in the debate between the active and passive approaches:
   a. The speed of adjustment of the nominal wage
   b. The speed of adjustment of expectations about inflation
   c. The existence of lags in policy creation and implementation
   d. Variability in the natural rate of unemployment over time

15. *(CaseStudy: Active versus Passive Presidential Candidates)* What were the main differences between candidates Bush and Clinton in the 1992 presidential campaign? Illustrate their ideas using the aggregate supply and demand model.

16. *(Problems with Active Policy)* Use an *AD-AS* diagram to illustrate and explain the short-run and long-run effects on the economy of the following situation: Both the natural rate of unemployment and the actual rate of unemployment are 5 percent. However, the government

believes that the natural rate of unemployment is 6 percent and that the economy is overheating. Therefore, it introduces a policy to reduce aggregate demand.

17. *(Policy Lags)* What lag in discretionary policy is described in each of the following statements? Why do long lags make discretionary policy less effective?
    a. The time from when the government determines that the economy is in recession until a tax cut is approved to reduce unemployment
    b. The time from when the money supply is increased until the resulting effect on the economy is felt
    c. The time from the start of a recession until the government identifies the existence and severity of the recession

d. The time from when the Fed decides to reduce the money supply until the money supply actually declines

18. *(Rational Expectations)* Using an *AD–AS* diagram, illustrate the short-run effects on prices, output, and unemployment of an increase in the money supply that is correctly anticipated by the public. Assume that the economy is initially at potential output.

19. *(Long-Run Phillips Curve)* Suppose the economy is at point *d* on the long-run Phillips curve shown in Exhibit 6. If that inflation rate is unacceptably high, how can policy makers get the inflation rate down? Would rational expectations help or hinder their efforts?

EXPERIENTIAL EXERCISES

20. *(Active Versus Passive Policy)* The Federal Reserve Bank of Minneapolis's *The Region* at http://woodrow.mpls.frb.fed.us/pubs/region/int.html features an ongoing series of interviews with prominent U.S. policy makers. Choose a Fed governor or a regional Reserve Bank president and try to determine whether that person leans more toward an active or a passive policy view. What specific policy views does that person advocate?

21. *(CaseStudy: Central Bank Independence and Price Stability)* The Bank for International Settlements maintains a list of links to central banks around the world at http://www.bis.org/cbanks.htm. Many of

those banks maintain English-language Web pages. Choose one or two nations and explore their central bank Web pages. How much independence do those banks have? To what extent are their functions and goals similar to those of the U.S. Federal Reserve System?

22. *(Wall Street Journal)* A good source for the latest information regarding macroeconomic policy is the Economy column that appears in the daily *Wall Street Journal*. Take a look at today's issue and review the latest hot topics. Then turn to the editorial pages, where the *Journal's* editorial board, contributors, and letter writers have their say.

Federal Budgets and Public Policy

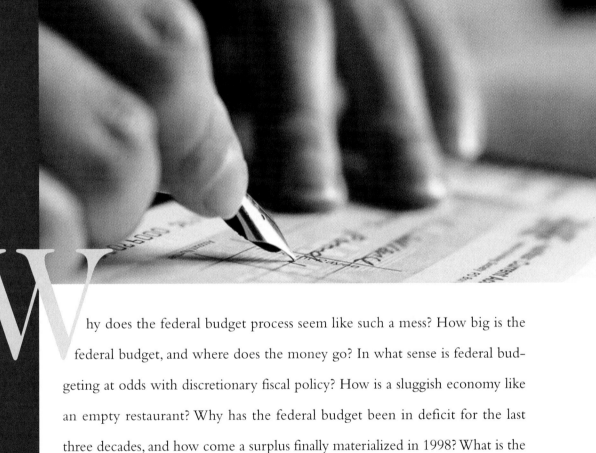

Why does the federal budget process seem like such a mess? How big is the federal budget, and where does the money go? In what sense is federal budgeting at odds with discretionary fiscal policy? How is a sluggish economy like an empty restaurant? Why has the federal budget been in deficit for the last three decades, and how come a surplus finally materialized in 1998? What is the federal debt and who bears the burden of that debt? Answers to these and other questions are examined in this chapter, which examines federal budgeting in theory and practice.

The word *budget* derives from the Old French word *bougette,* which means "little bag." The annual federal budget now exceeds $1,800,000,000,000.00—over $1.8 trillion dollars a year. That's big money! If this "little bag" contained

Visit the McEachern
Interactive Study Center
for this chapter at
tp://mcisc.swcollege.com

$100 bills, it would weigh over 19,000 *tons*! These $100 bills would fill over 670 trailer trucks or they could paper over a 10-lane highway stretching from Bangor, Maine, to San Diego, California. This budget could cover every U.S. family's mortgage and car payment every month. If the president's sole function were to pay the bills by writing million-dollar checks, to keep up with federal spending, our chief executive would have to write over three checks a minute, 24 hours a day, 365 days a year.

Government budgets have a tremendous impact on the economy. Government outlays at all levels amount to about one-third the size of GDP. Our focus in this chapter will be the federal budget, beginning with an examination of the federal budget process. We then consider budget deficits of the last three decades along with the resulting explosion of national debt. We will look at the source of the deficits, the effects of deficits on the economy, and why the deficits disappeared as of 1998. We also examine the impact of a higher national debt. Topics discussed in this chapter include:

- The budget process
- Rationale for deficits
- Impact of deficits

- Crowding out and crowding in
- The miraculous budget surplus
- The burden of the federal debt

Federal budget A plan for federal government outlays and revenues for a specified period, usually a year

THE FEDERAL BUDGET PROCESS

The **federal budget** is a plan for government outlays and revenues for a specified period, usually a year. Outlays include both government purchases (which we have referred to as G) and transfer payments. Social Security, Medicare, and welfare payments made up about half of federal outlays in fiscal year 1998. National defense accounted for 15.8 percent of the budget (down from 28.1 percent in 1987). And interest payments on the debt soaked up 14 percent of the budget, or about one in seven federal dollars, up from 7 percent in 1975.

The period covered by the federal budget is called the *fiscal year;* it runs from October 1 of one year to September 30 of the following year. Exhibit 1 shows the composition of federal outlays by major category since 1959. As you can see, defense spending has declined as a percentage of federal outlays, while Social Security and Medicare, programs aimed primarily at the elderly, have increased and now account for over one-third of the federal budget. For the last two decades, welfare spending, which consists of cash and in-kind transfer payments, has remained relatively constant as a share of all federal outlays, accounting for one-seventh of the federal budget.

The Presidential Role in the Budget Process

Before 1921, the federal budget played a minor role in the economy, with federal outlays, except during wartime, amounting to less than 3 percent of GDP (versus 19.2 percent in 1998). Federal agencies made budget requests directly to Congress, bypassing the president entirely. Legislation in 1921 created the Office of Management and Budget (OMB) to examine agency budget requests and to help the president develop a budget proposal.

The Employment Act of 1946 created the Council of Economic Advisers to forecast economic activity and assist the president in formulating an appro-

EXHIBIT 1

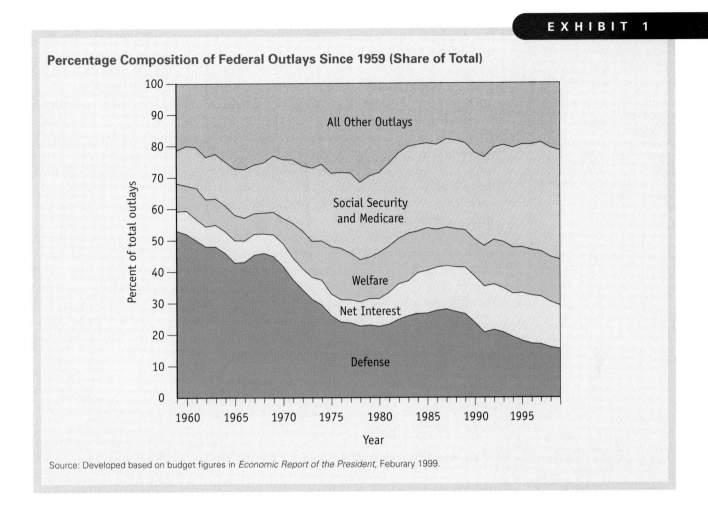

Percentage Composition of Federal Outlays Since 1959 (Share of Total)

All Other Outlays

Social Security and Medicare

Welfare

Net Interest

Defense

Percent of total outlays

Year

Source: Developed based on budget figures in *Economic Report of the President*, Feburary 1999.

priate fiscal policy. During the 1960s and 1970s, various measures were introduced by the executive branch to improve the evaluation of government programs. By the mid-1970s, the president had in place the staff and the procedures to translate policy into a budget proposal to be presented to Congress.

Development of the president's budget begins a year before it is submitted to Congress, with each agency preparing a budget request. The formal budget process begins early in the calendar year, when the president submits to Congress a pile of books called *The Budget of the United States Government* (the 1999 budget filled four volumes). This document details the president's proposals about what should be spent in the upcoming fiscal year and how this spending should be financed. At this stage, the president's budget is little more than detailed suggestions for congressional consideration. Soon after a budget is proposed, the *Economic Report of the President* is also transmitted to Congress. This report, required under the Employment Act of 1946 and written by the Council of Economic Advisers, reflects the administration's views about the state of the economy and includes fiscal policy recommendations for fostering "maximum employment, production, and purchasing power."

The Congressional Role in the Budget Process

The congressional budget cycle begins when the president presents a budget to Congress—in late January or early February. Budget committees in the House and the Senate then rework the President's budget and eventually agree on total outlays, spending by major category, and expected revenues. Once an overall budget outline has been approved by Congress as a **budget resolution,** this resolution is supposed to discipline the many congressional committees and subcommittees that authorize spending by establishing a framework to guide spending and revenue decisions. The budget cycle is supposed to end by October 1, when the new fiscal year begins. Thus the federal budget has a congressional gestation period of about nine months, although, as we have noted, the president's budget begins taking shape a year before the January submission.

The spending side of the budget is usually outlined in much greater detail than the revenue side. That's because most taxes are collected on the basis of certain rules and schedules that change infrequently. Of special interest is the bottom line, the relationship between *budgeted* outlays and *projected* revenues. The difference between outlays and revenues is one measure of the budget's fiscal impact. *When outlays exceed revenues, the budget is in deficit. A larger deficit stimulates aggregate demand. Alternatively, when revenues exceed outlays, the budget is in surplus. A larger surplus dampens aggregate demand.*

Problems with the Budget Process

The federal budget process sounds good on paper, but it does not work well in practice. There are several problems.

Continuing Resolutions Instead of Budget Decisions. The budget timetable discussed in the preceding section is often ignored by Congress. Because deadlines are frequently missed, budgets typically run from year to year based on **continuing resolutions,** which are agreements to allow agencies, in the absence of an approved budget, to spend at the rate of the previous year's budget. Poorly conceived programs continue through sheer inertia; successful programs cannot be expanded. On occasion, the president must shut down some government functions temporarily because not even the continuing resolution can be approved on time. For example, in late 1995 and early 1996, two government shutdowns closed most government offices for 27 days. Congress also failed to approve a continuing resolution before the start of the 1999 fiscal year.

Overlapping Committee Authority. Overlaps in budget authority among the many congressional committees and subcommittees require the executive branch of government to defend the same section of the president's budget before several committees in both the House and the Senate. Those responsible for running the federal government end up spending much of their time testifying before assorted congressional committees. Because several committees have jurisdiction over the same area, no committee really has final authority, so matters often remain unresolved even after extensive committee deliberations.

Budget resolution A congressional agreement about total outlays, spending by major category, and expected revenues, which guides spending and revenue decisions by the many congressional committees and subcommittees

Continuing resolutions Budget agreements that allow agencies, in the absence of an approved budget, to spend at the rate of the previous year's budget

Lengthy Budget Process. You can imagine the difficulty of using the budget as a tool of fiscal policy when the budget process takes so long. Given that the average recession lasts only about a year and that budget preparations begin more than a year and a half before the budget goes into effect, planning discretionary fiscal measures to address economic fluctuations is difficult. That's one reason why attempts to stimulate an ailing economy often seem so half-hearted; by the time Congress agrees on a fiscal remedy, the economy has often taken a turn for the better on its own.

Uncontrollable Budget Items. Congress has only limited control over much of the budget. Some budget items, such as interest on the national debt, cannot be changed in the near term. *About three-quarters of the budget outlays are determined by existing laws.* For example, once Congress establishes eligibility criteria, **entitlement programs,** such as Social Security and Medicare, take on a life of their own, with each annual appropriation simply reflecting the amount required to support the expected number of entitled beneficiaries. Congress has no say in such appropriations unless it chooses to change the eligibility criteria or the level of benefits. Most entitlement programs have such politically powerful constituencies that Congress is reluctant to mess with the structure.

Entitlement programs
Guaranteed benefits for those who qualify under government transfer programs such as Social Security and Medicare

Overly Detailed Budget. The federal budget is divided into thousands of accounts and subaccounts, which is why it fills four volumes. To the extent that the budget is a way of making political payoffs, such micromanagement allows elected officials to reward friends and punish enemies with great precision. For example, in recent budgets Congress has found $2.7 million for a freshwater catfish farm in Arkansas, $2.5 million to remove asbestos from a meat-packing plant in Iowa, and $10 million to build a ramp to the Milwaukee Brewers' stadium parking lot. Congress tends to budget in such minute detail that the big picture gets lost. *This detailed budgeting is not only time-consuming, but it also reduces the flexibility of the budget as a tool for discretionary fiscal policy.* When economic conditions change or when there is a shift in the demand for certain kinds of publicly provided goods, the federal government cannot easily reallocate funds from one account to another.

Suggested Budget Reforms

Several reforms have been suggested to improve the budget process. First, the annual budget could be converted into a two-year budget, or *biennial budget.* As it is, Congress spends nearly all of the year working on the budget. The executive branch is always dealing with three budgets: administering an approved budget, defending a proposed budget before congressional committees, and preparing the next budget for submission to Congress. If decisions were made for two years at a time, Congress would not be continually involved with budget deliberations, and executive branch heads could run their agencies rather than march from committee hearing to committee hearing. A two-year budget, however, would require longer-term economic forecasts of the economy and would be even less useful than a one-year budget as a tool of discretionary fiscal policy.

Another possible reform would be for Congress to simplify the budget document by concentrating on major groupings and eliminating line items. Each agency head could then be given an overall budget, along with the discretion to allocate funds in a manner consistent with the perceived demands for agency services. The drawback is that agency heads may have different priorities than those of elected representatives.

Another way of making more sense of the budget and its impact would be to sort federal spending into a capital budget and an operating budget. As it is, Congress approves a single budget that throws together the cost of new federal building with the payroll cost of federal employees. A *capital budget* would include spending on physical capital such as buildings, highways, dams, computers, and other government infrastructure. An *operating budget* would include spending on the payroll, building maintenance, computer paper, paper clips, and other ongoing expenses. We will return to this issue.

FEDERAL BUDGET DEFICITS

When government outlays—that is, government purchases plus transfer payments—exceed government revenue, the result is a *budget deficit,* a term first introduced in Chapter 5. Although the federal budget experienced a surplus in 1998, it had been in deficit every year but one since 1960. That's nearly four decades of deficits. To place deficits in perspective, let's first examine the economic rationale for deficit financing.

Rationale for Deficits

Deficit financing has been justified for outlays that increase the economy's productivity—capital outlays for investments such as highways, waterways, and dams. The cost of these capital projects should be borne in part by future taxpayers, who will also benefit from these investments. Hence there is some justification for borrowing to finance capital projects so that future taxpayers can help pay for them. This rationale is used to fund capital projects at the state and local level. But, as noted already, the federal government does not budget capital projects separately, so there is no link between deficits and capital budgets.

Before the Great Depression, federal deficits occurred only during wartime. Because wars involved much hardship, public officials were understandably reluctant to increase taxes much to finance war-related spending. Deficits incurred during wars were largely self-correcting, however, because after each war government spending dropped faster than government revenues.

The Depression led John Maynard Keynes to argue that government spending should compensate for any drop in investment spending. As you know, the Keynesian prescription for fighting an economic slump is for the federal government to stimulate aggregate demand through deficit spending. As a result of the Depression, automatic stabilizers were also introduced, which increased government outlays during recessions and decreased them during expansions. The federal deficit therefore increases during recessions because, as economic activity slows, unemployment rises, increasing government outlays for unemployment benefits and for other transfer payments. Furthermore, tax revenues decline during recessions. For example, as a result of the 1990–1991 recession, annual tax revenues from corporations fell by $14 billion between 1989 and 1992, while transfer payments for "income security" jumped by $60 billion. An economic expansion is the other side of the coin. As business activity expands, so do jobs, personal income, and corporate profits, causing federal revenue to swell. With reduced joblessness, transfer payments decline. Thus the federal deficit shrinks.

Budget Philosophies and Deficits

Several budget philosophies have emerged over the years. Fiscal policy prior to the Great Depression aimed at maintaining an **annually balanced budget,** except during wartime. Since tax revenues rise during expansions and fall during recessions, the annually balanced budget means the federal government must increase spending during expansions and reduce spending during recessions. But such spending will worsen fluctuations in the business cycle, overheating the economy during expansions and increasing unemployment during recessions.

A second budget philosophy calls for a **cyclically balanced budget,** which means budget deficits during recessions and budget surpluses during expansions. Fiscal policy would thereby dampen swings in the business cycle without increasing the national debt. Nearly all state governments have established "rainy day" funds to build up budget surpluses during the good times for use during hard times.

A third budget philosophy is **functional finance,** which says that policy makers should be less concerned with balancing the budget annually, or even over the business cycle, than with ensuring that the economy produces its potential output. This philosophy argues that one of the federal government's primary responsibilities is to promote stability at the economy's potential level of output. If the budgets needed to keep the economy operating at its potential GDP involve chronic deficits, so be it. Since the Great Depression, budgets in this country have seldom balanced. *Although budget deficits have been larger during recessions than during expansions, the federal budget has been in deficit in all but nine years since 1931.*

Annually balanced budget Budget philosophy prior to the Great Depression; aimed at equating revenues with outlays, except during times of war

Cyclically balanced budget A budget philosophy calling for budget deficits during recessions to be financed by budget surpluses during expansions

Functional finance A budget philosophy aiming fiscal policy at achieving potential GDP, rather than balancing budgets either annually or over the business cycle

Deficits in the 1980s

In 1981, President Reagan secured a three-year budget resolution that included a large tax cut along with increases in defense spending. Some so-called *supply-side* economists argued that tax cuts would stimulate enough economic activity to keep tax revenues from falling. The congressional budget resolution adopted in 1981 was based on an assumption that unspecified spending cuts would bring the two sides of the budget into balance, but the promised cuts in spending never materialized.

Moreover, overly optimistic revenue projections—so-called rosy scenarios—were built into the budget. For example, the budget projected that real GDP would grow by 5.2 percent in 1982, but the economy fell into a recession and, instead, output dropped by 2.1 percent. The recession caused the automatic stabilizers to kick in, thereby reducing revenues and increasing spending still more. Since spending was underestimated and revenue overestimated, the deficit in 1982 amounted to about 4 percent of GDP, at the time one of the largest peacetime deficits in U.S. history.

The deficit served as a backdrop for budget debates in the early 1980s. President Reagan's budget strategy called for increases in defense spending, but he promised to veto any new taxes or any cuts in Social Security. The deficit climbed to 6.1 percent of GDP in 1983. In short, the government had cut tax rates but did not cut expenditures. *Federal revenues declined relative to GDP, but federal spending rose relative to GDP.* Exhibit 2 shows federal budget deficits and the lone surplus since 1970 relative to GDP. As you can see, the deficit as a percentage of GDP climbed in the early 1980s, declined somewhat as the economy improved after the recession of 1982, then increased in 1990 with the onset of another recession. But after bottoming out in 1991, the deficit decreased each year until blooming into a surplus in 1998. That's the short history of modern deficits. The longer story comes next.

EXHIBIT 2

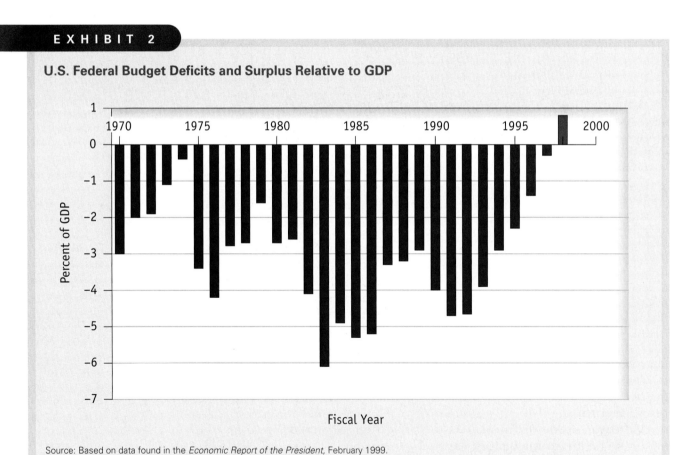

U.S. Federal Budget Deficits and Surplus Relative to GDP

Fiscal Year

Source: Based on data found in the *Economic Report of the President,* February 1999.

Why Did Deficits Persist So Long?

As we have seen, the huge deficits of the 1980s and early 1990s were caused by a combination of tax cuts and spending increases. But why has the budget been in deficit for all but nine years since 1931? Why did federal budget deficits become so much a part of the federal budget scene? The most obvious answer is that Congress is not required to balance the budget. In contrast, in 49 states the legislatures are required to balance their budgets.

Let's consider one widely accepted model of the public sector. Elected officials attempt to maximize political support, including votes and campaign contributions. Voters like public spending programs but hate paying taxes, so spending programs win support and taxes lose support. Because of this asymmetry, candidates attempt to maximize their chances of getting elected by offering a budget that is long on benefits but short on taxes.

Moreover, the many fragmented congressional committees push their favorite programs with little concern about the overall budget. For example, a defense bill recently included 18 F-14D fighter jets and 36 V-22 Osprey aircraft because the planes were produced by firms located in key congressional districts. The Pentagon did not want the planes.

The Relationship Between Deficits and Other Aggregate Variables

During the era of high deficits, there was much talk in the news media about the relationships among deficits, interest rates, and inflation. To develop a clearer understanding of these links, let's go back to our model of aggregate demand and aggregate supply. We begin with a balanced federal budget and an economy producing its potential GDP (point *a* in Exhibit 3). The short-run aggregate supply curve is based on long-term labor contracts reflecting an expected price level of 130.

Suppose an unexpected decline in private-sector spending reduces aggregate demand. Recent research suggests that each percentage point added to the unemployment rate cuts output by two percentage points. As employment and output decline, the automatic stabilizers kick in, reducing tax revenues and increasing transfer payments. These stabilizers keep aggregate demand from falling as much as it would without them. Still, the aggregate demand curve shifts from *AD* to *AD'*, resulting in a short-run equilibrium with an output of $7.8 trillion. This combination of reduced tax revenues and increased government outlays results in a budget deficit. According to research, every 1 percent increase in the unemployment rate increases the federal deficit by over $30 billion.

Now let's consider the association between this deficit, triggered as it is by automatic stabilizers, and what happens to real output, the price level, and interest rates. You can see from Exhibit 3 that a deficit resulting from a decline in private-sector spending occurs with falling real output and a falling price level, or reduced inflation. With regard to the interest rate, when output and the price level decline, the transactions demand for money declines as well, so the interest rate tends to fall. Thus, *a decline in private-sector spending triggers automatic stabilizers that result in a federal budget deficit. This deficit is associated with a lower price level, lower output, and lover interest rates.*

EXHIBIT 3

Deficits and Other Measures of the Economy's Performance

At point *a*, the federal budget is in balance and output is at potential. A decline in aggregate demand to *AD'* triggers automatic stabilizers. Tax revenues fall, transfer payments increase, and the budget moves to a deficit position. In this case, the deficit is associated with falling output and a falling price level.

With the economy now at point *b*, suppose policy makers stimulate aggregate demand through expansionary fiscal policy. Tax revenues fall, government expenditures increase, and the deficit grows larger. Here the deficit is associated with rising output and a rising price level.

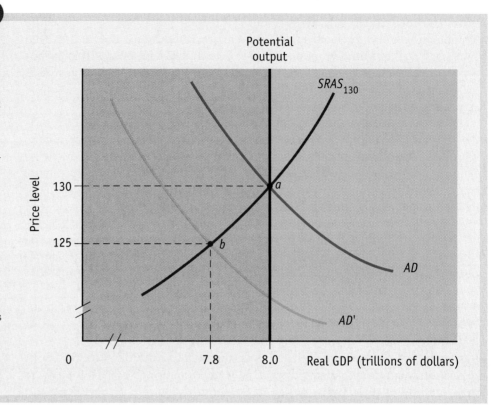

At point *b*, the economy is in recession, with a short-run equilibrium output that is below the economy's potential. Policy makers can either do nothing, waiting for natural market forces to correct the problem of unemployment, or they can intervene in some way. Recall that activists believe that if government takes no action, the movement back to potential output could be long and painful, with much unemployment and much forgone output. Advocates of passive policy believe that government intervention involves unpredictable lags and may affect aggregate demand only after the economy has naturally returned to its potential.

Suppose the government increases its spending, financing this increase by selling bonds to the public, a move that puts upward pressure on interest rates. According to the activist view, the appropriate increase in government spending could stimulate aggregate demand just enough to return the economy to its potential GDP. The effects of this policy would be represented in Exhibit 3 by a movement from point *b* back to point *a*. In essence, increased government demand offsets the decline in private-sector demand.

What is the relationship between the higher deficit that results from this discretionary fiscal policy and the other macroeconomic measures? This higher deficit is associated with greater output and a higher price level. The interest rate rises not only because the Treasury sells bonds to finance the deficit but also because the higher price and output levels increase the demand for money.

Thus, *a deficit that arises from discretionary fiscal policy is associated with a higher real output, a higher price level, and a higher interest rate.*

We can conclude that there is no necessary relationship between deficits and various measures of economic performance. Deficits resulted initially from automatic stabilizers and then from discretionary fiscal policy, but the results of each deficit on real output, the price level, and interest rates differ. The results differ because the source of the deficit differs.

Crowding Out and Crowding In

Why do we care about the effect deficits have on interest rates? Recall that interest rates are a key determinant of investment, and investment is critical to economic growth. What's more, year-to-year fluctuations in investment spending are the primary source of shifts in aggregate demand. Let's look at the impact of deficit spending on business investment.

Suppose the federal government decides to expand the interstate highway system with a construction program that involves deficit spending of $10 billion. To pay for the new system, the Treasury sells government securities, or IOUs. The government's increased demand for credit raises interest rates in the market for loanable funds. Higher interest rates in turn discourage, or *crowd out,* some private investment, reducing the deficit expansionary effect. The extent of **crowding out** is a matter of debate. Some argue that although government borrowing may displace some private-sector borrowing, discretionary fiscal policy will result in a net increase in aggregate demand, leading to greater output and employment in the short run. Others believe the crowding out is more extensive, so borrowing from the public in this way could result in little or no net increase in aggregate demand and output.

Although crowding out is likely to occur to some degree, there is another possibility. If the economy is operating well below its potential, the additional fiscal stimulus provided by deficit spending could encourage firms to invest more and could thus result in a higher level of investment. Recall that an important determinant of investment spending is business expectations. A government deficit could stimulate a weak economy, increasing aggregate demand, boosting employment, and putting a sunny face on business expectations. As business expectations grow more favorable, firms could become more willing to invest. The Japanese government has recently proposed deficit spending as a way of stimulating private-sector spending. This ability of government deficits to stimulate private investment is sometimes called **crowding in,** to distinguish it from crowding out.

Were you ever unwilling to patronize a restaurant because it was too crowded? You simply did not want to put up with the hassle and long wait and were thus "crowded out." As that baseball-player-turned-philosopher Yogi Berra said, "No one goes there nowadays. It's too crowded." Similarly, large government deficits may "crowd out" some investors by driving up interest rates. On the other hand, did you ever pass up an unfamiliar restaurant because the place seemed dead—it had few customers? Perhaps you wondered why so few people chose to eat there. If you had seen just a few more customers, you might have stopped in—you might have been willing to "crowd in." Similarly, businesses may be reluctant to invest in a seemingly lifeless economy. The economic

Crowding out The displacement of interest-sensitive private investment that occurs when increased government deficit spending drives up interest rates

Crowding in The potential for government spending to stimulate private investment in an otherwise sluggish economy

stimulus resulting from deficit spending could encourage some investors to "crowd in."

The Twin Deficits

To finance the huge deficits of the early 1980s, the U.S. Treasury had to sell a lot of bonds, driving up the market interest rate. With U.S. interest rates relatively high, foreigners were more willing to buy dollar-denominated bonds. To buy them, foreigners had to exchange their currencies for dollars. This greater demand for dollars caused the dollar to appreciate relative to foreign currencies during the first half of the 1980s. The rising value of the dollar made foreign goods cheaper in the United States and U.S. goods more expensive abroad. Thus, U.S. imports increased and U.S. exports decreased, so the foreign trade deficit increased.

The higher trade deficits meant that foreigners were accumulating dollars. With these dollars, they purchased U.S. assets, including U.S. government bonds, and thereby helped fund the giant federal deficits. The increase in funds from abroad in the 1980s was both good news and bad news for the U.S. economy. The good news was that the supply of foreign funds increased investment in the United States over what would have occurred in the absence of these funds. Ask people what they think of foreign investment in their town; they will likely say it's great.

But the foreign supply of funds to some extent simply offsets a decline in U.S. saving. Such a pattern could pose problems in the long run. The United States has surrendered a certain amount of control over its economy to foreign investors. And the return on foreign investments in the United States flows abroad.

The Miraculous Budget Surplus

In 1990 federal outlays were 22.4 percent as large as GDP; federal revenue was 18.8 percent the size of GDP. The difference represented a substantial deficit of 3.6 percent relative to GDP. By 1998 federal revenue exceeded federal outlays, yielding a surplus of $70 billion, or 0.8 percent relative to GDP. What happened between 1990 and 1998 that erased the deficit?

Tax Increases. With concern about the deficit growing, Congress and President Bush agreed to the 1990 Budget Enforcement Act, a package of spending cuts and tax increases aimed at trimming the projected deficit. Ironically, that tax increase not only may have cost President Bush reelection in 1992, but it also helped create the surplus in 1998, which President Clinton took credit for. President Clinton, for his part, increased taxes substantially on high-income households in 1993. The highest marginal tax rate jumped from 31 percent to 39.6 percent. Certain exemptions for high-income households were also reduced or eliminated, raising the effective marginal rate at the top to about 42 percent. Meanwhile the economy experienced a vigorous recovery during the 1990s, fueled by growing consumer spending and the strongest stock market in history. The combined effects of these tax increases and a strengthening economy raised federal revenue from 18.8 percent of GDP in 1990 to 21.8 percent in 1998.

Reduced Growth in Federal Outlays. Because of spending restrictions imposed by the 1990 Budget Enforcement Act, the rate of growth in federal outlays slowed compared to the 1980s. The collapse of the Soviet Union reduced U.S. military commitments abroad and resulted in a 30 percent drop in defense spending between 1990 and 1998 in inflation-adjusted dollars. The size of the armed forces dropped from 2.1 million people in 1990 to 1.4 million in 1998. The number of nondefense federal employees declined by 62,000, or about 5 percent, between 1990 and 1998. Part of the impetus for slower growth came from Republicans, who attained a congressional majority in 1994. Since then, inflation-adjusted domestic spending has been flat. Another beneficial factor has been the decline in interest rates on U.S. government securities. By late 1998, these rates had declined to their lowest level in 30 years, saving the federal government billions in interest charges on the national debt. Federal outlays dropped from 22.4 percent relative to GDP in 1990 to 21.0 percent in 1998.

Not-Quite-Perfect Picture. Thanks to the tax-rate increases and the strong economy, tax revenues gushed into Washington, growing an average of 8.0 percent per year between 1993 and 1998. Meanwhile, federal outlays remained in check, growing only 3.8 percent per year. By 1998 that combination created a federal budget surplus of $70 billion, a reversal of fortune from a deficit that had topped $290 billion only six years earlier.

But the results are not quite as rosy as they appear, so hold the champagne for now. The first surplus in three decades would have been a $30 billion deficit had it not been for about $100 billion in surplus generated by the Social Security program, as discussed in the following case study.

Reforming Social Security

CaseStudy

Public Policy

The National Academy of Social Insurance is a nonpartisan research organization formed to study Social Security and Medicare. Its Web site includes a "Social Security Sourcebook" page at http://www.nasi.org/source/reso.htm. Read "Social Security Briefs" to learn more about particular reforms suggested for Social Security. There is also a glossary of terms to help you sort out the jargon.

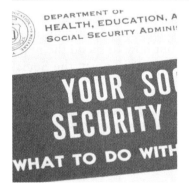

Social Security is a federal redistribution program that collects payroll taxes from current workers to provide pensions for current retirees. Annual benefits in 1998 averaged $8,772 for individual retirees and $15,456 for couples. Social Security consists of two plans, each with its own tax structure. The pension program is paid from the old-age, survivors, and disability insurance (OASDI) tax, which in 1998 applied at a rate of 6.2 percent each on employee and employer to the first $68,400 earned, so the combined maximum tax that year was $8,881.60. Hospital care for the elderly is paid from the Medicare tax, which applies at a rate of 1.45 percent each on employee and employer, with no cap on the earnings taxed, so the Medicare tax on Harrison Ford's earnings of $20 million per movie totals $580,000.

During the first 50 years of the program, whenever tax revenues exceeded the cost of the program, Congress either raised benefits, expanded eligibility, or spent the surplus on something else. In the early 1980s, analysts began to fathom the tremendous impact of the baby boom generation on such a pay-as-you-go program. When baby boomers begin retiring in large numbers around 2020, the

erations because future debt service payments no longer remain in the country. Foreigners are owed about one-fifth of the debt held by the public.

Crowding Out and Capital Formation

We have seen that government borrowing can drive up interest rates, crowding out some private investment by making it more costly. The long-run effects of deficit spending depend on how the government spends the borrowed dollars. If additional outlays are oriented toward investments such as improving interstate highways or educating the workforce, the public investment may be as productive as any private investment forgone. Hence, there may be no harmful effects on the economy's long-run productive capabilities. If, however, the additional borrowed dollars go toward current consumption, such as farm subsidies or federal retirement benefits, the economy's capital formation will be less than it would otherwise be. With less investment today, there will be a smaller endowment of capital equipment and technology for future generations. U.S. private investment declined from about 16 percent of GDP in 1984 to 12 percent in 1991. But since 1991 private investment has rebounded to about 16 percent of GDP in 1998. So private investment increased as the federal deficit decreased.

Ironically, despite the large federal deficits of the 1980s and early 1990s, government investments in roads, bridges, and airports—so-called *public capital*—has declined. In 1970, the value of the nation's public capital stock was about 50 percent of GDP; this figure has declined to about 40 percent today. So public investment has declined. Some argue that declining investment in the public infrastructure serves as a drag on productivity growth. For example, the failure to invest sufficiently in airports and in the air traffic control system has resulted in congested airports and flight delays.

Thus government deficits of one generation can affect the standard of living of the next. And some argue that our current measure of the national debt does not capture all burdens passed on to future generations. For example, Martin Feldstein, a Harvard economist, believes that unfunded liabilities of government retirement programs, such as Social Security, should be included in the debt. Such an inclusion would triple the measure of the national debt. A model that considers some intergenerational issues is discussed in the following case study.

An Intergenerational View of Deficits and Debt

CaseStudy

Public Policy

Across Generations is an archive of articles from *Pioneer Press* (St. Paul, MN) dealing with intergenerational issues, Social Security in particular. Link to http://www.pioneerplanet.com/archive/gen/index.htm and explore the numerous themes listed along the right-side menu

Robert Barro, another economist from Harvard, has developed a model that assumes parents are concerned about the welfare of their children, who, in turn, are concerned about the welfare of *their* children, and so on for generations. Thus, the welfare of all generations is tied together. According to Barro, parents concerned about future generations will reduce the burden of federal debt on future generations and reduce the stimulative effect of deficit spending.

Here's his argument. When the government incurs deficits, this keeps current taxes lower than they would otherwise be, but taxes in the future must increase to service the resulting debt. If there is no regard for the welfare of future generations, then the older people are, the more attractive debt becomes relative to taxes. Older people can enjoy the benefits of public spending now, but will not live long enough to finance the debt through higher taxes or lower benefits. If people are concerned about their children's welfare, however, they will be more reluctant to run deficits now and thereby raise future taxes.

Parents can undo the harm that deficit financing imposes on their children by consuming less now and saving more. As governments substitute deficits for taxes, parents will consume less and save more to increase gifts and bequests to their children. If increases in household saving just offset increases in federal deficits, deficit spending will not increase aggregate demand, because the decline in consumption will negate the fiscal stimulus provided by deficits. This intergenerational transfer offsets the future burden of higher debt and neutralizes the effect of deficit spending on aggregate demand, output, and employment.

The large budget deficits of the last two decades, caused in part by tax cuts, seem to provide a natural experiment for testing Barro's theory of government debt. The evidence fails to support his theory, since the large federal deficits coincided with low national saving rates. Yet defenders of Barro's view say that maybe the saving rate was low because people were optimistic about future economic growth, an optimism that was reflected by a huge increase in the stock market. Or maybe the saving rate was low because people believed the tax cuts would result not in higher future taxes but in lower government spending, as President Reagan promised.

But there are other reasons to be skeptical about Barro's theory. First, individuals without children may not be concerned about the welfare of future generations. Second, the theory assumes that people are well informed about federal spending and tax policies and about the future consequences of current policies; most people are in fact poorly informed about such matters. One survey found that only one in ten adults polled had any idea about the size of the federal deficit. In the poll taken in 1995, when the federal deficit was around $165 billion, only one in ten adults said correctly that the deficit was between $100 billion and $400 billion.

Sources: Robert J. Barro, "Are Government Bonds Net Worth?" *Journal of Political Economy* 82 (November/December 1974): 1095–1117; Robert J. Barro, "The Ricardian Approach to Budget Deficits," *Journal of Economic Perspectives* 3 (Spring 1989): 37; and Jay Mathews, "How High Is the Deficit, the Dow? Most in Survey Didn't Know," *Hartford Courant* (19 October 1995).

bar. The site also provides links to additional Internet resources such as the Third Millenium at http://www.thirdmil.org/, an organization of generation Xers proposing solutions to long-term problems facing the U.S.

CONCLUSION

John Maynard Keynes introduced the idea that federal deficit spending is an appropriate fiscal policy when private aggregate demand is insufficient to achieve potential output. The federal budget has not been the same since. Until the last year or so, the federal budget had been in deficit every year but one since 1960.

And beginning in the early 1980s, giant federal deficits dominated the fiscal policy debate. But after peaking at $290 billion in 1992, the deficit came down because of higher tax rates on high-income households, reduced federal outlays (especially for defense), and a rip-roaring economy and stock market. Whether chronic deficits have been eliminated remains to be seen.

SUMMARY

1. The federal budget process suffers from a variety of problems, including overlapping committee jurisdictions, lengthy budget deliberations, extensive use of continuing resolutions, budgeting in too much detail, and a lack of year-to-year control over most of the budget. Suggested improvements include instituting a biennial budget, budgeting in less detail, and distinguishing between a capital budget and an operating budget.

2. Deficits usually rise during wars and severe recessions, but deficits remained large during the economic expansion of the 1980s. The deficits arose from a combination of tax cuts during the early 1980s and growth in federal spending. As a percentage of GDP, the national debt has doubled since 1980.

3. There is no clear, consistent relationship between deficits and other measures of macroeconomic performance, such as output, the price level, and interest rates. If a fall in aggregate demand results in a recession, deficits increase because of automatic stabilizers, but output, the inflation rate, and the interest rate all decline. If discretionary fiscal policy is used to rekindle aggregate demand, deficits increase; so do output, the price level, and the interest rate.

4. To the extent that deficits crowd out private capital formation, this decline in private investment reduces the economy's ability to grow. Foreign holdings of debt also impose a burden on future generations because future payments to service this debt are paid to foreigners and consequently are not available to U.S. citizens. Thus the deficits of one generation can reduce the standard of living of the next.

5. After peaking at $290 billion in 1992, the federal deficit turned into a surplus by 1998 because of higher tax rates, reduced outlays especially for defense, declining interest rates, and a strengthening economy.

QUESTIONS FOR REVIEW

1. *(The Federal Budget Process)* The budgets passed by Congress and signed by the president show the relationship between *budgeted* expenditures and *projected* revenues. Why does the budget require a forecast of the state of the economy? Under what circumstances would the actual government spending and tax revenue fail to match the budget as approved?

2. *(The Federal Budget Process)* In what sense is the executive branch of the U.S. government always dealing with three budgets?

3. *(Problems with the Budget Process)* In terms of the policy lags described in Chapter 16, discuss the following problems with the budget process:
   a. Continuing resolutions
   b. Overlapping committee authority

   c. Uncontrollable budget items
   d. An overly detailed budget

4. *(Budget Philosophies)* Explain the differences among an annually balanced budget, a cyclically balanced budget, and functional finance. How does each affect economic fluctuations?

5. *(Budget Philosophies)* One alternative to balancing the budget annually or cyclically is to produce a government budget that would be balanced if the economy were at potential output. Given the cyclical nature of government tax revenues and spending, how would the resulting budget deficit or surplus vary over the business cycle?

6. *(Budget Philosophies)* The functional finance approach to budget deficits would set the federal budget to promote

an economy operating at potential output. What problems would you expect if the country were to employ this kind of budgetary philosophy?

7. *(Deficits and Other Aggregate Variables)* Distinguish between (1) the short-run changes in real output, the price level, and the interest rate associated with deficits caused by automatic stabilizers and (2) the short-run effects associated with deficits caused by discretionary fiscal policy. .

8. *(Crowding Out)* Is it possible for U.S. federal budget deficits to crowd out investment spending in other countries? How could German or British investment be hurt by large U.S. budget deficits?

9. *(Crowding Out)* How might federal deficits crowd out private domestic investment? How could this crowding out affect future living standards?

10. *(Interest on the Debt)* The percentage of federal income tax revenues necessary to service the debt increased from 20 percent in 1978 to 30 percent in 1998. What problems has that created for public officials and spending programs?

11. *(Burden of the Debt)* Suppose that government budget deficits are financed to a considerable extent by foreign sources. How does this create a potential burden for the domestic economy in the future?

12. *(The Twin Deficits)* How is the U.S. budget deficit related to the trade deficit?

13. *(The Miraculous Budget Surplus)* Why did the federal budget go from a huge deficit in 1992 to a surplus in 1998? Explain the factors that contributed to the turnaround.

14. *(CaseStudy: Reforming Social Security)* Why is the Social Security program headed for trouble? When will the trouble begin? What possible solutions have been proposed?

15. *(Crowding Out and Capital Formation)* In earlier chapters, we've seen that the government can increase GDP in the short run by running a government budget deficit. What are some of the longer-term effects of deficit spending?

16. *(CaseStudy: An Intergenerational View of Deficits and Debt)* Explain why Robert Barro argues that if parents are concerned about the future welfare of their children, the effects of deficit spending will be neutralized.

PROBLEMS AND EXERCISES

17. *(The National Debt)* Try the following exercises to better understand how the national debt is related to the government's budget deficit.
    a. Assume that the gross national debt initially is equal to $3 trillion and the federal government then runs a deficit of $300 billion:
       i. What is the new level of gross national debt?
       ii. If 100 percent of the deficit is financed by the sale of securities to federal agencies, what happens to the amount of debt held by the public? What happens to the level of gross debt?
       iii. If GDP increased by 5 percent in the same year that the deficit is run, what happens to gross debt as a percent of GDP? What happens to the level of debt held by the public as a percent of GDP?

    b. Now suppose that the gross national debt initially is equal to $2.5 trillion and the federal government then runs a deficit of $100 billion:
       i. What is the new level of gross national debt?
       ii. If 100 percent of this deficit is financed by the sale of securities to the public, what happens to the level of debt held by the public? What happens to the level of gross debt?
       iii. If GDP increases by 6 percent in the same year as the deficit is run, what happens to gross debt as a percent of GDP? What happens to the level of debt held by the public as a percent of GDP?

EXPERIENTIAL EXERCISES

18. *(Federal Budget Deficits)* Try your hand at balancing the federal budget. Visit the National Budget Simulation at UC Berkeley's Center for Community Economic Research at http://socrates.berkeley.edu:3333/budget/budget.html.

    a. Develop a budget and see what happens. Were you successful in balancing the budget? If not, how much of a deficit or surplus did you end up with? What does this exercise tell you about the process of creating a balanced budget?

    b. Reexamine the budget cuts or increases you made. What problems would such changes pose for a politician facing reelection?

    c. This budget simulator allows you only to change spending and tax expenditures over a one-year period. What problems does this pose to finding a realistic economic solution for balancing the budget?

19. *(CaseStudy: Reforming Social Security)* Visit South-Western College Publishing's EconDebates Online at http://www.swcollege.com/bef/mceachern/mceachern.html. Review the materials on "Will Social Security survive into the 21st century?" What are some of the macroeconomic implications of Social Security reform?

20. *(Wall Street Journal)* You learned that the government pays billions of dollars in interest each year to finance the national debt. Those debt payments are sensitive to changes in the nominal interest rate. Check the "Treasury Issues" table in the Money and Investing section of today's *Wall Street Journal*. Have interest rates on Treasury bonds and bills been increasing or decreasing lately? What are the implications of interest rate changes for bond prices and for debt finance?

International Trade

This morning you pulled up your Levi jeans from Mexico, pulled over your Benetton sweater from Italy, and laced up your Nikes from Indonesia. After a breakfast that included bananas from Honduras and coffee from Brazil, you climbed into your Volvo from Sweden fueled by Saudi Arabian oil and headed for a lecture by a visiting professor from Hungary. If the United States is such a rich and productive nation, why do we import so many goods and services? Why don't we produce everything ourselves? And why do some groups try to restrict foreign trade? Answers to these and other questions are addressed in this chapter.

The world is a giant shopping mall, and Americans are big spenders. Americans buy Japanese cars, French wine, Swiss clocks, European vacations, and

Visit the McEachern Interactive Study Center for this chapter at http://mcisc.swcollege.com

thousands of other goods and services from around the globe. But foreigners spend a lot on American products too—grain, personal computers, aircraft, movies, trips to Disney World, and thousands of other goods and services. In this chapter, we examine the gains from international trade and the effects of trade restrictions on the allocation of resources. The analysis is based on the familiar tools of supply and demand. Topics discussed in this chapter include:

- Gains from trade
- Absolute and comparative advantage revisited
- Tariffs

- Import quotas
- Welfare loss from trade restrictions
- Arguments for trade restrictions

THE GAINS FROM TRADE

A family from Virginia that sits down for a meal of Kansas prime rib, Idaho potatoes, and California string beans, with Georgia peach cobbler for desert is benefiting from interstate trade. You already understand why the residents of one state trade with those of another. Back in Chapter 2, you learned about the gains arising from specialization and exchange. You may recall the discussion of how you and your roommate could maximize output by specializing in typing or ironing. The law of comparative advantage says that the individual with the lowest opportunity cost of producing a particular output should specialize in producing that output. Just as individuals benefit from specialization and exchange, so do states and, indeed, nations. To reap the gains that arise from specialized production, countries engage in international trade. *With trade, each country can concentrate on producing those goods and services that involve the least opportunity cost.*

A Profile of Imports and Exports

Some nations are more involved in international trade than others, just as some states are more involved in interstate trade than others. For example, exports account for about half of the gross domestic product (GDP) in Holland; about one-third of the GDP in Germany, Sweden, and Switzerland; and about one-quarter of the GDP in Canada and the United Kingdom. Despite the perception that Japan has a giant export sector, only about 13 percent of Japanese production is exported.

In the United States, exports of goods and services amounted to about 11 percent of GDP in 1998. Although small relative to GDP, exports play a growing role in the U.S. economy. The four main U.S. exports are (1) high-technology manufactured products, such as computer software and hardware, aircraft, telecommunication equipment, and military equipment; (2) industrial supplies and materials; (3) agricultural products, especially corn and soybeans; and (4) entertainment products, such as movies and recorded music.

The United States depends on imports for some key inputs. For example, our position as the world's largest producer of aluminum depends on our importing vast amounts of bauxite. Most of our platinum and chromium and all of our manganese, mica, diamonds, and nickel are imported. Two-thirds of U.S. imports are (1) manufactured consumer goods, such as automobiles from Japan and Germany and electronic equipment from Taiwan, and (2) capital goods, such as high-tech printing presses from Germany. *U.S. imports of goods and services amounted to about 13 percent relative to GDP in 1998.*

The big change in U.S. exports over the last 25 years has been a growth in the dollar value of machinery exports; nearly half of the capital goods produced in the United States are exported. The primary change in U.S. imports over the last 25 years has been the increase in spending on foreign oil. Canada is our largest trading partner, followed by Japan and Mexico. Other important trading partners include Germany, Great Britain, South Korea, France, Hong Kong, Italy, and Brazil.

Production Possibilities Without Trade

The rationale behind some international trade is obvious. The United States grows no coffee beans because our climate is not suited to coffee. It is more revealing, however, to examine the gains from trade where the cost advantage is not so obvious. Suppose that just two goods—food and clothing—are produced and consumed and that there are only two countries in the world—the United States, with a labor force of 100 million workers, and the mythical country of Izodia, with 200 million workers. The conclusions we derive from this simple model will have general relevance to the pattern of international trade.

Exhibit 1 presents each country's production possibilities table, based on the size of the labor force and the productivity of workers in each country. We assume a given technology and that labor is fully and efficiently employed. Since no trade occurs between countries, Exhibit 1 presents each country's *consumption possibilities* table as well, reflecting each country's consumption alternatives.

The production numbers imply that each worker in the United States can produce either 6 units of food or 3 units of clothing per day. If all 100 million U.S. workers produce food, 600 million units can be produced per day, as reflected by combination U_1 in part (a) of Exhibit 1. If all U.S. workers produce clothing, U.S. output would be 300 million units per day, as reflected by combination U_6.

EXHIBIT 1

Production Possibilities Schedules for the United States and Izodia

(a) United States

| Units Produced (per worker per day) | Production Possibilities with 100 Million Workers (millions of units per day) | | | | | |
	U_1	U_2	U_3	U_4	U_5	U_6
Food　6	600	480	360	240	120	0
Clothing　3	0	60	120	180	240	300

(b) Izodia

| Units Produced (per worker per day) | Production Possibilities with 200 Million Workers (millions of units per day) | | | | | |
	I_1	I_2	I_3	I_4	I_5	I_6
Food　1	200	160	120	80	40	0
Clothing　2	0	80	160	240	320	400

Combinations in between represent alternatives if some workers produce food and some produce clothing. Because a U.S. worker can produce either 6 units of food or 3 units of clothing, *his opportunity cost of 1 more unit of food is ½ unit of clothing.*

Suppose Izodian workers are less educated, work with less capital, and farm less fertile land than U.S. workers. So each Izodian can produce only 1 unit of food or 2 units of clothing per day. If all 200 million Izodian workers specialize in food, they can produce 200 million units of food per day, as reflected by combination I_1 in part (b) of Exhibit 1. If all Izodian workers produce clothing, total output is 400 million units of clothing per day, as reflected by combination I_6. Some intermediate production possibilities are also listed in the exhibit. Because an Izodian worker can produce either 1 unit of food or 2 units of clothing, *her opportunity cost of 1 more unit of food is 2 units of clothing.*

We can convert the data in Exhibit 1 to a production possibilities frontier for each country, as is shown in Exhibit 2. In each diagram, the amount of food produced is measured on the vertical axis and the amount of clothing is measured on the horizontal axis. U.S. combinations are shown in panel (a) by U_1, U_2, and so on; Izodian combinations are designated in panel (b) by I_1, I_2, and so on. Because we assume that resources are perfectly adaptable to the production of each commodity, each production possibilities curve is a straight line reflecting constant opportunity cost.

Exhibit 2 illustrates—in red—the possible combinations of food and clothing that residents of each country can produce and consume if all resources are fully and efficiently employed and there is no trade between the two countries. **Autarky** is the situation of national self-sufficiency, in which there is no economic interaction with foreigners. Suppose that U.S. producers maximize profit

Autarky A situation of national self-sufficiency in which there is no economic interaction with foreigners

EXHIBIT 2

Production Possibilities Frontiers for the United States and Izodia (in millions of units per day)

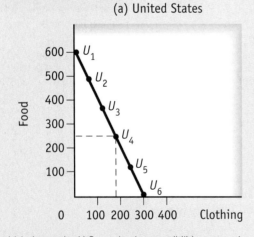 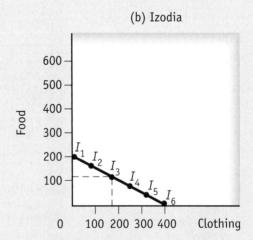

Panel (a) shows the U.S. production possibilities curve; its slope indicates that the opportunity cost of an additional unit of food is 1/2 unit of clothing. Panel (b) shows production possibilities in Izodia; an additional unit of food costs 2 units of clothing. Food is relatively cheaper to produce in the United States.

and U.S. consumers maximize utility with the combination of 240 million units of food and 180 million units of clothing—combination U_4. This combination will be called the *autarky equilibrium*. Suppose also that Izodians have an autarky equilibrium, identified as combination I_3, of 120 million units of food and 160 million units of clothing.

Consumption Possibilities Based on Comparative Advantage

In our example, each U.S. worker can produce both more clothing and more food per day than can each Izodian worker. U.S. workers therefore have an *absolute advantage* in the production of both goods because a U.S. worker can produce each good in less time than can an Izodian worker. With an absolute advantage in the production of both commodities, should the U.S. economy remain in autarky—that is, self-sufficient in both food and clothing productions—or could there be gains from trade?

As long as the opportunity cost of the two goods differs between the two countries, there are gains from specialization and trade. The opportunity cost of producing 1 more unit of food in the United States is ½ unit of clothing, compared to 2 units of clothing in Izodia. *According to the law of comparative advantage, each country should specialize in producing the good with the lower opportunity cost.* Since the opportunity cost of producing food is lower in the United States than in Izodia, both countries will gain if the United States specializes in producing food and exports some to Izodia, and Izodia specializes in producing clothing and exports some to the United States.

Before countries can trade, they must somehow determine how much of one good will be exchanged for another—that is, they must establish the **terms of trade.** Suppose that market forces shape terms of trade whereby 1 unit of clothing exchanges for 1 unit of food. Based on those terms of trade, Americans trade 1 unit of food to Izodians for 1 unit of clothing. To produce 1 unit of clothing Americans would have to sacrifice 2 units of food. Likewise, Izodians sacrifice 1 unit of clothing by trading clothing to Americans for 1 unit of food, which is only half what Izodians would sacrifice to produce 1 unit of food themselves.

Terms of trade How much of one good exchanges for a unit of another good

Exhibit 3 shows that with 1 unit of food trading for 1 unit of clothing, Americans and Izodians can consume anywhere along or below their blue consumption possibilities frontiers. *The consumption possibilities frontier* shows a nation's alternative combinations of goods available as a result of production and foreign trade. (Note that the U.S. consumption possibilities curve does not extend to the right of 400 million units of clothing, since that is the most the Izodians can produce.) The amount each country actually consumes will depend on its relative preferences for food and clothing. Suppose Americans select point *U* in panel (a) and Izodians select point *I* in panel (b).

Without trade, the United States produced and consumed 240 million units of food and 180 million units of clothing. With trade, the United States specializes in food by producing 600 million units; Americans eat 400 million units and exchange the remaining 200 million for 200 million units of Izodian clothing. This consumption combination is reflected by point *U* in panel (a). Through exchange, Americans increase their consumption of both food and clothing.

EXHIBIT 3

Production (and Consumption) Possibilities Frontiers with Trade (in millions of units per day)

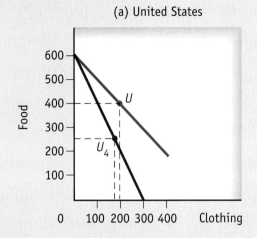

(a) United States

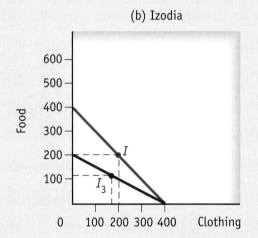

(b) Izodia

If Izodia and the United States can trade at the rate of 1 unit of clothing for 1 unit of food, both can benefit. Consumption possibilities at those terms of trade are shown by the blue lines. The United States was previously producing and consuming combination U_4. By trading with Izodia, it can produce only food and still consume combination U—a combination that contains more food and more clothing than combination U_4 does. Likewise, Izodia can attain the preferred combination I by trading its clothing for U.S. food. Both countries are better off as a result of international trade.

Without trade, Izodians produced and consumed 120 million units of food and 160 million units of clothing. With trade, Izodians specialize in clothing to produce 400 million units; Izodians wear 200 million units of clothing and exchange the remaining 200 million units for 200 million units of food. This consumption combination is shown by point I in panel (b). Izodians, like Americans, are able to increase their consumption of both food and clothing through trade. How is this possible?

Since Izodians are relatively more efficient in the production of clothing and Americans relatively more efficient in the production of food, total output increases when each country specializes. Specifically, without specialization, total world production was 360 million units of food and 340 million units of clothing. With specialization, food production increases to 600 million units and clothing production increases to 400 million units. The only constraint on trade is that, for each good, *total world production must equal total world consumption*. In our two-country world, this means that the amount of food the United States exports must equal the amount of food Izodia imports. The same goes for Izodia's exports of clothing.

Thus, both countries have more goods and services after trade. *Although the United States has an absolute advantage in both goods, differences in the opportunity cost of production between the two nations ensure that specialization and exchange will result in mutual gains.* Remember that comparative advantage, not absolute advantage, is the source of gains from trade.

We simplified trade relations in our example to highlight the gains from specialization and exchange. We assumed that each country would completely specialize in producing a particular good, that resources were equally adaptable to the production of either good, that the costs of transporting the goods from one country to another were inconsequential, and that there were no problems in arriving at the terms of trade. The world is not that simple (for example, we don't expect a country to produce just one good), but the law of comparative advantage still points to gains from trade.

Reasons for International Specialization

Countries trade with one another—or, more precisely, people and firms in one country trade with those in another—because each side expects to gain from the exchange. How do we know what each country should produce and what goods should be traded?

Differences in Resource Endowments. Trade is often prompted by differences in resource endowments. Two key resources are labor and capital. Countries differ not only in their amounts of labor and capital but in the qualities of those resources. A well-educated and well-trained labor force is more productive than an uneducated and unskilled one. Similarly, capital that reflects the most recent technological developments is more productive than nonexistent or obsolete capital. Some countries, such as the United States and Japan, have an educated labor force and an abundant stock of modern capital. Both resources result in greater productivity per worker, making each nation quite competitive in producing goods that require skilled labor and sophisticated capital.

Some countries are blessed with an abundance of fertile land and favorable growing seasons. The United States, for example, has been called the "bread-basket of the world" because of its rich farmland. Honduras has the ideal climate for growing bananas. Coffee is grown best in the climate and elevation of Colombia, Brazil, and Jamaica. Thus, the United States exports corn and imports coffee and bananas. Differences in the seasons across countries also serve as a basis for trade. For example, during the winter months, Americans import fruit from Chile and Canadian tourists travel to Florida for sun and fun. During the summer months, Americans export fruit to Chile and American tourists travel to Canada for fishing and camping.

Mineral resources are often concentrated in particular countries: oil in Saudi Arabia, bauxite in Jamaica, diamonds in South Africa. The United States has abundant coal supplies, but not enough oil to satisfy domestic demand. Thus the United States exports coal and imports oil. More generally, *countries export those products that they can produce more cheaply in return for those that are unavailable domestically or are more costly to produce than to buy from other countries.*

Economies of Scale. If production is subject to *economies of scale*—that is, if the average cost falls as the rate of production increases—countries can gain from trade if each nation specializes. Such specialization allows each nation to produce at a greater output rate, which reduces average production costs. The primary reason for establishing the single integrated market in Western Europe is to offer European producers a large, open market of over 320 million consumers so that producers can increase production, experience economies of scale, and in the process become more competitive in international markets.

NetBookmark

What goods and services does the United States trade? With whom? Who are our largest trading partners? Answers to these and many other trade-related questions can be found by cruising through the U.S. Census Bureau's Trade Data Web site at http://www.census.gov/foreign-trade/www/tradedata.html.

Differences in Tastes. Even if all countries had identical resource endowments and combined those resources with equal efficiency, each country would still gain from trade as long as tastes and preferences differed among countries. Consumption patterns differ. For example, the per-capita consumption of beer in Germany is more than double that in Portugal or Sweden. The French drink three times as much wine as Danes do. The Danes consume twice as much pork as Americans do. Americans consume twice as much chicken as Hungarians do. Soft drinks are four times more popular in the United States than in Western Europe. The English like tea; Americans coffee. Algeria has an ideal climate for growing grapes, but its large Muslim population abstains from alcohol. Thus Algeria exports wine.

TRADE RESTRICTIONS

Despite the benefits of international trade, nearly all countries at one time or another erect barriers to impede or block free trade among nations. Trade restrictions usually benefit domestic producers but harm domestic consumers. In this section, we will consider the effects of restrictions and the reasons they are imposed.

Consumer and Producer Surplus

Before we consider the net effect of world trade on social welfare, let's develop a framework for describing the benefits that consumers and producers derive from exchange. To do this, let's consider a hypothetical market for chicken shown in Exhibit 4. The height of the demand curve reflects the amount that consumers are willing and able to pay for each additional pound of chicken. In effect, the height of the demand curve shows the *marginal benefit* consumers expect from each pound of chicken. For example, the demand curve indicates that some consumers are willing to pay $1.50 or more per pound for the first few pounds of chicken. But all consumers get to buy chicken at the market-clearing price, which in Exhibit 4 is only $0.50 per pound. The blue shaded triangle below the demand curve and above the market price reflects the *consumer surplus,* which is the difference between the maximum sum of money consumers would pay for 60 pounds of chicken per day and the actual sum they do pay. Consumers thus get a bonus, or a surplus, from market exchange. We all enjoy a consumer surplus from most products we consume.

There is a similar surplus on the producer side. The height of the supply curve reflects the minimum amount of money that producers are willing and able to accept for each additional pound of chicken. That is, the height of the supply curve shows the *marginal cost* producers incur in supplying each additional pound of chicken. For example, the supply curve indicates that some producers incur a marginal cost of $0.25 or less per pound for supplying the first few pounds of chicken. But all producers get to sell chicken for the market-clearing price—in this case, $0.50 per pound. The gold shaded triangle above the supply curve and below the market price reflects the *producer surplus,* which is the difference between the actual sum of money producers receive for 60 pounds of chicken and the minimum sum they would accept for that quantity.

EXHIBIT 4

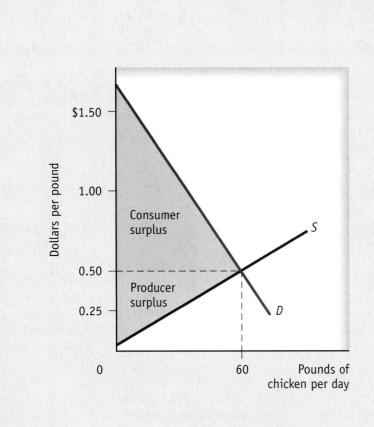

Consumer Surplus and Producer Surplus

Consumer surplus, shown by the blue shaded triangle, shows the net benefits consumers reap by being able to purchase 60 pounds of chicken at $0.50 per pound. Some consumers would have been willing to pay $1.50 or more per pound for the first few pounds. Consumer surplus measures the difference between the maximum sum of money consumers would pay for 60 pounds of chicken and the actual sum they pay. Producer surplus, shown by the gold shaded triangle, shows the net benefits producers reap by being able to sell 60 pounds of chicken at $0.50 per pound. Some producers would have been willing to supply chicken for $0.25 per pound or less. Producer surplus measures the difference between the actual sum of money producers receive for 60 pounds of chicken and the minimum amount they would accept for this amount of chicken.

The point is that market exchange usually yields a surplus, or a bonus, to both producers and consumers. In the balance of the chapter, we focus on how restrictions on international trade affect consumer surplus and producer surplus.

Tariffs

A *tariff*, a term first introduced in Chapter 4, is a tax on imports. (Tariffs can also be applied to exports, but we will focus on import tariffs.) A tariff can be either *specific*, such as a tariff of $5 per barrel of oil, or *ad valorem*, a percentage of the price of imports at the port of entry. Consider the effects of a specific tariff on a particular good. In Exhibit 5, *D* is the domestic demand for sugar and *S* is the supply provided by domestic producers. Suppose that the world price of sugar is $0.10 per pound, as it was in 1998. The **world price** is the price determined by the world supply and world demand for a product. It is the price at which any supplier can sell output on the world market and at which any demander can purchase output on the world market.

World price The price at which a good is traded internationally; determined by the world supply and demand for the good

EXHIBIT 5

Effect of a Tariff

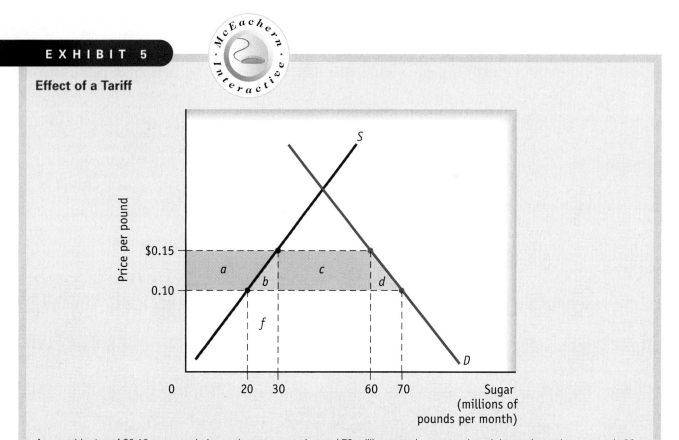

At a world price of $0.10 per pound, domestic consumers demand 70 million pounds per month and domestic producers supply 20 million pounds per month; the difference is imported. With the imposition of a $0.05 per pound tariff, the domestic price rises to $0.15 per pound, domestic producers increase production to 30 million pounds, and domestic consumers cut back to 60 million pounds. Imports fall to 30 million pounds. At the higher domestic price, consumers are worse off; their loss of consumer surplus is the sum of areas *a, b, c,* and *d.* Area *a* represents an increase in producer surplus: a transfer from consumers to producers. Areas *b* and *f* reflect the portion of additional revenues to producers that is just offset by the higher production costs of expanding domestic output by 10 million pounds. Area *c* shows government revenue from the tariff. The net welfare loss to society is the sum of area *d,* which reflects the loss of consumer surplus resulting from the drop in consumption, and area *b,* which reflects the higher marginal cost of domestically producing output that could have been produced more cheaply abroad.

With free trade, domestic consumers can buy any amount desired at the world price, so the quantity demanded is 70 million pounds per month, of which 20 million pounds are supplied by domestic producers and 50 million pounds are imported. Domestic producers cannot charge more than the world price, since domestic buyers can purchase as much sugar as they want at $0.10 per pound in the world market.

Now suppose that a specific tariff of $0.05 is imposed on each pound of sugar imported, raising the price of imported sugar from $0.10 to $0.15 per pound. Domestic producers can therefore raise their price to $0.15 per pound as well without losing sales to imports. At the higher price, the quantity supplied by domestic producers increases to 30 million pounds per month, but the quantity demanded by domestic consumers declines to 60 million pounds per month. Because the quantity demanded has declined and the quantity supplied by domestic producers has increased, imports decline from 50 million to 30 million pounds per month.

Since the price is higher after the tariff, consumers are worse off. The loss in consumer surplus is identified in Exhibit 5 by the blue and red shaded areas. Because both the domestic price and the quantity of sugar supplied by domestic producers have increased, the total revenue received by domestic producers increases by the areas *a* plus *b* plus *f*. But only the light-blue shaded area, *a*, represents an increase in producer surplus. The increase in revenue represented by the areas *b* plus *f* merely offsets the higher marginal cost of expanding domestic production from 20 million to 30 million pounds. The red shaded triangle, *b*, represents part of the net welfare loss to the domestic economy, because those 10 million pounds could have been purchased from abroad for $0.10 per pound rather than produced domestically at a higher marginal cost.

Government revenue from the tariff is identified by the light-blue shaded area, *c*, which equals the tariff of $0.05 per pound multiplied by the 30 million pounds that are imported, or $1.5 million per month. Tariff revenue represents a loss to consumers, but since the tariff is revenue to the government, this loss can potentially be offset by a reduction in taxes or an increase in public services. The red-shaded triangle, *d*, shows a loss in consumer surplus resulting from the fact that less sugar is consumed at the higher price. This loss in consumer surplus is not redistributed as a gain to anyone else, so area *d* reflects part of the net welfare loss of the tariff. Therefore, the two red-shaded triangles, *b* and *d*, show the domestic economy's net welfare loss of the tariff; the *two triangles measure a net loss in consumer surplus that is not offset by a net gain to anyone else.*

Of the total loss in consumer surplus (areas *a, b, c,* and *d*) resulting from the tariff, area *a* is redistributed from consumers to domestic producers, area *c* becomes tariff revenue for the government, and the two red-shaded triangles, *b* and *d*, reflect a net loss in social welfare because of the tariff.

Import Quotas

An *import quota* is a legal limit on the quantity of a particular commodity that can be imported. Quotas often target exports from certain countries. For example, a quota may limit automobile imports from Japan or shoe imports from Brazil. To have an impact on the market, or to be *effective,* a quota must restrict imports to less than the amount imported with free trade.

Let's consider the impact of a quota on the domestic market for sugar. In panel (a) of Exhibit 6, the domestic supply curve of sugar is *S* and the domestic demand curve is *D*. Suppose again that the world price of sugar is $0.10 per pound. With free trade, that price would prevail in the domestic market, and a total of 70 million pounds per month would be demanded. Domestic producers would supply 20 million pounds and importers would supply 50 million pounds. With a quota of 50 million pounds or more per month, the domestic price would remain the same as the world price of $0.10 per pound, and domestic sales would be 70 million pounds per month. In short, a quota of at least 50 million pounds would have no effect. A more stringent quota, however, would reduce the supply of imports, which, as we will see, would raise the domestic price.

Suppose that a quota of 30 million pounds per month is established. As long as the price in the U.S. market is at or above the world price of $0.10 per pound, foreign producers supply 30 million pounds to the U.S. market. So at

EXHIBIT 6

Effect of a Quota

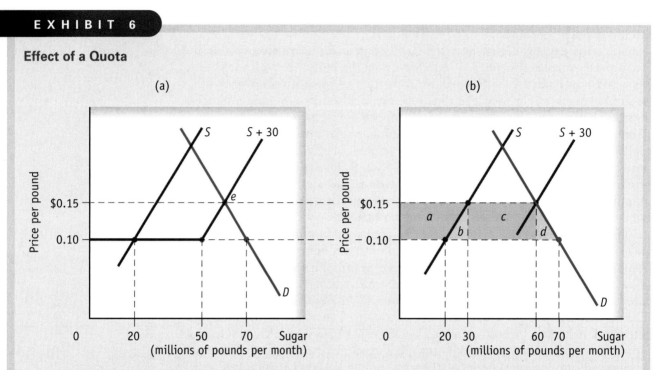

In panel (a), *D* is the domestic demand curve and *S* is the domestic supply curve. When the government establishes a sugar quota of 30 million pounds per year, the supply curve from both domestic production and imports becomes horizontal at the world price of $0.10 per pound and remains horizontal until the supply reaches 50 million pounds. For higher prices, the supply curve equals the horizontal sum of the domestic supply curve, *S,* and the quota. The new domestic price, $0.15 per pound, is determined by the intersection of the new supply curve, *S* + 30, with the domestic demand curve, *D.* Panel (b) shows the welfare effect of the quota. As a result of the higher domestic price, consumer surplus is reduced by the amount of shaded area. Area *a* represents a transfer from domestic consumers to domestic producers. Rectangular area *c* shows the gain to those who can import sugar at the world price and sell it at the higher domestic price. Triangular area *b* reflects a net loss; it represents the amount by which the cost of producing an extra 10 million pounds of sugar in the United States exceeds the cost of buying it from abroad. Area *d* also reflects a net loss—a reduction in consumer surplus as consumption falls. Thus, the blue-shaded areas illustrate the loss in consumer surplus that is captured by domestic producers and those who are permitted to fulfill the quota, and the red-shaded triangles illustrate the minimum net welfare cost.

prices at or above $0.10 per pound, the total supply of sugar to the domestic market is found by adding 30 million pounds of sugar to the amount supplied by domestic producers. At the world price of $0.10 per pound, domestic producers supply 20 million pounds, and importers supply the quota of 30 million pounds, for a total quantity supplied of 50 million pounds. At prices above $0.10, domestic producers can and do expand their quantity supplied in the U.S. market, but imports are restricted to the quota of 30 million pounds.

Domestic and foreign producers will never sell their output for less than $0.10 per pound in the U.S. market because they can always sell for that price on the world market. Thus the supply curve that sums both domestic production and imports becomes horizontal at the world price of $0.10 per pound and remains horizontal until the quantity supplied reaches 50 million pounds. For prices above $0.10 per pound, the supply curve equals the horizontal sum of the supply curve of domestic producers, *S,* and the quota of 30 million pounds. The domestic price is found where this new supply curve intersects the domes-

well-defined group of producers who can clearly identify the source of their gains. *One reason trade restrictions get introduced is that most of those harmed by restrictions do not know they are losers, whereas beneficiaries know what's at stake.*

Producers have an interest in trade legislation, but consumers remain largely ignorant. Consumers purchase thousands of different goods and thus have no special interest in the effects of trade policy on any particular good. Congress tends to support the group that makes the most noise, so trade restrictions persist, despite the clear gains from free trade.

SUMMARY

1. Even if a country has an absolute advantage in producing all goods, that country should specialize in producing the goods in which it has a comparative advantage. If each country specializes and trades according to the law of comparative advantage, all countries will have greater consumption possibilities.

2. Tariff revenues go to the government and could be used to lower taxes. Quotas confer benefits on those with the right to buy the good at the world price and sell it at the higher domestic price. Both restrictions harm domestic consumers more than they help domestic producers, although tariffs at least yield domestic government revenue.

3. Despite the gains from free trade and the net welfare losses arising from tariffs and quotas, trade restrictions have been a part of trade policy for hundreds of years. The General Agreement on Tariffs and Trade (GATT) was an international treaty ratified in 1947 to reduce tariffs. Subsequent rounds of negotiations promoted lower tariffs and discouraged trade restrictions. The Uruguay Round, ratified by 123 countries in 1994, created the World Trade Organization (WTO) to succeed GATT.

4. Reasons given for instituting trade restrictions include promoting national defense, giving infant industries time to grow, preventing foreign producers from dumping goods in domestic markets, protecting domestic jobs, and allowing declining industries time to phase out.

QUESTIONS FOR REVIEW

1. *(Profile of Imports and Exports)* What are the major U.S. exports and imports? How does international trade affect consumption possibilities?

2. *(Gains from Trade)* Complete each of the following sentences:
   a. When a nation has no economic interaction with foreigners and produces everything it consumes, the nation is in a state of _____.
   b. According to the law of comparative advantage, each nation should specialize in producing the goods in which it has the lowest _____.
   c. The amount of one good that a nation can exchange for one unit of another good is known as the _____.
   d. Specializing according to comparative advantage and trading with other nations results in _____.

3. *(Reasons for International Specialization)* What determines which goods a country should produce and export?

4. *(Tariffs)* High tariffs usually lead to black markets and smuggling. How is government revenue reduced by such activity? Relate your answer to the graph in Exhibit 5 in this chapter. Does smuggling have any social benefits?

5. *(Trade Restrictions)* Exhibits 5 and 6 show net losses to the economy of a country that imposes tariffs or quotas on imported sugar. What kinds of gains and losses would occur in the economies of countries that export sugar?

6. *(CaseStudy: The World Trade Organization)* What is the World Trade Organization (WTO) and how does it help foster multilateral trade? (Check the WTO website at http://www.wto.org/).

7. *(Arguments for Trade Restrictions)* Explain the national defense, declining industries, and infant industry arguments for protecting a domestic industry from international competition.

8. *(Arguments for Trade Restrictions)* Firms hurt by cheap imports typically argue that restricting trade will save U.S. jobs. What's wrong with this argument? Are there ever any reasons to support such trade restrictions?

9. *(**Case**Study: Enforcing Trade Restrictions)* Increasingly, goods are manufactured using a variety of domestic and imported parts or resources. What problem does this create in enforcing such trade restrictions?

PROBLEMS AND EXERCISES

10. *(Comparative Advantage)* Suppose that each U.S. worker can produce 8 units of food or 2 units of clothing daily. in Fredonia, which has the same number of workers, each worker can produce 7 units of food or 1 unit of clothing daily. Why does the United States have an absolute advantage in both goods? Which country enjoys a comparative advantage in food? Why?

11. *(Comparative Advantage)* The consumption possibilities frontiers shown in Exhibit 3 assume terms of trade of 1 unit of clothing for 1 unit of food. What would the consumption possibilities frontiers look like if the terms of trade were 1 unit of clothing for 2 units of food?

12. *(Import Quotas)* What is an effective import quota? Using a supply-and-demand diagram, illustrate and explain the net welfare loss from imposing such a quota. Under what circumstances would the net welfare loss from an import quota exceed the net welfare loss from an equivalent tariff (one that results in the same price and import level as the quota)?

13. *(Trade Restrictions)* Suppose that the world price for steel is below the U.S. domestic price, but the government requires that all steel used in the United States be domestically produced.
    a. Use a diagram like the one in Exhibit 5 to show the gains and loses from such a policy.
    b. How could you estimate the net welfare loss (deadweight loss) from such a diagram?
    c. What response to such a policy would you expect from industries (like automobile producers) that use U.S. steel?
    d. What government revenues are generated by this policy.

EXPERIENTIAL EXERCISES

14. *(Arguments for Trade Restrictions)* Visit the Office of the U.S. Trade representative at http://www.ustr.gov/. The U.S. Trade Representative is a Cabinet member who acts as the principal trade advisor, negotiator, and spokesperson for the president on trade and related investment matters. Look at some of the most recent press releases. What are some of the trade-related issues the United States is currently facing?

15. *(Antidumping Argument)* Thomas Klitgaard and Karen Schiele have analyzed dumping in their article "Free Trade or Fair Trade: The Dumping Issue." Current Issues in Economics and Finance, (August 1998). Download this article at http://www.ny.frb.org/rmaghome/curr-iss/ci4-8.htm. How can we tell whether foreign firms are selling products in the U.S. at a price below the cost of production?

16. *(Wall Street Journal)* The *Wall Street Journal* is one of the world's best sources of information regarding international trade. A good place to look is the International page inside the First Section of each day's *Journal*. Look at today's issue and find an article dealing with trade barriers—tariffs, quotas, and so on. Model the trade barrier using a graph, and try to determine who are the beneficiaries and who bears the costs. If you are lucky, the article will provide sufficient information to allow you to actually estimate costs and benefits in dollar terms.

International Finance

What do we mean when we talk about a "strong dollar"? How come U.S. consumers favor a strong dollar more than U.S. producers? Should we worry when we hear about a rising U.S. trade deficit? And what about the new European currency, the euro? Answers to these and other questions are explored in this chapter, which focuses on international finance.

A U.S. firm that plans to buy a German printing press will be quoted a price in euros. Suppose that machine costs one million euros. How many dollars is that? The cost in dollars will depend on the current exchange rate. When buyers and sellers from two countries trade, two currencies are usually involved. Supporting the flows of goods and services are flows of currencies that connect all international transactions.

The *exchange rate* between two currencies—the price of one in terms of the other—is the means by which the price of a good produced in one country gets translated into the price to the buyer in another country. The willingness of buyers and sellers to strike deals, therefore, depends on the rate of exchange between currencies. In this chapter we examine the international transactions that determine the relative value of one currency in terms of another. Topics discussed in this chapter include:

- Balance of payments
- Trade deficits and surpluses
- Foreign exchange markets
- Floating exchange rates
- Purchasing power parity

- Fixed exchange rates
- The international monetary system
- Managed float
- Bretton Woods agreement

BALANCE OF PAYMENTS

A country's gross domestic product measures the flow of economic activity that occurs within that country during a given period. To account for dealings abroad, countries also keep track of their international transactions. A country's *balance of payments,* as introduced in Chapter 4, summarizes all economic transactions that occur during a given time period between residents of that country and residents of other countries. *Residents* include individuals, firms, and governments.

International Economic Transactions

Balance-of-payments statements measure economic transactions that occur between countries, whether they involve goods and services, real or financial assets, or transfer payments. Because it reflects the volume of transactions that occur during a particular time period, usually a year, the balance of payments measures a *flow.*

Some transactions included in the balance-of-payments account do not involve payments of money. For example, if *Time* magazine ships a new printing press to its Australian subsidiary, no payment occurs, yet an economic transaction involving another country has taken place and must be included in the balance-of-payments account. Similarly, if CARE sends food to Africa, or if the Pentagon sends military assistance to Israel, these transactions must be captured in the balance of payments. So remember, although we speak of the *balance of payments,* a more descriptive phrase would be the *balance of economic transactions.*

Balance-of-payments accounts are maintained according to the principles of *double-entry bookkeeping,* in which entries on one side of the ledger are called *debits,* and entries on the other side are called *credits.* As we will see, the balance-of-payments accounts are made up of several individual accounts; a deficit in one or more accounts must be offset by a surplus in the other accounts. Thus the total debits must be in balance with, or equal to, the total credits—hence the expression *balance* of payments. The balance of payments involves a comparison during a given time period, such as a year, between the outflow of payments to the rest of the world, which are entered as debits, and the inflow of receipts from the rest of the world, which are entered as credits. The next few sections describe the major accounts in the balance of payments.

Merchandise Trade Balance

The *merchandise trade balance,* a term first introduced in Chapter 4, equals the value of merchandise exported minus the value of merchandise imported. The merchandise account reflects trade in tangible products (stuff you can drop on your toe), such as French wine and U.S. computers, and is often referred to simply as the *trade balance.* The value of U.S. merchandise exports is listed as a credit in the U.S. balance-of-payments account because U.S. residents must *be paid* for the exported goods. The value of U.S. merchandise imports is listed as a debit in the balance-of-payments account because U.S. residents must *pay* for the imported goods.

If the value of merchandise exports exceeds the value of merchandise imports, there is a *surplus* in the merchandise trade balance, or, more simply, a *trade surplus.* If the value of merchandise imports exceeds the value of merchandise exports, there is a *deficit* in the merchandise trade balance, or a *trade deficit.* The merchandise trade balance, which is reported monthly, influences foreign exchange markets, the stock market, and other financial markets. The trade balance depends on a variety of factors, including the relative strength and competitiveness of the domestic economy compared to other economies and the relative value of the domestic currency compared to other currencies.

The U.S. merchandise trade balance since 1979 is presented in Exhibit 1. Because imports have exceeded exports every year, the balance has been in deficit, as is reflected by the bottom line. Note that during recessions, which are indicated by shading, imports growth are relatively flat, as is the trade deficit. Between 1983 and 1990, and since 1991, the U.S. economy has expanded. *When the domestic economy expands, spending on all goods increases, so imports have increased.* In 1998 the merchandise trade deficit exceeded $300 billion, a record level.

Balance on Goods and Services

The merchandise trade balance focuses on the flow of goods, but services are also traded internationally. *Services* are intangibles, such as transportation, insurance, banking, consulting, and tourist expenditures. Services also include the income earned from foreign investments less the income earned by foreigners from their investment in the U.S. economy. Services are often called "invisibles," because they are not tangible—not something you can drop on your toe. The value of U.S. service exports, such as when an Irish tourist visits New York City, is listed as a credit in the U.S. balance-of-payments account because U.S. residents receive payments for these services. The value of U.S. service imports, such as when a computer specialist in Ireland enters policy information for a Connecticut insurer, is listed as a debit in the balance of payments account because U.S. residents must pay for the imported services.

The **balance on goods and services** is the difference between the value of exports of goods and services and the value of imports of goods and services. Currently-produced goods and services that are sold or otherwise provided to foreigners form part of U.S. output. The production of these goods and services generates income during the current period. Conversely, imports of goods and services form part of the nation's current expenditures—part of consumption, investment, and government expenditures. Allocating imports to each of the

*Net*Bookmark

The Bureau of Economic Analysis reports data on U.S. international accounts at http://www.bea.doc.gov/bea/ai1.htm. Review the most recent edition of U.S. International Transactions. What are the trends in the current and capital accounts, and in trade in goods and services? Which are in deficit, which in surplus? How has the value of the dollar been changing? What relationship is there between the state of these accounts and the value of the dollar?

Balance on goods and services The section of a country's balance of payments account that measures the difference in value between a country's exports of goods and services and its imports of goods and services

EXHIBIT 1

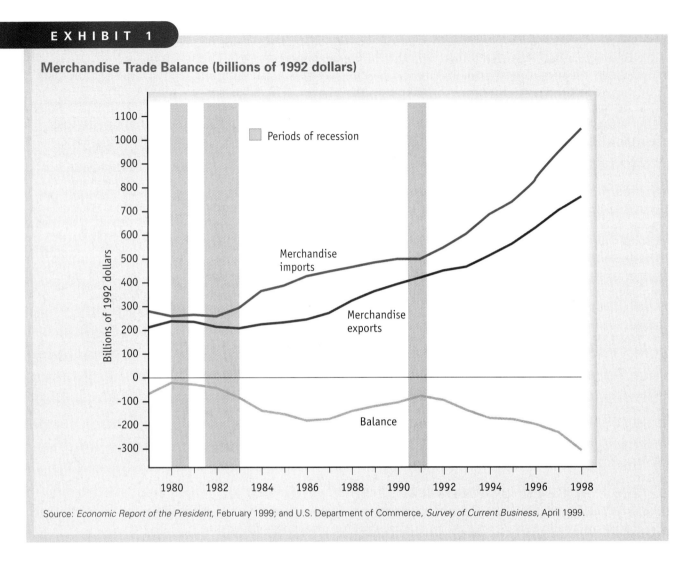

Merchandise Trade Balance (billions of 1992 dollars)

Source: *Economic Report of the President,* February 1999; and U.S. Department of Commerce, *Survey of Current Business,* April 1999.

major expenditure components is an accounting nightmare, so we usually just subtract imports from exports to yield *net exports.* Thus the U.S. gross domestic product in a given year equals total expenditures for consumption, investment, government purchases, and net exports.

Unilateral Transfers

Unilateral transfers consist of government transfers to foreign residents, foreign aid, personal gifts to friends and relatives abroad, personal and institutional charitable donations, and the like. For example, money sent abroad by a U.S. resident to friends or relatives would be included in U.S. unilateral transfers and would be a debit in the balance of payments account. U.S. **net unilateral transfers** equal the unilateral transfers received from abroad by U.S. residents minus the unilateral transfers sent to foreign residents. U.S. net unilateral transfers have been negative each year since World War II, except for 1991, when the U.S. government received sizable transfers from foreign governments to support the Persian Gulf war.

Net unilateral transfers
The unilateral transfers (gifts and grants) received from abroad by residents of a country minus the unilateral transfers residents send abroad

The United States places no restrictions on money sent out of the country.[1] Other countries, particularly developing countries, strictly limit the amount of money that may be sent abroad. More generally, developing countries often restrict the convertibility of their currency into other currencies.

When we add net unilateral transfers to the exports of goods and services minus the imports of goods and services, we get the **balance on current account,** which is reported quarterly. Thus, *the current account includes all transactions in currently produced goods and services plus net unilateral transfers.* It can be negative, reflecting a current account deficit; positive, reflecting a current account surplus; or zero.

Capital Account

Whereas the current account records international transactions involving the flows of goods, services, and unilateral transfers, the **capital account** records international transactions involving the flow of financial assets, such as borrowing, lending, and investments. For example, U.S. investors purchase foreign assets in order to earn a higher rate of return and to diversify their portfolios. When economists talk about capital, they usually mean the physical and human resources employed to produce goods and services. But sometimes *capital* is used as another word for *money*—money used to acquire financial assets, such as stocks, bonds, bank balances, and money used to make direct investments in foreign plants and equipment. U.S. capital outflows result when Americans purchase foreign assets. U.S. capital inflows result from foreign purchases of U.S. assets.

Between 1917 and 1982, the United States was a net capital exporter, and the net return on all this foreign investment over the years improved our balance on current account. In 1983, high real interest rates in the United States (relative to those in the rest of the world) resulted in a net inflow of capital for the first time in 65 years. A net inflow of capital shows up as a surplus in the capital account. Since then, U.S. imports of capital have exceeded exports of capital nearly every year, meaning that Americans owe foreigners more and more. *The United States is now the world's largest net debtor nation.* This is not as bad as it sounds, since foreign investment in the United States adds to America's productive capacity and promotes employment. But the return on foreign investment in the United States flows to foreigners, not to Americans.

The **official reserve transactions account** indicates the net amount of international reserves that shift among central banks to settle international transactions. (Many government publications show this not as a separate account but as part of the capital account.) International reserves consist of gold, dollars, euros, other major currencies, and a special-purpose reserve currency called *Special Drawing Rights*, or *SDRs*.

Statistical Discrepancy

As we have seen, the U.S. balance of payments is a record of all transactions between U.S. residents and foreign residents over a specified period. It is easier to

Balance on current account The section of a country's balance-of-payments account that measures the sum of the country's net unilateral transfers and its balance on goods and services

Capital account The record of a country's international transactions involving purchases or sales of financial and real assets

Official reserve transactions account The section of a country's balance-of-payments account that reflects the flow of gold, Special Drawing Rights, and currencies among central banks

---

1 Federal authorities do, however, require reporting the source of cash exports of $10,000 or more. This measure is aimed at reducing money laundering overseas.

describe this record than to compile it. Despite efforts to capture all international transactions, some go unreported. Yet as the name *balance of payments* suggests, debits must equal credits—the entire balance of payments account must by definition be in balance. This idea that debits equal credits is expressed in a double-entry bookkeeping system in which debits are recorded on one side of the ledger and credits are recorded on the other side. To ensure that the two sides of the ledger balance, a residual account called the *statistical discrepancy* was created. An excess of credits in all other accounts is offset by an equivalent debit in the statistical discrepancy account, or an excess of debits in all other accounts is offset by an equivalent credit in the discrepancy account. So you might think of the statistical discrepancy as the "fudge factor." The statistical discrepancy provides analysts with both a measure of the net error in the balance of payments data and a means of satisfying the double-entry bookkeeping requirement that total debits must equal total credits.

Deficits and Surpluses

Nations, like households, operate under a cash-flow constraint. Expenditures cannot exceed income plus cash on hand and borrowed funds. We have distinguished between *current* transactions, which are the income and expenditures from exports, imports, and unilateral transfers, and *capital* transactions, which reflect international investments and borrowing. Any surplus or deficit in one account must be balanced by other changes in the balance of payments accounts. The current account has been in deficit since 1982, meaning that the sum of U.S. imports and unilateral transfers to foreigners has exceeded the sum spent by foreigners on our exports and sent as unilateral transfers to us.

Exhibit 2 presents the U.S. balance of payments statement for 1998. All transactions requiring payments from foreigners to U.S. residents are entered as credits, indicated by a plus sign (+), because they result in a flow of funds from foreign residents to U.S. residents. All transactions requiring payments to foreigners from U.S. residents are entered as debits, indicated by a minus sign (−), because they result in a flow of funds from U.S. residents to foreign residents. As you can see, a surplus in the capital account offsets deficits in the current account, in the official reserve transactions account, and in the statistical discrepancy.

Foreign exchange is the currency of another country that is needed to carry out international transactions. A country runs a deficit in its current account when the amount of foreign exchange that country gets from exporting goods and services and from receipts of unilateral transfers falls short of the amount needed to pay for its imports and to make unilateral transfers. The additional foreign exchange required must come from either a net capital inflow (international borrowing, foreign purchases of domestic stocks and bonds, and so forth) or through official government transactions in foreign currency. If a country runs a current account surplus, the foreign exchange received from selling exports and from unilateral transfers exceeds the amount required to pay for imports and to make unilateral transfers. This excess foreign exchange could be held in a bank account, converted to the domestic currency, or used to purchase foreign stocks, bonds, or other foreign investments.

When all transactions are considered, the balance of payments must always balance, though specific accounts may not. A deficit in a particular account

EXHIBIT 2

U.S. Balance of Payments: 1998 (billions of dollars)

Item	
Current Account	
1. Merchandise exports	+671.0
2. Merchandise imports	−919.0
3. Trade balance (1 + 2)	−248.0
4. Service exports	+503.0
5. Service imports	−446.6
6. Goods and services balance (3 + 4 + 5)	−191.6
7. Net unilateral transfers	−41.9
8. Current account balance (6 + 7)	−233.5
Capital Account	
9. Outflow of U. S. capital	−297.8
10. Inflow of foreign capital	+564.6
11. Capital account balance (9 + 10)	+266.8
Official Reserve Transactions Account	
12. Change in U. S. official assets abroad	−7.6
13. Change in foreign official assets in U. S.	−22.1
14. Official reserve balance (12 + 13)	−29.7
15. Statistical discrepancy	−3.6
TOTAL (8 + 11 + 14 + 15)	**0.0**

Source: *Survey of Current Business*, U. S. Department of Commerce, April 1999.

should not necessarily be viewed as a source of concern, nor should a surplus be a source of satisfaction. The deficit in the U.S. current account in recent years has been offset by a net inflow of capital from abroad. As a result of the net inflow of capital, foreigners are acquiring more claims on U.S. assets.

FOREIGN EXCHANGE RATES AND MARKETS

Now that you have some idea about the international flow of products and investment funds, we can take a closer look at the forces that determine the underlying value of the currencies involved in these transactions. We begin by looking at exchange rates and the market for foreign exchange.

Foreign Exchange

Foreign exchange, recall, is foreign currency needed to carry out international transactions. The **exchange rate** is the price of one currency measured in terms of another currency. Exchange rates are determined by the interaction of the households, firms, private financial institutions, governments, and central banks that buy and sell foreign exchange. The exchange rate fluctuates to equate

Exchange rate The price of one country's currency measured in terms of another country's currency

the quantity of foreign exchange demanded with the quantity supplied. Typically, foreign exchange is made up of bank deposits denominated in the foreign currency. When foreign travel is involved, foreign exchange may consist of foreign paper money.

The foreign exchange market incorporates all the arrangements used to buy and sell foreign exchange. This market is not so much a physical place as it is a network of telephones and computers connecting large banks all over the world. Perhaps you have seen pictures of foreign exchange traders in New York, Frankfurt, London, or Tokyo amid a tangle of phone lines. The foreign exchange market is like an all-night diner—it never closes. Some trading center is always open somewhere in the world.

We will consider the market for the euro in terms of the dollar. But first a bit about the euro, since it may be new to you. In January 1999, the euro became the official common currency of eleven European countries, now known collectively as the euro zone or *Euroland.* By 2002, the national currencies of Germany, France, Italy, Austria, Spain, Portugal, Finland, Ireland, Belgium, Luxembourg, and the Netherlands are scheduled to disappear. In the mean time, the euro will be interchangeable with the local currency at a fixed rate.

Currency depreciation
With respect to the dollar, an increase in the number of dollars needed to purchase 1 unit of foreign exchange

Currency appreciation
With respect to the dollar, a decrease in the number of dollars needed to purchase 1 unit of foreign exchange

The price, or exchange rate, of the euro in terms of the dollar is the number of dollars required to purchase one euro. An increase in the number of dollars needed to purchase a euro indicates a weakening, or a **depreciation,** of the dollar. A decrease in the number of dollars needed to purchase a euro indicates a strengthening, or an **appreciation,** of the dollar. Put another way, a decrease in the number of euros needed to purchase a dollar is a depreciation of the dollar, and an increase in the number of euros needed to purchase a dollar is an appreciation of the dollar.

Since the exchange rate is a price, it can be determined using the conventional tools of supply and demand: the equilibrium price of foreign exchange is the one that equates quantity demanded with quantity supplied. To simplify the analysis, let's suppose that the United States and Euroland make up the entire world, so the supply and demand for euros is the supply and demand for foreign exchange from the U.S. perspective.

Demand for Foreign Exchange

U.S. residents need euros to pay for goods and services produced in Euroland, to invest in assets there, to make loans to Euroland, or simply to send cash gifts to friends or relatives there. Whenever U.S. residents need euros, they must buy them in the foreign exchange market, which could be their local bank, paying for them with dollars.

Exhibit 3 depicts a market for foreign exchange—in this case, for euros. The horizontal axis identifies the quantity of foreign exchange, measured here in millions of euros. The vertical axis identifies the price per unit of foreign exchange, measured here as the number of dollars required to purchase each euro. The demand curve for foreign exchange, identified as *D,* shows the inverse relationship between the dollar price of the euro and the quantity of euros demanded, other things constant. Some of the factors held constant along the demand curve are the incomes and preferences of U.S. consumers, the expected inflation rates in the United States and Euroland, the euro price of goods in Euroland, and interest rates in the United States and Euroland. People have many

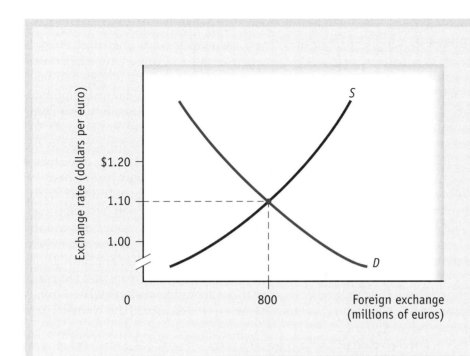

EXHIBIT 3

The Foreign Exchange Market

The fewer dollars needed to purchase 1 unit of foreign exchange, the lower the price of foreign goods and the greater the quantity of foreign goods demanded. The greater the demand for foreign goods, the greater the amount of foreign exchange demanded. The demand curve for foreign exchange slopes downward. An increase in the exchange rate makes U.S. products cheaper for foreigners. The increased demand for U.S. goods implies an increase in the quantity of foreign exchange supplied. The supply curve of foreign exchange slopes upward.

different reasons for demanding foreign exchange, but in the aggregate, the lower the dollar price of foreign exchange, other things constant, the greater the quantity demanded.

A drop in the dollar price of foreign exchange, in this case the euro, means that fewer dollars are needed to purchase each euro, so the dollar prices of Euroland products (such as German cars, Italian shoes, French wine, along with investments in Euroland), which have price tags listed in euros, become cheaper. The cheaper it is to buy euros, the lower the dollar price of Euroland products to U.S. residents, so the greater the quantity of euros demanded by U.S. residents, other things constant. For example, a cheap enough euro might persuade you to tour Rome, climb the Austrian Alps, wander the museums of Paris, or crawl the pubs of Dublin.

Supply of Foreign Exchange

The supply of foreign exchange is generated by the desire of foreign residents to acquire dollars—that is, to exchange euros for dollars. Foreign residents want dollars to buy U.S. goods and services, to buy U.S. assets, to make loans in dollars, or to make cash gifts in dollars to their U.S. friends and relatives. Also, citizens of countries suffering from economic and political turmoil, such as Malaysia, Indonesia, and South Korea, may want to buy dollars as a hedge against the depreciation and instability of their own currencies. The dollar has long been accepted as an international medium of exchange. It is also the currency of choice in the world markets for oil and for illegal drugs. But the euro may challenge that dominance, in part because the largest euro denomination, the 500 euro note, is worth about five times more than the top dollar note, the

$100 bill (hence, with euro notes, it would be five times easier to smuggle, say, a million dollars).

Europeans supply euros in the foreign exchange market to acquire the dollars they need. An increase in the dollar-per-euro exchange rate, other things constant, makes U.S. products cheaper for foreigners, since foreign residents need fewer euros to get the same number of dollars. For example, suppose a Dell computer sells for $1,100. If the exchange rate is $1.10 per euro, that computer costs 1,000 euros; if the exchange rate is $1.25 per euro, it costs only 880 euros. The number of Dell computers demanded in Euroland increases as the dollar-per-euro exchange rate increases, other things constant, so more euros will be supplied on the foreign exchange market to buy dollars.

More generally, the higher the dollar-per-euro exchange rate, other things constant, the greater the quantity of euros supplied to the foreign exchange market. The positive relationship between the dollar-per-euro exchange rate and the quantity of euros supplied on the foreign exchange market is expressed in Exhibit 3 by the upward-sloping supply curve for foreign exchange (again, euros in our example).[2] The supply curve is drawn holding other things constant, including Euroland incomes and preferences, expectations about the rates of inflation in Euroland and the United States, and interest rates in Euroland and the United States.

Determining the Exchange Rate

Exhibit 3 brings together the supply and demand for foreign exchange to determine the exchange rate. At an exchange rate of $1.10 per euro, the quantity of euros demanded equals the quantity of euros supplied—in our example, 800 million euros. Once achieved, this equilibrium exchange rate will remain constant until a change occurs in one of the factors that affect supply or demand. If the exchange rate is allowed to adjust freely, or to *float,* in response to market forces, the market will clear continually, as the quantities of foreign exchange demanded and supplied are equated.

What if the initial equilibrium is upset by a change in one of the underlying forces that affect supply or demand? For example, suppose an increase in U.S. income causes Americans to increase their demand for all normal goods, including Euroland goods and services. Such an increase in income will shift the U.S. demand curve for foreign exchange to the right, as Americans seek more euros to buy more Italian marble, Dutch chocolate, French couture, German machines, and euro securities.

This increased demand for euros is shown in Exhibit 4 by a shift to the right in the demand curve for foreign exchange. The supply curve does not change. The shift of the demand curve from D to D' leads to an increase in the exchange rate from $1.10 per euro to $1.15 per euro. Thus the euro increases in value, or appreciates, while the dollar falls in value, or depreciates. The higher exchange value of the euro prompts some Euroland residents to purchase more American products, which are now cheaper in terms of the euro. In our

---

2   As the exchange rate rises, Europeans have a greater incentive to buy more U.S. goods and services because their prices in terms of euros have decreased. As more is bought at lower prices, however, the total expenditure of euros rises only if the percentage increase in quantities of U.S. products demanded by the Europeans exceeds the percentage decrease in the prices in terms of euros. If the percentage increase in quantities demanded is less than the percentage decrease in the price in terms of euros, the supply curve of euros will slope downward.

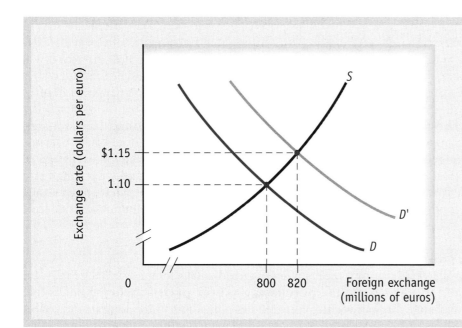

EXHIBIT 4

Effect on the Foreign Exchange Market of an Increase in Demand for Euros

The intersection of supply curve *S* and demand curve *D* determines the exchange rate. At an exchange rate of $1.10 per euro, the quantity of euros demanded equals the quantity supplied. An increase in the demand for euros from *D* to *D'* leads to an increase in the exchange rate from $1.10 to $1.15 per euro.

example, the equilibrium quantity of euros increases from 800 million to 820 million.

Any increase in the demand for foreign exchange or any decrease in its supply, other things constant, causes an increase in the number of dollars required to purchase one unit of foreign exchange, which is a depreciation of the dollar. On the other hand, any decrease in the demand for foreign exchange or any increase in its supply, other things constant, causes a reduction in the number of dollars required to purchase one unit of foreign exchange, which is an appreciation of the dollar.

Arbitrageurs and Speculators

Exchange rates between specific currencies are nearly identical at any given time in the different markets around the world. For example, the price of a dollar in terms of the euro is the same in New York, Frankfurt, Tokyo, London, Zurich, Istanbul, and other financial centers. This equality is ensured by **arbitrageurs**—dealers who take advantage of any temporary difference in exchange rates between markets by buying low and selling high. Their actions help to equalize exchange rates across markets. For example, if one euro costs $1.09 in New York and $1.10 in Frankfurt, an arbitrageur could buy, say, $10,000,000 worth of euros in New York and at the same time sell them in Frankfurt for $10,091,743, thereby earning $91,743 minus the transaction costs of executing the trades. Because exchange rate differences tend to be very small and because of transaction costs, an arbitrageur has to trade huge amounts to make enough profit to survive.

Because an arbitrageur buys and sells simultaneously, relatively little risk is involved. In our example, the arbitrageur increased the demand for euros in

Arbitrageur A person who takes advantage of temporary geographic differences in the exchange rate by simultaneously purchasing a currency in one market and selling it in another market

New York and increased the supply of euros in Frankfurt. Therefore, the actions of arbitrageurs increase the dollar price of euros in New York and decrease it in Frankfurt, thereby eliminating the differential. Even a tiny difference in exchange rates across markets will prompt arbitrageurs to act, and this action will quickly eliminate discrepancies in exchange rates across markets. Exchange rates may still change because of market forces, but they tend to change in all markets simultaneously.

The demand and supply of foreign exchange arises from many sources: from importers and exporters, investors in foreign assets, central banks, tourists, arbitrageurs, and speculators. **Speculators** buy or sell foreign exchange in hopes of profiting by trading the currency at a more favorable exchange rate later. By taking risks, speculators aim to profit from market fluctuations—they try to buy low and sell high. In contrast, arbitrageurs take little risk, since they *simultaneously* buy and sell a currency in different markets.

Purchasing Power Parity

As long as trade across borders is unrestricted and as long as exchange rates are allowed to adjust freely, the **purchasing power parity theory** predicts that the exchange rate between two currencies will adjust in the long run to reflect price-level differences between the two currency regions. *A given basket of internationally traded goods should therefore sell for similar amounts around the world (except for differences reflecting transportation costs and the like).* Suppose a basket of internationally traded commodities that sells for $11,000 in the United States sells for 10,000 euro in Euroland. According to the purchasing power parity theory, the equilibrium exchange rate between the dollar and the euro should be $1.10. If this were not the case—if the exchange rate were, say, $1.00 per euro—then the basket of goods could be purchased in Euroland for 10,000 euro and sold in the United States for $11,000. The $11,000 could then be exchanged for 11,000 euro, yielding a profit of 1,000 euro (minus any transaction costs). Selling dollars and buying euros drives up the dollar price of euros.

The purchasing power parity theory is more of a long-run predictor than a day-to-day predictor of the relationship between changes in the price level and the exchange rate. For example, a country's currency generally appreciates when its inflation rate is lower than the rest of the world's and depreciates when its inflation rate is higher. Likewise, a country's currency generally appreciates when its real interest rates are higher than the rest of the world, since foreigners are more willing to buy and hold investments denominated in that currency. As a case in point, the dollar appreciated during the first half of the 1980s, when real U.S. interest rates were relatively high, and depreciated in the early 1990s, when real U.S. interest rates were relatively low.

Because of trade barriers, central bank intervention in exchange markets, and the fact that many products are not traded or are not comparable across countries, the purchasing power parity theory usually does not explain exchange rates at a particular point in time. For example, if you went shopping in Zurich, you would soon notice that one dollar's worth of Swiss francs buys less than that dollar will buy in the United States. The following case study considers the theory in light of the price of Big Macs around the globe.

Speculator A person who buys or sells foreign exchange in hopes of profiting from fluctuations in the exchange rate over time

Purchasing power parity (PPP) theory The theory that exchange rates between two countries will adjust in the long run to reflect price level differences between the countries

The Big Mac Price Index

CaseStudy

Other Times,
Other Places

The *Economist* has published a focus article titled "Ten Years of the Big Mac Index." It is available at http://www. economist.com/editorial/ freeforall/focus/bigmac_ webonly.html. From there you can also access the latest edition of the index. Which currencies have had the largest changes in value? Which currencies went from being overvalued to undervalued between 1989 and 1998? Compare the index numbers among countries that are adopting the new euro as their currency. How close are they to one another?

As you have already learned, the purchasing power parity (PPP) theory says that, in the long run, the exchange rate between two currencies should move toward the rate that equalizes the prices, in each country, of an identical basket of internationally traded goods. A light-hearted test of the theory has been developed by the *Economist* magazine, which each year compares prices across countries of a "market basket" consisting simply of one McDonald's Big Mac—a product that, although not internationally traded, is made using the same recipe in more than 100 countries. The *Economist* begins with the price of a Big Mac in the local currency, then converts that price into dollars based on the actual exchange rate prevailing at the time. A comparison of the dollar price of Big Macs across countries offers a crude test of the PPP theory, which predicts that these prices should move toward equality in the long run.

Exhibit 5 lists the dollar price of a Big Mac on March 30, 1999, in each of 31 countries plus an average for the 11 countries in Euroland. By comparing the price of a Big Mac in the United States with prices in other countries, we can derive a crude measure of whether particular currencies are undervalued or overvalued relative to the dollar. For example, because the price of a Big Mac in Switzerland, at $3.97, was 51 percent higher than the U.S. price of $2.43, the Swiss franc seemed overvalued by 63 percent compared to the dollar. The same approach suggests that the Danish krona was 47 percent overvalued, the Israeli shekel 42 percent overvalued, and the British pound 26 percent overvalued. The cheapest Big Mac was in Malaysia, where recent devaluations because of the "Asian contagion" cut the price to $1.19, or 51 percent below the U.S. level.

Big Mac prices around the world have been converging in recent years. In 1995 the price of a Big Mac in Switzerland was tops in the world, 124 percent above the U.S. price. By 1999, the Swiss price was still tops but only 63 percent above the U.S. price. At the bottom end, the lowest price in 1995 was 55 percent below the U.S. price. By 1999 the lowest price was only 51 percent below the U.S. price. Finally, in 1995 the price of a Big Mac in Japan was double the U.S. price. In 1999, the Japanese price was about the same as the U.S. price. So prices around the world have converged since 1995 in a way consistent with the PPP theory.

Still, prices in 1999 ranged from 63 percent above to 51 percent below the U.S. price. Some may view this misalignment as a rejection of the PPP theory, but that theory relates only to traded goods. The Big Mac is not traded internationally. A large share of the total cost of a Big Mac is rent, which varies substantially across countries. Local prices may also be distorted by taxes and trade barriers, such as a tariff on beef. Furthermore, prices for similar goods vary across the United States even though we all use dollars here. For example, housing prices are higher in the Northeast and the West Coast than in the Midwest and the South. Still, the Big Mac index offers a crude test of the PPP theory.

EXHIBIT 5

Big Mac Prices Around the World on March 30, 1999

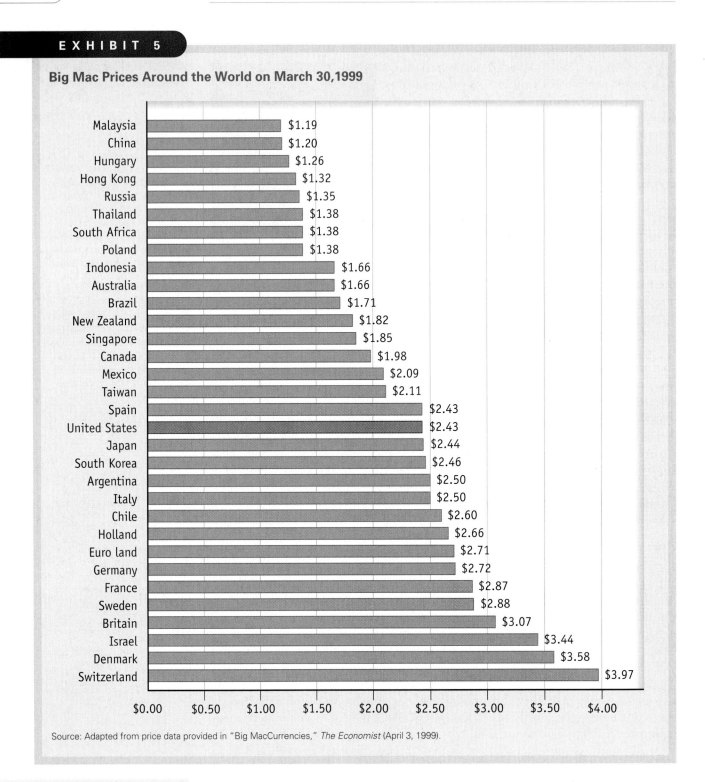

Source: Adapted from price data provided in "Big MacCurrencies," *The Economist* (April 3, 1999).

Sources: "Big MacCurrencies," *Economist* (3 April 1999); "Big MacCurrencies," *Economist* (15 April 1995); and Peter Liu and Paul Burkett, "Instability in Short-Run Adjustments to Purchasing Power Parity: Results for Selected Latin American Countries," *Applied Economics* (October 1995): 973–83.

Flexible Exchange Rates

For the most part, we have been discussing a system of **flexible exchange rates,** in which each exchange rate is determined by the forces of supply and demand. Flexible, or *floating,* exchange rates adjust continually to the myriad forces that buffet the foreign exchange market. Consider how the exchange rate is linked to the balance of payments accounts. Debit entries in the current and capital accounts increase the demand for foreign exchange, resulting in a depreciation of the dollar. Credit entries in these accounts increase the supply of foreign exchange, resulting in an appreciation of the dollar.

Flexible exchange rates Rates determined by the forces of supply and demand without government intervention

Fixed Exchange Rates

When exchange rates are flexible, government officials usually have little direct role in foreign exchange markets. But if government officials try to set exchange rates, active and ongoing central bank intervention is necessary to establish and maintain these **fixed exchange rates.** Suppose the European Central Bank selects what it thinks is an appropriate rate of exchange between the dollar and the euro. It attempts to *fix,* or to "peg," the exchange rate within a narrow band around the particular value selected. If the value of the euro threatens to drop below the minimum acceptable exchange rate, monetary authorities will sell dollars and buy euros in foreign exchange markets. This increased demand for the euro will keep its value up relative to the dollar. Conversely, if the value of the euro threatens to climb above the maximum acceptable exchange rate, monetary authorities will sell euros and buy dollars, thereby keeping the dollar price of the euro down. Through such intervention in the foreign exchange market, monetary authorities can stabilize the exchange rate, keeping it within the specified band.

Fixed exchange rates Rates pegged within a narrow range of values by central banks' ongoing purchases and sales of currencies

If monetary officials must keep selling foreign exchange to maintain the pegged rate, they risk running out of foreign exchange reserves. When this threat occurs, the government has several options for eliminating the exchange rate disequilibrium. First, the pegged exchange rate can be increased, which is a **devaluation** of the domestic currency. (A decrease in the pegged exchange rate is called a **revaluation.**) Second, the government can attempt to reduce the domestic demand for foreign exchange directly by imposing restrictions on imports or on capital outflows. China and many other developing countries do this. Third, the government can adopt contractionary fiscal or monetary policies to reduce the country's income level, increase interest rates, or reduce inflation relative to that of the country's trading partners, thereby indirectly decreasing the demand for foreign exchange. Several Asian economies, such as Korea and Indonesia, pursued such policies to stabilize their currencies in 1998. Finally, the government can allow the disequilibrium to persist and ration the available foreign currency through some form of foreign exchange control.

Currency devaluation An increase in the official pegged price of foreign exchange in terms of the domestic currency

Currency revaluation A reduction in the official pegged price of foreign exchange in terms of the domestic currency

We have now concluded our introduction to international finance in theory. Let's examine how international finance works in practice.

DEVELOPMENT OF THE INTERNATIONAL MONETARY SYSTEM

From 1879 to 1914, the international financial system operated under a **gold standard,** whereby the major currencies were convertible into gold at a fixed

Gold standard An arrangement whereby the currencies of most countries are convertible into gold at a fixed rate

rate. For example, the U.S. dollar could be redeemed at the U.S. Treasury for one-twentieth of an ounce of gold. The British pound could be redeemed at the British Exchequer, or treasury, for one-fourth of an ounce of gold. Since each pound could buy five times as much gold as each dollar, one pound exchanged for $5.

The gold standard provided a predictable exchange rate, one that did not vary as long as currencies could be redeemed for gold at the announced rate. But the money supply in each country was determined in part by the flow of gold between countries, so each country's monetary policy was influenced by the supply of gold. A balance-of-payments deficit resulted in a loss of gold, which theoretically caused a country's money supply to drop. A balance-of-payments surplus resulted in an increase in gold, which theoretically caused a country's money supply to rise. The supply of money throughout the world also depended to some extent on the vagaries of gold discoveries. When gold production was so slow that the money supply did not keep pace with the growth in economic activity, the result was a drop in the price level, or *deflation*. When gold production grew so much that the growth of the money supply exceeded the growth in economic activity, the result was a rise in the price level, or *inflation*. For example, gold discoveries in Alaska and South Africa in the late 1890s expanded the U.S. money supply, leading to inflation.

The Bretton Woods Agreement

During World War I, many countries could no longer convert their currencies into gold, and the gold standard eventually collapsed, disrupting international trade during the 1920s and 1930s. Once an Allied victory in World War II appeared certain, the Allies met in Bretton Woods, New Hampshire, in July of 1944, to formulate a new international monetary system. Because the United States was not ravaged by World War II and had a strong economy, the dollar was selected as the key reserve currency in the new international monetary system. All exchange rates were fixed in terms of the dollar, and the United States, which held most of the world's gold reserves, stood ready to convert foreign holdings of dollars into gold at a rate of $35 per ounce. Even though exchange rates were fixed by the Bretton Woods accord, *other* countries could adjust *their* exchange rates relative to the U.S. dollar if they found a fundamental disequilibrium in their balance of payments—that is, if a country faced a large and persistent deficit or surplus.

International Monetary Fund (IMF) An international organization that establishes rules for maintaining the international monetary system and makes loans to countries with temporary balance of payments problems

The Bretton Woods agreement also created the **International Monetary Fund (IMF)** to set rules for maintaining the international monetary system and to make loans to countries with temporary balance of payments problems. IMF loans to Russia, to Brazil, and to struggling Asian economies, such as Indonesia and South Korea, have been in the news lately. The IMF, which today has more than 150 member countries, also standardized financial reporting for international trade and finance.

Demise of the Bretton Woods System

During the latter part of the 1960s, inflation began heating up in the United States, and the higher U.S. prices meant that those exchanging foreign currencies for dollars at the official exchange rates found these dollars bought less in U.S. goods and services. Because of U.S. inflation, the dollar had become *over-*

valued at the official exchange rate, meaning that the gold value of the dollar exceeded the exchange value of the dollar. With the dollar overvalued, foreigners redeemed more dollars for gold. To stop this outflow of gold, something had to give. On August 15, 1971, President Richard Nixon closed the "gold window," refusing to exchange gold for dollars. In December 1971, the 10 richest countries of the world met in Washington and devalued the dollar by 8 percent. The hope at the time was that this devaluation would put the dollar on firmer footing and would save the "dollar standard." With prices rising at different rates around the world, however, an international monetary system based on fixed exchange rates was doomed.

In 1971, U.S. merchandise imports exceeded merchandise exports for the first time since World War II. When the trade deficit tripled in 1972, it became clear that the dollar was still overvalued. In early 1973, the dollar was devalued another 10 percent, but this did not quiet foreign exchange markets. The dollar, for three decades the anchor of the international monetary system, suddenly looked vulnerable, and speculators began betting the dollar would fall even more. Dollars were exchanged for German marks because the mark appeared to be the most stable currency. Monetary officials at the Bundesbank, Germany's central bank, exchanged marks for dollars in an attempt to defend the official exchange rate and to prevent an appreciation of the mark. Why didn't Germany want the mark to appreciate? Appreciation of the mark would make German goods more expensive abroad and foreign goods cheaper in Germany, thereby reducing German exports and increasing German imports. This would reduce German output and employment. But after selling $10 billion worth of marks, the German central bank gave up defending the dollar. As soon as the value of the dollar was allowed to float against the mark, the Bretton Woods system, already on shaky ground, collapsed.

The Current System: Managed Float

The Bretton Woods system has been replaced by a **managed float system,** which combines features of a freely floating exchange rate with sporadic intervention by central banks as a way of moderating exchange rate fluctuations among the world's major currencies. Most smaller countries, particularly developing countries, peg their currencies to one of the major currencies (such as the U.S. dollar) or to a "basket" of major currencies. What's more, in developing countries, private international borrowing and lending are severely restricted; governments may allow residents to purchase foreign exchange only for certain purposes. In some countries, different exchange rates apply to different categories of transactions.

The exchange rate between the Japanese yen and the U.S. dollar has been relatively unstable, particularly because of international speculation about official efforts to stabilize that exchange rate. Major criticisms of flexible exchange rates are that (1) they are inflationary, since they free monetary authorities to pursue expansionary policies, and (2) they have often been volatile, especially since the late 1970s. This volatility creates uncertainty and risk for importers and exporters, increasing the transaction costs of international trade and thus reducing its volume. Furthermore, exchange rate volatility can lead to wrenching changes in the competitiveness of a country's export sector and of those domestic producers who must compete with imports. These changes in

Managed float system An exchange rate system that combines features of freely floating rates with intervention by central banks

competitiveness cause swings in employment, resulting in louder calls for import restrictions.

Policy makers are always on the lookout for an international monetary system that will perform better than the current managed float system, with its fluctuating currency values. *Their ideal is a system that will foster international trade, lower inflation, and promote a more stable world economy.* International finance ministers have acknowledged that the world must find an international standard and establish greater exchange rate stability.

The wild swings in exchange rates that sometimes occur with flexible exchange rates have caused policy makers to intervene to reduce undesirable fluctuations, as discussed in the following case study about financial troubles in Asia.

The Asian Contagion

CaseStudy

Other Times, Other Places

The Institute for International Economics Policy Brief, "The Depressing News from Asia" at http://www.iie.com/NEWSLETR/news98-5.htm, predicts the impact of the Asian financial crisis on other countries. Notice how it uses various scenarios involving different potential changes in key variables. How is the crisis expected to affect industrialized economies, and the United States in particular? Other economists' views and analyses were published in the Summer 1998 edition of the Brookings Institution magazine accessible through http://www.brook.edu/pub/review/oldtoc.htm.

It started in Thailand in early 1997, when a booming economy ran into trouble because of a decline in exports and over-lending in the property sector. Speculators began betting that the Thai currency, the baht, was in for a fall. The Thai central bank attempted to defend the baht's value, which at the time was tied to the U.S. dollar, by buying baht and selling foreign reserves. As the central bank's foreign reserves dwindled, the government decided in July 1997 to let the baht float. It immediately went into free-fall, losing 40 percent of its value against the dollar in a matter of weeks. With the baht worth so much less, Thai businesses and the government had difficulty paying foreign loans, most of which were denominated in dollars.

The crisis prompted a $17-billion bailout supervised by the International Monetary Fund (IMF) aimed at helping Thailand pay back some foreign debts. But problems in Thailand deepened, as outside credit agencies continued to downgrade Thai debt. Trouble soon spread to neighboring Indonesia, Malaysia, South Korea, Hong Kong, Singapore, and even mighty Japan, as the so-called Asian Contagion ripped through the region. South Korea and Indonesia were forced to seek IMF assistance; Indonesia was promised $40 billion in loans and South Korea, $58 billion, the most costly rescue package in history. In exchange for the aid, both countries agreed to cut government spending and open up their markets to foreign goods and foreign investors.

In Japan, where the economy had been struggling since 1990, matters worsened. In November 1997, four large financial institutions went bankrupt, the yen suffered its biggest drop against the dollar in years, and the stock market continued its eight-year slide. In June 1998, Japanese officials confirmed that national output had declined two quarters in a row and thus the country was officially in recession. For the full fiscal year, Japan's GDP declined, the first officially acknowledged annual drop since the oil shocks of the mid-1970s.

A big problem overhanging the Japanese economy was a trillion dollars worth of bad debts in the banking system. Banks had extended real estate loans during the booming 1980s. But when property values crashed, the loans could not be repaid, so the banks were in big trouble. Japan, the second-largest economy in the world (after the United States), is by far the largest economy in Asia. A weakened Japan threatened the fragile economies of Asia as they tried to recover from financial chaos. A weakened economy meant Japan would buy less from its Asian neighbors, and a weakened yen meant Japanese exports would be cheaper on world markets, thus competing with exports from elsewhere in Asia.

Faced with growing problems in Asia, the U.S. government joined forces with the Japanese government on June 17, 1998 to intervene in currency markets and spent $2 billion buying yen. In return for help from the United States, Japan agreed to allow more companies to fail by abandoning the system whereby the government forced stronger companies to bail out weaker ones.

By increasing the demand for yen, the U.S. intervention reversed the slide in the yen's value. In one day the yen-per-dollar exchange rate appreciated from 143.3 yen to 136.6, or by 4.7 percent. This was the first U.S. intervention in world currency markets in nearly three years. As the yen appreciated against the dollar, other currencies in Asia also stabilized. By the end of April 1999, the yen had appreciated to 118 yen to the dollar, and Asia was showing preliminary signs of recovery.

Sources: David Wessel, "Wealthy Nations Are Trying to Save Japan from Itself," *Wall Street Journal* (18 June 1998); "Stocks Stumble Across Asia as Yen Hits Lowest Since '90," *Wall Street Journal* (11 June 1998); "Asia's Symptoms," *Economist* (13 June 1998): 14; "Will Tokyo Finally Clean House?" *Economist* (27 June 1998): 71–72; and Fareed Zakaria, "Will Asia Turn Against the West?" *New York Times* (10 July 1998).

CONCLUSION

At one time the United States was largely self-sufficient. A technological lead over the rest of the world, an abundance of natural resources, a well-trained work force, a modern and extensive capital stock, and a currency as good as gold made the United States the envy of the world, with an economy that produced 40 percent of the world's output in the 1950s.

The situation has changed. The United States is now very much a part of the world economy, not only as the largest exporter but also as the largest importer. Although the dollar remains the unit of transaction in many international settlements—OPEC, for example, still states oil prices in dollars—the wild gyrations of exchange rates have made those involved in international finance wary of putting all their eggs in one basket. The euro could replace the dollar as the currency of choice on world markets.

The international monetary system is now going through a difficult adjustment period as it continues to grope for a new source of stability nearly three decades after the collapse of the Bretton Woods agreement.

SUMMARY

1. The balance of payments reflects all economic transactions across national borders. The current account measures the flows of (1) merchandise; (2) services, including investment income, military transactions, and tourism; and (3) unilateral transfers, or public and private transfer payments to foreign residents. The capital account measures international flows involving purchases or sales of financial and real assets.

2. Currencies support the flow of goods and services across international borders. The interaction of the supply and demand for foreign exchange determines the equilibrium exchange rate.

3. Under a system of floating exchange rates, the value of the dollar relative to foreign exchange varies over time. An increase in the demand for foreign exchange or a reduction in its supply, other things constant, will cause an increase in the value of foreign exchange relative to the dollar, which is a depreciation of the dollar. Conversely, a reduction in the demand for foreign exchange or an increase in its supply will cause a decrease in the value of foreign exchange relative to the dollar, which is an appreciation of the dollar.

4. Under a system of fixed exchange rates, monetary authorities usually try to stabilize the exchange rate, keeping it between a specified ceiling and floor.

5. For much of this century, the international monetary system was based on fixed exchange rates. A managed float system has been in effect for the major currencies since the demise of the Bretton Woods system in the early 1970s. Although central banks have often tried to stabilize exchange rates, recent swings in exchange rates have troubled policy maker.

QUESTIONS FOR REVIEW

1. *(Balance of Payments)* Suppose the United States ran a balance on goods and services surplus by exporting goods and services while importing nothing.
   a. How would such a surplus be offset elsewhere in the balance-of-payments accounts?
   b. If the level of U.S. production does not depend on the balance on goods and services, how would running this surplus affect our *current* standard of living?
   c. What is the relationship between total debits and total credits in the goods and services balance?
   d. When all international economic transactions are considered, what must be true about the sum of debits and credits?
   e. What is the role of the statistical discrepancy account?

2. *(Foreign Exchange)* What is the difference between a depreciation of the dollar and a devaluation of the dollar?

3. *(Purchasing Power Parity)* According to the theory of purchasing power parity, what will happen to the value of the dollar (against foreign currencies) if the U.S. price level doubles and price levels in other countries remain constant? Why is the theory more suitable to analyzing events in the long run?

4. *(Case**Study:** The Big Mac Index)* The Big Mac Index computed by the *Economist* has found the U.S. dollar to be undervalued against some other major currencies, which seems to call for a rejection of the purchasing power parity theory. Explain why this index may not be a valid test of the theory.

5. *(The Current System: Managed Float)* What is a managed float? What are the disadvantages of freely floating exchange rates that led countries to the managed float system?

6. *(Merchandise Trade Balance)* Explain why U.S. recessions (which are not at the same time world recessions) tend to reduce the U.S. trade deficit.

PROBLEMS AND EXERCISES

7. *(Balance of Payments)* The following are hypothetical data for the U.S. balance of payments. Use the data to calculate each of the following:
   a. Merchandise trade balance
   b. Balance on goods and services
   c. Balance on current account
   d. Capital account balance
   e. Official reserve transactions account balance
   f. Statistical discrepancy

	Billions of Dollars
Merchandise exports	350.0
Merchandise imports	-425.0
Service exports	170.0
Service imports	-145.0
Net unilateral transfers	-21.5
Outflow of U.S. capital	-45.0
Inflow of foreign capital	70.0

Decrease in U.S. official assets abroad	2.5
Increase in foreign official assets in U.S.	35.0

8. *(Balance of Payments)* Explain where in the U.S. balance of payments an entry would be made for each of the following:
   a. A Hong Kong financier buys some U.S. corporate stock
   b. A U.S. tourist in Paris buys some perfume to take home
   c. A Japanese company sells machinery to a pineapple company in Hawaii
   d. U.S. farmers make a gift of food to starving children in Ethiopia
   e. The U.S. Treasury sells a thirty-year bond to a Saudi Arabian prince
   f. A U.S. tourist flies to France on Air France
   g. A U.S. company sells insurance to a foreign firm

9. *(Determining the Exchange Rate)* Use these data to answer the following questions about the market for British pounds:

Price of pounds (in $)	Quantity Demanded (of pounds)	Quantity Supplied (of pounds)
$4.00	50	100
3.00	75	75
2.00	100	50

   a. Draw the supply and demand curves for pounds, and determine the equilibrium exchange rate (dollars per pound).
   b. Suppose that the supply of pounds doubles. Draw the new supply curve.
   c. What is the new equilibrium exchange rate?
   d. Has the dollar appreciated or depreciated?
   e. What happens to U.S. imports of British goods?

EXPERIENTIAL EXERCISES

10. *(Foreign Exchange Rates and Markets)* Trade among European nations will be bolstered by the introduction of a common European currency called the euro. Not surprisingly, there is a special Web page devoted to the introduction of the euro—EmuNet at http://www.euro-emu.co.uk/. Go to the EmuNet home page to review the latest developments in the introduction of the euro.

11. *(CaseStudy: The Asian Contagion)* Yahoo, an online search engine, maintains a page devoted to the Asian financial crisis. Visit this page at http://headlines.yahoo.com/Full_Coverage/World/Asian_ Economic_Woes/ and determine whether the crisis seems to be easing or getting worse.

12. *(Wall Street Journal)* The latest data on exchange rates appear in the Currency Trading column in the daily *Wall Street Journal*. You can find it in the Money & Investing section. Try tracking a particular foreign currency over the course of several weeks. Has the dollar been appreciating or depreciating relative to that currency? Try to explain why it has been appreciating or depreciating.

CHAPTER

20

Developing and Transitional Economies

Visit the McEachern
Interactive Study Center
for this chapter at
http://mcisc.swcollege.com

People around the world face the day under very different circumstances. Many Americans rise from a comfortable bed in a nice home, select the day's clothing from a wardrobe, choose from a variety of breakfast foods, and drive to school or to work in one of the family's personal automobiles. But most of the world's nearly six billion people have little housing, clothing, or food. They own no automobile, and many have no formal job. Their health is poor, as is their education. Many cannot read or write. An estimated one billion people need glasses but can't afford them. Why are some countries so poor while others are so rich? What determines the wealth of nations?

In this chapter, we sort out rich nations from poor ones and try to explain the difference. Although there is no widely accepted theory of economic development, one approach that seems to be gaining favor lately is the introduction of market forces, especially in formerly socialist countries. Around the world, the demise of central planning has been stunning and pervasive. We close the chapter with a discussion of these rich experiments—these works in progress. Topics discussed in this chapter include:

- Developing countries
- Obstacles to development
- Import substitution
- Export promotion
- Foreign aid
- Transitional economies
- Big bang versus gradualism
- Privatization

WORLDS APART

Differences in economic activity among countries are profound. For example, the United States, with its 270 million people, has a gross domestic product that exceeds the *combined* output of 2.7 billion people living in poor countries. The United States, with only 5 percent of the world's population, produces more than does the poorer half of the world's population.

Countries are classified in a variety of ways based on their level of economic development. The yardstick most often used to compare living standards across nations is *output per capita*. The World Bank, an economic development institution affiliated with the United Nations, attempts to estimate comparable output per capita figures and then uses these figures to classify economies. The World Bank divides countries into three major groups based on their per capita output: low-income economies, middle-income economies, and high-income economies.

Developing and Industrial Economies

The low- and middle-income economies are usually referred to as **developing countries**, and the high-income economies are usually referred to as **industrial market countries** (though some of the high-income countries have incomes based primarily on oil and are viewed as still developing). A few primarily socialist countries, such as Cuba, North Korea, and Libya, do not report data on their economic status and consequently are classified by the World Bank as *nonreporting countries*.

Developing countries usually have a high rate of illiteracy, high unemployment, extensive underemployment, rapid population growth, and exports consisting primarily of agricultural products and raw materials. On average, about two-thirds of the labor force in developing countries is in agriculture. Because farming methods are relatively primitive, farm productivity is low and most people barely subsist. Industrial market countries or *developed countries* are the economically advanced capitalist countries of Western Europe, North America, Australia, New Zealand, and Japan. They were the first to experience long-term economic growth during the 19th century.

The measure of output used by the World Bank to classify countries is gross national product (GNP) per capita. GNP measures the market value of all goods and services produced by resources supplied by the countries' residents and firms, regardless of the location of the resource. For example, U.S. GNP includes profit earned by a Ford factory in Great Britain but excludes profits earned by a Toyota factory in the United States.

Developing countries Nations typified by high rates of illiteracy, high unemployment, high fertility rates, and exports of primary products

Industrial market countries Economically advanced capitalist countries of Western Europe, North America, Australia, New Zealand, and Japan; also known as developed countries

Data on total population, GNP per capita, and growth in private consumption per capita are summarized in Exhibit 1 for all reporting countries with a population of 1 million or more. GNP per capita figures have been adjusted to reflect the actual purchasing power of the native currency in its respective economy. The idea is to measure the actual GNP per capita for each country. Low-income countries made up about one-third of the 5.8 billion people on Earth in 1997, middle-income countries accounted for half, and high-income countries accounted for only one-sixth.

India and China are two population giants shown separately in Exhibit 1. Together they account for more than one-third of the world's population, but produce only about one-twentieth of the world's output. India's GNP per capita of $1,650 in 1997 was slightly above the average of $1,400 for all low-income economies. India's 1.6 percent average growth rate in private consumption per capita between 1980 and 1996 was above the 1.0 percent average for all low-income economies. China's GNP per capita of $3,570 was below the average of $4,550 for all middle-income economies, but its growth rate in private consumption exceeded that of all middle-income economies. High-income economies averaged $22,770 per capita in 1997, or about 16 times the average for low-income economies—quite a difference.

Exhibit 2 presents GNP per capita in 1997 for selected countries, arranged from top to bottom in descending order. Again, figures have been adjusted by the United Nations to reflect the actual purchasing power of the native currency in its respective economy. The United States, the top-ranked country, had a GNP per capita that was 7.5 times that of Paraguay. But GNP per capita in Paraguay, in turn, was 7.5 times that of Sierra Leone, the poorest country in the world. Residents of Paraguay likely feel poor relative to industrialized nations, but they appear well off compared to the poorest developing nations. Per capita GNP in the United States was 56 times greater than in Sierra Leone. Thus there is a tremendous range in productive performance around the world.

Health and Nutrition

Differences in stages of development among countries are reflected in a number of ways besides per capita income levels. For example, many people in

---

EXHIBIT 1

Population, GNP per Capita, and Annual Growth Rate in Private Consumption per Capita

Source: Based on data presented by the World Bank in *World Development Report 1998/99* (New York: Oxford University Press, 1998), Tables 1 and 2. Data are for countries with populations of 1 million or more.

Classification	Population, 1997 (millions)	GNP per Capita 1997 Dollars	Annual Growth Rate, in Private Consumption per Capita, 1980–1996 (percent)
1. Low–income economies	2,048	1,400	1.0
India	961	1,650	1.6
2. Middle-income economies	2,855	4,550	2.8
China	1,227	3,570	4.5
3. High-income economies	926	22,770	1.4

EXHIBIT 2

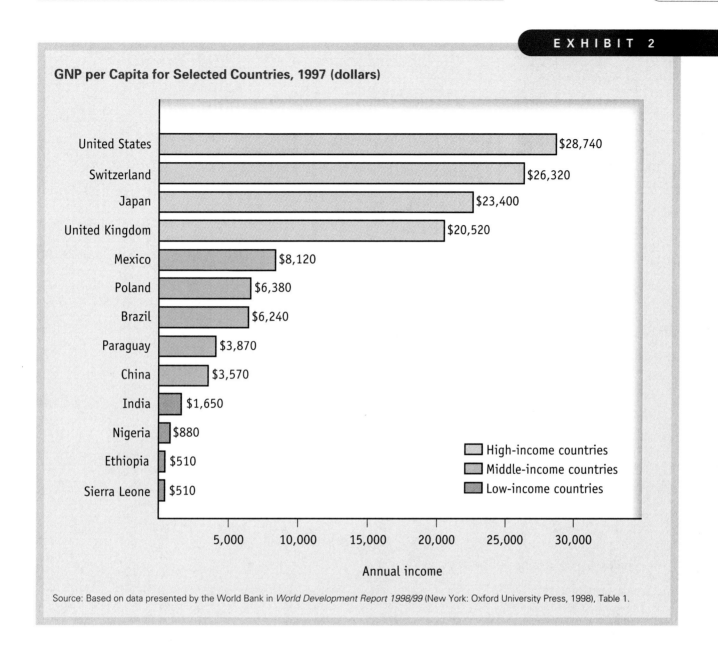

GNP per Capita for Selected Countries, 1997 (dollars)

Country	GNP per Capita
United States	$28,740
Switzerland	$26,320
Japan	$23,400
United Kingdom	$20,520
Mexico	$8,120
Poland	$6,380
Brazil	$6,240
Paraguay	$3,870
China	$3,570
India	$1,650
Nigeria	$880
Ethiopia	$510
Sierra Leone	$510

High-income countries
Middle-income countries
Low-income countries

Annual income

Source: Based on data presented by the World Bank in *World Development Report 1998/99* (New York: Oxford University Press, 1998), Table 1.

developing countries suffer from poor health as a result of malnutrition and disease. AIDS is devastating some developing countries, particularly those in central and east Africa. Life expectancy at birth in 1996 averaged 59 years in low-income economies, 68 years in middle-income economies, and 77 years in high-income economies. Average life expectancy ranged from 37 years in Sierra Leone to 80 years in Japan.

Infant Mortality. Health differences among countries are reflected in infant mortality rates. Mortality rates for selected countries are presented as Exhibit 3.

EXHIBIT 3

Mortality Rate up to Age 5 per 1,000 Live Births for Selected Countries: 1996

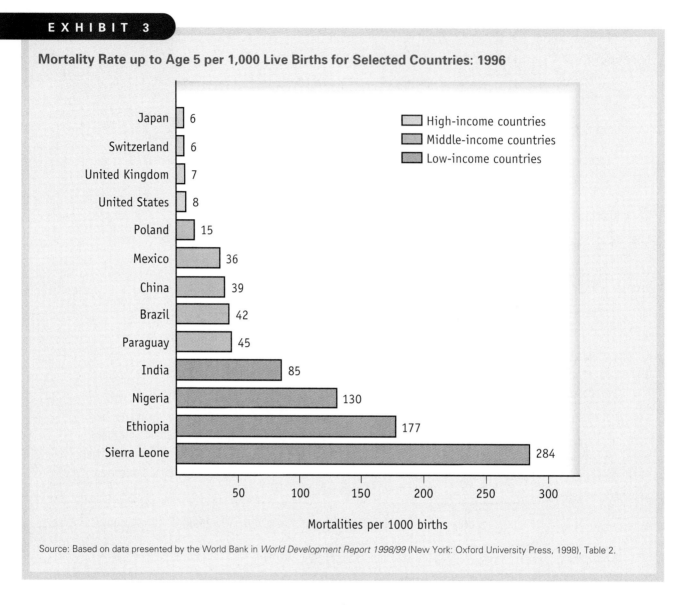

Source: Based on data presented by the World Bank in *World Development Report 1998/99* (New York: Oxford University Press, 1998), Table 2.

As might be expected, countries with the longest life expectancies also have the lowest infant mortality rates. Similarly, the countries with the shortest life expectancies have the highest infant mortality rates. The infant mortality rate in Sierra Leone is at least 35 times the rates in Japan, Switzerland, the United Kingdom, and the United States.

Malnutrition. Many people living in Africa, South Asia, and the Indian subcontinent often do not have enough food to maintain good nutrition. Those in the very poorest countries consume only half the calories of those in high-income countries. Even if an infant survives the first year, malnutrition can turn normal childhood diseases, such as measles, into life-threatening events. Malnutrition is a primary or contributing factor in more than half of all deaths among children under five in low-income countries. Diseases that are well controlled in the industrial countries—malaria, whooping cough, polio, dysentery, typhoid, and cholera—become epidemics in poor countries. Many of these diseases are water borne, because residents of urban areas in less-developed countries are often unable to obtain safe drinking water.

High Birth Rates

Developing countries are identified not only by their low incomes and high mortality rates but also by their high birth rates. This year, about 80 million of the 90 million people added to the world's population will be born in developing countries. In fact, the birth rate is one of the clearest ways of distinguishing between industrial and developing countries. Few developing countries have a total fertility rate per woman of less than 2.2 births, but no industrial country has a fertility rate above that level.

Exhibit 4 presents total fertility rates per woman for 1980 and 1996. Note that fertility rates for all groups declined between the two years. Note also that fertility rates are highest in the low-income economies and lowest in the high-income economies. The fertility rate dropped most in India, where it went from 5.0 in 1980 to 3.1 in 1996. Fertility rates dropped the least in high-income economies, where they were already relatively low in 1980.

Families tend to be larger in developing countries because children are viewed as a source of farm labor and as economic and social security as the parents age. Most developing countries have no pension or social security system for the aged. The higher infant mortality rates in poorer countries also engender higher birth rates, as parents strive to ensure a sufficiently large family.

Sub-Saharan African countries are the poorest in the world and have the fastest-growing populations. Because of high fertility rates in developing countries, children under 15 make up almost half their total population. In industrial countries, children make up only about a quarter of the population. Italy recently became the first country in history to have more people over the age of 60 than under the age of 20. Germany, Greece, and Spain will soon join Italy.[1]

EXHIBIT 4

Total Fertility Rates: Births per Woman

The total fertility rate is the number of children that would be born to a woman if she were to live to the end of her childbearing years and to bear children in accordance with current age-specific fertility rates.

Classification	1980	1996
1. Low-income economies	5.6	4.1
India	5.0	3.1
Sub-Saharan Africa	6.6	5.6
2. Middle-income economies	3.2	2.3
China	2.5	1.4
3. High-income economies	1.9	1.7

Source: Based on data presented by the World Bank in *World Development Report 1998/99* (New York: Oxford University Press, 1998), Table 7.

---

1 As reported in Michael Specter, "Population Implosion Worries a Graying Europe," *New York Times* (10 July 1998).

In some developing countries, the population growth rate has exceeded the real GNP growth rate, so the standard of living as measured by per capita GNP has declined. Still, even in the poorest of countries, attitudes about family size are changing. According the United Nations, the birth rate during a typical woman's lifetime in a developing country has fallen since 1965 from six children to three children. Evidence from developing countries more generally indicates that when women have better employment opportunities outside the home, fertility rates decline. And as women become better educated, they tend to earn more and have fewer children.

Women in Developing Countries

Throughout the world, poverty is greater among women than men, particularly women who head households. The percentage of households headed by women varies from country to country, but exceeds 40 percent in some areas of the Caribbean and Africa. Because women often must work in the home as well as in the labor market, poverty can impose a special hardship on them. In many cultures, women's responsibilities include gathering firewood and carrying water, tasks that are especially burdensome if firewood is scarce and water is far from home.

Women in developing countries tend to be less educated than men. In the countries of sub-Saharan Africa and South Asia, for example, only half as many women as men complete high school. And in Indonesia, girls are six times more likely than boys to drop out of school before the fourth grade. Women have fewer employment opportunities and earn lower wages than men do. For example, Sudan's Muslim fundamentalist government bans women from working in public places after 5:00 P.M. In Algeria, Egypt, Jordan, Libya, and Saudi Arabia, women account for only about one-quarter of the labor force. Women are often on the fringes of the labor market, working long hours in agriculture. They also have less access to other resources, such as land, capital, and technology. Worse yet, according to social workers and press reports, during the recent economic crisis in Asia, some peasant girls were sold to traders who in turn sold them to brothels in places like Bangkok, Thailand.[2]

PRODUCTIVITY: KEY TO DEVELOPMENT

We have examined some symptoms of poverty in developing countries, but not why poor countries are poor. At the risk of appearing simplistic, we might say that poor countries are poor because they do not produce many goods and services. In this section, we will examine why some developing countries experience such low productivity.

Low Labor Productivity

Labor productivity, measured in terms of output per worker, is low in low-income countries. Why? Labor productivity depends on the quality of the labor and on the amount of capital, land, and other resources that combine with labor. For example, one certified public accountant with a computer and specialized

---

2 As reported in Nicholas D. Kristof, "Asian Crisis Deals Setbacks to Women," *New York Times* (11 June 1998). This story tells of a 15-year-old sold by her grandmother for $40.

software can sort out a company's finances more quickly and more accurately than can a thousand high-school–educated file clerks with pencils and paper.

One way a country raises its productivity is by investing more in human and physical capital. This investment must be financed by either domestic savings or foreign funds. Income per capita is often too low in developing countries to permit extensive investments to be financed with internal funds. In poor countries with unstable governments, the wealthy minority frequently invests in more stable foreign economies. Thus there are few domestic funds available for investment in either human or physical capital; without sufficient capital, workers are less productive.

Technology and Education

What exactly is the contribution of education to the process of economic development? Education makes people more receptive to new ideas and methods. Countries with the most advanced educational systems were also the first to develop. In this century, the leader in schooling and economic development has been the United States. In Latin America, Argentina was the most educationally advanced nation 100 years ago, and it is one of the most developed Latin American nations today. The growth of education in Japan during the 19th century contributed to a ready acceptance of technology and thus to Japan's remarkable economic growth in the 20th century.

If knowledge is insufficient, other resources may not be used efficiently. For example, a country may be endowed with fertile land, but farmers may lack knowledge of irrigation and fertilization techniques. Or farmers may not know how to rotate crops and avoid soil depletion. In low-income countries, about 60 percent of adults were illiterate in 1995, compared to less than 5 percent in high-income countries.

Child labor in developing countries reduces educational opportunities. In Pakistan, for example, the education system can accommodate only one-third of the country's school-age children. More than 10 million Pakistani children work full-time—half of whom are less than 10 years old.[3] Worldwide, more than 200 million children under 14 years of age work full-time.

Inefficient Use of Labor

Another feature of developing countries is that they use labor less efficiently than developed nations. Unemployment and underemployment reflect inefficient uses of labor. *Underemployment* occurs when skilled workers are employed in low-skill jobs or when people are working less than they would like—a worker seeking full-time employment may find only a part-time job. *Unemployment* occurs when those willing and able to work cannot find jobs.

Unemployment is measured primarily in urban areas, because in rural areas farm work is usually an outlet for labor even if many workers are underemployed there. The unemployment rate in developing nations on average is about 10 to 15 percent of the urban labor force. Unemployment among young workers—those aged 15 to 24—is typically twice that of older workers. In developing nations, about 30 percent of the combined urban and rural work forces is either unemployed or underemployed.

---

3 Pakistani children in the lowest castes become laborers almost as soon as they can walk. See Jonathan Silvers, "Child Labor in Pakistan," *Atlantic Monthly* (February 1996).

In some developing countries, the average farm is as small as two acres. Productivity is also low because few other inputs, such as capital and fertilizer, are used. Even where more land is available, the absence of capital limits the amount of land that can be farmed. *Although about two-thirds of the labor force in developing countries works in agriculture, only about one-third of GNP in these countries stems from agriculture.* In the United States, where farmers account for only 2.5 percent of the labor force, a farmer with modern equipment can farm hundreds of acres. In developing countries a farmer with a hand plow or an ox-drawn plow can farm maybe 10 to 20 acres. As you would expect, U.S. farmers, though one-fortieth of the workforce, grow enough to feed a nation and to lead the world in farm exports.

Low productivity obviously results in low income, but low income can, in turn, affect worker productivity. Low income means less saving and less saving means less investment in human and physical capital. Low income can also mean poor nutrition during the formative years, which can retard mental and physical development. These difficult beginnings may be aggravated by poor diet and insufficient health care in later life, making workers poorly suited for regular employment. Thus, *low income and low productivity may reinforce each other in a vicious cycle.* Poverty can result in less saving, less capital formation, an inadequate diet, and insufficient attention to health care—all of which can reduce a worker's productive ability.

Natural Resources

Some countries are richer than others because they are blessed with natural resources. The difference is most striking when we compare countries with oil reserves and those without. Some developing countries of the Middle East are classified as high-income economies because they are lucky enough to be sitting atop major oil reserves. But oil-rich countries are the exception. Many developing countries, such as Chad and Ethiopia, have little in the way of natural resources. Most developing countries without oil reserves were in trouble when oil prices rose. Oil had to be imported, and these imports drained the oil-poor countries of precious foreign exchange.

Financial Institutions

Another requirement for development is an adequate and trusted system of financial institutions. An important source of funds for investment is the savings of households and firms. People in developing countries often have little confidence in their currency because some governments finance a large fraction of public outlays by printing money. This practice results in high inflation and sometimes very high inflation, or hyperinflation, as occurred recently in Russia. High and unpredictable inflation discourages saving and hurts development.

Developing countries have special problems because banks are often not held in high regard. At the first sign of economic problems, many depositors withdraw their funds. Since banks cannot rely on a continuous supply of deposits, they cannot make loans for extended periods. Also governments often impose ceilings on the interest rates that lenders can charge, forcing lenders to ration credit among borrowers. If financial institutions fail to serve as intermediaries between borrowers and lenders, the resulting lack of funds for investment becomes an obstacle to growth.

Capital Infrastructure

Some development economists believe that the most important ingredient in economic development is the administrative competence of the government. Production and exchange rely on an infrastructure of communication and transportation networks provided by the public sector. Roads, bridges, airports, harbors, and other transportation facilities are vital to commercial activity. Reliable mail service, telephone communication, clean water, and electricity are also essential for advanced production techniques. Imagine how difficult it would be to run even a personal computer if the supply of electricity and phone service were continually interrupted, as is often the case in developing countries. Many developing countries have serious deficiencies in their infrastructures. And some of the poorest countries in Africa have been ravaged by internal strife. For example, Ethiopia, one of the poorest countries in the world, has been caught up in a war with the break-away province of Eritrea. Both sides have spent millions on jet fighters, even though neither has any qualified pilots to fly the new planes.

Entrepreneurial Ability

An economy can have abundant supplies of land, labor, and capital, but without entrepreneurial ability, the other resources will not be combined efficiently to produce goods and services. Unless a country has a class of entrepreneurs who are able to bring together resources and take the risk of profit or loss, development may never begin. Many developing countries were once under colonial rule, a system of government that offered the local population little opportunity to develop entrepreneurial skills.

Government Monopolies

Government officials often decide that local private-sector entrepreneurs are unable to generate the kind of economic growth the country needs. State enterprises are therefore created to do what government believes the free market cannot do. State-owned enterprises may have objectives other than producing goods efficiently—objectives that could include maximizing employment and providing jobs for friends and relatives of government officials, as discussed in the following case study.

Crony Capitalism in Indonesia—All in the Family

CaseStudy

Other Times, Other Places

Indonesia is a country of more than 200 million people spread across some 13,000 islands in the Indian Ocean. The country is rich in natural resources, including oil, yet economic development has been hampered by bureaucratic red tape and corruption. At the center was President Suharto, who ruled the nation as a virtual dictator between 1965 and his forced resignation in 1998. Over the years, he conferred monopoly privileges on family and friends.

Based on the strength of government-granted monopolies, President Suharto and his

Is crony capitalism an example of market failure or government failure? "TRB From Washington: Super Markets," by Charles Lane in the *New Republic,* takes the latter view, citing Indonesia and Russia as examples. See http://www. thenewrepublic.com/ magazines/tnr/archive/1198/ 110298/trb110298.html. What else does he blame for the financial crisis? What good does he think might follow from it?

six children were able to build an economic empire valued at more than $4 billion, spanning over 2,000 Indonesian companies. Because of government-imposed monopolies, the prices of products in Indonesia were higher than those prevailing on the world market. For example, friends and relatives held the exclusive rights to import steel, plastic, tin, cotton, industrial machinery, cement, and other key resources. In 1990 one of Suharto's sons and some business partners were awarded an exclusive license to import, buy, and sell cloves, a spice used in cooking and to flavor tobacco in Indonesian cigarettes. To finance the monopoly, the central Bank of Indonesia advanced the group $325 million in loans and credits, or half the Bank's annual budget for agricultural subsidies. At the time the son claimed, "We're doing it for the good of the farmers." The monopoly purchased cloves from farmers for less than the world price and sold the cloves to cigarette manufacturers for twice the world price. The monopoly was a hugely profitable.

These monopolies reduced competition, increased costs to consumers, and hindered the development of an export sector that could compete on the world market. In this environment, a combination of "crony capitalism" and nepotism, political connections become more important than ability or expertise; free enterprise was thereby discouraged. Businesses were better off developing political contacts than producing goods and services more efficiently.

By the time Suharto resigned in 1998, the Indonesian economy was in shambles. Economic output declined 12 percent in the first half of 1998. The government had taken over 70 percent of the nation's banks. The national currency, the rupiah, had fallen 80 percent against the dollar. And half the population was living below the poverty level. Some of this was caused, no doubt, by the economic malaise sweeping through Asia, but Indonesia was hit hardest because its economy had been distorted for so long.

Sources: Maggie Farley, "A Familiar Scent of Monopoly," *Los Angeles Times* (21 March 1998); Steven Erlanger, "Suharto's Cling to Power Undermines His Legacy," *New York Times* (22 May 1998); Peter Waldman, "Hand in Glove: How Suharto's Circle, Mining Firm Did So Well Together," *Wall Street Journal* (29 September 1998); and "The World's Working Rich," *Forbes* (6 July 1998): 198–199.

INTERNATIONAL TRADE AND DEVELOPMENT

Developing countries need to trade with developed countries in order to acquire the capital and technology that will increase labor productivity on the farm, in the factory, in the office, and in the home. To import capital and technology, developing countries must first acquire the funds, or foreign exchange, needed to pay for imports. Exports usually generate more than half of the annual flow of foreign exchange in developing countries. Foreign aid and private investment make up the rest.

Primary products, such as agricultural goods and other raw materials, make up the bulk of exports from developing countries, just as manufactured goods make up the bulk of exports from developed countries. Developing countries must export a large amount of raw materials in order to buy back the finished products made from these same materials. Another problem is that the prices of primary products, such as coffee, cocoa, sugar, and rubber, fluctuate more widely than do the prices of finished goods, because crop production fluctuates with the weather.

A third problem of developing countries has been their deteriorating trade position. In recent years, the prices of raw materials have fallen as demand has softened (in part because of the troubles in Asia) and as substitutes have been developed for products such as rubber. Since the prices of manufactured imported goods have not dropped as much, developing countries receive less money from exports than they spend on imports, resulting in trade deficits. To reduce these deficits, developing countries have tried to restrict imports. Because imported food often is critical to survival, developing countries are more likely to cut imports of capital goods—the very items needed to promote long-term growth and productivity. Thus many developing countries cannot afford the modern machinery that will help them become more productive. Developing countries must also confront industrial countries' trade restrictions, such as tariffs and quotas, which often discriminate against primary products. For example, the United States strictly limits sugar imports. *Developing countries' share of world trade has fallen since 1950.*

Import Substitution Versus Export Promotion

Economic development frequently involves a shift from the production of raw materials and agricultural products to manufacturing. If a country is fortunate, this transformation occurs gradually through natural market forces. Sometimes the shift is pushed along by government. Many developing countries, including Argentina and India, pursued a policy called **import substitution**, whereby the country manufactures products that until then had been imported. To insulate domestic producers from foreign competition, the government imposes tariffs and import quotas. This development strategy became popular for several reasons. First, demand already existed for these products, so the "what to produce" question was readily answered. Second, by reducing imports, the approach addressed the lack of foreign exchange so common among developing countries. Third, import substitution nurtured infant industries, providing them a protected market. Finally, import substitution was popular with those who supplied capital, labor, and other resources to the favored domestic industries.

Import substitution A development strategy that emphasizes domestic manufacturing of products that are currently imported

Like all protection measures, however, import substitution erases the gains from specialization and comparative advantage among countries. Often the developing country replaced relatively low-cost foreign goods with high-cost domestic goods. And domestic producers, insulated from foreign competition, usually fail to grow efficient. Even the balance-of-payments picture did not improve, because other countries often retaliated with their own trade restrictions.

Critics of the import-substitution approach claim that export promotion is a surer path to economic development. **Export promotion** is a development strategy that concentrates on producing for the export market. This approach begins with relatively simple products, such as textiles. As a developing country builds its technological and educational base—that is, as the developing economy learns by doing—producers can then export more complex products. Economists tend to favor export promotion over import substitution because the emphasis is on comparative advantage and trade expansion rather than trade restriction. Export promotion also forces producers to grow more efficient in order to compete

Export promotion A development strategy that concentrates on producing for the export market

on world markets. Recent research shows that global competition has a profound effect on domestic efficiency.[4] What's more, export promotion requires less government intervention in the market than does import substitution.

Export promotion has been the more successful development strategy, as reflected for example by the newly industrialized countries of East Asia, which in recent decades have grown much more quickly than import-substituting countries such as Argentina, India, and Peru. Since 1965 the four Asian newly industrialized economies raised their average real income from 20 percent of the high income countries' level to 70 percent. Most Latin American nations, which for decades had favored import substitution, are now pursuing free trade agreements with the United States. Even India is in the process of dismantling trade barriers, although the emphasis has been on importing high-technology capital goods. One slogan of Indian trade officials is "Microchips, yes! Potato chips, no!"

Migration and the Brain Drain

Migration plays an important role in the economies of developing countries. A major source of foreign exchange in some countries is the money sent home by migrants who find jobs in industrial countries. Thus migration provides a valuable safety valve for poor countries. But there is a downside. Often the best and the brightest professionals, such as doctors, nurses, and engineers, migrate to developed countries. Since human capital is such a key resource, this "brain drain" hurts the developing economy.

Trade Liberalization and Special Interests

Although most people would benefit from freer international trade, some would be worse off. Consequently, governments in some developing countries have difficulty pursuing policies conducive to development. Often the gains from economic development are widespread, but the beneficiaries, such as consumers, do not recognize their potential gains. On the other hand, the losers tend to be concentrated, such as producers in an industry that had been sheltered from foreign competition, and they know quite well the source of their losses. So the government often lacks the political backing to remove impediments to development, because the potential losers fight reforms that might harm their livelihood while the potential winners remain largely unaware of what's at stake. What's more, consumers have difficulty organizing even if they become aware of what's going on. A recent study by the World Bank suggests a strong link in Africa between governments that cater to special-interest groups and low rates of economic growth.

Nonetheless, many developing countries have been opening their borders to freer trade. People around the world have been exposed to information about the opportunities and goods available on world markets. So consumers want the goods and firms want the technology and capital that are available abroad. Both groups want government to ease trade restrictions. Studies by the World Bank and others have underscored the successes of countries that have adopted trade liberalization policies.

---

4 See Martin Baily and Hans Gersbach, "Efficiency in Manufacturing and the Need for Global Competition," in *Brookings Papers on Economic Activity: Microeconomics,* M. Baily, P. Reiss, and C. Winston, eds. (Washington D.C.: Brookings Institution, 1995): 307–347.

FOREIGN AID AND ECONOMIC DEVELOPMENT

We have already seen that because poor countries do not generate enough savings to fund an adequate level of investment, these countries often rely on foreign financing. Private international borrowing and lending are heavily restricted by the governments of developing countries. Governments may allow residents to purchase foreign exchange only for certain purposes. In some developing countries, different exchange rates apply to different categories of transactions. Thus the local currency is not easily convertible into other currencies. Some developing countries also require foreign investors to find a local partner who must be granted controlling interest. All these restrictions discourage foreign investment. In this section, we will look primarily at foreign aid and its link to economic development.

Foreign Aid

Foreign aid is any international transfer made on *concessional* (i.e., especially favorable) terms for the purposes of promoting economic development. Foreign aid includes grants, which need not be repaid, and loans extended on more favorable repayment terms than the recipient could normally secure. Concessional loans have lower interest rates, longer repayment periods, or grace periods during which repayments are reduced or waived (similar to some student loans). Foreign aid can take the form of money, capital goods, technical assistance, food, and so forth.

Foreign aid An international transfer made on especially favorable terms for the purpose of promoting economic development

Some foreign aid is granted by a specific country, such as the United States, to another specific country, such as the Philippines. Country-to-country aid is called *bilateral* assistance. Other foreign aid goes through international bodies such as the World Bank. Assistance provided by organizations that use funds from a number of countries is called *multilateral*. For example, the World Bank provides loans and grants to support activities that are viewed as prerequisites for development, such as health and education programs or basic development projects like dams, roads, and communications networks. And the International Monetary Fund extends loans to countries that have trouble with their balance of payments, with recent loans to Indonesia, Korea, and Brazil.

During the last four decades, the United States has provided the developing world with over $400 billion in aid. Since 1961, most U.S. aid has been coordinated by the U.S. Agency for International Development (AID), which is part of the U.S. Department of State. This agency concentrates primarily on health, education, and agriculture, providing both technical assistance and loans. AID emphasizes long-range plans to meet the basic needs of the poor and to promote self-sufficiency. Foreign aid is a controversial, though relatively small, part of the federal budget. Since 1993, official U.S. aid has been less than 0.2 percent of U.S. GDP, compared to an average of 0.3 percent from 21 other industrialized nations.

Does Foreign Aid Promote Economic Development?

In general, foreign aid provides additional purchasing power and thus the possibility of increased investment, capital imports, and consumption. But it remains unclear whether foreign aid *supplements* domestic saving, thus increasing investment, or simply *substitutes* for domestic saving, thereby increasing consumption rather than investment. What is clear is that foreign aid often becomes a source of discretionary funds that benefit not the poor but their leaders. More than 90 percent of the funds distributed by AID go to governments, whose leaders assume responsibility for distributing these funds.

Much bilateral funding is tied to purchases of goods and services from the donor nation, and such programs can sometimes be counterproductive. For example, in the 1950s, the United States began the Food for Peace program, which helped sell U.S. farm products abroad, but some governments sold that food to finance poorly conceived projects. Worse yet, the availability of low-priced food drove down farm prices in the developing countries, hurting farmers there.

Foreign aid may have raised the standard of living in some developing countries, but it has not necessarily increased their ability to become self-supporting at that higher standard of living. Many countries that receive aid are doing less of what they had done well. Their agricultural sectors have suffered. For example, though we should be careful when drawing conclusions about causality, per capita food production in Africa has fallen since 1960. Outside aid has often insulated government officials from the fundamental troubles of their own economies. No country receiving U.S. aid in the past 20 years has moved up in status from developing to industrial. And most countries today that have achieved industrial status did so without foreign aid.

Because of disappointment with the results of government aid, the trend is toward channeling funds through private nonprofit agencies such as CARE. More than half of the flow of aid now goes through private channels.

The privatization of foreign aid follows a larger trend toward privatization around the world. We discuss that important development in the balance of this chapter.

TRANSITIONAL ECONOMIES

As we have seen, there is no widely accepted theory of economic development, but around the world markets are replacing central plans in once-socialist countries. Economic developments in these emerging market economies have tremendous significance for those who study economics. Like geologists, economists must rely primarily on natural experiments to figure out how things work. *The attempt to replace central planning with markets is one of the greatest economic experiments in history.* In the study of geology, this would be comparable to a huge earthquake. In this section, we take a look at these so-called transitional economies.

Types of Economic Systems
First, let's briefly review economic systems. In Chapter 2, we considered the three questions that every economic system must answer: what to produce, how to produce it, and for whom to produce it. Laws regarding resource ownership and the role of government in resource allocation determine the "rules of the game"—the incentives and constraints that guide the behavior of individual decision makers. Economic systems can be classified based on the ownership of resources, the way resources are allocated to produce goods and services, and the incentives used to motivate people.

As we discussed in Chapter 2, resources in *capitalist* systems are owned mostly by individuals and are allocated through market coordination. In socialist economies, resources other than labor are owned by the state. For example, a country such as Cuba or North Korea carefully limits the private ownership of resources such as land and capital. Each country employs a slightly different system of resource ownership, resource allocation, and individual incentives to answer the three economic questions.

So under capitalism, the rules of the game include private ownership of most resources and the coordination of economic activity by price signals generated by market forces; market coordination answers the three questions. Under socialism, the rules of the game include government ownership of most resources and the allocation of resources through central plans.

Enterprises and Soft Budget Constraints

In the socialist system, enterprises that earn a "profit" see that profit appropriated by the state. Firms that end up with a loss find that loss covered by a state subsidy. Thus socialist enterprises face what has been called a **soft budget constraint**. This can lead to inefficiency, a lack of response to changes in supply or demand, and poor investment decisions. Quality has also been a problem under central planning, because plant managers would rather meet production quotas than satisfy consumer demand. For example, plant managers do not score extra bureaucratic points by producing garments that are in style and in popular sizes. Tales of shoddy products in socialist systems abound.

Soft budget constraint The budget condition faced by socialist enterprises that are subsidized if they lose money

Most prices in centrally planned economies are established not by market forces but by central planners. As a result, consumers have little to say about what to produce. Once set, prices tend to be inflexible. For example, in the former Soviet Union, the price of a cabbage slicer was stamped on the metal at the factory. In the spirit of equity, Soviet planners priced most consumer goods below the market-clearing level, so shortages (or "interruptions in supply," as they were called) were common. As of 1990, the price of bread had not changed since 1954, and that price in 1990 amounted to only 7 percent of bread's production cost. Meat prices had not changed since 1962. Some rents had not changed in 60 years.

Capitalist economies equate quantity supplied with quantity demanded through the *invisible hand* of market coordination; centrally planned economies use the *visible hand* of bureaucratic coordination assisted by taxes and subsidies. If quantity supplied and quantity demanded are not in balance, something has to give. In a capitalist system, what gives is the price. In a centrally planned economy, what usually gives is the central plan itself. A common problem in the Soviet system was that the amount produced often fell short of planned production. When the quantity supplied fell below the planned amount, central planners reduced the amount supplied to each sector, cutting critical sectors such as heavy industry and the military the least and cutting lower-priority sectors such as consumer products the most. Evidence of shortages of consumer goods included long waiting lines at retail stores; empty store shelves; the "tips," or bribes, shop operators expected for supplying scarce consumer goods; and higher prices for goods on the black market. Shoppers would sometimes wait in line all night and into the next day. Consumers often relied on "connections" through acquaintances to obtain most goods and services. Scarce goods were frequently diverted to the black market.

Another distinction between socialist economies and capitalist economies involves the ownership of resources. The following case study considers the effect of ownership on the efficient use of resources.

Ownership and Resource Use

Because most property is owned by the state in a socialist economy, nobody in particular owns it. Because there are no individual owners, resources are often wasted. For example, in the former Soviet Union, about one-third of the harvest reportedly deteriorated before it reached retailers. Likewise, to meet Soviet planning goals, oil producers often pumped large pools of oil reserves so quickly that the remaining oil became inaccessible. Soviet workers usually had little regard for equipment that belonged to the state. New trucks or tractors might be dismantled for parts, or working equipment might be sent to a scrap plant. Pilfering of state-owned property, though officially a serious crime, was a high art and a favorite sport. As an old Soviet saying goes, "If you don't steal from the State, you are stealing from your family."

A narrow focus on meeting the objectives of the central plan also imposed a heavy cost on the environment. The Aral Sea, which is about the size of Lake Michigan, has been called "a salinated cesspool." Thousands of barrels of nuclear waste were dumped into Soviet rivers and seas. The 1986 Chernobyl reactor meltdown still poses a threat of nuclear contamination; similar reactors continue to supply energy to Russia, Ukraine, and Lithuania. In a drive for military supremacy, the Soviet government set off 125 nuclear explosions *above* ground. The resulting bomb craters later filled with water, forming contaminated lakes.

In contrast to the treatment of state property, Soviet citizens took extremely good care of their personal property. For example, personal cars were so well maintained that they lasted 20 years or more on average—twice the official projected automobile life. The incentives of private ownership were also evident in agriculture, where farmers typically worked as a group on a *collective*. But each farmer on the collective was also allowed a small plot of land on which to cultivate crops for personal consumption or for sale at prices determined in unregulated markets. Despite the small size of the plots and high taxes on earnings from these plots, farmers produced a disproportionate share of output on private plots. Privately farmed plots constituted only 3 percent of the Soviet Union's farmland, but they supplied 30 percent of all meat, milk, and vegetables and 60 percent of all potatoes.

Perhaps the benefits of privately held resources are no better illustrated than where countries were divided by ideology: West and East Germany before unification, South and North Korea, and Taiwan and mainland China. In each case the economies began with similar human and physical resources, but income per capita diverged sharply, with the market economies outperforming the centrally planned markets. For example, despite recent turmoil in Asia, per capita income in South Korea was still at least five times greater than in North Korea, a communist country.

Recognizing the incentive power of private property, even the most die-hard socialist economies now allow some free-market activity. For example, Cuba allows foreigners to buy Cuban companies and repatriate profits earned in Cuba. On a more down-to-earth level, hundreds of farmers' markets have been established in Cuba to sell everything from live goats to tropical fruit. And for the first time in fifty years, in 1998 China announced plans to allow urban residents the ability to buy homes. But sale prices will still be dictated by the government. The point is that the personal incentives provided by private property usually promote a more efficient use of that property than does state, or common, ownership.

Sources: "Stuck in a Rut," *Wall Street Journal* (23 June 1998); Esther Dyson, *Release 2.0 : A Design for Living in the Digital Age* (New York: Broadway Books, 1997); Erik Eckholm, "China Spells Out Rules On New National Housing Policy," *New York Times* (19 June 1998); Vito Echevarria, "Capitalism Grows in Cuba," *New American News Service* (30 April 1998); and "Viewing Cuba's Market Culture," *Times-Picayune* (29 April 1998).

MARKETS AND INSTITUTIONS

A study of economic systems underscores the importance of institutions in the course of development. *Institutions*, or "rules of the game," are the incentives and constraints that structure political, economic, and social interaction. They consist of (1) formal rules of behavior, such as a constitution, laws, and property rights, and (2) informal constraints on behavior, such as sanctions, manners, customs, traditions, and codes of conduct. Throughout history, institutions have been devised by people to create order and reduce uncertainty in exchange. Thus underlying the surface of economic behavior is a grid of informal, often unconscious, habits, customs, and norms that make the functioning of markets possible. *A reliable system of property rights and enforceable contracts are prerequisites for creating incentives that support a healthy market economy.*

Together with the standard constraints of economics, such as income, resource availability, and prices, institutions shape the incentive structure of an economy. As the incentive structure evolves, it can direct economic change toward growth, stagnation, or decline. Economic history is largely a story of economies that have failed to produce a set of economic rules of the game that lead to sustained economic growth. After all, more than three-quarters of the world's economies are still trying to develop—still trying to get their act together.

Customs and conventions can sometimes be obstacles to development. In developed market economies, resource owners tend to supply their resources where they are most valued; but in developing countries, links to the family or clan may be the most important consideration. For example, in some cultures, children are expected to remain in their father's occupation even though some are better suited to other lines of work. Family businesses may resist growth because such growth would involve hiring people from outside the family.

Institutions and Economic Development

Institutions shape the incentive structure of an economy, but, as we have already noted, most countries in the world have failed to produce a set of economic rules of the game that lead to sustained economic growth. Although political and judicial decisions may change formal rules overnight, informal constraints embodied in customs, traditions, and codes of conduct are more immune to deliberate policies. For example, respect for the law cannot be legislated.

Prior to the market reforms in the former Soviet Union, widespread corruption and a lack of faith in formal institutions were woven into the social fabric. Workers bribed officials to get good jobs and consumers bribed clerks to get desired products. Bribery became a way of life, a way of dealing with the distortions that arise when prices are not allowed to allocate resources efficiently.

In centrally planned economies, the exchange relationship was typically personal, based as it was on bureaucratic ties on the production side and inside connections on the consumption side. But in the United States and other market economies, successful institutional evolution permits the *impersonal* exchange necessary to capture the potential economic benefits of specialization and modern technology. Impersonal exchange allows for a far greater division of labor, but it requires a richer and more stable institutional setting.

The Big Bang Versus Gradualism

The Hungarian economist Janos Kornai believes that a market order should be grown from the bottom up. First, small-scale capitalism in farming, trade, light manufacturing, and services thrives. These grass-roots markets can serve as a foundation for the privatization of larger industrial sectors. Large industrial enterprises should quickly find the market-clearing price so that input and output decisions are consistent with market preferences. In the meantime, state-owned enterprises should be run more like businesses in which state directors attempt to maximize profit. Money-losing enterprises should be phased out. This "bottom-up" approach proposed by Kornai could be termed **gradualism**, which can be contrasted with a **big-bang** approach, whereby the transition from central planning to a market economy would take place in a matter of months.

One example of gradualism is taking place in China. In 1978, the government began dismantling agricultural communes in favor of a "household-responsibility" system of small-farm agriculture. Land was assigned to individual families, which could keep any excess production after meeting specific state-imposed goals. Initially the system was to be applied only to the poorest 20 percent of rural areas. Once the positive effects became apparent, however, the system spread on its own. Eventually farmers established their own wholesale and retail marketing systems and were allowed to sell directly to urban areas at market-clearing prices. This gave rise to a market for truckers to buy, transport, and resell farm products. Over the next seven years, agricultural output increased by an impressive 8 to 10 percent per year.

In structuring the transition from central planning to a market system, economists are feeling their way. Nobel prize-winner Friedrich von Hayek argued that competitive markets provide instant information about the price and quantity resulting from the interaction of supply and demand. But central planning provides no way to discover what the equilibrium price and quantity should be. And the more rigid prices become, the less information they convey. According to Hayek, not only is finding equilibrium price and quantity a discovery process, but developing appropriate rules of the game to nurture market activity is also a discovery process. Both discovery processes are especially

Gradualism A "bottom-up" approach to moving from a centrally planned to a market economy emphasizing established markets at the most decentralized level first, such as on small farms or in light industry

Big-bang theory The argument that the transition from a centrally planned to a market economy should be broad and swift, taking place in a matter of months

difficult for transitional economies, which usually have no history of market interaction and no established record of codified law or rules of conduct for market participants. For example, based on China's success with privately run farms, Russia's 1993 constitution guaranteed the right to buy and sell land. But that guarantee was never fleshed out with supporting legislation. Thus farm cooperatives in Russia today operate much as they did in the Soviet days. Hayek believed that *government's role should be to help establish competitive markets by identifying and codifying the conventions of trade and by protecting property rights.*

Privatization

Privatization is the process of turning public enterprises into private enterprises. It is the opposite of *nationalization*. For example, Russian privatization began in April 1992 with the sale of municipally owned shops. Although most property in countries of the former Soviet Union is nominally owned by the state, it often remains unclear who has the authority to sell the property and who should receive the proceeds. This ambiguity results in cases in which the same property has been purchased from different officials by different buyers. Yet *there is no clear legal process for resolving title disputes.* Worse still, some enterprises have been stripped of their assets by self-serving managers, a process that derisively came to be called "spontaneous" privatization. The necessarily complex process of privatization will be undermined if the general population perceives it to be unfair.

Privatization The process of turning public enterprises into private enterprises

Transparent Finances

Privatization requires modern accounting and other information systems, the training of competent managers, and the installation of adequate facilities for telecommunication, computing, travel, and transportation. This transformation cannot be accomplished overnight. Consider just the accounting problem. A market economy depends on financial accounting rules as well as on an independent system for auditing financial reports. The needed information must show up in a company's balance sheet and income statement. Prospective buyers of enterprises need such information, as do banks and other lenders. Thus, a firm's finances should be **transparent**, meaning someone should be able to look at the books and the balance sheet and tell exactly what's going on.

Transparent finances A firm's financial records that clearly indicate the economic health of the company

By all reports, the accounting systems of most formerly socialist firms are almost worthless. For decades, data had been aimed more at central planners, who wanted to know about *physical* flows, than at someone who wanted to know about the efficiency and financial promise of the firm. So there is much information, but little that is relevant. Incidentally, the major advantage of the market economy is that it minimizes the need for the kind of resource-flow data that had been reported under central planning. Prices convey most of the information necessary to coordinate economic activity among firms.

Institutional Requirements of Efficient Markets

Some may look at the initial instability that resulted from the dismantling of socialist states and argue that the move toward markets has been a failure. But in the former Soviet Union the state dismantled central controls before institutions such as property rights, customs, codes of conduct, and a legal system were in place. For example, more than half of the 17-year-olds surveyed in Russia saw nothing wrong with looking for a job that offered opportunities to collect bribes and nearly half believed it acceptable to take what they wanted by force.[5]

Tax laws are applied unevenly and the rates change frequently. For example, the personal income tax in Russia jumped from a graduated rate topping at 13 percent to a flat rate of 60 percent and then to a graduated rate topping at 40 percent. Most Russians evade taxes—only one million people filed income tax returns in 1997, a tiny fraction of the 147 million population.[6] Corporate taxes appear just as arbitrary in Russia, with politically connected companies paying little or no taxes. The head of Russia's Statistics Service was fired in 1998 after his arrest for helping big companies evade taxes.[7] Harvard economist and Russian expert Marshall Goldman argues that "tax evasion by both enterprises and individuals is a source of pride dating back to czarist times."[8] Millions of Russians carry out their business in the underground economy.

The shift from central planning to a market economy is easier said than done. Simply loosening constraints to create private property may not be enough for successful reform. The development of supporting institutions is essential, but *there is no unified economic theory of how to construct the institutions that are central to the success of capitalism.* Most so-called economists employed in Soviet-type systems did not understand even the basics of how markets work. They had been trained to regard the alleged "anarchy" of the market as a primary defect of capitalism.

A more fundamental problem is that, although Western economic theory focuses on the operation of efficient markets, *even market economists usually do not understand the institutional requirements of efficient markets.* Market economists often take the necessary institutions for granted. Those involved in the transition must develop a deeper appreciation for the institutions that nurture and support impersonal market activity.

So the jury is still out on the transition to markets. Exhibit 5 presents, for some key transitional economies, the GNP per capita in 1997 based on the purchasing power of the domestic currency. Notice the dramatic differences across these economies, with per capita GNP in the Czech Republic more than five times greater than that of the Ukraine. By way of comparison, U.S. GNP per capita in 1997 was $28,740, or about 150 percent above the Czech Republic, the most successful transitional economy.

Lessons about the nature of economic processes will likely emerge from the analysis of these transitional economies. The course of economic reform will provide insights into both the potential and the limits of economics itself.

---

5 As reported by James Meek, "For Youth, Bribery a Matter of 'Maybe' Rather than 'Nyet,'" *Sydney Morning Herald* (21 March 1998).
6 Michael R. Gordon, "Russia's New Enforcer of Taxes Is Taking On a Land of Evaders," *New York Times* (4 July 1998).
7 "Russia's Finance: Taxman in a Tank," *Economist* (13 June 1998): 72.
8 Marshall Goldman, "Russian Tax Evasion Is Source of Pride," letter to the editor, *New York Times* (9 August 1998).

EXHIBIT 5

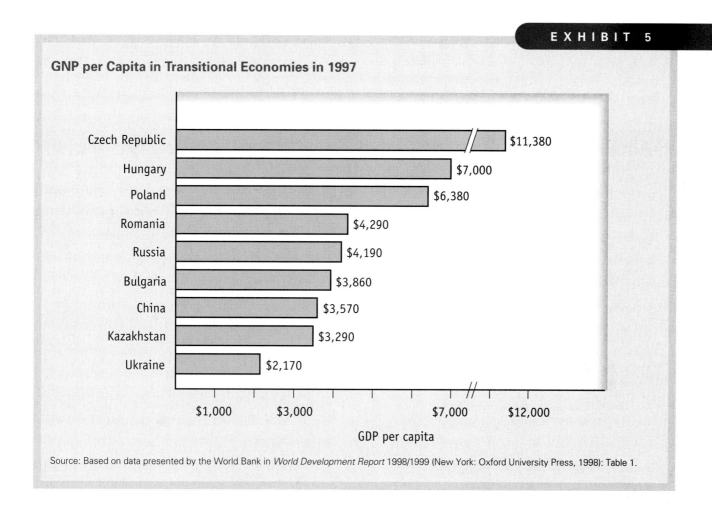

GNP per Capita in Transitional Economies in 1997

- Czech Republic — $11,380
- Hungary — $7,000
- Poland — $6,380
- Romania — $4,290
- Russia — $4,190
- Bulgaria — $3,860
- China — $3,570
- Kazakhstan — $3,290
- Ukraine — $2,170

GDP per capita

Source: Based on data presented by the World Bank in *World Development Report* 1998/1999 (New York: Oxford University Press, 1998): Table 1.

CONCLUSION

Because no single theory of economic development has become widely accepted, this chapter has been more descriptive than theoretical. We can readily define the features that distinguish developing from industrial economies, but we are less sure how to foster growth and development. Economic history is largely a story of economies that have failed to produce a set of economic rules of the game that lead to sustained economic growth.

Perhaps the most elusive ingredients for development are the formal and informal institutions that promote economic activity: the laws, customs, conventions, and other institutional elements that encourage people to undertake productive activity. A stable political environment with well-defined property rights is important. Little private sector investment will occur if potential investors believe their capital might be appropriated by government, destroyed by civil unrest, or stolen by thieves. Education is also key to development, both because of its direct effect on productivity and because those who are more educated tend to be more receptive to new ideas. A physical infrastructure of transportation and communication systems and utilities is needed to link economic participants. And trusted financial institutions help link savers and borrowers. Finally, a country needs entrepreneurs with the vision to move the economy forward. Some newly emerging industrial countries prove that economic development is achievable, though not necessarily easy.

SUMMARY

1. Developing countries are distinguished by low levels of output per capita, poor health and nutrition, high fertility rates, low levels of education, and saving rates that are too low to finance sufficient investment.

2. Worker productivity is low in developing countries because the stocks of physical and human capital are low, technological advances are not widely diffused throughout the economy, natural resources and entrepreneurial ability are scarce, financial markets are not well developed, some talented professionals migrate to high-income countries, formal and informal institutions do not provide sufficient incentives for market activity, and governments may serve the interests of the group in power rather than the public interest.

3. The key to growth and a rising standard of living is increased productivity. To foster productivity, developing nations must stimulate investment, support education and training programs, and provide the infrastructure necessary to promote economic development.

4. Increases in productivity do not occur without prior saving, but most people in developing countries have such low incomes that there is little opportunity to save. Even if some higher-income people have the money to save, financial institutions in developing countries are not well developed, and savings are often sent abroad, where there is a more stable investment climate.

5. Foreign aid has been a mixed blessing for most developing countries. In some cases, that aid has helped countries build the roads, bridges, schools, and other capital infrastructure necessary for development. In other cases, foreign aid has simply increased consumption and insulated government from painful but necessary reforms. Worse still, subsidized food from abroad has undermined domestic agriculture.

6. Major reforms have been introduced in recent years in formerly socialist economies to decentralize decision making, to provide greater production incentives to workers, and to introduce competitive markets. But in many cases, central controls were dismantled before the institutional framework had developed to support a market economy.

QUESTIONS FOR REVIEW

1. *(Worlds Apart)* Compare developing and industrial market economies on the basis of each of the following general economic characteristics, and relate the differences to the process of development:
    a. Diversity of the industrial base
    b. Distribution of resource ownership
    c. Educational level of the labor force

2. *(Developing Countries)* How would you explain why agricultural productivity in developing countries is usually low?

3. *(Classification of Economies)* What are the arguments for using real per capita GNP to compare living standards between countries? What weakness does this measure have?

4. *(Productivity and Development)* Among the problems that hinder growth in developing economies are poor infrastructure, lack of financial institutions and a sound money supply, a low saving rate, poor capital base, and lack of foreign exchange. Explain how these problems are interconnected.

5. *(**Case**Study: Crony Capitalism in Indonesia)* How did President Suharto and his family undermine the economy of Indonesia? Did the Indonesian economy have any special features that made it vulnerable to crony capitalism?

6. *(International Trade and Development)* From the perspective of citizens in a developing country, what are some of the benefits and drawbacks of international trade?

7. *(Foreign Aid and Economic Development)* Foreign aid, if it is to be successful in enhancing economic development, must lead to a more productive economy. Describe some of the problems in achieving such an objective through foreign aid.

8. *(Foreign Aid and Economic Development)* It is widely recognized that foreign aid that promotes productivity in developing economies is superior to merely shipping products like food to these countries. Yet the latter is the approach frequently taken. Why do you think this is the case?

9. *(Types of Economic Systems)* One of the questions every economic system must answer is for whom products are produced. How is the answer determined in a market system? How is it answered in a centrally planned system?

10. *(Transitional Economies)* What special problems are being faced by Eastern European economies as they make the transition from central planning to free markets?

11. *(CaseStudy: Ownership and Resource Use)* In what ways were the incentives of private ownership evident even in the Soviet Union?

12. *(Markets and Institutions)* Why is a system of well-defined and enforceable property rights crucial when a country is converting to a market-based system of resource allocation?

13. *(Big Bang Versus Gradualism)* Explain the difference between the big bang and gradualism approaches to moving from central planning to market coordination.

PROBLEMS AND EXERCISES

14. *(Worlds Apart)* Per capita GNP most recently is about 56 times greater in the richest country on Earth than in the poorest country. Suppose per capita GNP grows an average of 2 percent per year in the richest country and 4 percent per year in the poorest country. Assuming such growth rates continue indefinitely into the future, how many years would it take before the per capita GNP in the poorest country reaches that of the richest country?

15. *(Import Substitution versus Export Promotion)* Using supply and demand curves for a particular good, show why domestic producers who supply a good that competes with imports would prefer an import-substitution approach to trade policy rather than an export-promotion approach. Which policy would domestic consumers prefer and why?

EXPERIENTIAL EXERCISES

16. *(Foreign Aid)* Review the most recent *World Bank News,* a weekly publication of events, activities, and initiatives involving the World Bank at http://www.world.bank.org/html/extdr/extcs/news.html. Review one report specific to a developing country. What is the World Bank doing to help this country? In return for assistance, what has the developing country done, or what does it plan to do?

17. *(Transitional Economies)* The World Bank's *Transition Newsletter* at http://www.worldbank.org/html/ prddr/trans/WEB/trans.htm is a good source for the latest information on economies in transition. Review the latest issue of the *Newsletter.* What are some of the special problems currently faced by transitional economies?

18. *(Wall Street Journal)* Go to the Money & Investing section of today's *Wall Street Journal* and find an article relating to a developing or transitional economy. What kinds of changes are described there? What are the implications of those changes for investors in the United States?

Glossary

Glossary

Ability-to-pay-tax principle Those with a greater ability to pay should pay more tax

Absolute advantage The ability to produce something using fewer resources than other producers use

Actual investment The amount of investment actually undertaken during a year; equals planned investment plus unplanned changes in inventories

Adverse supply shocks Unexpected events that reduce aggregate supply, sometimes only temporarily

Aggregate demand curve A curve representing the relationship between the economy's price level and the amount of aggregate output demanded per period, other things being held constant

Aggregate demand The relationship between the price level in the economy and the quantity of aggregate output demanded, other things held constant

Aggregate expenditure line A relationship showing, for a given price level, planned spending at each level of income; the total of C + I + G + (X − M) at each level of income

Aggregate expenditure Total spending on final goods and services during a given time period, usually a year

Aggregate income The sum of all income earned by resource suppliers in an economy during a given time period

Aggregate output A composite measure of all final goods and services produced in an economy during a given time period; real GDP

Aggregate supply curve A curve representing the relationship between the economy's price level and the amount of aggregate output supplied per period, other things held constant

Alternative goods Other goods that use some of the same resources as used to produce the good in question

Annually balanced budget Budget philosophy prior to the Great Depression; aimed at equating revenues with outlays, except during times of war

Applied research Research that seeks to answer particular questions or to apply scientific discoveries to the development of specific products

Arbitrageur A person who takes advantage of temporary geographic differences in the exchange rate by simultaneously purchasing a currency in one market and selling it in another market

Asset Anything of value that is owned

Association-is-causation fallacy The incorrect idea that if two variables are associated in time, one must necessarily cause the other

Asymmetric information Unequal information known by each party to a transaction; borrowers usually have more information about their credit worthiness than do lenders

Autarky A situation of national self-sufficiency in which there is no economic interaction with foreigners

Automatic stabilizers Structural features of government spending and taxation that smooth fluctuations in disposable income, and hence consumption, over the business cycle

Autonomous A term that means "independent"; autonomous investment is independent of the level of income

B

Balance of payments A record of all economic transactions between residents of one country and residents of the rest of the world during a given time period

Balance on current account The section of a country's balance-of-payments account that measures the sum of the country's net unilateral transfers and its balance on goods and services

Balance on goods and services The section of a country's balance-of-payments account that measures the difference in value between a country's exports of goods and services and its imports of goods and services

Balance sheet A financial statement that shows assets, liabilities, and net worth at a given point in time; since assets must equal liabilities plus net worth, the statement is in balance.

Bank holding company A corporation that owns banks

Bank notes Papers promising a specific amount of gold or silver to bearers who presented them to issuing banks for redemption; an early type of money

Barter The direct exchange of one good for another without the use of money

Base year The year with which other years are compared when constructing an index; the index equals 100 in the base year

Basic research The search for knowledge without regard to how that knowledge will be used

Behavioral assumption An assumption that describes the expected behavior of economic decision makers

Beneficial supply shocks Unexpected events that increase aggregate supply, sometimes only temporarily

Benefits-received tax principle Those who receive more benefits from the government program funded by a tax should pay more tax

Big-bang theory The argument that the transition from a centrally planned to a market economy should be broad and swift, taking place in a matter of months

Budget resolution A congressional agreement about total outlays, spending by major category, and expected revenues, which guides spending and revenue decisions by the many congressional committees and subcommittees

C

Capital All buildings, equipment, and human skill used to produce goods and services

Capital account The record of a country's international transactions involving purchases or sales of financial and real assets

Change in demand A shift in a given demand curve caused by a change in any of the determinants of demand for the good other than its price

Change in quantity demanded A movement along the demand curve in response to a change in the price, other things constant

Change in quantity supplied A movement along the supply curve in response to a change in the price, other things constant

Change in supply A shift in a given supply curve caused by a change in one of the determinants of the supply of the good other than its price

Checkable deposits Deposits in financial institutions against which checks can be written

Circular flow model A diagram that outlines the flow of resources, products, income, and revenue among households, firms, governments, and the rest of the world

Classical economists A group of 18th and 195h-century economists who believed that recessions were short-run phenomena that corrected themselves through natural market forces; thus they believed the economy was self-correcting

Classical economists A group of 18th- and 19th-century economists who believed that recessions were short-run phenomena that corrected themselves through natural market forces; thus they believed the economy was self-correcting

Cold turkey The announcement and execution of tough measures to reduce high inflation

Commercial banks Depository institutions that make short-term loans primarily to businesses

Commodity money Anything that serves both as money and as a commodity

Comparative advantage The ability to produce something at a lower opportunity cost than other producers face

Complements Goods that are related in such a way that an increase in the price of one leads to a decrease in the demand for the other

Consumer price index (CPI) A measure of the cost of a fixed "market basket" of consumer goods and services

Consumption All household purchases of final goods and services

Consumption function The relationship between the level of income in an economy and the amount households plan to spend on consumption, other things constant

Continuing resolutions Budget agreements that allow agencies, in the absence of an approved budget, to spend at the rate of the previous year's budget

Contractionary gap The amount by which actual output in the short run falls below the economy's potential output

Convergence A theory that the standard of living in economies around the world will grow more similar over time, with poorer countries catching up with richer countries

Coordination failure A situation in which workers and employers fail to achieve an outcome that all would prefer; and are unable to jointly choose strategies that would result in a more preferred outcome

Corporate profits A component of national income measuring the net revenues received by incorporated businesses before corporate income taxes are subtracted

Corporation A legal entity owned by stockholders whose liability is limited to the value of their stock

Cost-push inflation A sustained rise in the price level caused by reductions in aggregate supply

Crowding in The potential for government spending to stimulate private investment in an otherwise sluggish economy

Crowding out The displacement of interest-sensitive private investment that occurs when increased government deficit spending drives up interest rates

Currency appreciation A decrease in the number of dollars needed to purchase 1 unit of foreign exchange

Currency depreciation An increase in the number of dollars needed to purchase 1 unit of foreign exchange

Currency devaluation An increase in the official pegged price of foreign exchange in terms of the domestic currency

Currency revaluation A reduction in the official pegged price of foreign exchange in terms of the domestic currency

Cyclical unemployment Unemployment that fluctuates with the business cycle, increasing during recessions and decreasing during expansions

Cyclically balanced budget A budget philosophy calling for budget deficits during recessions to be financed by budget surpluses during expansions

D

Decision-making lag The time needed to decide what to do once a macroeconomic problem is identified

Deflation A sustained decrease in the price level

Demand A relation showing the quantities of a good that consumers are willing and able to buy at various prices during a given period of time, other things constant

Demand curve A curve showing the quantities of a particular good demanded at various possible prices during a given time period, other things constant

Demand deposits Accounts at financial institutions that pay no interest and on which depositors can write checks to obtain their deposits at any time

Demand for money The relationship between how much money people want to hold and the interest rate

Demand-pull inflation A sustained rise in the price level caused by increases in aggregate demand

Demand-side economics Macroeconomic policy that focuses on changing aggregate demand as a way of promoting full employment and price stability

Depository institutions Commercial banks and thrift institutions that accept deposits from the public

Depreciation The value of capital stock used up during a year in producing GDP

Depression A severe reduction in an economy's total production accompanied by high unemployment lasting more than a year

Developing countries Nations typified by high rates of illiteracy, high unemployment, high fertility rates, and exports of primary products

Discount rate The interest rate charged by the Fed for loans to banks

Discouraged worker A person who has dropped out of the labor force because of lack of success in finding a job

Discretionary fiscal policy The deliberate manipulation of government purchases, taxation, and transfers in order to promote macroeconomic goals such as full employment, price stability, and economic growth

Disequilibrium A mismatch between quantity supplied and quantity demanded as the market seeks equilibrium

Disinflation A reduction in the rate of inflation

Disposable income (DI) The income households have available to spend or save after paying taxes and receiving transfer payments

Division of labor The organization of production of a product into separate tasks in which people specialize

Double coincidence of wants A situation in which two traders are willing to exchange their products directly

Double counting The mistake of including the value of intermediate goods plus the value of final goods in gross domestic product, counting the value of the same good more than once

Dumping Selling a commodity abroad at a price that is below its cost of production or below the price charged in the domestic market

E

Economic fluctuations The rise and fall of economic activity relative to the long-term growth trend of the economy; also called business cycles

Economic growth A shift outward in the production possibilities frontier; an increase in the economy's ability to produce goods and services

Economic system The set of mechanisms and institutions that resolve the what, how, and for whom questions

Economic theory, economic model A simplification of reality used to make predictions about the real world

Economics The study of how people use their scarce resources in an attempt to satisfy their unlimited wants

Economy The structure of economic life or economic activity in a community, a region, a country, a group of countries, or the world

Effectiveness lag The time necessary for changes in monetary or fiscal policy to have an effect on the economy

Efficiency The condition that exists when there is no way resources can be reallocated to increase the production of one good without decreasing the production of another

Efficiency wage theory The idea that keeping wages above the level required to attract a sufficient pool of workers makes workers compete to get and keep their jobs and results in greater productivity

Employee compensation A component of national income made up of wages and salaries plus payments by employers to cover Social Security taxes, medical insurance, and other fringe benefits

Entitlement programs Guaranteed benefits for those who qualify under government transfer programs such as Social Security and Medicare

Entrepreneurial ability Managerial and organizational skills combined with the willingness to take risks

Equation of exchange The quantity of money, M, multiplied by its velocity, V, equals nominal GDP, which is the product of the price level, P, and real GDP, Y.

Equilibrium The condition that exists in a market when the plans of the buyers match the plans of the sellers; the market clears

Excess reserves Bank reserves in excess of required reserves

Exchange rate The price of one country's currency measured in terms of another country's currency

Expansion A phase of economic activity during which there is an increase in the economy's total production

Expansionary gap The amount by which actual output in the short run exceeds the economy's potential output

Expenditure approach to GDP A method of calculating GDP by adding up spending on all final goods and services produced during the year

Export promotion A development strategy that concentrates on producing for the export market

Externality A cost or a benefit that falls on third parties and is therefore ignored by the two parties to the market transaction

F

Fallacy of composition The incorrect belief that what is true for the individual, or part, must necessarily be true for the group, or whole

Federal budget A plan for federal government outlays and revenues for a specified period, usually a year

Federal funds market A market for overnight lending and borrowing of reserves among banks; the market for reserves on account with the Fed

Federal funds rate The interest rate prevailing in the federal funds market; the interest rate banks charge one another for overnight borrowing

Federal Reserve System The central bank and monetary authority of the United States; also known as "the Fed"

Fiat money Money not redeemable for any commodity; its status as money is conferred by the government

Final goods and services Goods and services sold to final, or ultimate, users

Financial intermediaries Institutions that serve as go-betweens, accepting funds from savers and lending them to borrowers

Financial markets Banks and other institutions that facilitate the flow of loanable funds from savers to borrowers

Firms Economic units, formed by profit-seeking entrepreneurs who employ resources to produce goods and services for sale

Fiscal policy The use of government purchases, transfer payments, taxes, and borrowing to influence aggregate economic activity

Fixed exchange rates Rates pegged within a narrow range of values by central banks' ongoing purchases and sales of currencies

Flexible exchange rates Rates determined by the forces of supply and demand without government intervention

Flow A variable that measures the amount of something over an interval of time, such as the amount of money you spend on food per week

Foreign aid An international transfer made on especially favorable terms for the purpose of promoting economic development

Foreign exchange Foreign currency needed to carry out international transactions

Fractional reserve banking system A banking system in which only a portion of deposits is backed by reserves

Frictional unemployment Unemployment that arises because of the time needed to match qualified job seekers with available job openings

Full employment The level of employment when there is no cyclical unemployment

Functional finance A budget philosophy aiming fiscal policy at achieving potential GDP rather than balancing budgets either annually or over the business cycle

G

GDP price index A comprehensive price index of all goods and services included in the gross domestic product

General Agreement on Tariffs and Trade (GATT) An international tariff-reduction treaty adopted in 1947 that resulted in a series of negotiated "rounds" aimed at freer trade; the Uruguay Round created GATT's successor, the World Trade Organization (WTO)

Gold standard An arrangement whereby the currencies of most countries are convertible into gold at a fixed rate

Good A tangible item that is used to satisfy wants

Government budget deficit A flow variable that measures the amount by which total government outlays exceed total government revenues in a particular period

Government debt A stock variable that measures the net accumulation of prior budget deficits

Government purchase function The relationship between government purchases and the level of income in the economy, other things constant

Government purchases Spending for goods and services by all levels of government; government outlays minus transfer payments

Government subsidies Government transfers to businesses

Gradualism A "bottom-up" approach to moving from a centrally planned to a market economy emphasizing established markets at the most decentralized level first, such as on small farms or in light industry

Gresham's Law People tend to trade away inferior money and hoard the best

Gross domestic product, or **GDP** The market value of all final goods and services produced by resources located in the United States, regardless of who owns those resources.

H

Householder The key decision maker in the household

Hyperinflation A very high rate of inflation

Hypothesis A statement about relationships among key variables

I

Implementation lag The time needed to introduce a change in monetary or fiscal policy

Import substitution A development strategy that emphasizes domestic manufacturing of products that are currently imported

Income approach to GDP A method of calculating GDP by adding up all payments to owners of resources used to produce output during the year

Income effect A fall in the price of a good increases consumers' real income, making the consumers more able to purchase all goods; for normal goods, the quantity demanded increases

Income-expenditure model A relationship between aggregate income and aggregate spending that determines, for a given price level, where income equals planned spending

Indirect business taxes Federal, state, and local business taxes that are partially or entirely shifted to other taxpayers; taxes on sales and on property are examples.

Industrial market countries Economically advanced capitalist countries of Western Europe, North America, Australia, New Zealand, and Japan; also known as developed countries

Industrial policy The view that government—using taxes, subsidies, regulations, and coordination—should nurture the industries and technologies of the future, to give domestic industries an advantage over foreign competition

Industrial Revolution Development of large-scale factory production that began in Great Britain around 1750 and spread to the rest of Europe, North America, and Australia

Inferior good A good for which demand decreases as consumer incomes rise

Inflation A sustained increase in the economy's average price level

Injection Any payment of income other than by firms or any spending other than by domestic households; includes investment, government purchases, transfer payments, and exports

Interest rate Interest per year as a percentage of the amount loaned

Interest The dollar amount paid by borrowers to lenders to forgo present consumption; the payment resource owners receive for the use of their capital

Intermediate goods and services Goods and services purchased for further reprocessing and resale

International Monetary Fund (IMF) An international organization that establishes rules for maintaining the international monetary system and makes loans to countries with temporary balance of payments problem.

Inventories Producers' stocks of finished or in-process goods

Investment The purchase of new plants, new equipment, new buildings, new residences, and net additions to inventories

Investment function The relationship between the amount businesses plan to invest and the level of income in the economy, other things constant

L

Labor The physical and mental effort of humans used to produce goods and services

Labor force Individuals 16 years of age and older who are either working or actively looking for work

Labor force participation rate The ratio of the number in the labor force to the adult population

Labor productivity Output per unit of labor; measured as total output divided by the number of units of labor employed to produce that output

Land Plots of ground and other natural resources used to produce goods and services

Law of comparative advantage The individual, firm, region, or country with the lowest opportunity cost of producing a particular good should specialize in producing that good.

Law of demand The quantity of a good demanded during a given time period is inversely related to its price, other things constant

Law of increasing opportunity cost To produce each additional increment of a particular good, a successively larger increment of an alternative good must be sacrificed if the economy's resources are already being used efficiently

Law of supply The quantity of a product supplied in a given time period is usually directly related to its price, other things constant

Leakage Any diversion of income from the domestic spending stream; includes saving, taxes, and imports

Legal tender Anything that creditors are required to accept as payment for debts

Liability Anything that is owed to another individual or institution

Liquidity A measure of the ease with which an asset can be converted into money without significant loss in its value

Long run A period during which wage contracts and resource price agreements can be renegotiated

Long-run aggregate supply (LRAS) curve The vertical line drawn at the economy's potential output; aggregate supply when there are no price surprises

Long-run equilibrium Combination of price level and real GDP, where (1) the actual price level equals the expected price level, (2) quantity supplied equals potential output, and (3) quantity supplied equals quantity demanded

Long-run Phillips curve A vertical line drawn at the economy's natural rate of unemployment that traces equilibrium points that can occur when employers and workers have the time to adjust fully to any unexpected change in aggregate demand

M

M1 A measure of the money supply consisting of currency and coins held by the nonbanking public, checkable deposits, and travelers checks

M2 A monetary aggregate consisting of M1 plus savings deposits, small time deposits, and money market mutual funds

M3 A monetary aggregate consisting of M2 plus large-denomination time deposits

Macroeconomics The study of the economic behavior of entire economies

Managed float system An exchange rate system that combines features of freely floating rates with intervention by central banks

Marginal A term meaning incremental, additional, or extra; used to describe the result of a change in an economic variable

Marginal propensity to consume The fraction of a change in income that is spent on consumption; the change in consumption spending divided by the change in income that caused it

Marginal propensity to import (MPM) The fraction of a change in income that is spent on imports; the change in import spending divided by the change in income that caused it

Marginal propensity to save (MPS) The fraction of a change in income that is saved; the change in saving divided by the change in income that caused it

Marginal propensity to save The fraction of a change in income that is saved; the change in saving divided by the change in income that caused it

Marginal tax rate The percentage of each additional dollar of income that goes to taxes

Market A set of arrangements through which buyers and sellers carry out exchange at mutually agreeable terms

Market failure A condition that arises when unrestrained operation of markets yields socially undesirable results

Medium of exchange Anything that facilitates trade by being generally accepted by all parties in payment for goods or services

Merchandise trade balance The value of a country's exported goods minus the value of its imported goods during a given time period

Microeconomics The study of the economic behavior in particular markets, such as the market for computers or for unskilled labor

Mixed system An economic system characterized by private ownership of some resources and public ownership of other resources; some markets are unregulated and others are regulated.

Monetary aggregates Measures of the economy's money supply

Monetary policy Regulation of the money supply in order to influence aggregate economic activity

Money Anything that is generally accepted in exchange for goods and services

Money market mutual fund A collection of short-term interest-earning assets purchased with funds collected from many shareholders

Money multiplier The multiple by which the money supply increases as a result of an increase in excess reserves in the banking system

Monopoly A sole producer of a product for which there are no close substitutes

N

National debt The net accumulation of federal budget deficits

National income The amount of national income earned by suppliers of resources employed to produce gross national product; net domestic product plus net earnings of U.S. resources abroad minus indirect business taxes (net of subsidies)

Natural monopoly One firm that can serve the entire market at a lower per-unit cost than can two or more firms

Natural rate hypothesis The natural rate of unemployment is largely independent of the stimulus provided by monetary or fiscal policy

Natural rate of unemployment The unemployment rate that occurs when the economy is producing its potential level of output

Net domestic product Gross domestic product minus depreciation

Net export function The relationship between net exports and the level of income in the economy, other things constant

Net exports The value of a country's exports minus the value of its imports

Net interest A component of national income made up of interest received by households, excluding interest paid by consumers to businesses and interest paid by government

Net taxes (NT) Taxes minus transfer payments

Net unilateral transfers The unilateral transfers (gifts and grants) received from abroad by residents of a country minus the unilateral transfers residents send abroad

Net wealth The value of a household's assets minus its liabilities

Net worth Assets minus liabilities

Nominal GDP GDP based on prices prevailing at the time of the transaction; current-dollar GDP

Nominal rate of interest The interest rate expressed in current dollars as a percentage of the amount loaned; the interest rate on a loan agreement

Nominal wage The wage measured in terms of current dollars; the dollar amount on a paycheck

Normal good A good for which demand increases as consumer incomes rise

Normative economic statement A statement that represents an opinion, which cannot be proved or disproved

O

Official reserve transactions account The section of a country's balance-of-payments account that reflects the flow of gold, Special Drawing Rights, and currencies among central banks

Open-market operations Purchases and sales of government securities by the Federal Reserve in an effort to influence the money supply

Open-market purchase The purchase of U.S. government bonds by the Federal Reserve, for the purpose of increasing the money supply

Open-market sale The sale of U.S. government bonds by the Federal Reserve for the purpose of reducing the money supply

Opportunity cost The value of the best alternative forgone when an item or activity is chosen

Other-things-constant assumption The assumption, when focusing on key economic variables, that other variables remain unchanged

Output per capita Total output in the economy divided by the population

P

Partnership A firm with multiple owners who share the firm's profits and each of whom bears unlimited liability for the firm's debts

Per-worker production function The relationship between the amount of capital per worker in the economy and the output per worker

Permanent income Income that individuals expect to receive on average over the long term

Personal income The amount of before-tax income received by households; national income less income earned but not received plus income received but not earned

Phillips curve A curve showing possible combinations of the inflation rate and the unemployment rate

Physical capital Manufactured items used to produce goods and services

Planned investment The amount of investment firms plan to undertake during a year

Political business cycles Economic fluctuations that result when discretionary policy is manipulated for political gain

Positive economic statement A statement that can be proved or disproved by reference to facts

Potential output The economy's maximum sustainable output level, given the supply of resources, technology, and production incentives; the output level when there are no surprises about the price level

Price ceiling A maximum legal price above which a good or service cannot be sold; to be effective, a price ceiling must be set below the equilibrium price

Price floor A minimum legal price below which a good or service cannot be sold; to be effective, a price floor must be set above the equilibrium price

Price index A number that shows the average price of a market basket of goods; changes in a price index over time changes in the average price level

Price level A composite measure reflecting the prices of all goods and services in the economy relative to prices in a base year

Privatization The process of turning public enterprises into private enterprises

Product market A market in which goods and services are bought and sold

Production possibilities frontier (PPF) A curve showing alternative combinations of goods that can be produced when available resources are used efficiently

Productivity The ratio of a specific measure of output to a specific measure of input, such as output per hour of labor

Profit The payment resource owners receive for their entrepreneurial ability; the total revenue from sales minus the total cost of resources employed by the entrepreneur

Progressive taxation The tax as a percentage of income increases as income increases.

Proportional income tax Taxes remain a constant percentage of income as income increases

Proportional taxation The tax as a percentage of income remains constant as income increases; also called a flat-rate tax

Proprietor's income A component of national income made up of earnings of farmers and other unincorporated businesses

Public good A good that, once produced, is available for all to consume, regardless of who pays and who does not

Purchasing power parity (PPP) theory The theory that exchange rates between two countries will adjust in the long run to reflect price level differences between the countries

Pure command system An economic system characterized by public ownership of resources and centralized economic planning

Pure market system An economic system characterized by private ownership of resources and the use of prices to coordinate economic activity in unregulated markets

Q

Quantity theory of money If the velocity of money is stable or at least predictable, then changes in the money supply have predictable effects on nominal GDP

Quota A legal limit on the quantity of a particular product that can be imported or exported

R

Rational expectations A school of thought that claims people form expectations based on all available information, including the probable future actions of government policy makers

Real GDP GDP adjusted for changes in the price level

Real income Income measured in terms of the goods and services it can buy

Real rate of interest The interest rate expressed in dollars of constant purchasing power as a percentage of the amount loaned; the nominal rate of interest minus the inflation rate

Real wage The wage measured in terms of dollars of constant purchasing power; hence, the wage measured in terms of the quantity of goods and services it will purchase

Recession A period of decline in total output usually lasting at least six months and marked by contractions in many sectors of the economy

Recognition lag The time needed to identify a macroeconomic problem and assess its seriousness

Regressive taxation The tax as a percentage of income decreases as income increases

Relevant resources Resources used to produce the good in question

Rent The payment resource owners receive for the use of their land

Rental income of persons A component of national income consisting mainly of the imputed rental value of owner-occupied housing

Required reserve ratio The ratio of reserves to deposits that banks are required, by regulation, to hold

Required reserves The dollar amount of reserves a bank is legally required to hold

Reserves Funds that banks use to satisfy the cash demands of their customers and the reserve requirements of the Fed; reserves consist of deposits at the Fed plus currency physically held by banks

Residential construction Building new permanent homes or dwelling places

Resource market A market in which resources are bought and sold

Resources The inputs, or factors of production, used to produce the goods and services that humans want; resources consist of labor, capital, land, and entrepreneurial ability

S

Saving function The relationship between saving and the level of income in the economy, other things constant

Savings deposits Deposits that earn interest but have no specific maturity date

Scarcity When the amount people desire exceeds the amount available at a zero price

Seasonal unemployment Unemployment caused by seasonal shifts in labor supply and demand

Secondary effects Unintended consequences of economic actions that develop slowly over time as people react to events

Seigniorage The difference between the face value of money and the cost of supplying it; the "profit" from issuing money

Service An activity that is used to satisfy wants

Short run A period during which at least some resource prices, especially those for labor, are fixed by agreement

Short-run aggregate supply (SRAS) curve A curve that shows the direct relationship between the price level and the quantity of aggregate output supplied in the short run, other things constant

Short-run equilibrium Combination of price level and real GDP, where the aggregate demand curve intersects the short-run aggregate supply curve

Short-run Phillips curve A curve, based on an expected inflation rate, that reflects an inverse relationship between the inflation rate and the level of unemployment

Shortage An excess of quantity demanded compared to quantity supplied at a given price; a shortage puts upward pressure on price

Simple money multiplier The reciprocal of the required reserve ratio, or $1/r$; the maximum multiple of excess reserves by which the money supply can increase

Simple spending multiplier The ratio of a change in real GDP demanded to the initial change in expenditure that brought it about; the numerical value of the simple spending multiplier is $1/(1 - MPC)$; it is called "simple" because consumption is the only component that varies with income.

Simple tax multiplier The ratio of a change in real GDP demanded to the initial change in autonomous net taxes that brought it about; the numerical value of the simple tax multiplier is $-MPC/(1 - MPC)$

Soft budget constraint The budget condition faced by socialist enterprises that are subsidized if they lose money

Sole proprietorship A firm with a single owner who has the right to all profits and who bears unlimited liability for the firm's debts

Specialization of labor Focusing an individual's efforts on a particular product or a single task

Speculator A person who buys or sells foreign exchange in hopes of profiting from fluctuations in the exchange rate over time

Stagflation A contraction, or *stag*nation, of a nation's output accompanied by in*flation* in the price level

Stock A variable that measures the amount of something at a particular point in time, such as the amount of food in your refrigerator or the amount of money you have with you right now

Store of value Anything that retains its purchasing power over time

Structural unemployment Unemployment that arises because (1) the skills demanded by employers do not match the skills of the unemployed, or (2) the unemployed do not live where the jobs are located

Substitutes Goods Goods that are related in such a way that an increase in the price of one leads to an increase in the demand for the other

Substitution effect When the price of a good falls, consumers will substitute that good for other goods, which are now relatively more expensive

Sunk cost A cost that has already been incurred in the past and, hence, a cost that is irrelevant to present and future economic decisions

Supply A relation showing the quantities of a good producers are willing and able to sell at various prices during a given time period, other things constant

Supply curve A curve showing the quantities of a good supplied at various prices, other things constant

Supply shocks Unexpected events that affect aggregate supply, sometimes only temporarily

Supply-side economics Macroeconomic policy that focuses on increasing aggregate supply through tax cuts or other changes to increase production incentives

Surplus An excess of quantity supplied compared to quantity demanded at a given price; a surplus puts downward pressure on the price

T

Tariff A tax on imports or exports

Tastes Consumer preferences; likes and dislikes in consumption

Tax incidence The distribution of tax burden among taxpayers

Terms of trade How much of one good exchanges for a unit of another good

Thrift institutions, or thrifts Savings and loan institutions, mutual savings banks, and credit unions; depository institutions that make long-term loans primarily to households

Time deposits Deposits that earn a fixed rate of interest if held for the specified period, which can range anywhere from several months to several years

Time-inconsistency problem The problem that arises when policy makers have an incentive to announce one policy to influence expectations but then to pursue a different policy once those expectations have been formed and acted upon

Token money The name given to money whose face value exceeds the cost of producing it

Transaction costs The costs of time and information required to carry out market exchange

Transfer payments Cash or in-kind benefits given to individuals as outright grants from the government

Transparent finances A firm's financial records that clearly indicate the economic health of the company

U

Underemployment A situation in which workers are overqualified for their jobs or work fewer hours than they would prefer

Underground economy An expression used to describe all market exchange that goes unreported either because it is illegal or because those involved want to evade taxes

Unemployment insurance Cash transfers provided to unemployed workers who actively seek employment and who meet other qualifications

Unemployment rate The number of unemployed individuals expressed as a percentage of the labor force

Unit of account A common unit for measuring the value of every good or service

Utility The satisfaction received from consumption; satisfaction, sense of well-being

V

Value added The difference at each stage of production between the value of a product and cost of intermediate goods bought from other firms

Variable A measure, such as price or quantity, that can take on different possible values

Velocity of money The average number of times per year a dollar is used to purchase final goods and services

W

Wages The payment resource owners receive for their labor

World price The price at which a good is traded internationally; determined by the world supply and demand for the good

World Trade Organization (WTO) The legal and institutional foundation of the multilateral trading system that succeeded GATT in 1995

Index

Note: The letter *d* after an entry indicates marginal *definition; e* indicates *exhibit; i* indicates *Internet address.*

Photo Credits